Democracy in South Asia

This volume examines the state of democracy in South Asia after the first two decades of the millennium. It shows how the inroads made by democracy that surged through South Asia at the turn of the century arrived at a crucial juncture after two decades. The Taliban regaining strength in Afghanistan, tricky civil-military relations in Pakistan, the political stand-off in Nepal, as well as the undermining of civil rights in other countries point to the deepening challenges to democracy in the region. At the same time the region presents many positives to be taken forward and opportunities to be cashed in on. The chapters in the volume map the gains made and challenges faced by each South Asian country, especially since 2000. Going beyond the usual regional powers like India, Pakistan, Bangladesh and Sri Lanka, the volume also includes detailed analysis of the state of democracy and future trajectories of Nepal, Afghanistan, Bhutan and the Maldives.

The volume will be of great interest to scholars, researchers and students of politics and international relations and South Asian studies.

Aijaz Ashraf Wani is Associate Professor at Department of Political Science, University of Kashmir.

Arshid Iqbal Dar is Assistant Professor in the Centre for International Relations, Islamic University of Science and Technology (IUST).

Democracy in South Asia

Edited by
Aijaz Ashraf Wani and Arshid Iqbal Dar

LONDON AND NEW YORK

First published 2025
by Routledge
4 Park Square, Milton Park, Abingdon, Oxon OX14 4RN

and by Routledge
605 Third Avenue, New York, NY 10158

Routledge is an imprint of the Taylor & Francis Group, an informa business

© 2025 selection and editorial matter, Aijaz Ashraf Wani and Arshid Iqbal Dar; individual chapters, the contributors

The right of Aijaz Ashraf Wani and Arshid Iqbal Dar to be identified as the authors of the editorial material, and of the authors for their individual chapters, has been asserted in accordance with sections 77 and 78 of the Copyright, Designs and Patents Act 1988.

All rights reserved. No part of this book may be reprinted or reproduced or utilised in any form or by any electronic, mechanical, or other means, now known or hereafter invented, including photocopying and recording, or in any information storage or retrieval system, without permission in writing from the publishers.

Trademark notice: Product or corporate names may be trademarks or registered trademarks, and are used only for identification and explanation without intent to infringe.

British Library Cataloguing in Publication Data
A catalogue record for this book is available from the British Library

ISBN: 978-1-032-19655-8 (hbk)
ISBN: 978-1-032-19917-7 (pbk)
ISBN: 978-1-003-26146-9 (ebk)

DOI: 10.4324/9781003261469

Typeset in Sabon
by Taylor & Francis Books

For the people of South Asia, with the hope and prayers to witness a peaceful and prosperous future; and to our parents who made enormous sacrifices to secure our future and educated us to be humane.

Contents

List of illustrations	ix
List of contributors	x
Acknowledgments	xiii

1 Introduction   1
AIJAZ ASHRAF WANI AND ARSHID IQBAL DAR

2 Democracy Denied: The False Promise of Afghanistan's
Constitutions   31
JENNIFER BRICK MURTAZASHVILI

3 The Making of an Autocratic Regime: Democratic Backsliding in
Bangladesh   51
ALI RIAZ

4 Removals of Elected and Appointed Public Officials in Bhutan:
Democratic Recession or Consolidation?   76
SONAM KINGA

5 Democracy in India: Continuities, Realignments, and Promises   105
ANUP SHEKHAR CHAKRABORTY

6 Democracy in the Maldives: Unpacking the "Democratization-
Backsliding" Rollercoaster   134
ARSHID IQBAL DAR AND AIJAZ ASHRAF WANI

7 Nepal's Tryst with Democracy: Internal Dynamics, External
Influences   163
ABIJIT SHARMA

viii *Contents*

8 Democratization in Pakistan and Its Challenges   185
   MARIAM MUFTI AND KAZMA CHAUDHRY

9 Constitutional Amendments (2001–2022) and Democracy in
   Sri Lanka   207
   NADARAJAH PUSHPARAJAH AND MALINI BALAMAYURAN

   Index   223

Illustrations

Figures

3.1 Bangladeshi Elections: Party Participation, Voter Turnout, and Unopposed Candidates, 1973–2014	62
3.2 Freedom of Expression in Bangladesh, 2009–2018	64
3.3 Enforced Disappearances and Extrajudicial Killings in Bangladesh, 2009–2018	65
3.4 Democracy Score, Competitiveness in Participation, and Political Competition, 2009–2018	66
3.5 Bangladesh's GDP Growth Rate, 1996–2018	68

Tables

3.1 Model of Democratic Backsliding	59
3.2 Bangladeshi Model of Democratic Backsliding	60
3.3 Election Results 2018	70

Contributors

Aijaz Ashraf Wani (PhD) is Associate Professor at the Department of Political Science, University of Kashmir. He is the author of *What Happened to Governance in Kashmir?* (Oxford University Press, 2019) and co-editor of *Government and Politics of Jammu and Kashmir: From Princely State to Union Territory* (Sage, 2022). His research interest lies in Governance and Public Policy, Democracy, J&K Politics, Indian Politics and South Asia. His research has appeared in national and international journals, including the *Journal of Borderlands Studies, Studies in Indian Politics, Indian Journal of Public Administration, South Asian Survey, Economic and Political Weekly, Indian Historic Review, Urban India,* etc. He also has chapters in books published by Routledge, Orient Blackswan and Palgrave Macmillan. He has completed two major research projects sponsored by the Indian Council of Social Science Research (ICSSR), New Delhi, and is working on another research project on the theme of Urban Governance, funded by ICSSR. He has also completed a number of minor projects on Electoral Studies sponsored by the Centre for the Study of Developing Societies (CSDS), New Delhi.

Arshid Iqbal Dar (PhD) is Assistant Professor in the Centre for International Relations, Islamic University of Science and Technology (IUST). He teaches IR Theory, Non-Western IR, Foreign Policy of India, Geopolitics, and Governance and Security. His research interest lies in Theories of IR, Foreign Policy Analysis, South Asia, and India-US, India-China and Indo-Pacific relations. His research has appeared in various refereed and peer-reviewed journals, including *Asian Survey, Asian Affairs, Israel Affairs, India Quarterly, Journal of Borderland Studies* and *Chinese Political Science Review.*

Ali Riaz is a Distinguished Professor of Political Science at Illinois State University, a Nonresident Senior Fellow of Atlantic Council, and the President of the American Institute of Bangladesh Studies (AIBS). He served as a Visiting Researcher at the Varieties of Democracy Institute (V-Dem) at Sweden (2023) and as a Public Policy Scholar at the Woodrow Wilson International Center for Scholars at Washington, DC (2013). His area of interests are

South Asian politics, democratization, violent extremism and Bangladeshi politics. He has numerous publications, including *The Charade: Bangladesh's 2024 Election* (2024), *Pathways for Autocratization: The Tumultuous Journey of Bangladeshi Politics* (2024); *How Autocrats Rise: Sequences of Democratic Backsliding* (co-authored with Md Sohel Rana, 2024) and *Trials and Tribulations: Politics, Economy and Foreign Affairs of Bangladesh* (2023).

Sonam Kinga is the Inaugural Research Fellow at the Royal Institute of Governance and Strategic Studies based in Phuntsholing, Bhutan. He was earlier the Chairman of Druk Gyalpo's Institute, Visiting Scholar at the Graduate School of Asian and African Area Studies at Kyoto University, Visiting Research Fellow at the Institute of Developing Economies (IDE) in Tokyo and founding member and researcher at The Centre for Bhutan Studies. He represented Tashigang Dzongkhag in the National Council, Parliament of Bhutan for ten years. In his first term, he served as the Deputy Chairperson and in second term, as the Chairperson. He has received the prestigious honor of Red Scarf in 2012 and Gold Medal (National Order of Merit) in 2014 from His Majesty the King. His research interests primarily focus on Bhutanese history, politics, culture and foreign relations. His works include *Changes in Bhutanese Social Structure* (2002), *Polity Kingship and Democracy* (2009) and *Democratic Transition in Bhutan* (2019) published by IDE, Bhutan's Ministry of Education and Routledge, respectively.

Jennifer Brick Murtazashvili is Director of the Center for Governance and Markets and Professor Public and International Affairs at the University of Pittsburgh. She serves as a nonresident scholar at the Carnegie Endowment for International Peace, a distinguished scholar of peace and international order at the Institute for Humane Studies and is a contributing editor at *National Interest* magazine. She is author of *Informal Order and the State in Afghanistan* (Cambridge University Press), and co-author (with Ilia Murtazashvili) of *Land, the State, and War: Property Institutions and Political Order in Afghanistan* (Cambridge University Press).

Mariam Mufti is an Associate Professor of Political Science at the University of Waterloo, Canada. She has published articles in peer-reviewed journals such as *Comparative Politics* and *Publius*, and co-edited the volume *Pakistan's Political Parties: Surviving between Dictatorship and Democracy* (Georgetown University Press, 2020). She has also appeared in *The Dictator's Playbook* on PBS (2018) and *How to Be a Tyrant* on Netflix (2021).

Anup Shekhar Chakraborty is an Associate Professor in the Department of Political Science, North-Eastern Hill University (NEHU), Shillong, Meghalaya, and member of the Mahanirban Calcutta Research Group (MCRG), Kolkata. He has over 17 years of teaching and research experience. Much of his works focus on the Himalayan region and India's Northeast. His latest co-edited books include: *Indigeneity, Development and Sustainability – Perspectives from Northeast India* (with Dr. Anjan Chakrabarti and Dr. Gorky

xii *List of contributors*

Chakraborty, Springer Nature, 2024); *Queer and the Vernacular Languages in India: Studies in Contemporary Texts and Culture* (with Kaustav Chakraborty, Routledge, 2023); and *Death and Dying in Northeast India: Indigeneity and Afterlife* (with Parjanya Sen, Routledge, 2023). He serves as one of the Guest Editors of the *Special Issue on "LGBTQ+ People in Situations of Forced Displacement"* (*Oxford Journal of Refugee Studies*, Oxford, UK); and the *Special Issue on "Politics and the People in India: Modern and Historical Perspectives"* (*Humanities and Social Science Communications/Palgrave Communications*, Springer Nature, UK).

Nadarajah Pushparajah is a Senior Lecturer in Political Science at the Department of Social Sciences, Eastern University, Sri Lanka. He received his PhD from the Scuola Superiore Sant'Anna, Pisa, Italy and LLM degree from NUIG, Ireland. Pushparajah worked as a Post-Doctoral Research Fellow at the Institutum Iurisprudentiae, Academia Sinica (February–November 2018) and the KoGuan Law School, Shanghai Jiao Tong University (June 2015–June 2017). His research interests mainly include human rights, humanitarian law, international politics, constitution-making, democracy and transitional justice.

Malini Balamayuran is a Senior Lecturer at the Department of Political Science, University of Peradeniya, Sri Lanka. She obtained her PhD in Social Sciences from the University of Western Sydney, Australia and MA in Political Science from the University of Hawaii at Manoa, USA. Her research interests primarily focus on extremism, terrorism, ethnic mobilisation and disaster capitalism.

Abijit Sharma has a decade of experience working in the Nepali development sector, focusing on research and monitoring and evaluation. He writes frequently on matters pertaining to politics, foreign policy and development issues on national as well as international media. Abijit holds an undergraduate degree in Political Science (Honors) from Delhi University, Delhi (India); a postgraduate degree in Sociology from Tribhuwan University, Kathmandu (Nepal); and a postgraduate degree in International Economic Law from East China University of Political Science and Law, Shanghai (China).

Kazma Chaudhry graduated from the University of Waterloo with a bachelor's degree in Psychology. She also minored in Political Science with a regional specialization in South Asia under the supervision of Dr. Mariam Mufti. She recently graduated from Carleton University with an MA in Human-Computer Interaction, and published her master's thesis research at the *2023 European Symposium on Usable Security*.

Acknowledgments

The idea for this volume originated in March 2021 during our evening walks around the famous Dal Lake. As a matter of habit, we would go for an evening walk almost every day and take up some academic or general topic for discussion. During one such walk South Asia in general came up for discussion. One of us was teaching a course on South Asia to master's students, and as we would often discuss our teaching and research assignments, so it came up for discussion. For the next couple of weeks South Asia remained the topic of discussion; and why not? After all, South Asia as a region is so fascinating that one can go on and on discussing its dynamics—historical, political, cultural, economic and so on. We specifically discussed democracy in South Asia at great length—its past, present and imagined future. What began as a casual discussion gradually started taking a serious academic turn. Firstly, we thought of a research paper. But the more we went on discussing the theme, the more we realized that it needed more than a research article to capture the dynamics. We also acknowledged the merit in having country-specific experts to write the chapters. Thus was born the idea of an edited volume.

Special words of gratitude to the following scholars for accepting our invitation to contribute to this volume and demonstrating enormous patience during the whole process. Thank you so much Ali Raiz, Sonam Kinga, Jannifer Brick Murtazashvili, Mariam Mufti, Kazma Chaudhry, Malini Balamayuran, Nadarajah Pushparajah, Anup Shekhar Chakraborty and Abijit Sharma. This volume could not have acquired the academic richness that it possesses now without your efforts.

Our heartfelt thanks to the reviewers for their encouraging words as well as for providing very useful suggestions. While making improvements in the light of their suggestions, the work has substantially improved.

This work is the outcome of the immense help we received from our teachers, colleagues, friends, family and well-wishers. While it is not possible to name them all here, we are sure they know it. We express our deep sense of gratitude to all of them. Our unconditional love and thanks to our parents for making us what we are.

Special thanks to all our students whose company we enjoy the most. It is they who keep pushing us to learn more.

Last but not the least, our heartfelt gratitude to the whole Routledge family for their support. Special thanks to Aakash Chakrabarty and Brinda Sen for showing exemplary patience and support in the preparation of this volume.

1 Introduction

Aijaz Ashraf Wani and Arshid Iqbal Dar

Understanding Democracy

Democracy is essentially a contested concept with too many meanings attached to it. Consequently, we can never reach any one agreed-upon definition because the definition carries different social, moral, and political connotations. Michael Saward in his book *Democratic Design* (2021) summarized it very eloquently:

> I have learned over the years that when people talk about democracy—in parliament committee rooms, at a university seminar, in cafes or pubs, or around the dinner table—there is often only one thing they will agree on: that they cannot or will not agree. Democracy's place, value, and meaning are disputed, and the arguments can be emotive. Do we really have it (whoever the "we" is—the local school committee, the town, the country, the world)? Did we ever? Which politicians or others are on the side of democracy, and which are not? And what really *is* democracy, anyway?
>
> (Saward, 2021: Xi)

The seriousness of conceptual confusion in the literature can be understood by the fact that David Collier and Steven Levitsky would identify more than 550 "subtypes" of democracy while reviewing around 150 studies (Collier and Levitsky, 1997). For Larry Diamond, while very few of these subtypes just identify particular institutional features or varieties of full democracy, several of these signify "diminished" forms of democracy (Diamond, 1997: 6). Nevertheless, as Bernard Crick reckons, "we cannot live without it" (Crick, 2002: 1). In his *In Defense of Politics* (1962), Crick considers democracy as "the most promiscuous word"; he uses the analogy of a Greek or Roman nymph as well as an Athenian minor god. For him, "democracy being everyone's mistress somehow keeps her magic even when a lover perceives that her favours are being illicitly shared by many others" (Crick, 1962: 51). Much earlier in a parliamentary debate in 1947 Winston Churchill argued that "no one pretends that democracy is perfect or all-wise. Indeed it has been said that democracy is the worst form of Government except for all those other forms that have been tried from time to time" (Churchill, 1947). What Churchill and Crick said decades

DOI: 10.4324/9781003261469-1

2 Introduction

ago has become a commonplace thesis because, as Renske Doorenspleet had argued very recently, "it appears no other types of political systems have been functioning better than the democratic as it has neither a serious opponent, nor a real alternative" (Doorenspleet, 2018: 1). So democracy continues, to use the words of Larry Diamond, to be broadly the sole legitimate form of government in the world (Diamond, 2014). This edited volume is not about the conceptual understanding of democracy and its value as the best form of government. Rather, we are interested in raising and trying to investigate questions such as, is the allure of democracy fading away? If so, why? Further, like multiple meanings of what we mean by "democracy", are there also multiple meanings of what is called the "decline of democracy"? It may be mentioned at the outset that when we refer to democracy we are precisely referring to "liberal democracy" and we are taking South Asia as a case study. Therefore, any serious attempt to conceptualize and theorize democracy is beyond the scope of this text. Nevertheless, a review of the academic and scholarly attempts at examining and theorizing democracy and democratization throughout the globe cannot be left out. Further, in order to have a more or less comprehensive understanding of the current discourse, especially on the crisis/decline of democracy, it is important to examine and understand the trajectory of democracy and democratization. To put it differently, in order to understand what went wrong with liberal democracy, this introduction employs a historical approach to get through the noise and noose of democracy especially in the post–World War II era.

Notwithstanding the contested nature of democracy, scholars from time to time have attempted to understand it as a concept, an ideology or a theory (Grugel and Bishop, 2013; 12). For Mackensie, "as an ideology democracy represents a set of political ideas that underscore the best viable form of social organization' (MacKensie, 1994). Accordingly, it can then be understood as an ideal. To be a democrat is to have confidence in humans, to trust that they have inalienable rights to make choices for themselves, and to be devoted to the perception that everybody is equal in some fundamental and crucial way (Grugel and Bishop, 2013: 12). For Saward, not only is democracy as an idea and practice very diverse and open-ended, but also potentially prone to radical thinking for new conditions. The fragile nature of the idea of democracy invites challenges and creates chances for those who wish to bring it into contexts that don't have it, or reform it in contexts where it already exists. The flexible nature of democratic ideas and practices creates opportunities that inspire novel thinking and experimentation. However, this very characteristic of flexibility that makes democracy adaptable has to be carefully navigated as the new ideas and practices also need to be democratic—we have to clearly and carefully define the scope of the concept (Saward, 2021: xiv). This impelled Charles Tilly to argue that "in order to take democracy seriously, we tend to grasp what we are speaking about" (Tilly, 2007: 7). Tilly's four-fold way of defining the concept of democracy is very useful here as it captures most of the academic and scholarly examination of democracy. According to Tilly, scholars of

Introduction 3

democratization and democracy commonly choose, covertly or overtly, among four core types of definitions: constitutional, substantive, procedural, and process-oriented (Andrews and Chapman, 1995; Collier and Levitsky, 1997; Held, 1996; Inkeles, 1991; O'Donnell, 1999; Schmitter and Karl, 1991). For Tilly, a constitutional approach focuses on laws which are enacted by a regime with regard to political activity. It underscores that the rights of minorities and individuals are respected because the constitution defines and regulates the power of political authority. In contrast to a legal perspective, this approach allows looking through history and recognizing changes among republics, oligarchies, monarchies, and many others. In democracies, moreover, this approach is very useful in differentiating between presidential systems, constitutional monarchies, and parliament-centered arrangements, as well as for analyzing variations between federal and unitary structures. For Tilly, the constitutional criterion has several advantages for large-scale historical comparisons, particularly the relative visibility of constitutional forms (Tilly, 2007: 7).

The substantive approaches pay attention to the conditions of life and politics a particular regime endorses. Whether rights exist on paper doesn't count; whether they have the actual meaning for people is what underscores the litmus test for a democracy (Grugel and Bishop, 2013: 7). For Mary Kaldor and Ivan Vejvoda,

> substantive democracy [is] a process that has to constantly reproduce a way to regulate the power relations in such a manner so as to maximize the opportunities for individuals to affect their living conditions, enabling them to take part in and influence the debates pertaining to the key decisions which influence the society.
>
> (Kaldor and Vejvoda 1997: 67)

For Tilly substantive conceptualization of democracy underlines two troubles: firstly, how does one deal with the tradeoffs among several estimable substantive principles? If a particular regime is extremely poor but its citizens are roughly equal, should we consider it as more democratic compared to a fairly wealthy but hugely unequal regime? Secondly, to focus on the likely outcomes of politics hampers any attempt to understand whether political arrangements like democracy promote more desirable substantive results than others (Tilly, 2007: 7–8). The advocates of procedural understanding of democracy emphasize a small array of governmental practices to delineate whether a regime can be said to be democratic. Originally, the procedural conception of democracy intentionally portrayed it as a bulwark for liberty. Joseph Schumpeter has been widely acknowledged as the founder of the procedural approach for measuring democratic performance. He was in favor of a "realist" model of democracy which he defined as "an institutional arrangement to arrive at political decisions wherein individuals obtain the power to choose by means of a competitive struggle for the people's vote" (Schumpeter, 1947: 250). Schumpeter's notion of democracy was just a set of political procedures and institutions divorced from

4 *Introduction*

any broader ideal conceptions. His minimalist procedural norm was modified by later social scientists by adding additional criteria to identify and measure political democracy. However, the central organizing standard for most of the adherents of the procedural approach is "elections" and they ask whether truly competitive elections involving large numbers of citizens regularly produce changes in the government's policy and personnel. Amy Gutmann and Dennis Thompson, while making a case for deliberative democracy, criticize the procedural democracy as incomplete. For them, "not only does it neglect the values of constitutional democracy but also ignores the processes emphasized by deliberative democracy" (Gutmann and Thompson, 1996: 33).

Finally, in contrast to hitherto discussed constitutional, procedural, and substantive variants of democracy, the process-oriented approach identifies a minimum set of processes that are required to be in continuous motion for a specific situation to be qualified as democratic. In his book *On Democracy* (1998), Robert Dahl in his classic statement has identified five criteria for a democratic process:

(I) **Effective participation.** Before an association adopts a policy, all its members must be having equal and effective opportunities to make their views known to other members about what the policy should be.

(II) **Voting equality.** When the moment of final decision arrives about the policy to be made, every member must possess an equal and effective opportunity to vote, and all votes must then be counted as equal.

(III) **Enlightened understanding.** Within reasonable limits as to time for learning about the relevant alternative policies and their possible consequences, each member must have equal and effective opportunities.

(IV) **Control of the agenda.** The members must have the exclusive opportunity to decide how and, if they choose, what matters are to be placed on the agenda. So the democratic process required by the above-mentioned three criteria is never closed. The policies of the association are always open to change if the members so choose.

(V) **Inclusion of adults.** The full rights of citizens implied by the above four criteria must be possessed by almost all, or at any rate most, adult permanent residents. However, argues Dahl, this criterion was unacceptable to most of the adherents of democracy (Dahl, 1998: 37–38).

For Dahl, the opportunity for these five criteria to exist is provided only by democracy. Even when these criteria do not lay down any rules for their implementation in a particular democracy, they are quintessentially process-oriented. Notwithstanding his focus on a process-oriented approach, applied to "large-scale democracy", Dahl shifted towards institutions, which he understood as consisting of practices that endure. He introduced the notion of "polyarchal democracy", which according to him installs six distinct institutions: free, fair, and frequent elections, elected officials, alternative sources of information, freedom of expression, associational autonomy, and inclusive

Introduction 5

citizenship (Dahl, 1998: 85; Dahl, 2005: 188–189). In his *A Preface to Democratic Theory* (2006), Dahl, in an elaborative statement on polyarchal democracy, identifies its eight definitional characteristics, which he further subdivides into four periods. They are: the voting period, pre-voting period, post-voting period, and inter-election stage. Dahl's eight characteristics that define the polyarchal democracy include:

> every member of society expresses a preference through voting; all votes are weighted the same; the preference with a majority wins; the opportunity to submit alternatives; all individuals possess the same information about alternative preferences; the winning preference should be implemented or inducted requiring the losing preference to be removed; orders of elected officials are executed; and that all inter-election decisions should follow these characteristics.
>
> (Dahl, 2006: 67–71)

A polyarchy in its most basic form is a political system which, besides electing leaders through free, fair, competitive, and relatively inclusive electoral system, must also ensure freedoms (such as freedom of expression and organization) to make these elections meaningful (Bass, 2005: 638). In this way Dahl rejected the procedural—substantive dichotomy—because for him, a democratic process may fail to achieve desirable results or, put simply, may find it difficult to properly balance between the procedural and substantive values (Dahl, 1989: 175).

Dahl's analysis of democracy is important because nobody has thought more about it than him. His influence shapes discussions on democracy more than any other theorist. Not only do his eight criteria of polyarchy open the possibility of hybrid regimes or even flawed democracies, but they also imply that the contemporary version of liberal democracy has room to become even more democratic.

As already pointed out in the beginning, this introduction traces the historical trajectory of liberal democracy especially since the end of World War II. The logic for the same has been aptly summarized by Jean Grugel, who argues:

> After 1945 democracy was successfully married to liberalism. Liberal democracy was no longer seen as one strand of democracy: it was presented as the only version there was. Liberal democracy was presented in opposition to both Communism (seen as an ideology and a geopolitical force) and Fascism over which democracy was thought to have triumphed.
>
> (Grugel, 2002: 17)

Similarly, Larry Diamond reckons that when scholars and policy experts refer to the term "democracy" today, they are referring to a purely political idea, which he conceptualized as "liberal democracy" in which the individual and group liberties are not only strong but also well protected (Diamond, 1997: 6). Building on the conceptualization of Lawrence Whitehead (1988), Schmitter and

6 *Introduction*

Karl (1991) and Dahl (1971; 1982), Diamond has identified nine components of a liberal democracy as:

(I)   Control of the state and its key decisions and allocations lies, in fact as well as in constitutional theory, with elected officials (and not democratically unaccountable actors or foreign powers); in particular, the military is subordinate to the authority of elected civilian officials.

(II) Executive power is constrained, constitutionally and in fact, by the autonomous power of other government institutions (such as an independent judiciary, parliament, and other mechanisms of horizontal accountability).

(III) Not only are electoral outcomes uncertain, with a significant opposition vote and the presumption of party alternation in government over time, but no group that adheres to constitutional principles is denied the right to form a party and contest elections (even if electoral thresholds and other rules exclude smaller parties from winning representation in parliament).

(IV) Cultural, ethnic, religious, and other minority groups (as well as traditionally disadvantaged or disempowered majorities) are not prohibited (legally or in practice) from expressing their interests in the political process nor from using their language and culture.

(V)   Beyond parties and intermittent elections, citizens have multiple ongoing channels and means for the expression and representation of their interests and values, including a diverse array of autonomous associations, movements, and groupings that they have the freedom to form and join.

(VI) In addition to associational freedom and pluralism, there exist alternative sources of information (including independent media) to which citizens have (politically) unfettered access.

(VII) Individuals also have substantial freedom of belief, opinion, discussion, speech, publication, assembly, demonstration, and petition.

(VIII) Citizens are politically equal under the law (even though they are invariably unequal in their political resources), and the above individual and group liberties are effectively protected by an independent, nondiscriminatory judiciary whose decisions are enforced and respected by other centers of power.

(IX) The rule of law protects citizens from unjustified detention, exile, terror, torture, or undue interference in their personal lives not only by the state but by organized antistate forces as well.

(Diamond, 1997: 13–14)

One of the most commonly employed contemporary measures of liberal democracy is the annual survey of freedom, started by the non-profit organization Freedom House in 1973. The Freedom House evaluation criterion incorporates some substantive judgments regarding the extent to which a particular country's citizens enjoy political rights and civil liberties. However, for the

Introduction 7

judgment of a particular country as an "electoral democracy" the Freedom House mostly employs a procedural approach. It considers a political system as an electoral democracy if it has a competitive multiparty system, universal adult franchise, regular free and fair elections, and access of political parties to the electorate through the use of media and open political campaigning (Karatnycky et al., 2003).

The elements of polyarchy of Dahl and liberal democracy, especially political rights and civil liberties, as advocated by Diamond, incorporate most of the criteria by which Freedom House annually rates every country of the world. The political rights and civil liberties are separately measured on a 7-point scale, where rating of 1 indicates most free, and 7 indicates the least free. The combination of two scales, as most of the recent quantitative analyses of democracy have done, produces a total score ranging from 2 to 14, or an average score from 1 to 7. Those countries that are averaging 2.5 or lower are considered "free", those scoring 3 to 5.5 are "partly free", and those at the lower end (5.5 to 7, as measured by a more discriminating raw-point score) are considered "not free". For Diamond, the "free" rating in the Freedom House survey is the best, most sensitive and objective empirical indicator available on "liberal democracy" (Diamond, 1997: 14). More interestingly, the conceptual distinctiveness of political rights and civil liberties has enabled the Freedom House to be in a better position to reveal how societies can come up with political systems that are unevenly democratic. Even if there is generally a high degree of correlation between the political and civil dimensions measured, substantial discrepancies do sometimes occur. As demonstrated by the recent trends in much of Latin America and Eastern Europe, where political rights are believed to be fairly secure, for civil liberties the trajectory is too far from complete. To describe those electoral democracies where there is no respect for the rule of law and no protection for civil rights, and where no checks and balances restrain the power of different branches of government, Fareed Zakaria famously introduced the term "illiberal democracy" (Zakaria, 1997). Finally, identifying the rarer reverse phenomenon of "liberal autocracy", in which citizens have access to some civil liberties and rule of law but have fewer political rights, has been made very easy by the Freedom House survey data (Bass, 2005: 639). Notwithstanding the contestations, the Freedom House survey largely represents the reference point for looking at the health of liberal democracy in the contemporary world.

Democratization and the "Waves" Metaphor

If the concept of democracy is contested, so is democratization. Instead of getting caught in the bottomless ocean of democratization, we will rather restrict our analysis primarily to the notion of "waves". That said, a cursory understanding of democratization as a concept is too important to be completely left out. Democratization has generally been defined as a process through which a political regime becomes democratic. It is what Laurence Whitehead argues as

8 *Introduction*

"a dynamic, open-ended complex process involving progress towards a more consensual, rule based and participatory politics" (Whitehead, 2002; 27). To simplify for our purposes here democratization is taken to mean the gradual process of the global spread of democracy and in our case liberal democracy. Since the 19th century, democracy has unfolded gradually across the globe and this process of democratization has neither been linear nor uncontested. Its causes have varied across time and space. For Grugel and Bishop, if it were class that drove the process of democratization in the 19th century, by the 1980s and 1990s it was the complex mix of state building, social conflict, and external influence that would underpin it (Grugel and Bishop, 2013: 32). The analytical device which has become a conventional part of the story of democratization is the notion of the "wave". In *The Third Wave: Democratization in the Late Twentieth Century*, Harvard Political Scientist Samuel P. Huntington famously distinguished between three waves of democratization and two waves of de-democratization (Huntington, 1991). Since the publication of his book, Huntington's wave metaphor has been employed often to capture the major trends in regime change across the globe in the direction to or from democracy (Berg-Schlosser, 1998; Diamond, 1996; Doorenspleet, 2000; Kurzman, 1998). Before going on to analyze the democratization process as it unfolded through the "wave" metaphor, it is pertinent to discuss first the idea of the wave itself. To quote Huntington:

> A wave of democratization is a group of transitions from nondemocratic to democratic regimes that occur within a specified period of time and that significantly outnumber transitions in the opposite direction during that period of time. A wave also involves liberalization or partial democratization in political systems that do not become fully democratic. Each of the first two waves of democratization was followed by reverse waves in which some but not all of the countries that had previously made the transition to democracy reverted to nondemocratic rule.
>
> (Huntington, 1991; 15–16)

While examining Huntington's wave analogy, Charles Kurzman has conceptualized it in at least three ways: 1) when the global level of democracy rises; 2) when there would be periods of net positive transitions to democracy; and 3) when there is any linked set of transitions to democracy. The notion of "waves", argues Kurzman, carries with it the consequence of continuous oscillation. Whether the analogy is used to mean an electromagnetic wave or a simple wave in water, the image indicates that any forward positive democratic oscillation will be balanced by future downward cycles. It is in fact their imminent demise which defines the essence of waves; if they don't reverse or crash, they would no longer remain waves and one would have to abandon the metaphor (Kurzman, 1998; 42–43).

As for as the unfolding of the democratization process—actual rise and global spread of democracy—across several historical periods is concerned,

Introduction 9

John Ikenberry in his latest book *A World Safe for Democracy: Liberal Internationalism and the Crises of Global Order* (2020) argues that scholars generally take recourse to the sequence of waves (Ikenberry, 2020). The first long wave of democratization as per Huntington began in the early 19th century, which roughly ran from 1828 to the early 1920s. During this wave, there was a gradual increase in the number of democratic governments (Diamond, 2011: 299). The first democratic transitions during the first wave developed slowly and were encouraged by the 19th century European and American political movements. During the 19th and early 20th centuries, as many as 29 countries joined the democratic world (Ikenberry, 2020: 49). Notwithstanding the challenges during this time, liberal democracy was in a process of expansion. It was challenged by the notion of socialist democracy, which was based on the concept of popular rule in the context of a socialist organization of society and the economy. To put it another way, communism was an influential anti-capitalist ideology. However, the most significant challenge to liberal democracy as well as to communism came from fascism (Grugel and Bishop, 2013: 33). To quote Huntington, "The dominant political development of the 1920s and the 1930s was the shift away from democracy and either the return to traditional forms of authoritarian rule or the introduction of new mass based, more brutal and pervasive forms of totalitarianism (Huntington, 1991: 17). Huntington believes that the reversals occurred mostly in those countries where democracy *and* the country itself were new. These countries had undergone the democratization process just before or after the first World War. In Huntington's estimation, out of the 17 countries that adopted democracy between 1910 and 1931, only four would survive by the end of 1930s (ibid.). It was the rise of Benito Mussolini and Hitler in Italy and Germany, respectively, and other related developments across Europe which brought the first wave to an end. For Huntington, in what he refers to as the first reverse wave, which began in 1926 and lasted until 1942, democratic political systems collapsed in Italy, Germany, Argentina, Spain, and some of the fledgling democracies in Eastern Europe. Even the newly introduced democracy of Japan (1920s) was supplanted by military rule in the early 1930s. These democratic reversals if anything reflected the rise of fascist, communist, and militaristic ideologies. Interestingly Huntington believed that World War I, which was fought to make the world safe for democracy, instead "unleashed both Left and Right movements that were intent on destroying it" (Huntington, 1991: 17–18).

The second wave of democratization identified by Huntington was significantly shorter. Its commencement signaled the end of World War II. The Allied powers inaugurated democratic institutions in the occupied territories of Japan, Germany, and Austria. Although Soviet pressure snuffed out inchoate democracy in Czechoslovakia and Hungary, in the late 1940s and early 1950s Turkey and Greece moved toward democracy. During this wave most Latin American countries also witnessed democratization. Furthermore, the democratic upsurge in this wave that peaked in 1960s was a product of the postwar decolonization process as many new states were born. However, not every

10 *Introduction*

newly born postcolonial state embraced democracy. For example, in the case of Asia, or to be more precise South Asia, Huntington refers to Pakistan as an example of democracy never really taking hold and being formally abandoned in 1958. However, India and Sri Lanka continued the democratic march for a decade or more (ibid.: 19). During the second wave, the number of democracies reached 36 (Ikenberry, 2020: 49), which accounted for 32% as compared to 20% of all nations during the first reverse wave in 1942 (Kurzman, 1998: 43). It was in the early 1960s that, according to Huntington, the second wave of democratization was exhausted and another reverse wave began. The political developments and regime transitions were tilting towards authoritarianism by the late 1950s and the change was most dramatic in Latin America (Huntington, 1991: 19). The democratic consolidation from the 1960s to 1970s was patchy especially in the developing world where the clutch of harsher dictatorships increased in an unprecedented way. The Argentinian and Guatemalan dictatorships as a case in point were as repressive and violent as the 30–40-year-old fascist regimes of Europe (Grugel and Bishop, 2013: 33). In the case of South Asia, martial law was imposed in 1958 in Pakistan and in 1975 democratic practices were suspended in India with the declaration of emergency. The second reverse wave reduced the number of democracies to 30 from 36 (25% from 32%) from the peak of first wave (Huntington, 1991).

The Only Game in Town: Democratization through the "Third Wave" and Beyond

The "third wave" of democratization, which Huntington believed would carry democracy on an almost irresistible global tide—moving on from one triumph to the next—began with Portugal's democratization in 1974, which was quickly followed by Spain and Greece. During this wave countries in Latin America, East Asia and Southern Europe made democratic transitions. By any measure, as Diamond argues, whether it is the number of democracies in the world or the proportion of the world's regimes that are democratic, democracy has expanded dramatically since the third wave began in 1974 (Diamond, 1997: 20). The number of democracies more than doubled during this wave. According to the Freedom House database, the third wave began with a trough of 96 in 1975 and reached its peak of 118 in 1992. This wave, as per Doh Chull Shin, had been revolutionary in the sense that it impacted every form of regime—Islam, communism, Confucianism—and all other forms of authoritarianism; and truly global in the sense that it reached almost every corner of the world. By transforming democracy into the "only game in town", the third wave, in short, as Shin reckons, fully qualifies for the designation as "the global democratic revolution" (Shin, 1994: 150–151). Huntington has identified five key factors shaping the massive transformation of democratization characterizing the third wave. They are:

Introduction 11

(I) the deepening legitimacy problems of authoritarian systems. This was made worse by the fact that nondemocratic regimes tend to depend excessively on performance legitimacy. A number of nondemocratic regimes were undermined either by poor economic performance in the wake of oil-price rises in the 1970s or by military defeat;

(II) rising expectations following the economic boom of the 1960s, leading to demands for raised living standards and education, especially among the middle classes;

(III) the liberalization of the Catholic Church following the Second Vatican Council of 1963–1965, assisting the transformation of national churches (and individual church leaders) and making it possible for them to act as proponents of reform;

(IV) the changing policies of global organizations such as the European Union, and of actors such as Gorbachev and the shift in US policy towards endorsing an agenda of democratization and human rights; and

(V) demonstration effects, or snowballing, the result of the global growth of communication networks (Huntington, 1991: 45–46).

Although Huntington's analysis of the third wave ended in the beginning of the 1990s, liberal democracy seemed to be on an irresistible march. In just four years the proportion of the world's democratic states increased massively, from 43% in 1990 to more than 57% in 1994. This percentage was much higher than the 38% of the 1920s and 35% of the 1960s—the maximum that these democratic waves could achieve (Doorenspleet, 2000: 392). The remarkable global spread of democracy, which almost doubled from 30% in the early 1980s to almost 60% by the dawn of the 21st century, led Simmons, Dobbin, and Garrett call this the "headline statistic of the late twentieth century" (Ikenberry, 2020: 265). The year 2006 was the high watermark for liberal democracy, as their number reached to 121, which was nearly 63% of all states (Diamond, 2011: 299). For Aurel Croissant and Jeffrey Haynes, the period from 1975 to 2005 saw the spread of democratic institutions in an unprecedented way in human history. Even those societies that had no earlier experience of democratic traditions and did not seem to possess the socio-economic prerequisites for successful democratization witnessed the introduction of democratic institutions in this period (Croissant and Haynes, 2021: 1). The euphoria of liberal democracy's triumph after the fall of the Berlin Wall and the collapse of Soviet Union led the American Political Scientist Francis Fukuyama to proclaim the "end of history" and the triumph of liberal democracy, which he thought to be the end point of man's ideological evolution. In fact, Fukuyama considered the universalization of Western liberal democracy as the final form of government (Fukuyama, 1989: 4). Since liberal democracy, according to him, was now the only viable option, there was no need to search for alternatives. Moving beyond the legitimacy and its ideological appeal, in what he termed a "democratic movement", Marc F. Plattner observed that, even in economic and military strength, democracy enjoyed superiority. For him, there was no easily

12   *Introduction*

discernible, powerful, nondemocratic, economic, political, or ideological challenger on the horizon. Plattner reckoned that even if we are yet to arrive at Fukuyama's "end of history", we have nevertheless entered into a unrelenting period of peaceful democratic hegemony—a kind of "Pax Democratica" (Plattner, 1991: 40). The democratization in post-Soviet states was in particular seen as a "fourth wave" of democracy by Doorenspleet (2005). This is considered a wave because there was democratization in a region which had remained untouched by any previous wave. Most of Eastern Europe, including Poland, Ukraine, and Hungary, turned into democracies. The breakup of the former Soviet Union created new independent countries and added new democracies to the world map. For Doorenspleet the post-communist transitions in Eastern Europe in particular differed notably from the earlier waves of democratization, as during those waves democratic transitions were less frequent (Gleditsch, 2006: 288).

Democratization in Asia through the "Third Wave": Lessons from South Asia

The hitherto democratic experience of Asia has been described by scholars as an "exception" (Grugel, 2002; Lee, 2002; Diamond, 2013; Croissant and Haynes, 2021). It is argued that the first wave of democratization before and after the World War I left the region untouched. The second wave led to the establishment of few electoral democracies like India and Sri Lanka. Only one liberal democracy, that of Japan, with much American pressure, was established. However, even Japan failed to pass the "two-turnover test" until August 1993 (Croissant and Haynes, 2021: 6). Asia before the 1980s, argues Grugel, was characterized by very different political systems than the West. Its leadership style and economic and social systems were remarkably different. The example of China and many other Asian countries is cited to substantiate the difference. Not only was China socialist, but even Asian capitalism was considered as different from that of European or Anglo-American variants. Asian capitalism had a strong role for the state in shaping and directing firms and national markets. The non-socialist Asian political systems, including the formal liberal democracy of Japan, were seen through the prism of exemplifying "Asian values". The rigid ideological divergence between East and West has been purposely exaggerated owing to its utility for the ruling elite in Asia and for policy-makers in the West (Grugel, 2002: 217–218). Asia's rushed socioeconomic development since the 1960s, argues Croissant, has produced a form of "compressed modernity", which has strained the social fabric of societies and as such neglected the region's democratic process (Croissant, 2020: 5).

However, like the rest of the world, the third wave of democratization also engulfed Asia. It reached Asia in the mid-1980s. Besides the surge of opposition movements, some Asian countries progressed towards electoral democracy. Ten Asian countries experienced transition to democracy during this wave. India was the first one to (re)democratize in 1977, after the second reverse wave during the emergency, and there was a domino effect on their Asian neighbors.

Introduction 13

For instance, Sri Lanka democratized in 1983, the Philippines in 1987, South Korea and Pakistan in 1988, Thailand and Mongolia in 1990, Bangladesh and Nepal in 1991, and finally Taiwan in 1992 (Heo and Hahm, 2012: 11). However, the Asian democratic surge during the third wave not only differed from the West, but was also marked with various intricacies and nuances from country to country. Consequently, Junhan Lee contended that the conventional theories of democratization fail to explain the Asian transitions. His analysis demonstrated that factors like economic development, economic crisis, civic culture, and the colonialism of Britain did not impact the Asian democratic surge. Instead, Lee found the factor of "political protest" as one of the significant driving forces of the Asian democratization process during the third wave. For him, the Asian people, tired of the legitimacy crisis of their respective regimes in power, demanded the resignation of their authoritarian leaders. Depending upon their country-specific political conditions, they also demanded free elections, repeal of martial law, and other constitutional changes. Forced to concede to the demands of their people meant the beginning of political liberalization (Lee, 2002: 831). Regarding the overall experience of protest politics during the third wave, which triggered Asian democratization, Lee has proposed some common features. Firstly, the series of political demonstrations, which spread from capitals to many major cities in each country, were sparked by college students. Secondly, the backbone of Asian pro-democracy movements was the region's middle class. Thirdly, the role of many opposition leaders was crucial as they formed a national pro-democracy organization which they used to orchestrate the demonstrations joined by students and middle-class people. Finally, the political demonstrations led to a snowball effect, at the domestic as well as the international level, which continued until the demands of pro-democracy movement were met (Lee, 2002: 836).

The third wave of democracy also swept through South Asia, raising apprehensions and anticipations about how democracy would treat the region, and vice versa. Regardless of the consistent question marks about India's effectiveness in pursuing the regime's "own professional goals", it has managed to function as a democracy since its independence (Kohli, 1987: 8). The economic reforms of the 1990s appeared to be compatible with providing more space for political competitors in a landscape long dominated by the Congress party. India's neighbors were gradually taking steps to follow its lead towards greater democracy. Bangladesh's tryst with the third wave of democracy started with the ending of 15 years of military rule in December 1990 through a people's movement. Khaleda Zia's taking over as the first female prime minister, if anything, underscored great promise towards democratization with political and substantial liberalization reforms (Widmalm, 2021: 3). Commenting on the euphoria and optimism regarding democratization in Bangladesh, Ali Riaz argues:

> the uprising not only brought down the government but also brought an end to the era of civilian and military authoritarianism ... it raised the hopes for democratization. The expectation was based on the lessons from

14 *Introduction*

the prodemocracy movement, particularly an agreement signed by all political parties at the height of the movement promising to adhere to the fundamental canons of liberal democracy such as fair elections, freedom of assembly, and freedom of press among others.

(Riaz, 2021: 181)

Pakistan, experiencing periods of procedural democracy on account of national elections held during 1971–77 and 1980–99, became a reference point of a third wave; however, the seizure of power by the military on 12 October 1999 marked the single most serious reversal during the period (Diamond, 2000: 92). Besides these three big countries, the trajectory of democratization in other countries like Sri Lanka, Nepal, Bhutan, Maldives and Afghanistan during the third wave underscore the fact that the South Asian trajectory of democratization and consolidation differed widely from country to country (Adeney and Wyatt, 2004: 2). Peter R. DeSouza et al. have aptly summed up South Asia's response to the third wave of democracy, stating:

South Asia does not fully fit into the story of the global triumph of democracy. The countries in this region have not experienced a linear progression toward democracy; more often than not, theirs has been a story of forward movements followed by setbacks and regression.

(DeSouza et al., 2008: 85)

Similarly, Larry Diamond also argues that during the third wave South Asia experienced significant oscillation. To a considerable level he holds Pakistan responsible for this due to the country's repeated democratic failures and its protracted descent into institutional decay. This is mainly because of military domination, extremism, and the incurable corruption and fecklessness of politicians and civilian political parties. Yet another sad story of South Asia during the third wave, argues Diamond, has been the steady decay of democracy in Sri Lanka. The country's descent from a stable democracy into an illiberal state and finally a highly corrupt and abusive electoral autocracy (as a result of the civil war) presents another classic case of democratic reversal during the third wave. However, not only has democracy remained sturdy and vibrant in India, but even Bangladesh, after a brief interruption, once again returned to democracy (Diamond, 2013: 97).

The non-linear democratic trajectory of South Asia, with few exceptions, has been an anomaly for the third wave euphoria in respect of the global triumph of democracy. South Asian countries without any exception, as Madhavi Bhasin argues, witnessed three regime changes:

(I) cyclical: alteration between democracy and authoritarianism;
(II) second-try pattern: weak democracy gives way to authoritarianism, which is replaced by stronger democracy; or
(III) interrupted democracy: temporary suspension of a democratic system and then its resumption (Bhasin, 2009: 1).

Introduction 15

While, on the one hand, the uniqueness of the "attempts at democracy" in South Asia presents an analytical challenge for democratization theorists, on the other hand, it provides an unprecedented lesson of the region's consistent desire for democracy despite recurring failures. The peculiarity of South Asian democratization has led Bhasin to call it the beginning of a "fourth wave of democracy" (Bhasin, 2009). Apart from the gradual democratic opening in Afghanistan with the Bonn Conference 2001, a long spell of military rule in Pakistan came to an end by late 2007. The tragic assassination of Benazir Bhutto, just after she had returned from exile and become the country's most popular civilian leader, marked the beginning of a first peaceful transition towards democracy, and thus Pakistan managed to pass Huntington's "two-turnover test" (Widmalm, 2021: 3). The small archipelagic nation of Maldives, by overthrowing Asia's longest serving dictator, experienced its first free and fair multiparty elections in 2008, marking the moonset of authoritarianism and the sunrise of democracy. Bhutan also saw what came to be regarded as world history's smoothest democratic transition in 2008, paving the way for so-called "culturally guided democracy". The democratic nation-building in Bhutan was undertaken by exploring the cultural connectivity among the people (Bhasin, 2009: 8). After decades of war and its civil war in 2009, Sri Lanka entered a more peaceful era, creating circumstances for re-starting the halted process of democratization. More surprisingly, in 2008, Nepal—through the collective choreography of political forces and the Maoists—experienced what came to be characterized as the most unanticipated political transformation of the current century. Besides the abolition of the 250-year-old institution of monarchy, the steering of the new era of democracy in Nepal in an unprecedented manner allowed the former guerrillas (Nepali Maoists) to join the electoral process and even head the new government.

Although examining the current dynamics of South Asia's democratic trajectory forms the core of this volume, we shall return to provide a brief overview of this at the end of the final section. For now we will turn to a brief discussion of the current discourse on the global decline of liberal democracy.

"Democracy under Siege": The Global Decline of Liberal Democracy

The euphoria of the third wave of democratization in recent times has turned into what can be referred as a "Rip Van Winkle" sentiment, since liberal democracy finds itself under siege (Repucci and Slipowitz, 2021). It is no longer the only political game in town, as its post– World War II ascent has come to a halt, thereby making its fate more uncertain. It has been argued that the sanguinity encouraged by the force of the third wave of democratization, including Fukuyama's bolder assertion of relegating the reverse wave of autocratization to the history books, was premature (Youngs et al., 2019: 2). This turnaround has been aptly summed up by Marc F. Plattner, who observed:

> those same principles and practices, which by the 1990s seemed to have fully regained their former attraction and to have spread to a much wider

16 *Introduction*

> range of countries than ever before, now seem again to be losing their luster. Today liberal democracy is clearly on the defensive. Authoritarian regimes of various stripes are showing a new boldness, and they appear to be growing stronger as the confidence and vigor of the democracies wane.
>
> (Plattner, 2017: 6)

In fact, new liberal democratic pessimism has gained traction. The growing autocratization has marked an important shift in the focus of research as well. The questions of democratic transition and consolidation are not only seriously challenged but in fact have been replaced by the growing challenge of auto-cratization and comparative authoritarianism as primary research focus (Croissant and Haynes, 2021: 2). A 2019 survey by Pew Research reported that about 51% of people around the world are dissatisfied with how democracy is working in their countries, in contrast to 45% who are satisfied (Pew Research Center, 2019). This democratic recession, as it has been called, has been there now for more than a decade and a half. The world's renowned organizations, such as Freedom House, Economist Intelligence Unit, Bertelsmann Transformation Index (BTI), and V-Dem have been documenting the global decline in democracy. Scholars, political leaders, and even commentators around the world today have recognized its growing vulnerability. Almost every week there are publications in the form of newspaper columns, journal articles, or books drawing our attention to this perilous state of democracy (Plattner, 2017: 6–7). If anything, it requires serious consideration as to how democracy arrived at this critical juncture.

To begin with, the promise of a "fourth wave of democratization" didn't materialize and its expansion simply stopped. The proportion of democracies since the "high watermark for global democracy"—that is, 2006—gradually declined. The year 2019 marked the low point of democracy since the end of the Cold War, as during this year for the first time we witnessed the majority of people around the world *not* living in a democratic setup. In 2019 BTI for the first time since 2004 recorded a slip towards more autocratization. Out of 137 country cases, 70 were autocracies, and only 67 were considered democracies. Hauke Hartmann, BTI project manager at the Bertelsmann Foundation, considers it the worst of the political transformations that his 15 years of work has measured (Hille, 2022). Invoking the wave metaphor, this democratic reversal has been dubbed by some scholars as the "third wave of autocratization" (Lührmann and Lindberg, 2019). The "autocratization virus" has shown an accelerating trend, as demonstrated by the 2021 V-Dem Democracy Report entitled *Autocratization Turns Viral*. According to the report, the share of world's population living in autocracies and autocratizing countries has increased from 48% to 68% and 6% to 34%, respectively, from 2010 to 2020 (V-Dem, 2021). The "resurgent authoritarianism", as it has been called, has fueled the malaise of democracy both in the West and East. If the major established democracies have turned inward, the leading authoritarian regimes have turned outward. More worryingly, it is no longer the "soft power" of

Introduction 17

democracies but surprisingly the "sharp power" of autocracies that seems to be alluring. The growing pessimism with democracy is also associated with the trend of continuous decline in various freedoms enjoyed by citizens. Freedom House in its 2023 report has counted the year 2022 as the 17th consecutive year of global decline of freedom—the key driver of global democratic decline (Freedom House, 2023: 1). The share of "Not Free" countries has dramatically risen since 2006.

Another observation that underscores the current discourse of the "global decline of democracy" is that of political fatigue and polarization increasingly affecting the established democracies of the West as well as "the Rest" (Croissant and Haynes, 2021: 3). The "polarization paradox" undermining the health of democracies has been well articulated by Thomas Carothers and Andrew O'Donohue in their 2019 edited volume *Democracies Divided: The Global Challenge of Political Polarization*. For them, the phenomenon of severe political polarization captures one of the important parts of the story of global democratic recession as it is gradually upsetting new and old democracies alike by generating rising societal anger and erosion of democratic norms (Carothers and O'Donohue, 2019). However, if their study finds "culture" or "identity politics" as the driving force of polarization, other studies have blamed the rise of global financial capitalism for challenging the "happy marriage" of liberal democracy with embedded capitalism, which has been the hallmark of democratic capitalism ever since World War II came to an end (Merkel, 2014; Przeworski, 2019). Furthermore, many recent democracies are undergoing increasing challenges of democratic erosion. Not only is the health of established democracies deteriorating, but more worryingly in non-democratic countries the authoritarian grip is hardening. Consequently, democratic openings are aborted and democratic moments are lost (Levitsky and Way, 2010).

It is important to point out that back in 1996, during the third wave of democratization, Huntington himself had thought about the likely challenges to liberal democracy. For him, the threat to the third wave democracies was not posed by revolutionaries or generals. Instead, they were threatened by political leaders or groups who after coming to power, after winning the elections, manipulate the democratic machinery to curtail or destroy it (Kneuer, 2021: 1443). As he reckoned, the problem with third wave democracies is erosion not overthrow, which he considered as the intermittent or gradual weakening of democracy by elected leaders (Huntington, 1996: 9). Likewise, the gradual erosion of freedoms, guarantees, and other vital processes of democracy have been called by O'Donnell as the "slow death" of democracy (De la Torre and Ortiz Lemos, 2016: 1). In contemporary times scholars have attempted to cut through the trajectory of the phenomenon of the slow death of democracy. Accordingly, the scholarly literature has seen the emergence of various new and markedly different conceptual categories, such as "democratic regression", "democratic recession", "democratic backsliding", "democratic erosion", "democratic decoupling", and so on. The following section discusses some of these most prevalent and often used conceptual categories underscoring the literature on

18 *Introduction*

global democratic pessimism. However, there is a caveat: we do not offer a comparative analysis by delineating the similarities and differences, nor do we engage with the question of choice as to which one is more appropriate. Rather, we aim to offer just an overview of these concepts and terms and leave it to the contributors to decide their appropriateness and usage. To put it differently, this edited volume can best be described as a case of a "plausibility probe" and hence we keep it open and flexible for the contributors to engage with the concepts and terms as per the plausibility of the country they are looking at as a case study.

Many Facets of Democratic Decline: Recapitulating the Conceptual Toolkit

Among various titles under which the global decline of democracy has been studied, the earliest one to be used in the evolving debate, and the one which came to be characterized as a more general concept, is *democratic regression*. Gero Erdmann and Marianne Kneuer define the term democratic regression as a "reverse process", that is, transition from democracy (Erdmann and Kneuer, 2013). They have offered three discrete forms of the term democratic regression. Firstly, it involves the loss of democratic quality in established democracies. Secondly, it involves the erosion of democracies into hybrid regimes. And thirdly, it includes the breakdown of democracies into outright dictatorships. These three forms of democratic regression can take two basic routes: slow death (democratic erosion and loss of democratic quality) or rapid death (breakdown). Erdmann and Kneuer argue that the phenomenon of rapid death or breakdown of democracy has been well researched in the past and identifies the slow death or the gradual erosion of democracy as the new research agenda (ibid.: 13). According to Larry Diamond, there is no single major explanation of the phenomenon of democratic regression that the world is currently experiencing. Yet a number of factors and agents can be identified. As he puts it,

> in most cases of democratic regression or failure, we can find familiar agents of destruction: elected political leaders, greedy for power and wealth, who knock away various types of constraints on their power and enlarge and entrench it in undemocratic ways.
>
> (Diamond, 2020: 9)

Diamond argues that in present times the democratic demise is hardly authored by military leaders, although occasionally military intervention may still happen as is the case of Thailand and Egypt (and behind the scenes, in Pakistan). Instead, democracy in today's world is under serious civilian assault. The prominent figures of democratic breakdowns are politicians and polarizing political parties. Moreover, typically the authoritarian politician, instead of being the product of political polarization, is its main generator. As Diamond points out:

Introduction 19

The populist politicians rise to power by inflaming divisions and mobilizing the good, deserving "people" against corrupt elites—the professional or "deep" state and their effete, educated handmaidens in the other (liberal) political parties—as well as a host of alien threats, such as international institutions, refugees and migrants, and "undeserving" minorities who really don't "belong" in the country.

(Diamond, 2020: 9–11)

For Diamond, who uses the terms *regression* and *recession* interchangeably, the world since 2006 has been in mild but prolonged democratic recession. For him, beyond the absence of advancement or modest erosion of freedom and democracy at global level, four other causes of concern have emerged. Firstly, the rate of democratic breakdown is accelerating rapidly. Secondly, in a number of strategically important and large emerging market economies, which Diamond calls "swing states", the stability and quality of democracy is declining. Thirdly, in a number of big and strategically significant countries authoritarianism has been deepening. Finally, the United States and other established democracies besides performing very poorly lack the self-confidence and will to effectively promote democracy abroad (Diamond, 2015: 144). The crux of Diamond's reckoning is that quality of liberal democracy is declining and so are its institutions. His notion of democratic recession is in fact used analogously to economic recession, involving the decline in the economy. Consequently, the process of democratic recession is incremental and gradual. The process very often starts with the erosion of qualities of democracy and gives rise to a "hybrid regime", combining the traits of both democracy and authoritarianism. While it has been commonplace to assume that electoral problems are at the root of democratic recession, there are other political elements like infringement of individual rights and the freedom of expression that are at the core of it.

Another facet of the global decline of democracy—as an important new research avenue—identified by David Waldner and Ellen Lust is that of *democratic backsliding*. They define backsliding more generally as a process of deteriorating democratic qualities within any regime. While it means the decline in the quality of democracy in democratic regimes, it entails the decline in the democratic qualities of governance in autocracies (Waldner and Lust, 2018: 95). While focusing on backsliding within democracies, Waldner and Lust comprehend it as a process occurring potentially through not a one-time coup de grace, but through a series of discontinuous incremental actions. Backsliding, as they argue, without openly abolishing universal franchise norms restricts participation and makes elections less competitive without undermining the electoral mechanism completely. It also loosens controls of accountability by eroding punishment and answerability norms. While answerability refers to the duty of public officials to publicize and justify their actions, punishment is the capacity of citizens or governing bodies to enforce negative consequences for undesirable actions or violations of authorized procedures (Waldner and Lust, 2018: 95). The basis of the backsliding phenomenon is the gradual process of weakening

20 Introduction

or piece-by-piece disassembling of democratic institutions without an all-out regime change. It is what Nancy Bermeo and Michael Coppedge refer to as the state-led debilitation or elimination of any of the political institutions that sustain an existing democracy (Bermeo, 2016; Coppedge, 2017). However, the condition for backsliding, they argue, is that a country must have passed a minimum threshold of democracy. The peculiarity about backsliding is that the duly elected incumbents are its drivers. Once an autocrat is in power, he or she takes undemocratic actions by removing the horizontal checks on the executive, violating the rights of citizens and in some extreme cases even going after the integrity of the electoral system itself. In essence, the notion of backsliding underscores that the conventional challenges of blatant auto-cratization, like election-day voting fraud and military coups, have been replaced by concealed forms of autocratization in the shape of executive aggrandizement, the strategic manipulation of disqualifying the opposition leaders, and harassing the opposition (Bermeo, 2016). However, as per this conceptualization, democratic backsliding doesn't mean autocratic consolida-tion, but it does entail episodes of democratic recession and breakdown (Croissant and Haynes, 2021: 5). As argued by Bermeo, "where backsliding takes the shape of gradual changes across a more restricted set of institutions, it is less likely to lead to all-out regime change and more likely to produce political systems that are hybrid or ambiguously democratic" (Bermeo, 2016: 6). It is in this context that some scholars have pointed to what they call "presidential hegemony" driving the backsliding phenomenon (Pérez-Liñán et al., 2019). Apart from what can be categorized mostly as the indigenous vari-ables of democratic backsliding, the extant literature also emphasizes the threat of authoritarian "sharp power", wherein the role of exporting auto-cracy by the modern-day resilient autocratic states like Russia, China, Iran, and Saudi Arabia is being invoked. It is argued that their growing influence in democratic countries gradually undermines democracy and thus leads to its backsliding (Walker, 2018; Wehrey, 2015).

Finally, the term *democratic erosion* has also been used extensively to capture the pattern of the slow death of global democracy. According to Marianne Kneuer, the democratic erosion occurs in the context of autocratization invol-ving two logics—and two paths: the "slow death" and the "rapid death". It is the former that has been more prevalent. Almost 70% of autocratization cases occurred through the route of the slow death of democracy. To capture this slow death of democracy, Kneuer prefers the term "erosion" to "backsliding" or other labels. As she puts it:

> the metaphor of erosion implies that, due to the force of a certain agent (like water or wind), an existing structure is hollowed out and conse-quently deteriorates. This means that there must indeed be a structure, that already exists, and that is then weakened actively by an agent.
>
> (Kneuer, 2021: 1446)

Building on this metaphor, she argues that democratic erosion occurs when an established democracy, a regime that for a certain time fulfills the essentials of democracy, faces a gradual dismantling of its democratic structure. For Kneuer, the concept of erosion is more appropriate than backsliding in pointing out the main factor driving the process (an erosion agent), the subject of the erosion (democracy), and the nature and direction of the process (gradual hollowing out). The term also helps to capture the final outcome of the process: a shell as a residue of the erosion process keeping up a façade of the earlier structure. Accordingly, the remaining shell has the propensity of being filled with a new content of different kinds (ibid.: 1446–1447). Likewise, for Melis G. Laebens and Anna Lührmann, democratic erosion occurs not when there is a suspension or abolishing of democratic institutions altogether but when democratically elected leaders considerably dent democratic institutions (that is, causes auto-cratization) by expanding or abusing their powers. For them one can know when autocratization has occurred or when democratic institutions have been undermined substantially only when there is a substantive decline in the extent to which the regime fulfills the criteria of Dahl's polyarchy, as discussed in the earlier section. It is only when the democratic institutions as proposed by Dahl are eroded in such a way that the country turns into an (electoral) autocracy that Laebens and Lührmann consider the key democratic institutions to be suspended or abolished. While conceiving the erosion of democracy as a sub-type of the larger autocratization process they argue that, driven by the demo-cratically elected incumbent's self-serving actions, it starts in democracies and ends without causing a democratic breakdown (Laebens and Lührmann, 2021: 910). Much like regression, backsliding and other labels, democratic erosion is not seen as a domestic matter only. The authoritarian rule's international dimension over the last decade demonstrates the entrenchment of the demo-cratic erosion between the domestic and international levels. It is applicable to both outward and inward directions. Accordingly, it can be assessed that the agents of erosion would link their domestic change mission with international ambitions or regional missions like region-building. They may even set out to promote actively their alternative model of rule in the geopolitical proximity. As Bermeo has reckoned, democratic erosions are "rational responses" to international inducements such as the stress on elections (Bermeo, 2016: 15). Thus, as Kneuer argues, erosion agents can be affected by external factors, which can be actor-based or structural, and impact their choices during the erosion process (Kneuer, 2021: 1447).

The aforementioned conceptual toolkit underscoring the global decline of democracy since 2006, notwithstanding the terminological variations, does exhibit a broad pattern with some obvious characteristics over which there seems to be unanimity among scholars and experts. Firstly, there is a broad consensus in the literature that democracy is declining slowly as compared to hitherto rapid democratic breakdowns. Secondly, the agents of democratic decline are mostly the elected populist politicians and polarized political parties than the conventional military interventions and coup d'états. Thirdly, the

22 Introduction

external variable of autocratic sharp power is further fueling the malaise of democracy. The resilience of autocracies like Russia, China and Saudi Arabia and their exportation of autocracy is conceived to be a major challenge to liberal democracy. Finally, the so-called democratic bastion states, especially the United States and other Western countries, besides failing to stand up to their own domestic challenges, are failing at the external front as well to promote democracy abroad.

Situating South Asia and *What to Follow*

The Freedom House in its 2022 report *Freedom in the World* makes a lamentable assessment of the global state of democracy. The report reads:

> Global freedom faces a dire threat. Around the world, the enemies of liberal democracy are accelerating their attacks. Authoritarian regimes have become more effective at co-opting or circumventing the norms and institutions meant to support basic liberties, and at providing aid to others who wish to do the same. In countries with long-established democracies, internal forces have exploited the shortcomings in their systems, distorting national politics to promote hatred, violence, and unbridled power. Those countries that have struggled in the space between democracy and authoritarianism, meanwhile, are increasingly tilting toward the latter.
>
> (Freedom House, 2022)

The report further warns that the global order is close to a tipping point, and the authoritarian model will triumph if the defenders of democracy fail to work together to help guarantee freedom for all. The report substantiates the alarming situation by its estimation that while since 2021 only 25 countries have shown improvement, a remarkable 60 countries have experienced decline. Almost 38% of the worldwide population lives in "Not Free" countries, the highest proportion since 1997. Only about 20% live in "Free" countries today (ibid.). The V-Dem's 2022 democracy report puts the current state of global democracy on par with the level in 1989. According to the report, the level of democracy that an average citizen in the world in the year 2021 enjoyed has fallen to 1989 levels. Accordingly, the democratic advances achieved in the last 30 years following the end of the Cold War have been destroyed. The regions of Eastern Europe, Latin America, the Caribbean, Central Asia, and Asia-Pacific make this decline evident (V-Dem, 2022). The overall Asian experience presents an ambiguous picture in the global decline of democracy debate. Croissant and Haynes point out that, "while the region compared to 30 or 40 years ago is much more democratic today … the recent data of many democratic barometers demonstrate a net decline of democracy by displaying [a] clearer sign of autocratization" (Croissant and Haynes, 2021: 6).

It is in this context, Diamond laments, that "sadly, the whole region of Asia appears now to be on the path of general democratic decline" (Diamond, 2020:

29). As far as South Asia is concerned, it is also seen as a region that has become part of what is termed the "third wave of autocratization" (Widmalm, 2021: 3). As per the Freedom House Index of 2022 there was no "Free" country in the region, which has not changed as per the 2023 report. If these reports are to be taken into consideration, the region is home to two "Not Free" countries—Myanmar and Afghanistan. Moreover, all countries, including India, are categorized as "Partly Free" (Freedom House, 2021). Arguing on similar lines a recent work concludes:

> South Asia is currently one of the world's regions where the level of democracy is declining sharply. Although the Indian subcontinent and its surrounding states are difficult to delimit in relation to the rest of Asia, the trend concerns India, Pakistan, Afghanistan, Bangladesh, Nepal, and Sri Lanka. Should we include Myanmar the impression would only deepen. Evidently, all states in this region either find it very hard to make significant gains in democratization, or have been caught in a seemingly unstoppable trend of autocratization.
>
> (Widmalm, 2021: 335)

It is argued that over the last ten years, Prime Minister Sheikh Hasina has pushed Bangladesh towards becoming a one-party state. Freedom of speech is being muffled in Pakistan and minorities are at risk in Sri Lanka. India is rapidly sinking in reports on democracy and liberal freedoms provided by Freedom House, Reporters Without Borders, Pen International, and Amnesty International. However, it is important to mention that the estimations of these institutions have not gone unchallenged on various grounds, particularly in India. The Economist, while determining 2021 to be a poor year for fair, free, and open societies in Asia, also laments the South Asian experience of democracy (The Economist, 2021). The year 2021 has been judged a poor one for democracy in South Asian. Even those political parties and politicians who came to power by winning elections pursued increasingly authoritarian policies intolerant of dissent (Dagia, 2022). The COVID-19 pandemic appeared to be a "blessing in disguise" for some of the governments of South Asia as it provided a pretext for pursuing authoritarian measures such as excessive surveillance and media crackdowns, as well as discriminatory restrictions on civil liberties. However, it is the return of the Taliban to power in Afghanistan in 2021 that is considered to be the biggest blow to South Asian democracy in recent times. Even though one may question the democratic trajectory of Afghanistan under President Ashraf Ghani, no one can deny that despite flaws, it was at least an elected government. The return of the Taliban has moved the democratic trajectory from bad to worse. In Pakistan the elected government led by Imran Khan's Pakistan Tehreek-e-Insaf (PTI) was overthrown by a military-orchestrated no-confidence motion, its leadership was jailed, and even the party was denied its symbol. In the 2024 elections, the PTI candidates were forced to fight the election as independents without a party symbol and there were widespread

24   *Introduction*

concerns raised on the fairness of the election (The Hindu, 2024). The role of the military in electoral politics has once again raised concerns about the future of democracy in Pakistan. In the Maldives, since 2008 no government can claim to have adhered to the democratic norms fully. Adding to this, the continuous tussle among political parties and the deep involvement of external forces keep the chances of a return to an autocratic regime open. In Bhutan, two judges and a top general were arrested over a suspected conspiracy to overthrow the chief justice and the military chief of the country. As for Nepal, former Prime Minister K.P. Sharma Oli and President Bidhya Devi Bhandari, by acting in complete disregard of various constitutional norms, procedures, and principles, have seriously dented democracy. Furthermore, the public trust in democratic institutions and processes in Nepal has been undermined by the terrible power struggle among its political parties. Therefore, the aforementioned democratic trajectory substantiates the claim that South Asia is going through a democratic crisis. However, it would be an exaggeration to place all the countries of the region within this single explanatory framework. Also, it may be noted that the argument of the crisis of democracy is seriously contested by the governments as well as sections of scholarship in countries like India. There is in fact a reverse claim, with valid justifications, that the democracy has strengthened as well as indigenized over a period of time. Furthermore, even if there is an overall decline of democracy in the region, its nature varies from country to country. For example, if Afghanistan and Sri Lanka represent democratic despair, Bhutan and Nepal still continue to be the democratic hope. Getting through the multilayered and multi-dynamic democratic trajectory of South Asia in recent times is what constitutes the crux of this edited volume.

Structure of the Volume

After this introduction, the remainder of the volume is structured as follows:

The contribution by Jennifer Brick Murtazashvili entitled "Democracy Denied: The False Promise of Afghanistan's Constitutions", contrary to the popularly held opinion regarding the democracy in Afghanistan, argues that democracy in Afghanistan did not fail. Instead, she argues that the democracy did not live up to its potential because it was never given a chance to thrive. The chapter identifies two reasons that have limited the potential of democracy in Afghanistan. First, the 2004 constitution never allowed Afghanistan's democracy to live up to its promise because the institutional arrangements that governed the post-2001 period failed to create incentives for participation in the state democratic system at the subnational level. Second, the staggering corruption in presidential and parliamentary elections disillusioned the citizens from the democratic project. While blaming the international community as well, she argues that political leaders in Kabul and its international patrons preferred to centralize authority around authoritarian institutions, rather than make concrete efforts to implement the "imperfect" democracy enshrined in the constitution. Accordingly, the state-building project denied the people of Afghanistan the democracy it promised.

Ali Riaz employs the theoretical construct of democratic backsliding in his contribution entitled "The Making of an Autocratic Regime: Democratic Backsliding in Bangladesh". The chapter focuses on the post-1990 developments with special reference to the rapid debilitation of the democratic institutions and practices after the Bangladesh Awami League (AL) came to power in 2009. By drawing on the elements of a three-stage model offered by Steven Levitsky and Daniel Ziblatt, he contends that in Bangladesh, the backsliding has taken course through changes in institutions like the electoral system, constitution, and judiciary, while constructing an ideology and using mobilizational capacity of the ruling party.

The chapter titled "Removals of Elected and Appointed Public Officials in Bhutan: Democratic Recession or Consolidation?" by Sonam Kinga looks at Bhutan as a case of democratic consolidation instead of democratic regression or recession. While focusing on one of the aspects, especially the adherence to the rule of law, the author illustrates the extent of democratic consolidation in Bhutan since its introduction 13 years ago. By using examples of the removals and resignations of very senior and highly positioned public officials who were either elected or appointed (which in an established democracy can been seen as signs of its decline), Sonam Kinga reckons that these were significant developments in the process of Bhutan's democratic consolidation. In other words, he argues that these removals and resignations attest to the political society's admirable commitment to due democratic process and rule of law, which he argues has been one of the main reasons for the success of consolidating Bhutan's nascent democracy.

In the chapter titled "Democracy in India: Continuities, Realignments and Promises", Anup Shekhar Chakraborty provides a nuanced analysis of the democratic trajectory of the world's largest democracy. Chakraborty weaves the continuities and realignments across ideologies, leaderships, party formations, and disintegrations to explore the democratic journey of the Indian state in recent times. By looking at Indian democracy as a "process", the chapter explores the future possibilities and promises while examining the recent trends under the current regime and explores how the democratic process has evolved into newer possibilities, as well as what happens to the Indian electorate—the *Jagrukta Sachet Janata Janardan*.

In our contribution, "Democracy in the Maldives: Unpacking the 'Democratization-Backsliding' Rollercoaster", by analyzing the island nation's democratic trajectory from 2008 onwards, we argue that it can best be described as a democratization-backsliding rollercoaster. By employing the theoretical prism of democratic backsliding, we try to explore a set of endogenous as well as exogenous variables that are driving forces behind this backsliding process. Among the endogenous variables the chapter identifies authoritarian residues, presidential hegemony and executive aggrandizement, and Islamic radicalism, and among the exogenous variables (which we describe as the tragedy of authoritarian leverage), the chapter explores the roles of China and Saudi Arabia.

26 Introduction

By considering the notion of backsliding, Abijit Sharma's chapter "Nepal's Tryst with Democracy: Internal Dynamics, External Influences" explores the recent democratic trajectory of Nepal. Sharma argues that Nepal has not been able to consolidate its democracy even seven decades after it was first ushered in (1951). Poor democratic consolidation has subsequently resulted in different forms of backsliding in the country. Sharma argues that Nepal's democratic backsliding has both an internal and external dimension. The chapter focuses on the role of Nepal's "pliant leadership" for encouraging internal problems as well as for encouraging the meddling by its two powerful neighbors, resulting in its democratic backsliding.

The chapter "Democratization in Pakistan and Its Challenges" by Mariam Mufti and Kazma Chaudhry employes an actor-centered approach to make a case for Pakistan continuing to be a hybrid regime despite its multiparty competition and regular elections. Pakistan persists as a hybrid regime rather than one progressing towards democracy. By employing an actor-centered approach, Mufti and Chaudhry bring to the forefront four major actors viz. British colonialism, the military, political elite, and international actor (United States), which have historically played roles in the development of a hybrid regime in Pakistan to protect their interests. Given some recent events in Pakistan's politics, they question if there is a fifth actor in the form of the judiciary, which might also be a contributing factor.

In their contribution "Constitutional Amendments (2001–2022) and Democracy in Sri Lanka", Nadarajah Pushparajah & Malini Balamayuran explore how constitutional amendments, normally seen as a constitutional means to improve and strengthen democracy, can also be used as a mechanism to undermine democracy by political leadership. By employing backsliding as a theoretical construct, the chapter explores the politics of constitutional amendments since 2001 and their impact on democracy in Sri Lanka. Selecting four constitutional amendments brought in since 2001, the chapter explores how governments exploited these amendments to consolidate political power rather than strengthen the democracy in the country. Having examined the consequences of democratic backsliding in Sri Lanka the chapter concludes with putting forward strategies to strengthen the process of democratization in post-war Sri Lanka.

Bibliography

Adeney, K. and Wyatt, A., 2004. "Democracy in South Asia: Getting beyond the structure-agency dichotomy". *Political Studies*, Vol. 52, No. 1: 1–18.

Andrews, G. and Chapman, H., eds, 1995. *The social construction of democracy, 1870–1990*. Springer.

Bass, J., 2005. "Democracy, measures of", in Leonard, K.K., ed., *Encyclopedia of social measurement*. Elsevier: 637–643.

Berg-Schlosser, D., 1998. "Conditions of authoritarianism, fascism and democracy in inter-war Europe: A cross-sectional and longitudinal analysis". *International Journal of Comparative Sociology*, Vol. 39, No. 4: 335–339.

Bermeo, N., 2016. "On democratic backsliding". *Journal of Democracy*, Vol. 27, No. 1: 5–19.

Bhasin, M., 2009. "South Asia and the fourth wave of democracy". Online, https://essaydocs.org/south-asia-and-the-fourth-wave-of-democracy.html.

Carothers, T. and O'Donohue, A., eds, 2019. *Democracies divided: The global challenge of political polarization*. Brookings Institution Press.

Churchill, W.S. 1947. "Debate Parliament Bill". HC Deb, vol. 444 cc203–321. November 11, http://hansard.millbanksystems.com/commons/1947/nov/11/parliament-bill#S5CV0444P0_19471111_HOC_292.

Collier, D. and Levitsky, S., 1997. "Democracy with adjectives: Conceptual innovation in comparative research". *World Politics*, Vol. 49, No. 3: 430–451.

Coppedge, M., 2017. "Eroding regimes: What, where, and when?". V-Dem Working Paper, No. 57, https://gupea.ub.gu.se/bitstream/handle/2077/54297/gupea_2077_54297_1.pdf?sequence=1&isAllowed=y.

Crick, B., 1962. *In defense of politics*. University of Chicago Press.

Crick, B., 2002. *Democracy: A very short introduction*. Oxford University Press.

Croissant, A., 2020. "The struggle for democracy in Asia–regression, resilience, revival". *Asia Policy Brief*. April, http://aei.pitt.edu/103242/.

Croissant, A. and Haynes, J., 2021. "Democratic regression in Asia: Introduction". *Democratization*, Vol. 28, No. 1: 1–21. Dagia, N., 2022. "2021 was a bad year for democracy in South Asia". *The Diplomat*, January 5.

Dahl, R.A., 1971. *Polyarchy: Participation and opposition*. Yale University Press.

Dahl, R.A., 1982. *Dilemmas of pluralist democracy: Autonomy vs. control*. Yale University Press.

Dahl, R.A., 1989. *Democracy and its critics*. Yale University Press.

Dahl, R.A., 1998. *On Democracy*. Yale University Press.

Dahl, R.A., 2005. "What political institutions does large-scale democracy require?" *Political Science Quarterly*, Vol. 120, No. 2: 187–197.

Dahl, R.A., 2006. *a preface to democratic theory*. University of Chicago Press.

De la Torre, C. and Ortiz Lemos, A., 2016. "Populist polarization and the slow death of democracy in Ecuador". *Democratization*, Vol. 23, No. 2: 221–241.

DeSouza, P.R., Palshikar, S., and Yadav, Y., 2008. "The democracy barometers (Part II): Surveying South Asia". *Journal of Democracy*, Vol. 19, No. 1: 84–96.

Diamond, L.J., 1996. "Is the third wave over?". *Journal of Democracy*, Vol. 7, No. 3: 20–37.

Diamond, L.J., 2000. "Is Pakistan the (reverse) wave of the future?" *Journal of Democracy*, Vol. 11, No. 3: 91–106.

Diamond, L., 1997. "Is the third wave over: An empirical assessment". *Helen Kellogg Institute for International Studies*, Working Paper, No. 236: 1–54. Diamond, L., 2011. "Democracy's third wave today". *Current History*, Vol. 110, No. 739: 299–307.

Diamond, L., 2013. "The flow and ebb of democracy's third wave". *Mongolian Journal of International Affairs*, Vol. 18: 94–104.

Diamond, L., 2014. "Chasing away the democracy blues". *Foreign Policy*. October 24.

Diamond, L., 2015. "Facing up to the democratic recession". *Journal of Democracy*, Vol. 26, No. 1: 141–155.

Diamond, L., 2020. "Democratic regression in comparative perspective: scope, methods, and causes". *Democratization*, Vol. 28, No. 1: 22–42.

Diamond, L., Plattner, M.F., Chu, Y.H., and Tien, H.M., eds, 1997. *Consolidating the third wave democracies* (Vol. 1). JHU Press. Doorenspleet, R., 2000. "Reassessing the three waves of democratization". *World Politics*, Vol. 52, No. 3: 384–406.

28 Introduction

Doorenspleet, R., 2005. *Democratic transitions: Exploring the structural sources of the fourth wave.* Lynne Rienner Publishers.

Doorenspleet, R., 2018. *Rethinking the value of democracy: A comparative perspective.* Springer.

Economic Intelligence Unit. 2020. "Democracy Index 2020: In sickness and in health?", https://www.eiu.com/n/campaigns/democracy-index-2020/.

Erdmann, G. and Kneuer, M., eds, 2013. *Regression of democracy?* Springer Science & Business Media.

Freedom House. 2022. "Freedom in the World 2022". Available at: https://freedomhouse.org/sites/default/files/2022-02/FIW_2022_PDF_Booklet_Digital_Final_Web.

Freedom House. 2023. "Freedom in the World 2023—marking 50 years in the struggle for democracy". Available at: https://freedomhouse.org/sites/default/files/2023-03/FIW_World_2023_DigtalPDF.pdf.

Fukuyama, F., 1989. "The end of history?" *The National Interest*, Vol. 16: 3–18.

Gleditsch, K.S., 2006. "Exploring the origins of transitions in the fourth wave". *International Studies Review*, Vol. 8, No. 2: 288–290.

Grugel, J., 2002. *Democratization: A critical introduction.* Palgrave Macmillan.

Grugel, J. and Bishop, M.L., 2013. *Democratization: A critical introduction.* Bloomsbury Publishing.

Gutmann, A. and Thompson, D., 1996. *Democracy and disagreement.* Belknap.

Held, D., 1996. *Models of democracy.* Stanford University Press.

Heo, U. and Hahm, S.D., 2012. "The third wave of democratization and economic performance in Asia: Theory and application". *Korea Observer*, Vol. 43, No. 1: 1–20.

Hille, P., 2022. "Democracy in decline worldwide". DW.com, February 23, https://www.dw.com/en/democracy-in-decline-worldwide/a-60878855.

Huntington, S.P., 1991. *The third wave: Democratization in the late twentieth century.* University of Oklahoma Press.

Huntington, S.P., 1996. "Democracy for the Long Haul". *Journal of Democracy*, Vol. 7, No. 2: 3–13.

Ikenberry, G.J., 2020. *A world safe for democracy: Liberal internationalism and the crises of global order.* Yale University Press.

Inkeles, A., ed., 1991. *On measuring democracy: Its consequences and concomitants.* Transaction Publishers.

Kaldor, M. and Vejvoda, I., 1997. "Democratization in central and east European countries". *International Affairs*, Vol. 73, No. 1: 59–82.

Karatnycky, A., Piano, A., and Puddington, A., eds., 2003. *Freedom in the world 2003: The annual survey of political rights and civil liberties.* Rowman & Littlefield.

Kneuer, M., 2021. "Unravelling democratic erosion: Who drives the slow death of democracy, and how?" *Democratization*, Vol. 28, No. 8: 1442–1462.

Kohli, A., 1987. *The state and poverty in India: The politics of reform.* Cambridge University Press.

Kurzman, C., 1998. "Waves of democratization". *Studies in Comparative International Development*, Vol. 33, No. 1: 42–64.

Laebens, M.G. and Lührmann, A., 2021. "What halts democratic erosion? The changing role of accountability". *Democratization*, Vol. 28, No. 5: 908–928.

Lee, J., 2002. "Primary causes of Asian democratization: Dispelling conventional myths". *Asian Survey*, Vol. 42, No. 6: 821–837.

Levitsky, S. and Way, L.A., 2010. *Competitive authoritarianism: Hybrid regimes after the Cold War.* Cambridge University Press.

Lührmann, A. and Lindberg, S.I., 2019. "A third wave of autocratization is here: What is new about it?" *Democratization*, Vol. 26, No. 7: 1095–1113.

MacKensie, I., 1994. "Introduction: The arena of ideology", in R. Ecleshall, V. Geoghegan, R. Jay, M. Kenny, I. Mackensie, and R. Wilford, eds, *Political ideologies*. Routledge.

Merkel, W., 2014. "Is there a crisis of democracy?" *Democratic Theory*, Vol. 1, No. 2: 11–25.

O'Donnell, G., 1995. "Democracy's future: Do economists know best?" *Journal of Democracy*, Vol. 6, No. 1: 23–28.

O'Donnell, G.A., 1999. *Counterpoints: Selected essays on authoritarianism and democratization*. University of Notre Dame Press.

Pérez-Liñán, A., Schmidt, N., and Vairo, D., 2019. "Presidential hegemony and democratic backsliding in Latin America, 1925–2016". *Democratization*, Vol. 26, No. 4: 606–625.

Pew Research Center. 2019. "Many across the globe are dissatisfied with how democracy is working". April 29, https://www.pewresearch.org/global/2019/04/29/many-across-the-globe-are-dissatisfied-with-how-democracy-is-working/.

Plattner, M.F., 1991. "The democratic moment". *Journal of Democracy*, Vol. 2, No. 4: 34–46.

Plattner, M.F., 2017. "Liberal democracy's fading allure". *Journal of Democracy*, Vol. 28, No. 4: 5–14.

Przeworski, A., 2019. *Crises of democracy*. Cambridge University Press.

Repucci, S. and Slipowitz, A., 2021. "Democracy under siege". Freedom House, https://freedomhouse.org/sites/default/files/2021-03/FIW2021_Abridged_03112021_FINAL.pdf.

Riaz, A., 2021. "The pathway of democratic backsliding in Bangladesh". *Democratization*, Vol. 28, No. 1: 179–197.

Saward, M., 2021. *Democratic design*. Oxford University Press.

Schmitter, P.C. and Karl, T.L., 1991. "What democracy is ... and is not". *Journal of Democracy*, Vol. 2, No. 3: 75–88.

Schumpeter, J.A., 1947. *Capitalism, socialism, and democracy*. 2nd edn. Harper and Brothers.

Shin, D.C., 1994. "On the third wave of democratization: A synthesis and evaluation of recent theory and research". *World Politics*, Vol. 47, No. 1: 135–170.

The Economist. 2021. "Democracy declined across Asia in 2021". December 18, https://www.economist.com/asia/2021/12/18/democracy-declined-across-asia-in-2021.

The Hindu. 2024. "U.S., U.K., and EU urge probe into Pakistan elections, express concerns". February 10, https://www.thehindu.com/news/international/us-uk-and-eu-urge-probe-into-pakistan-elections-express-concerns/article67830360.ece.

Tilly, C., 2007. *Democracy*. Cambridge University Press.

Varieties of Democracy. 2020. "Democracy report 2020: Autocratization surges—resistance grows". https://www.v-dem.net/static/website/files/dr/dr_2020.pdf.

V-Dem. 2021. "Autocratization turns viral: Democracy report 2021". March 22, https://www.v-dem.net/static/website/files/dr/dr_2021.pdf.

V-Dem. 2022. "Autocratization changing nature?". https://v-dem.net/media/publications/dr_2022.pdf.

Waldner, D. and Lust, E., 2018. "Unwelcome change: Coming to terms with democratic backsliding". *Annual Review of Political Science*, Vol. 21, No. 1: 93–113.

Walker, C., 2018. "What Is 'Sharp Power'?" *Journal of Democracy*, Vol. 29, No. 3: 9–23.

30 Introduction

Wehrey, F., 2015. "The authoritarian resurgence: Saudi Arabia's anxious autocrats". *Journal of Democracy*, Vol. 26, No. 2: 71–85.

Whitehead, L., 1988. *The consolidation of fragile democracies: A discussion with illustrations*. European Consortium for Political Research.

Whitehead, L., 2002. *Democratization: Theory and Experience*. Oxford University Press.

Widmalm, S., ed., 2021. *Routledge handbook of autocratization in South Asia*. Routledge.

Youngs, R., Aydın-Düzgit, S., Daly, T.G., Godfrey, K., Lindberg, S.I., Lührmann, A., and Petrova, T., 2019. *Post–Cold War democratic declines: The third wave of autocratization*. Carnegie Europe, June 27.

Zakaria, F., 1997. "The rise of illiberal democracy". *Foreign Affairs*. November–December, https://www.foreignaffairs.com/world/rise-illiberal-democracy.

2 Democracy Denied: The False Promise of Afghanistan's Constitutions[1]

Jennifer Brick Murtazashvili

Introduction

Democracy in Afghanistan did not fail. It did not live up to its potential because it was never given a chance to thrive. The blame for this is not to be found in its citizens, in its flourishing civil society, or in its vibrant media. It was limited for two main reasons. First, the 2004 constitution never allowed Afghanistan's democracy to live up to its promise as the institutional arrangements that governed the post-2001 period failed to create incentives for participation in the state democratic system at the subnational level. Constitutional provisions that could have allowed greater citizen participation through elections in their districts and cities were ignored by the country's leaders (J. Murtazashvili, 2016a). Second, staggering corruption in presidential and parliamentary elections disillusioned many from the democratic project (Chayes, 2021). The consequence of this was a dynamic political class that is concentrated in Kabul who have a vested interest in preserving democracy (SIGAR, 2016).

These groups understood the power of influence and advocacy because they were the few that could participate in this small window for contestation in Kabul. Outside of the capital, many felt betrayed by a system that, while delivering corrupt elections for the resident and National Assembly, retained features of previous authoritarian regimes. The international community bears enormous blame for this as well, as its massive financial support of these dynamics undermined the liberal state it sought to create (Bizhan, 2017). The bottom line is that political leaders in Kabul and its international patrons preferred to centralize authority around authoritarian institutions rather than implement the imperfect democracy enshrined in the constitution. The result is that the state-building project denied the people of Afghanistan the democracy it promised (J.B. Murtazashvili, 2022).

Survey data collected right before the collapse of the Afghan Republic indicate that many in Afghanistan did not believe that the constitution in its current form was worth preserving. Although most wanted to preserve Afghanistan as a republic rather than have it become an Islamic emirate, the vast majority believed that the peace agreement should bring substantial changes to political organization in the country. Just one-third believed the country should adopt a

DOI: 10.4324/9781003261469-2

32 *Democracy Denied: False Promise of Afghanistan's Constitutions*

fully Islamic legal basis and become an emirate, while most supported the country in its current form as a republic. Although most wanted the republican basis of law to remain, only 32 percent said that the republican constitution should serve as the basis of legal structures and law after a peace agreement (Heart of Asia Society, 2020). The explanation for these demands lies in Afghanistan's political system, which concentrated policymaking decisions in the capital alongside a bureaucratic structure designed for authoritarian rule that gave people outside the capital almost no voice in political decision-making or in policy choices (J. Murtazashvili and Qadam Shah, 2020).

While many believe that Afghanistan failed because there was no mass movement for democracy or that it was impossible because the country was so divided, this is not the case. From the onset of the republic, institutional rules stifled creation of an enduring civic society. For example, the single non-transferable voting system (SNTV) intentionally weakened the creation of political parties, disincentivizing them from playing a role in parliament. In the first parliamentary election in 2005, candidates were even banned from affiliating with political parties. With all political power concentrated in Kabul, there was little point in having formal civil society organizations engaged in advocacy work outside of the capital because the only place where they could influence politics was in the capital. Thus, Afghanistan's civil society endured through its customary governance structures.

When the government concentrated all its power in Kabul, there was almost no reason for a truly meaningful civil society to grow outside of the capital, but despite these incentives there was a vibrant informal civil society throughout the country. Formal civil society had little role in advocacy and because of formal rules that prevented them from influencing local policies, giving formal civil society little reason to organize—at least around matters of concern to government affairs. A consequence of this is that those who have the most to lose from the collapse of the current state were in the capital. The inability to extend meaningful participation and build local forms of accountability meant many Afghans had no stake in their governments at the subnational level. This represented a lost opportunity as so many Afghans clamored to change and wanted to participate in decisions in their communities.

The people of Afghanistan learned to live without the state (Ibrahimi, 2019). They learned to distrust democracy, but this does not mean that they are disinterested. On the contrary, many organize and lobby around ideas of local concern, but they use structures outside of the state to facilitate this cooperation. The great irony is that during the height of the state-building effort, the most dynamic civil society occurred in communities throughout the country, with almost no participation of the state. The inability of Kabul to harness this creative energy was the greatest lost opportunity of the past 20 years. The central government treated citizens as subjects who must be ruled (Sadr, 2020). A true lost opportunity to do things differently.

This chapter argues that democracy was not a failed effort in Afghanistan; instead, citizens were never given a fully democratic state in which their

Democracy Denied: False Promise of Afghanistan's Constitutions 33

participation was welcomed. The post-2001 political order did feature democratic elections, but these were narrow and never included voices at the local level, where Afghanistan has such a rich history of local involvement and a rich tradition of local democracy. The chapter then provides an overview of the democracy in Afghanistan under the Islamic Republic of Afghanistan. The next part of the chapter explores national-level politics, while the final part explores democracy at the subnational level. The final empirical section explores the consequence of the heavily centralized constitutional order for political order in Afghanistan by examining how centralization created incentives for the proliferation of state-created parallel governance structures.

The fact that the state was involved in engineering parallel structures to get around its own dysfunctional system tells us a great deal about the durability of state-backed governance organizations in Afghanistan. The second consequence of the heavily centralized system was that most meaningful civil society organizations in Afghanistan were centralized in the capital Kabul. Very few involved in politics had an opportunity to influence politics at the subnational level (at least through formal structures). Consequently, most support of the republican constitutional order was in Kabul and not in the provinces. The chapter concludes with a discussion of Afghanistan's political order under Taliban rule.

Concentration of Political Power in Afghanistan

The concentration of political decision-making in Kabul had several devastating consequences for the health of democracy in Afghanistan. First, it gave people of Afghanistan very limited opportunities to participate in democratic governance. Democracy is much more than elections.

What happens between elections is just as important as procedures used to select representatives. It is this period between elections that creates civic square and government legitimacy. The only place where people were able to participate in democratic governance was at the national level. This means that most political conversations and contestation occurred in Kabul between the educated elites, think tanks, parliament, government ministries, and state agencies. A consequence of this was that those who had a stake in the state and its future were largely concentrated in Kabul (Shayan, 2017). Those outside Kabul had few means to exercise their voice in politics and make decisions in their community. Therefore, they did not have a stake in keeping the system together because they were never able to have a real sense of ownership over what was created. This left Afghanistan as a country that was deeply divided, and urban–rural differences—especially differences between Kabul and the rest of the country—are an important driver of this divide. Although formal democracy has not lived up to its promise, the expansion of education and the constitutional support of democratic systems have had positive consequences.

Republican Afghanistan had much to celebrate. It had a civil society, deeply engaged political thinkers from across many political spectrums, and a

34 *Democracy Denied: False Promise of Afghanistan's Constitutions*

population that wanted to participate in the political process. Unfortunately, opportunities for participation were limited due to the lack of democratic institutions at the local level. Without opportunities for participation in local governance, the contours of the social contract remained largely unchanged from what they had been in the past. It is no small wonder, then, that people continued to fight for change. The Afghan government found itself in a very weak bargaining position with the Taliban. The weak military position of the state was partly a consequence of the inability to give those outside the capital a seat at the decision-making table.

The lack of opportunities for participation in the policy process in Afghanistan was striking given that the war in the country affected the rural population much more than those in Kabul. As a peace agreement with the United States and intra-Afghan talks were debated, there was a significant uptick in attacks in rural areas and a reduction of attacks in cities (Mashal and Rahim, 2020). Turnout for the final parliamentary elections were higher than presidential elections. Although there are many reasons for this, citizens may have perceived that their vote mattered more for the members of parliament (MPs). MPs were the only locally elected officials who played some role in public policymaking in the country. Reporting on the 2018 parliamentary election suggested that in many parts of the country, including Kabul, polls were not open due to insecurity. In much of the country, the Independent Elections Commission did not even set up voting stations because there was no security or support for the elections in these areas (Ruttig, 2018). Voting in the 2019 presidential election was the lowest since the adoption of the 2004 constitution. While people may value democracy, democracy as it was executed in Afghanistan, simply did not deliver for people.

In Afghanistan—and in so many other conflict-affected states that feature heavy international intervention—elections became the measure of democracy rather than more meaningful participation in the political process. Both domestic and international actors focused on successful presidential and National Assembly elections to measure the health of democracy in Afghanistan. This is a very imperfect measure as democracy is about much more than elections: it is about the role of citizens in the policymaking process. It is about oversight over officials. It is about the ability of citizens to have a voice in creating budgets from their taxpayer dollars, among so many other things. The constitution called for an elected president, National Assembly, as well as provincial, district, and village councils. Although the constitution mandated elections for district and village councils, more than 15 years after this document was drafted these elections were still not held.

Constitutional democracy failed to live up to its promise for several reasons, but the main reason is that the system created elections but those elections did not translate into the creation of bodies whereby citizens could hold officials accountable for their actions. The only exception to this is the National Assembly in Kabul. There are no bodies at the subnational level where citizens can participate in the crafting of public policy. They do not have the right to

Democracy Denied: False Promise of Afghanistan's Constitutions 35

make decisions over their own taxpayer resources at the local level. This is where democracy matters most. This is where it has been most absent. The constitution called for an elected president, National Assembly, as well as provincial, district, and village councils. Although the constitution mandated elections for district and village councils, after two decades, these elections were not held.

Democracy thus left an important vacuum in Afghanistan. The international donor community and factions within the Afghan government tried to fill this vacuum with donor projects like the National Solidarity Program and the Citizens' Charter. Although well intentioned, these programs sought to substitute for meaningful local participation. They built parallel structures supported by massive donor aid. In this way, donors supported the creation of a kind of rentier democracy at the local level that was not directly accountable to citizens or the government. It existed independently from it. It disappeared as quickly as the donor assistance.

The failure of the centralized governance system and its democratization project in Afghanistan represents another failed opportunity for the Afghan state to institutionalize its relationship and come to terms with society and their informal norms and functions. This exacerbated the attitude of society towards the state and made it much more unwilling to accommodate the state. In this sense, state failure remains a vicious cycle. In other words, it is the outcome of historical competition between the state and social forces and their failure to accommodate one another. The outcome of this process has been either centralization (when state has dominated) or anarchy because of the destruction of the center (when societal forces have dominated, for example in the 1990s).

The post-2001 centralization is a microcosm of this historical process for mutual domination where a heavily centralized state, with international support, manipulated the process in its favor rather than seeing a positive-sum result. Democracy in Afghanistan created a massive, winner-take-all competition that concentrated political power in the center. This led to increased polarization of the public and an increase in ethnic politics because it meant that power would be based on the ability to create factions. The inability to create opportunities for real democratic participation at the subnational level that gave citizens oversight into policies and programs at the local level was an unfortunate result of the post-2001 institutional design.

There are many reasons why an insurgency continues in Afghanistan; we would be quite remiss if we did not consider the ways in which the design of political institutions and inability to implement limited democratic rules concentrated opportunities for political participation in the capital, leaving the rest of the country out of the conversation.

National-Level Politics

Throughout its modern history, Afghanistan has had a political system that concentrates power in the center. Afghanistan's monarchs believed that to build the state, power must be concentrated in the center. This view is reflected in

36   *Democracy Denied: False Promise of Afghanistan's Constitutions*

Kabul until the collapse of the republic. Even President Ghani believed there was a sequence to political reform: consolidate the state at the center first, and only then can politics be devolved to localities. The sequencing assumes a kind of political maturity: when people are mature enough to submit to the rule of the center, only then can they have self-governance in their communities. The current trajectory of centralized rule is the product of the vision of Amir Dost Mohammad, but was accelerated by Abdur Rahman Khan, who ruled the country from 1880 until his death in 1901. He used a level of violence almost unprecedented by an Afghan leader to consolidate his personal rule. In terms of centralization, he ended the practice of appointing relatives of the monarch to run distant provinces. Although this informal system of governance had been around for decades if not centuries, he believed that Afghanistan's instability was tied up in this system. It allowed relatives of the king to amass bases of power outside of the capital, which they could then use to challenge the power of the monarch in the capital.

By putting an end to this system, Abdur Rahman moved to create a system of politics that was based on loyalty to him and that brought the most important decisions to the capital (Kakar, 1979). He used violent campaigns against informal customary leaders at the community level as part of his effort to gain quiescence. He viewed informal sources of authority, such as khans and customary leaders, as threats to state power. These individuals were threatening to the central government because they had sources of legitimacy that were not dependent upon the state. To Abdur Rahman, and others who followed him, legitimacy should emanate from the state. It could not be built from the bottom up.

Leaders who followed Abdur Rahman tended to view subnational politics in much the same way. Although there was some discussion of a more decentralized system in Afghanistan during the period before the 2004 Constitutional Loya Jirga (Rubin, 2004), the result of this process was the adoption of the current constitution, which is in most ways identical to the 1964 constitution, except that it replaces the monarchy with an elected president. The country was still to be governed through principles of centralism. The post-2004 constitutional order created very weak checks on a very strong executive. Given that the rules of the political game were based on the 1964 order, this should not have come as a surprise, as weak parliaments featuring weak parities have been a signature of the executive–legislative since that time (Weinbaum, 1972).

In contemporary Afghanistan, the parliament was weakened in two significant ways. First, the powers of the legislature to serve as an effective check on executive authority were very weak in comparison to a much stronger executive. Second, laws governing the elections of the parliament created the Single Non-Transferable Voting system relying on at-large constituencies in each province. This undermined strong representation of citizen interests in two ways. First, the system intentionally disincentivized the creation of strong political parties. During the first parliamentary elections in 2005, candidates were not allowed to associate with a political party.

Democracy Denied: False Promise of Afghanistan's Constitutions 37

Political parties are vital for the health of any democratic system. In addition to aggregating the interests of citizens, they also work to inform citizens, and develop positions that are independent of the executive. The creation of at-large districts created enormous confusion among citizens in respect of who represented you in the Wolesi Jirga (lower house of parliament). For example, there are eight seats reserved for Helmand Province. The electoral rules do not create district-level or other forms of constituencies below the level of province. It means that all members of parliament may come from the provincial capital. When citizens have more than one MP they can turn to, it creates diffused representation. People do not know who can best represent their interests in the elected body. It increases costs to citizens to raise concerns if it is not immediately clear to them who represents them. The weakness and lack of clarity about the roles and responsibilities of members of parliament created a system whereby individuals use these elected positions as performative positions.

Rather than enabling policy debates and deliberation, elections provided an opportunity for the most powerful and influential to extend or legitimize their power through other means (Coburn and Larson, 2014). They became venues for patronage and other informal politics. This is because members of parliament did not have incentives to rule as policymakers. Due to provincial-wide at-large districts, MPs basically have no constituencies. Most important lawmaking functions were given to a much stronger executive, which issues executive orders and proposes the budget. Parliament has emerged as a veto player in principle, but one that was not effective in contrast to the much stronger executive and a donor community that wanted to get things done quickly. Veto players are constraints on political power that by their very nature slow things down (Tsebelis, 2002).

There are very few meaningful institutional constraints on the executive in Afghanistan. Although the parliament has tried to assert itself more frequently in recent years, it is often ignored by both the government and the international community alike. For example, at the height of the COVID-19 crisis, the lower house of the National Assembly, the Wolesi Jirga, rejected President Ghani's proposed food relief program (*dastarkhan-e milli*) for fears that assistance would not reach those most in need. Despite parliament voting down this program, the government insisted that it had the right to implement the program (J.B. Murtazashvili and Qadam Shah, n.d.). The World Bank funded this program with $240 million in support. The parliament voted down the program, arguing that they did not believe the government would use the funds in a transparent manner (Ghubar, 2020). Donor willingness to support such a program considering the rejection by parliament of this program indicates that even donors who had spent such vast resources trying to create democracy in Afghanistan had no problem sidestepping it when it obstructed their vision.

38 *Democracy Denied: False Promise of Afghanistan's Constitutions*

Democracy and Accountability at the Subnational Level

Although Afghanistan strived to become a democratic state, the full potential of democracy was never felt because participatory decision-making, local oversight, and the ability to hold officials accountable have not been implemented at the subnational level. Furthermore, even if all the rules of the 2004 constitution were implemented, there would have been few venues for citizens to have a role in decision-making processes or hold officials accountable for their actions. This is because the post-2001 democratic order retained many vestiges of previous authoritarian regimes: all executive authorities at the subnational level are appointed by the center and are vertically accountable only to the center—not to the citizens. The constitution had no mechanisms to hold these appointed provincial governors, district governors, and mayors accountable to citizens.

Although democratic rules and procedures were used to select the president and the National Assembly, there was a deep gap in the ability of individuals and communities at the subnational level to select leaders and implement the policies at the local level that reflect local preferences. These elections featured vast amounts of fraud. The Independent Election Commission (IEC), which oversaw elections, was one of the most corrupt public bodies in Afghanistan. Many have accused the organization of playing ethnic politics, manipulating, and sometimes determining results based on ethnic favoritism. This significantly decreased voters' trust in the electoral system. This distrust could have played an important role in declining turnout and weakening representation system both at national and provincial levels (Callen and Long, 2015). Moreover, since members of the provincial units of the IEC were appointed from Kabul, those agents served the interests of the president.

Democracy at the provincial level in Afghanistan represented a great hope for many citizens after the fall of the Taliban government in 2001. But rather than seeing a striking change in the way they experience the state, governance represented a continuity with previous eras. A new regime was in place in Kabul, but the machinery of governance at the subnational level, where 75 percent of the population resides, was almost identical to previous authoritarian models. This was particularly striking if we look at the provincial government. After 2001, and continuing with the 2004 constitution, all provincial governors continued to be appointed by the president in Kabul. None of the provincial authorities at the subnational level were selected by citizens.

The constitution also created elected provincial councils. Although voters were promised something new with democracy and the election of provincial councils, what they were served by the state was familiar. The role of the provincial councils during the post-2001 period was identical to their role after the creation of the 1964 constitutional monarchy. They had no formal authority over the appointed provincial governors. Unlike provincial governors, provincial councils were elected by citizens. A challenge with these bodies is that they did not have the ability to override decisions made by provincial governors, they lacked policymaking authority, and they did not have oversight over

Democracy Denied: False Promise of Afghanistan's Constitutions 39

any decisions made at the district level. Citizens routinely complained that provincial council members did not serve the people, but instead existed to extract rents from aid, the state, and citizens (Brooks and Trebilcock, 2014; TOLOnews, 2013).

Citizens lacked confidence in provincial council members for many of the same reasons they distrusted members of parliament. Like MPs, provincial council members were selected on an at-large basis and lacked formal constituencies, which in turn led to an accountability crisis as citizens did not know which MPs served them.

The post-2001 constitution did not bring democracy to the district level, the lowest level of formal authority and the most crucial, as this is where people experience the state. Just as in previous eras, all district governors (woluswals) were appointed by the president (after having been vetted by the Independent Directorate for Local Governance (IDLG)). Since 2007, the civil service reforms meant that district governors must go through merit review to be appointed, but this did not mean that they were accountable to citizens. District governors were incredibly important actors because as the lowest level of government, they represented the face of the state to citizens. Many citizens have no idea who their provincial governor might be, but many do know their district leaders. The 2004 constitution also called for elected district councils, yet despite numerous promises by both Presidents Karzai and Ghani, district council elections were never held on a nation-wide basis. Officials pointed to the lack of security, the lack of resources, and most importantly the challenges faced in demarcating and delimiting district boundaries. Indeed, as recently as a few years ago, IDLG officials were unsure of exactly how many districts exist in Afghanistan.[2] The lack of elections for mayors represents one area where Afghanistan saw a pronounced democratic setback compared to the era of the constitutional monarchy in the 1960s. Just as the 1964 constitution promised elections for the leaders of Afghanistan's municipalities, so too did the 2004 constitution. Yet, this aspect of the constitution was never implemented. In 2009, President Hamid Karzai announced that mayoral elections would be held—as called for by the constitution—but this never happened (Katzman, 2015: 38).

Prior to 1964, there were several rounds of municipal elections held around the country. According to the 1947 Municipal Law, towns with populations over 10,000 people had institutions of self-governance. This law created elections for municipal councils based on nahiyas (wards) in each city. This law created Municipal Election Committees in each large town in Afghanistan that vetted candidates for these elections. By 1962, at least four rounds of these elections were held. Just as was the case with provincial council elections, municipal council elections were plagued with problems and corruption. Many never used secret ballots and used raising of hands to select candidates (Dupree, 1963).

Elections for provincial councils were held every four years. Mirroring the 1964 constitution, the 2004 constitution also called for the creation of elected village councils. As with the provincial and district councils, these elections never took place. As with the other elected councils it was never clear what

40 Democracy Denied: False Promise of Afghanistan's Constitutions

mandate such councils would have even if they were elected. The case of the village councils is even more puzzling. The constitution called for elected councils but did not call for elected village leaders. Typically, legislative councils have oversight or work in tandem with executives. In this case, the Afghan constitution created councils with an unclear mandate and which did not oversee other bodies (as is typically the case for elected councils that oversee executive authority).

Consequences

Proliferation of State-Created Parallel Structures

The failure to implement the constitution, especially with regard to district council elections, mayoral elections, and village council elections, meant that it was impossible to assess the full impact of democracy in Afghanistan. Representative democracy was never given a chance to demonstrate its ability to solve problems, aggregate citizen preferences, and hold politicians accountable. Consequently, most politics occurred through informal venues. The international donor community tried to paper over the lack of meaningful participation at the subnational level with a host of parallel structures that did not give citizens real or meaningful oversight over the government.

This was an extremely wasteful endeavor because it created ephemeral bodies that did not deliver on democratic promises. But these efforts were not successful because citizens recognized them as ephemeral. Furthermore, these bodies did not have the authority to do what people wanted them to do, which had a role in shaping policy outcomes. For example, the National Solidarity Program (NSP), which with more than $2 billion in support from the World Bank and other bilateral donors, sought to create more than 30,000 village development councils in communities throughout Afghanistan. This program ended in 2017. By the time the program concluded, much of Afghanistan's territory was not under government control. Many of the community development councils (CDCs) that were created no longer functioned because they were not in territory controlled by the government. Most importantly, their reason to exist—to spend donors' funds—no longer existed.

The World Bank's own assessment of the NSP was not positive (Beath, et al., 2015). It found that its efforts to create new community councils that were in parallel to existing customary structures undermined governance in communities where it worked. Specifically, it found that "the negative impact on perceived local governance quality indicates that the creation of new institutions in parallel to customary structures may not have the desired effect, particularly in cases in which the roles of new institutions are not well-defined" (Beath, et al., 2013). These findings, which were developed through a randomized control trial, illustrated that efforts to create new donor-supported organizations undermined existing forms of civil society in communities, namely customary authorities. The Citizens' Charter expanded the work of the NSP in rural areas to include both rural and urban areas. The project, also supported by the

World Bank with massive donor investments, viewed itself as a community-driven development project (Holmlund and Rao, 2021). It aims to provide every village and city in Afghanistan with basic services, based on community priorities. In addition to providing projects and grants, the Citizens' Charter sees itself as a project that monitors and evaluates government programs as they are implemented. It aims to gain government trust by reducing poverty and deepening the legitimacy of the Afghan state. Since the project was rolled out a few years ago, it has faced massive problems in implementation due to insecurity and corruption (Bjelica, 2020).

The international humanitarian community was not alone in building parallel structures to create venues for participatory processes at the subnational level. During the height of the counterinsurgency campaign of the United States and NATO countries, Western donors tried to support service provision through district councils (Terrones, 2014). Just like the international humanitarian community, the military community created its own parallel structures to provide services to citizens in a more targeted manner. These included Provincial Reconstruction Teams (PRTs) and District Stability Team (DSTs), whose impact and usefulness are still questioned. Tamim Asey (2019) argued that these donor-supported programs that sought to generate participation through development at the subnational level were not sustainable and were not successful because they relied so heavily on donor aid and donor management. These were also community development projects, he noted, and they were not drivers of the economic revitalization. In fact, he argues, these programs contributed to an "unsustainable subsidence economy in the rural parts of the country."

These programs were not just ineffective and wasteful, but they also served to undermine democracy because, as parallel structures, they diverted donor and public attention from what was constitutionally mandated: the creation of district councils and village councils. Rather than focusing on building the structures called for by the constitution, which gave citizens power over the government, it created parallel bodies that gave the illusion of participation but gave citizens no legal or constitutional oversight guaranteed to them. These parallel structures were thus illusory and ineffective (*BBC Monitoring Newsfile*, 2014). They did not win hearts and minds through their programs. They were not sustainable because they were based on cash infusions by donors rather than on giving citizens a voice over what matters most to them in local politics: their local administration. Participation at the subnational level is important. Aid projects like the NSP and Citizens' Charter created new councils that allowed people the opportunity to set priorities in the funding of local projects. Most, if not all, the funding for these projects came from the international community (Suhrke, 2013, 2011, 2008). These were not the funds of citizens. These were not taxpayer dollars.

While many donors were quite satisfied with the ability of citizens to play a role in deciding how funds should be spent, participation is important for many reasons besides setting spending priorities. Elected officials provide very important oversight that can help ameliorate corruption. Governments do much more

42   *Democracy Denied: False Promise of Afghanistan's Constitutions*

than distribute grants and aid. They solve problems. They are focal points for local collective action (Besley and Persson, 2009). In many democracies political parties should be involved in these issues because political parties play an important role not just in aggregating interests but also in educating voters on important policy issues.

Democratic Buy-in Concentrated in Kabul

What should be clear from the sections above is that Afghanistan had elements of an imperfect democracy. It was imperfect because most of the democratic aspects of the constitution have only been applied to politics at the national level. Subnational democracy was only partially implemented (through the creation of very weak provincial councils) (Jochem, et al., 2016). One consequence of this is that the groups who are most active in participating in Afghanistan democracy were clustered in Kabul, where the only meaningful participation in government exists.

While citizens may support factions in the government, it is unclear the extent to which citizens supported democracy in the country (Ahmadi, 2021). This is because many were not able to participate or benefit from democratic processes. The full spirit of democracy was able to flourish in the capital, where there were dozens of think tanks and civil society organizations that have gone beyond service delivery models, which is the most rudimentary form of civil society (Shayan, 2017). These organizations participated in sustained advocacy and data-driven policy formulation. Kabul had a diverse group of advocacy organizations that sought to influence national-level policy. Media organizations, especially television, featured vigorous debates about issues of national concern. Kabul featured a rotating door between think tank leaders and the government. Many people who emerged from civil society went on to government work. In this sense, Afghanistan emerged to be like many other healthy democracies. There was jockeying for influence with members of the government and even members of parliament as new rules were debated. The challenge was that so much of this rotation was limited to Kabul and did not exist far beyond it. Kabul was the seat of power and the place where important policy issues were debated. Due to challenges with constitutional design that make local-level policymaking unclear and the incomplete implementation of the constitution, these debates do not happen as vigorously as they should outside of the capital.

Formal, institutionalized civil society remained heavily concentrated in urban centers and in Kabul in particular. As a study on civil society by the Afghanistan Research and Evaluation Unit (AREU) pointed out, there were weak vertical relations with civil society organizations and people compared to horizontal relations with the government outside of Kabul. According to this report, "this point reassess[es] the important question of legitimacy, given the serious obstacles concerning the access to grassroots and rural civil society for supporting local voices" (Nemat and Werner, 2016: 28). The authors suggest that this created enormous legitimacy concerns for civil society organizations in the country. They argue that this Kabul–countryside gap was due to safety and security, and the fact that so many NGOs outside of Kabul were dependent on donor funding that is disappearing. The report noted that at the provincial level, a draft subnational governance policy allowed for bottom-up approaches to planning and budgeting, but this planning and budgeting approach would still have to go through line ministries (Qadam Shah, 2021).

The provincial governors, it is noted, were not engaged in this process. Reform proposals indicated some need for accountability, but that there was a legitimacy deficit at the district and village level because there were no formal channels of representation to the government at three levels. Furthermore, the government tried to engineer a community planning process that is still dominated by district-, provincial- and national-level planning and resource allocation (Nemat and Werner, 2016: 29).

An alternative explanation is that there are few reasons for individuals in rural areas to mobilize and participate in civil society if they are subjects of the state. As subjects, they have few opportunities to translate their policy and political preferences into real outcomes. Why would individuals work to overcome collective action dilemmas and form groups if the groups cannot have much influence on policy concerns? The lack of meaningful institutional reform has led to the continuation of the state's "old-style bureaucracy," with nepotism and corruption at the local level, because there are few opportunities baked into the political system for individuals outside of Kabul to have a meaningful influence on policy outcomes. In Kabul, there were many think tanks and civil society groups that had a large impact on the policy debates, but they had an unclear impact on policy itself. Leaders of civil society groups were often pulled from their organizations and asked to serve in the government. Organizations in Kabul could influence government decision-making in the capital because this was where decisions and policies were made. This influence happens, however, through a highly informal process that was based on personal networks and connections, not because of systematic opportunities for engagement in the policy process.

The consequence of the concentration of power inside of Afghanistan was the creation of a new political class in Kabul that had strong ties to the government and who were perceived to be out of touch with the lives of people in most of the country. Shortly before the collapse, Tamim Asey warned,

> Afghanistan's rapidly moving towards being an oligopoly, with extractive political power and economic institutions. The increasing amount of wealth and political power under control of a small minority of Afghanistan is increasingly marginalizing most of the country's population—largely in rural Afghanistan.
>
> (Asey, 2019)

According to the 2019 Asia Foundation Survey of the Afghanistan people, rural Afghans were more concerned with governance issues in respect of their

44 *Democracy Denied: False Promise of Afghanistan's Constitutions*

pessimism about the future (33 percent cited this as a major concern, vs. 27 percent in urban areas). The survey also shows that urban residents are historically much more likely to be satisfied with democracy than their rural counterparts (The Asia Foundation, 2020). The issue of centralization came up in the 2019 Asia Foundation Survey of the Afghan people. When asked what is important to protect as part of a peace agreement, support for preserving the current constitution, a "democratic system" and a "strong central government" were highest in Kabul than in other parts of the country.

Parliamentary elections became the elections that mattered most. It should not be surprising that turnout for the 2018 parliamentary elections in Afghanistan were higher than for the 2019 presidential elections (Cookman, 2020: 33). This is because members of parliament are the only elected officials outside of the president who have a role, albeit a small one, in the creation of public policy in the country. Therefore, having a say over who was represented in parliament was one of the only ways citizens could have a voice in matters of public policy. Yet, as noted earlier, parliament was very weak. The lack of opportunities for citizens to participate in local level democracy did not eliminate the demand of citizens for such participation. There is probably no country in the world that has developed more channels for local participation and problem-solving than Afghanistan.

The challenge with liberal state-building efforts, centered on strengthening democracy and the constitution, is that they did not reach out to Afghanistan's vibrant informal governance sector that is prevalent in so many customary bodies at the village and city level throughout the country (J.B. Murtazashvili, 2016; Barfield, 2008; J.B. Murtazashvili, 2021; Barfield, 2010).

Consequences for Taliban Rule

On August 15, 2021, the Taliban conquered Kabul and took over the seat of power—almost without a fight. For decades, Afghanistan's armed forces had put up a tremendous fight—losing tens of thousands of soldiers and countless civilians—seeking to fight the insurgency. By 2021, a society had grown weary of war, but more foundationally it had grown tired of the corruption and empty promises of a government and donor community that were unwilling to give citizens a greater seat at the table (Chayes, 2021). When the Taliban seized power, they began to dismantle—almost immediately—all the political institutions associated with democracy in the country. They eliminated both houses of the National Assembly and disbanded the Central Elections Commission. They also eliminated the Ministry of Women's Affairs and other government agencies that sought to build a more inclusive and democratic Afghanistan. This means that the democratic project—at least for now—is part of Afghan history.

The Taliban have moved to consolidate their power. They have stated in public that they believe democracy is antithetical to Islamic values, and thus, they have no plans of extending the vote or reestablishing democratic procedures in the near future (Watkins, 2021). Rather than govern inclusively, the

Democracy Denied: False Promise of Afghanistan's Constitutions 45

ruling group has relied upon a small cadre drawn from the leadership of its various factions to control the government. Almost all the political leaders appointed by the Taliban are ethnic Pashtuns. There is almost no representation of other ethnic groups in the Taliban government. The lack of representation caused deep consternation among the United States and European governments who focus bilateral relations with the ruling authority on promotion of democracy and gender rights. But the concerns about greater inclusivity do not stop with them.

It is also Afghanistan's most immediate neighbors that have expressed deep concern about the lack of inclusivity of the Taliban. This includes larger powers such as China and Russia (Evansky, 2022; Gannon, 2022; Umarov and Murtazashvili, 2022), but also smaller regional powers like Uzbekistan (Turkstra, 2021; Murtazashvili and Umarov, 2022). None of these countries are encouraging support formal democracy in Afghanistan, but they remain concerned that a political regime that relies on one ethnic group in such a diverse country is bound to fail. These larger powers and neighbors are concerned that the lack of representation in the government will generate larger conflict. They understand the dynamics of Afghan history, which has demonstrated that when one ethnic groups or small niche controls the government the state is bound to fail. Not only could it weaken in terms of its legitimacy, but rule by such an exclusive clique is also sure to breed violent conflict. Fearing violent spillover from Afghanistan, its neighbors are thus encouraging a much more inclusive government than the Taliban put into power after 2021.

Upon seizing power, the Taliban have been handed one of the most centralized states in the world, with most power concentrated in the capital. As an insurgent group that is learning how to govern, they face few incentives to decentralize power or give citizens greater voice in government. As a movement, they are working to consolidate their power and have shown very little interest in dividing power between the center and subnational units. The Taliban did attempt to include some ethnic minorities as they gained traction as an insurgency, but once they came to power, they did not give minorities important positions. The few who have been given positions have largely been forced out of power (Watkins, 2022).

As this chapter has demonstrated, the unwillingness to distribute and share power to the local level or among groups is not a new story for Afghanistan, but instead is part of a vicious cycle of history in Afghanistan (J. Murtazashvili, 2016b). Centralized state authorities concentrate power in the center at the expense of society. This generates disillusionment with the center and generates conflict. The vicious cycle operates in the following fashion. A new group comes to power and inherits a highly centralized state apparatus. Viewing their power as precarious, this group relies upon this centralized apparatus to execute its rule but also to eliminate potential rivals from power. This manner of rule alienates many and then drives some into the opposition. In the case of Afghanistan, this heavy centralization is usually accompanied by authoritarianism—thus any opposition must be violent in order to gain any traction or

46 *Democracy Denied: False Promise of Afghanistan's Constitutions*

sustain itself. Thus, Afghanistan finds itself in almost unending cycles of conflict because of the authoritarian nature of the centralized political institutions that dominate political life in the country—and that have dominated the country for more than a century (Simonsen, 2004). Until Afghanistan breaks out of this dynamic and moves to decentralize some authority and autonomy to its communities and districts, this cycle of violence is likely to continue.

Conclusion

Although democracy did not live up to its promise in Afghanistan, the public opinion data and evidence presented in this chapter should illustrate that most people in the country never gave up on a desire to participate in the political process. There was huge demand among citizens to participate in the policy-making process (Coburn and Larson, 2014). They were promised so many times that things would change, but that change never came about. The system installed after 2001 was a continuation of the old authoritarian system that existed prior to the Soviet invasion in 1979 (J. Murtazashvili, 2016b). It bears all the hallmarks of the constitutional monarchy of the 1964 constitution. This was a constitutional monarchy, but it was still an authoritarian regime. The constitution was never implemented. Most of the aspects of the constitution that called for democracy never came into being. It is striking that before 1964 there were even elections for municipal councils and for mayors around the country, something that was never achieved in the post-2001 period. The constitution of Afghanistan that was adopted in 2004 promised to bring democracy to the country. It was imperfectly implemented. Even if it had been implemented fully, it would only have brought limited democracy to the people. Because the constitution was based so heavily on its authoritarian antecedents, it did not create many opportunities for citizens to have oversight over government officials outside the capital, nor does it provide them opportunities to create public policies.

Democracy did not live up to its full potential in Afghanistan. Over the past 20 years, the country has seen the birth of an incredibly active civil society and media organizations. Yet so much of this is concentrated in the capital. This was not a consequence of capabilities outside of the capital; it was a consequence of institutional design. It was also a consequence of politicians and donors who preferred to concentrate power in the capital rather than diffuse it throughout the country.

People and groups living in the provinces had no opportunity to influence the policy process in their communities. They had no way to hold their local officials accountable. The ability to have a say in public policies, to be able to craft budgets that illustrate citizen priorities over taxpayer funds, and to oversee the work of public officials are fundamental parts of democracy. The liberal state-building project in Afghanistan executed democracy in a very narrow way: viewing it as elections for the president and the National Assembly. The constitution called for the election of weak bodies at the subnational level, but

Democracy Denied: False Promise of Afghanistan's Constitutions   47

those elections never took place. The people of Afghanistan remain ready to take on the gift of self-governance, but none of the country's constitutions gave them the authority to do so. Thus, the promise of democracy in Afghanistan is one that remains unfulfilled.

Notes

1 This chapter is based on an earlier version published by the Afghanistan Institute of Strategic Studies. The arguments in this paper are extended and developed for this chapter. It is republished with permission.
2 Interview, IDLG official, July 2013.

References

Ahmadi, Mohammad Amin. 2021. "An Assessment of the Possibility of Producing Consensus within the Parliamentary and Decentralized System of Democracy in Afghanistan." Kabul: Afghan Institute for Strategic Studies.

Asey, Tamim. 2019. "The Price of Inequality: The Dangerous Rural-Urban Divide in Afghanistan." *Global Security Review* (blog). March 5. https://globalsecurityreview. com/inequality-dangerous-rural-urban-divide-afghanistan/.

Barfield, Thomas J. 2008. "The Roots of Failure in Afghanistan." *Current History* 107 (713): 410.

Barfield, Thomas J. 2010. *Afghanistan: A Cultural and Political History*. Princeton, NJ: Princeton University Press.

BBC Monitoring Newsfile. 2014. "New Afghan Leader Vows to Put End to 'Parallel Governments,'" September 29. http://search.proquest.com.pitt.idm.oclc.org/docview/ 1566081246/D820FD4DDD684E38PQ?accountid=14709.

Beath, Andrew, Fotini Christia, and Ruben Enikolopov. 2013. "Randomized Impact Evaluation of Afghanistan's National Solidarity Programme." 81107. Washington, DC: The World Bank.

Beath, Andrew, Fotini Christia, and Ruben Enikolopov. 2015. *The National Solidarity Program: Assessing the Effects of Community-Driven Development in Afghanistan*. Policy Research Working Papers. The World Bank. https://doi.org/10.1596/ 1813-9450-7415.

Besley, Timothy J., and Torsten Persson. 2009. "State Capacity, Conflict and Development." *National Bureau of Economic Research Working Paper Series* No. 15088 (June). http://www.nber.org/papers/w15088.

Bizhan, Nematullah. 2017. *Aid Paradoxes in Afghanistan: Building and Undermining the State*. London: Routledge.

Bjelica, Jessica. 2020. "Is the Citizens' Charter the Right Vehicle for Reconciliation? The risks of monetising peace." Afghanistan Analysts Network—English. May 31. https:// www.afghanistan-analysts.org/en/reports/rights-freedom/is-the-citizens-charter-the-r ight-vehicle-for-reconciliation-the-risks-of-monetising-peace/.

Brooks, Chad, and Craig Trebilcock. 2014. "Fighting for Legitimacy in Afghanistan: The Creation of the Anti-Corruption Justice Center." *PRISM* 7 (1). http://cco.ndu.edu/News/ Article/1299577/fighting-for-legitimacy-in-afghanistan-the-creation-of-the-anti-corrup tion-just/.

48 *Democracy Denied: False Promise of Afghanistan's Constitutions*

Callen, Michael, and James D. Long. 2015. "Institutional Corruption and Election Fraud: Evidence from a Field Experiment in Afghanistan." *The American Economic Review* 105 (1): 354–381.

Chayes, Sarah. 2021. "Afghanistan's Corruption Was Made in America," September 3. https://www.foreignaffairs.com/articles/united-states/2021-09-03/afghanistans-corruption-was-made-in-america.

Coburn, Noah, and Anna Larson. 2014. *Derailing Democracy in Afghanistan: Elections in an Unstable Political Landscape.* New York: Columbia University Press.

Cookman, Colin. 2020. "Assessing Afghanistan's 2019 Presidential Election." Washington, DC: United States Institute of Peace. https://www.usip.org/publications/2020/08/assessing-afghanistans-2019-presidential-election.

Dupree, Louis. 1963. "Afghanistan's Slow March to Democracy: Reflections on Kabul's Municipal Balloting." *South Asia Series* 1 (7). Kabul: American Universities Field Staff.

Evansky, Ben. 2022. "China, Afghanistan's Taliban Forging a Closer Relationship, Former Diplomat Says." *Fox News*, May 3. https://www.foxnews.com/world/china-afghanistan-taliban-closer-relationship-former-diplomat.

Gannon, Kathy. 2022. "China's Foreign Minister Makes Surprise Stop in Afghanistan." AP News. March 24. https://apnews.com/article/afghanistan-business-china-economy-kabul-93160766eb7288c59d5673c712876092.

Ghubar, Gulabudin. 2020. "Losing House Vote, Govt Still Pushes Relief Plan." TOLOnews. July 26. https://tolonews.com/afghanistan/losing-house-vote-govt-still-pushes-relief-plan.

Heart of Asia Society. 2020. "Survey of Afghan Political Preferences Relevant to Intra-Afghan Peace Negotiations." Kabul. https://heartofasiasociety.org/wp-content/uploads/2020/09/HAS-Political-Survey_English-Version.pdf.

Holmlund, Marcus, and Vijayendra Rao. 2021. "Where and When Is Community-Driven Development (CDD) Effective?" World Bank Blog. October 26. https://blogs.worldbank.org/impactevaluations/where-and-when-community-driven-development-cdd-effective.

Ibrahimi, S. Yaqub. 2019. "Afghanistan's Political Development Dilemma: The Centralist State Versus a Centrifugal Society." *Journal of South Asian Development* 14 (1): 40–61. https://doi.org/10.1177/0973174119839843.

Jochem, Torsten, Ilia Murtazashvili, and Jennifer Murtazashvili. 2016. "Establishing Local Government in Fragile States: Experimental Evidence from Afghanistan." *World Development* 77 (January): 293–310. https://doi.org/10.1016/j.worlddev.2015.08.025.

Kakar, M. Hasan. 1979. *Government and Society in Afghanistan: The Reign of Amir Abd Al-Rahman Khan.* Austin, TX: University of Texas Press.

Katzman, Kenneth. 2015. "Afghanistan: Politics, Elections, and Government Performance." Washington, DC: Congressional Research Service.

Mashal, Mujib, and Najim Rahim. 2020. "Despite Calm in Afghan Cities, War in Villages Kills Dozens Daily." *The New York Times*, January 29. https://www.nytimes.com/2020/01/29/world/asia/afghanistan-taliban-peace-talks.html.

Murtazashvili, Jennifer. 2016a. "Subnational Governance in Afghanistan: Back to the Future." In *State Strengthening in Afghanistan: Lessons Learned, 2001–14*, edited by Scott Smith and Colin Cookman, 53–68. Washington, DC: United States Institute of Peace.

Murtazashvili, Jennifer. 2016b. "Afghanistan: A Vicious Cycle of State Failure." *Governance* 29 (2): 163–166. https://doi.org/10.1111/gove.12195.

Murtazashvili, Jennifer Brick. 2016. *Informal Order and the State in Afghanistan.* New York: Cambridge University Press.

Democracy Denied: False Promise of Afghanistan's Constitutions 49

Murtazashvili, Jennifer Brick. 2021. "The Endurance and Evolution of Afghan Customary Governance." *Current History* 120 (825): 140–145. https://doi.org/10.1525/curh.2021.120.825.140.

Murtazashvili, Jennifer Brick. 2022. "The Collapse of Afghanistan." *Journal of Democracy* 33 (1): 40–54. https://doi.org/10.1353/jod.2022.0003.

Murtazashvili, Jennifer Brick, and Mohammad Qadam Shah. n.d. "Defund Afghanistan." *Discourse Magazine.* https://www.discoursemagazine.com/politics/2020/07/21/defund-afghanistan/.

Murtazashvili, Jennifer, and Mohammad Qadam Shah. 2020. "Political Reform Urgently Needed in Afghanistan." *The Diplomat*, February 22. https://thediplomat.com/2020/02/political-reform-urgently-needed-in-afghanistan/.

Murtazashvili, Jennifer Brick, and Akram Umarov. 2022. "What Are the Implications of Uzbekistan's Rapprochement with the Taliban?" August 8. https://thediplomat.com/2022/08/what-are-the-implications-of-uzbekistans-rapprochement-with-the-taliban/.

Nemat, Orzala Ashraf, and Karin Werner. 2016. "The Role of Civil Society in Promoting Good Governance in Afghanistan." Kabul: Afghanistan Research and Evaluation Unit.

Qadam Shah, Mohammad. 2021. "The Politics of Budgetary Capture in Rentier States: Who Gets What, When and How in Afghanistan." *Central Asian Survey* 41 (1): 138–160. https://doi.org/10.1080/02634937.2021.1960487.

Rubin, Barnett R. 2004. "Crafting a Constitution for Afghanistan." *Journal of Democracy* 15 (3): 5–19.

Ruttig, Thomas. 2018. "Election Day One: A rural-urban divide emerging." Afghanistan Analysts Network—English. October 20. https://www.afghanistan-analysts.org/en/reports/rights-freedom/election-day-one-a-rural-urban-divide-emerging/.

Sadr, Omar. 2020. *Negotiating Cultural Diversity in Afghanistan.* London: Routledge.

Shayan, Zafar. 2017. "Challenges Facing Civil Society in Afghanistan." *Political Critique* (blog). April 20. http://politicalcritique.org/world/2017/civil-society-afghanistan/.

SIGAR. 2016. "Corruption in Conflict: Lessons from the U.S. Experience in Afghanistan." Washington, DC: Special Inspector General on Afghanistan Reconstruction. https://www.sigar.mil/pdf/lessonslearned/sigar-16-58-ll.pdf.

Simonsen, Sven Gunnar. 2004. "Ethnicising Afghanistan: Inclusion and Exclusion in Post-Bonn Institution Building." *Third World Quarterly* 25 (4): 707–729. https://doi.org/10.1080/01436590410001678942.

Suhrke, Astri. 2008. "Democratizing a Dependent State: The Case of Afghanistan." *Democratization* 15 (3): 630. https://doi.org/10.1080/13510340801972387.

Suhrke, Astri. 2011. *When More Is Less: The International Project in Afghanistan.* New York: Columbia University Press.

Suhrke, Astri. 2013. "Statebuilding in Afghanistan: A Contradictory Engagement." *Central Asian Survey* 32 (3): 271–286.

Terrones, Carlos. 2014. "Special Operations Forces' Turn: Recommendations for Leading the Way in Governance and Development in the Afghan Districts Post-DSTs." *Stability: International Journal of Security & Development* 3 (1): 16.

The Asia Foundation. 2020. "A Survey of the Afghan People: Afghanistan in 2019." The Asia Foundation. https://asiafoundation.org/wp-content/uploads/2019/12/2019_Afghan_Survey_Full-Report.pdf.

TOLOnews. 2013. "Rampant Corruption Forces Herat Provincial Governor to Resign." TOLOnews. June 27. /afghanistan/rampant-corruption-forces-herat-provincial-governor-resign.

50 Democracy Denied: False Promise of Afghanistan's Constitutions

Tsebelis, George. 2002. *Veto Players: How Political Institutions Work*. Princeton, NJ: Princeton University Press.

Turkstra, Alberto. 2021. "Uzbekistan Hosts Momentous Conference on Afghanistan." European Institute for Asian Studies. https://www.eias.org/news/uzbekistan-hosts-momentous-conference-on-afghanistan/.

Umarov, Akram, and Jennifer Brick Murtazashvili. 2022. "Where Russia's Afghanistan Policy Went Wrong." The National Interest. The Center for the National Interest. July 15. https://nationalinterest.org/feature/where-russia%E2%80%99s-afghanistan-policy-went-wrong-203566.

Watkins, Andrew. 2021. "The Taliban Rule at Three Months." *CTC Sentinel* 14 (9): 1–14.

Watkins, Andrew. 2022. "The Taliban One Year On." *CTC Sentinel* 15 (8): 1–16.

Weinbaum, Marvin G. 1972. "Afghanistan: Nonparty Parliamentary Democracy." *The Journal of Developing Areas* 7 (1): 57–74.

3 The Making of an Autocratic Regime: Democratic Backsliding in Bangladesh

Ali Riaz

Introduction

With democratic backsliding being a global phenomenon, two questions have become most pertinent: why does democracy backslide and how does the process unfold? Both warrant our attention, not only to understand the trend but also to chart the course to halt the process. It is now well known that democratic erosion doesn't happens in a day, nor is there a spectacular moment that can be marked as the beginning or end of the backsliding. Identifying the slow, yet consequential, process of reversal from the democratic pathway is a challenging task, but as Nancy Bermeo (2016, 14) aptly noted, 'we need to know more about how the slide backward into hybridity takes place.' This chapter aims to respond to this 'how' question. Although a global phenomenon, democratic institutions and practices unravel in a country; the particularity of the country shapes the pathway. This chapter intends to address the question as to how democracy backslides, using Bangladesh as a case study. Democratic backsliding is understood as 'the state-led debilitation or elimination of the political institutions sustaining an existing democracy' (Bermeo 2016, 5). The state-led process ensues when the incumbent political party begins to take steps towards weakening the institutions and practices of democracy. The process may or may not lead to regime change (Bakke and Sitter 2020, 3), but there are instances where the pathway leads to a transformation of the state. This chapter shows how the pathway has transformed the country into an autocracy.

Bangladesh has witnessed precipitous decline of democratic quality since 2014. The 2016 prediction of the Strategic Forecast that the country would shift toward a single party authoritarianism (Strategic Forecast 2016) seems to have come to pass through two consecutive rigged elections in 2014 and 2018. Ahead of the 2018 election, international media warned of the accelerating pace of authoritarianism (Economist 2018). In recent years various international organizations and analysts have categorized the country as 'authoritarian' (Savoia and Asadullah 2019; Blair 2020; Hossain 2020), 'competitive authoritarian' (Mostofa and Subedi 2021), 'moderate autocracy' (BTI 2022), and 'authoritarian regime' (IDEA 2022). I have previously described the country as a 'hybrid regime,' that is, a system which combines both democratic and authoritarian

DOI: 10.4324/9781003261469-3

52   The Making of an Autocratic Regime

traits (Riaz 2019). Despite the inherent fragility of democracy in Bangladesh due to recent democratization (i.e. 1991), the regression is neither accidental nor inevitable. In other words, Bangladesh is neither a case of institutional decay nor of democratic collapse, but rather an instance of gradual backsliding.

This chapter discusses the process of the incremental backsliding of democracy and argues that the process had begun after 2009, especially with a constitutional amendment in 2011 which annulled the caretaker government (CTG) provision. The CTG provision was the only guardrail against wholesale manipulation of the election. Comprehending the events and processes that contributed to the making of the autocratic regime in Bangladesh requires an understanding of how the country arrived at this stage. The country, after experiencing almost two decades of absence of democracy, under a civilian regime (1972–1975) and under various military leaders (1975–1990), entered the democratic era in 1991. During the subsequent 15 years, instead of consolidation, democracy eroded, and power began to be concentrated in the hands of the executive. A two-party system produced a competitive authoritarian system and paved the way for a promissory coup and the emergence of the military-backed regime, which ruled between 2007 and 2008. I further argue that after the assumption of power through a fair election in 2008, the AL took steps that transformed the country into a hegemonic authoritarian regime. While constitutional and institutional changes remain a key to this transformation, it is necessary that we also explore non-institutional aspects of the process. In Bangladesh, the backsliding has taken its course through changes in institutions such as the electoral system, constitution, and judiciary on the one hand, while constructing an ideology and using mobilizational capacity of the ruling party, on the other.

To unpack the stages of democratic backsliding after 2009 and Bangladesh's transformation into an autocratic state, I will draw on the elements of a three-stage model offered by Steven Levitsky and Daniel Ziblatt in their much-discussed book, *How Democracy Dies* (Levitsky and Ziblatt 2018), as a framework; however, rearranging the sequences of these elements are called for in the context of Bangladesh, which will allow us to retrace more fully the practices and mechanisms that comprise AL's authoritarian turn.

It is worth noting that the 1991 election, the first fairly held election, was one of the key moments of the political history of Bangladesh. Discussions on the political development between 1991 and 2009 will also allow us to see the marked differences between pre- and post-2009. The year 2009 should be marked as a watershed moment in the history of the country, because it provided a unique opportunity to chart a new course for the country's politics after two years of democratic disruption. In 2009, power was handed over to an elected government by the military-backed government. The military-backed government came into power as a result of a promissory coup, which was staged in January 2007. Promissory coups 'frame the ouster of an elected government as a defense of democratic legality and make a public promise to hold elections and restore democracy as soon as possible' (Bermeo 2016, 6).

The Making of an Autocratic Regime   53

However, these regimes often continue to hold on to power for a long period and the coup makers renege on their promises to restore democracy. Thanks to external pressure, a global economic crisis, growing popular discontent, and an inability of the regime to deliver on its promises of reforming the political system, Bangladesh's coup-makers stepped down.

Five sections follow the introduction. The first section provides a background, discussing the state of democracy between 1971 and 2009. The second section offers a theoretical framework of sequences of democratic backsliding drawing on Levitsky and Ziblatt (2018). The third section discusses the sequences of backsliding in Bangladesh between 2009 and 2018 under the Sheikh Hasina regime. The fourth section offers brief remarks on the post-2018 situation to demonstrate that an authoritarian system of governance became entrenched. The fifth section draws some conclusions. Discussions of the process and its defining features end in 2022, as by then the authoritarian rule had taken hold.

Background

A False Start and Military Rule: 1972–1990

Bangladesh emerged as an independent country in 1971, and the constitution (written in 1972) introduced a unicameral parliamentary system based on a first-past-the-post (FPTP) system with 300 directly elected representatives. Despite the promise of liberal democracy, the country witnessed a rigged election in 1973, moved away from a parliamentary system to the presidential system, and turned into a one-party populist authoritarian state in January 1975 through the 4th Amendment of the constitution. The government was replaced through a violent military coup in August when then-President Sheikh Mujibur Rahman, his family members, and associates were brutally killed – at their homes and inside the jail after being incarcerated. A number of coups and countercoups followed until November.

In the following 15 years, the country experienced military rule and several failed coups, witnessed the assassination of another president – Ziaur Rahman in 1981 – and the rise of another military leader – H. M. Ershad in early 1982. An eight-year-long pro-democracy movement, which brought all political parties closer and was spearheaded by three alliances, culminated in a popular uprising in December 1990 and deposed the pseudo-civilian military government (Maniruzzaman 1992).The uprising not only brought down the government but also brought an end to the era of civilian and military authoritarianism, which were the defining features of the first two decades of independent Bangladesh. The uprising raised hopes for democratization. The expectation was based on the lessons from the pro-democracy movement, particularly an agreement signed by all political parties at the height of the movement promising to adhere to the fundamental canons of liberal democracy such as fair elections, freedom of assembly, and freedom of press, among others.

54 *The Making of an Autocratic Regime*

The Beginning and the Erosion of Electoral Democracy: 1991–2001

A fair election and the peaceful transfer of power to an elected government in 1991 marked the beginning of the democratization process in Bangladesh; the transition from authoritarianism began in an almost textbook fashion. One can hardly escape the timing of the transition; democratization was sweeping across the globe, described as the 'Third Wave of Democracy' (Huntington 1993). A competitive, multiparty political system with universal adult suffrage and regularly contested elections suggested a promising start. Media became relatively free and promises of an independent judiciary were reiterated by all parties, particularly the two major parties – the incumbent Bangladesh Nationalist Party (BNP) and the opposition Bangladesh Awami League (AL). The constitutional amendment in 1991, to scrap the presidential system and re-introduce the parliamentary system, was a positive step towards accountability, as the presidential system had endowed unrestrained power to an individual (i.e., the president) with little or no accountability mechanism. Bangladesh's transition from an authoritarian system was dramatic in the sense that it didn't face any major stumbling block and the existing constitutional arrangement was sufficient for such a transition.

With these developments, Bangladesh became an electoral democracy. The defining characteristics of the electoral democracy are the following:

> A competitive, multiparty political system; universal adult suffrage for all citizens (with exceptions for restrictions that states may legitimately place on citizens as sanctions for criminal offenses); regularly contested elections conducted in conditions of ballot secrecy, reasonable ballot security, and in the absence of massive voter fraud that yields results that are representative of the public will; significant public access of major political parties to the electorate through the media and through generally open political campaigning.
>
> (Freedom House 2012)

The Varieties of Democracy Institute (V-Dem) identifies five indicators of electoral democracy – freedom of association, clean elections, freedom of expression and alternative sources of information, elected officials, and suffrage (V-Dem 2019). Additionally, an independent judiciary is essential for electoral democracy. In the initial years of democratization, Bangladesh fulfilled all these requirements. The agreement among political parties of all persuasions – from right-wing Islamists to left-wing socialists and all parties in-between – paved the way for the emergence of an electoral democracy. Political parties agreed that 'democracy is the only game in town.' The transition process, especially the introduction of the parliamentary system, had one wrinkle: the power of the president was transferred to the prime minister lock, stock, and barrel in addition to the prime minister's power under the parliamentary system, which created the opportunity for amassing unrestrained power in the hands of the prime minister.

The Making of an Autocratic Regime 55

After the first inclusive, fair election in 1991, which delivered a victory to the Bangladesh Nationalist Party (BNP), the opposition Bangladesh Awami League (AL) was unwilling to play by the rules, which unfortunately continued in the subsequent rounds of elections, although the roles of the two parties – the AL and the BNP – reversed every five years (Schaffer 2002). This is a marker of authoritarian behavior of both leaders – Sheikh Hasina and Khaleda Zia – and their respective parties. As noted by Levitsky and Ziblatt, four authoritarian behaviors that contribute to the demise of democracy include 'rejection of (or weak commitment to) democratic rules of the game' (Levitsky and Ziblatt 2018, 23). They specifically mentioned undermining the legitimacy of elections by refusing to accept credible election results as a test to measure a leader's commitment to democracy. The trust deficiency among the major political parties, especially AL and the BNP, engendered acrimony, street agitation, and violence, and the incessant wrangling among these two parties made the parliament dysfunctional. In late 1994, the opposition members of the 5th parliament resigned, demanding that a non-party caretaker government system be included as a permanent arrangement in the constitution to oversee the election. This en masse resignation made the parliament ineffective. The incumbent BNP showed an obdurate attitude and declined to make any changes; it insisted that the opposition adhere to the existing constitutional provisions (Hossain 1995). While the 5th parliament completed its term in late 1995, the impasse continued. In late 1995, the behavior of the opposition led by the AL and the incumbent BNP demonstrated their penchant for authoritarianism. On the one hand, the AL launched massive street agitations, repeatedly imposed *hartal* (general strike), and endorsed violence by their supporters – a key indicator of authoritarian behavior noted by Levitsky and Ziblatt (2018, 24). The incumbent BNP's use of heavy-handed measures against the opposition revealed its willingness to restrict or curtail civil liberties of the opposition (Levitsky and Ziblatt 2018, 24).

The incumbent finally went ahead with a non-inclusive election in February 1996, which elected a parliament with BNP members only. The 6th parliament incorporated the caretaker government system into the constitution through the 13th Amendment of the constitution and dissolved immediately. The incorporation of the caretaker government (CTG) in the constitution in 1996, although by a parliament with questionable legitimacy, allowed the establishment of a system of peaceful power transition. Despite such a significant step towards transfer of power through the June 1996 election, the parliament began to lose its importance, thanks to the boycott of the opposition and the ruling party's proclivity towards disregarding the opposition's demands. Instead of consolidating democracy, building democratic institutions, creating ways for vertical and horizontal accountability, and ensuring space for dissent, an all-powerful 'prime ministerial system' was created (Molla 2000, 15). The prime minister remained beyond any scrutiny and accountability because she holds several offices; in addition to being the prime minister, she is also the leader of the House, the leader of the parliamentary party of the majority party, and the

56   The Making of an Autocratic Regime

chief of the party. Article 70 of the Bangladesh constitution stipulates that a member of parliament will lose their membership if they vote against the party, are present in the parliament but abstain from voting, or abstain from any sitting, ignoring the direction of the party. This provision has provided complete control of the parliamentary party to the respective leaders. In the case of the prime minister, it allows her to exercise unrestrained power. The concentration of power in one office created the opportunity for the emergence of a constitutionally allowed authoritarian leader.

While the power became concentrated in one office at the top, politicization of administration became rampant, a phenomenon called 'partyarchy.' The ruling party was establishing 'monopolistic partyarchal governance.' Additionally, '[P]artisan control over the civil bureaucracy, state-owned electronic media, law enforcement agencies, institutions of horizontal accountability (Public Service Commission, Anti-Corruption Commission), the lower judiciary and … also the higher judiciary' (Hassan 2013) was normalized.

These tendencies of the political parties, both the AL and the BNP, produced an intolerant political culture that resulted in a gradual tilt towards authoritarianism, which I call semi-authoritarianism. Such characterization is based on three features: first, the overall political environment was marked by 'rhetorical acceptance of liberal democracy, (and some) political space for political parties and organizations of civil society to form, for an independent press to function to some extent, and for some political debate to take place' (Ottaway 2003); second, the dynastic nature of leadership with unlimited power to the party chiefs (Khaleda Zia of the BNP and Sheikh Hasina of the AL); and third, the tolerance of violence by their supporters and the denial of legitimacy of political opponents.

The Era of the Competitive Authoritarian Regime: 2001–2006

In 2004, when the BNP government passed the 14th Amendment of the constitution, the semi-authoritarian system began to transmute into a competitive authoritarian system. The constitution stipulated, pursuant to the 13th Amendment of 1996, that the immediate past chief justice would be the head of the caretaker government. The BNP raised the retirement age of the justices through the amendment to ensure that its preferred retired chief justice could be appointed as the head the next CTG.

> In competitive authoritarian regimes, formal democratic institutions are widely viewed as the principal means of obtaining and exercising political authority. Incumbents violate those rules so often and to such an extent, however, that the regime fails to meet conventional minimum standards for democracy.
>
> (Levitsky and Way 2002; 52)

The two-party system that emerged through the elections between 1991 and 2001, with an almost equal support base of these two parties – about 40 percent

The Making of an Autocratic Regime 57

of the popular vote (Riaz 2016) – made the system competitive and maintained an equilibrium. But the competition became increasingly vicious and the use of state power to persecute opponents through judicial and extrajudicial manners became the norm. Perhaps no other incidents exemplify the ruling party's penchant for extrajudicial measures better than the assassination attempt of the opposition leader Sheikh Hasina in August 2004 at a public rally. The cover-up by the BNP government was easily discernable after the incident and thus raised the question of its complicity. The opposition AL, on the other hand, through-out the period had adopted the strategy of repeated street agitation instead of making parliament the center of politics.

Elections are an important element of democracy and democratization. But it assumes a greater significance and becomes a high-stakes event in a competitive authoritarian system. In a competitive authoritarian system, elections become high-stakes exercises because they are the only source of legitimacy; ensuring a 'victory in elections – whether the elections are fair or not' (Kilinc 2017) turns out to be the principal objective. Machinations to influence the 2007 election by the incumbent BNP through manipulating the caretaker system bears testimony to this. As the time to appoint the CTG arrived in October 2006, the opposition political parties under the leadership of the AL vowed not to accept the immediate-past chief justice and launched agitations. When the former chief justice declined, the president assumed the position of the head of the government in addition to his responsibility as the head of state. Although legally permissible, it became evident that he was acting at the behest of the BNP to influence the elections scheduled in early 2007 (Hagerty 2007). *Hartals* (general strikes), demonstrations, heightened violence, and international pressure paved the way for the military to step in and install a caretaker government. The military takeover, albeit in civilian garb, averted large-scale bloodshed but it brought an end to the democratic processes. The flawed practice, which was already being eroded from within, faced a sudden, unexpected defeat.

The violence perpetrated by the activists received very little condemnation from the party leadership; instead the leaders of these parties tacitly condoned it. Although the intervention initially had the public support and blessings of the international community, domestic discontent, the Asian economic crisis, inability to deliver on the promised reforms in politics, the ill-conceived idea of removing two leaders (Khaleda Zia and Sheikh Hasina) from politics (Montlake 2007), and pressure from international actors forced the military to hold an election in late 2008, which produced a two-thirds majority victory for the Awami League, and Bangladesh returned to the competitive authoritarian system of governance. Explanation of the subsequent development requires an understanding of the stages of backsliding.

The Stages of Democratic Backsliding: A Framework

The process of democratic backsliding is not episodic but incremental, that is, 'a discontinuous series of incremental actions' (Waldner and Lust 2018, 95) that

58   The Making of an Autocratic Regime

debilitate democratic institutions. These actions '[make] elections less competitive without entirely undermining the electoral mechanism, [restrict] participation without explicitly abolishing norms of constitutive democracy, and [loosen] constraints of accountability by eroding norms of answerability and punishment' (Waldner and Lust 2018, 95). However, how the process unfolds and how various stages play out are seldom explored in the existing literature. Bermeo's suggestion that it occurs in three ways – promissory coups, executive aggrandizement, and strategic manipulation of election (Bermeo 2016, 7–8) – informs us of various aspects but leaves us with the question whether there is any sequence to these features.

It is evident from the recent incidents of backsliding in various countries around the world that these aspects are neither mutually exclusive nor sequential. This lacuna of the existing literature is addressed by Levitsky and Ziblatt and a model has been offered. They argue that there are three stages of democratic backsliding. These stages are: Stage 1 – target the 'referees'; Stage 2 – target opponents of the government; and Stage 3 – change the "rules of the game" (Levitsky and Ziblatt 2018, 78). Their model suggests that in the first stage, the incumbent targets the institutions that are essential to protecting the neutrality of the state and the rights of citizens. This is done with the objective of gaining control of law enforcement institutions, including the judiciary, law enforcement, and tax and regulatory agencies. The ruling party, particularly its leader, intends to ensure the unconditional loyalty of these institutions. By establishing complete control over these institutions, not only does the incumbent make these institutions ineffective, but they turn them into weapons against the opposition; these institutions become instruments for providing impunity to the extrajudicial activities of ruling party activists and state institutions. The damning effect of this action is the removal of any semblance of accountability.

In the second stage, opposition parties, the media, and civil society organizations are silenced. This stage ensues either concurrently with the first stage or immediately after the first stage has reached a level of comfort with the incumbent. It is in this context that we can remember Freedom House's description of what has happened between 2006 and 2019 – 'More authoritarian powers are now banning opposition groups or jailing their leaders, dispensing with term limits, and tightening the screws on any independent media that remain' (Freedom House 2019). It is important to note that these new authoritarian rulers usually neither outrightly proscribe the major opposition nor eliminate them. However, there are a few exceptions to this general pattern. The Hun Sen regime in Cambodia has banned the opposition parties twice in 2018 and 2023. Similarly, in Belarus the Lukashenko regime banned several political parties in 2023. In all instances, these regimes have used the highest courts to do their bidding. In most other instances, opposition parties are weakened to the extent that they are suffocated. This can be described as 'strategic silencing.' Ensuring the subservience of the media has been an important aspect of the process. Freedom House has noted that beyond the electoral process, the most significant impact of democratic backsliding has

The Making of an Autocratic Regime   59

been on freedom of expression (Freedom House 2019). Either they are domesticated or they are coerced into compliance. Restrictive laws are legislated and used in this stage to create fear among journalists. With the emergence of social media, restrictions on print or electronic media are no longer enough to control the message. That is why we have witnessed the phenomenon called 'digital authoritarianism.'

The third stage of backsliding is the ruling party establishing complete control over the state and the polity. This is achieved through changes in the constitution and legislative bodies. It is in this stage that electoral systems are shaped in such a manner that it delivers victory to the incumbent, even without any apparent electoral fraud. A schematic presentation of their argument follows (Table 3.1):

Table 3.1 Model of Democratic Backsliding

Stage	*Goals*	*Methods*
Stage 1		
Target the 'referees' of the state (the judiciary, law enforcement, and tax and regulation agencies)	Ensure loyalty of the institutions, so that the incumbent can protect the government (ruling party and leader) and attack opponents	• Bribery and blackmail • Replace civil servants with loyalists • Impeach judges • Court packing (appointing party people in the court) • Create new institutions
Stage 2		
Target opponents of the government (political opponents, critical media, business leaders, etc.)	Demoralize and weaken the opposition, and dissuade criticism of the government	• Bribery and blackmail • Charge opponents with invented or exaggerated criminal activities
Stage 3		
Change the rules of governing (legislation, constitution, and electoral system)	Ensure continued political dominance of the governmental political party (incumbent)	• Gerrymandering (manipulation of electoral constituency to favor a party) • Alter the electoral rules • Introduce legislation to favor the ruling party

Source: Levitsky and Ziblatt (2018, 78).

Sequences of Backsliding in Bangladesh (2009–2018)

While I agree with Levitsky and Ziblatt about the elements of each stage and process of backsliding, I note that Bangladesh experienced different sequencing. In the case of Bangladesh, the process started with the change in the

60   *The Making of an Autocratic Regime*

constitution, which allowed a non-inclusive election, followed by the persecution of opposition leaders and limiting the freedom of expression and targeting institutions, such as the judiciary and law enforcement agencies. The sequences of the process follow (Table 3.2):

Table 3.2 Bangladeshi Model of Democratic Backsliding

Stage	*Goals*	*Methods*	
Stage 1			
Change the rules of governing (legislation, constitution, and electoral system)	• Ensure dominance of the incumbent over the election • Ensure a subservient legislative body • Enhance the power of the executive body • Free the executive branch from accountability	• Introduce legislation in favor of the ruling party	• Removal of the caretaker government through the constitutional amendment in 2011
Stage 2			
Target opponents of the government (political opponents, critical media, business leaders, etc.)	• Demoralize and weaken the opposition • Dissuade criticism of the government	• Bribery and blackmail • Charge opponents with invented or exaggerated criminal activities	• Frivolous cases against the leaders of the opposition, particularly the BNP • Amendment of the ICT Act 2006 in 2013, adding the draconian provision of limiting freedom of press
Stage 3			
Target the 'referees' of the state (the judiciary, law enforcement, and tax and regulation agencies)	• Ensure loyalty of the institutions, so that the incumbent can protect the government (ruling party and leader) and attack opponents	• Bribery and blackmail • Replace civil servants with loyalists • Impeach judges • Court packing (appointing party people in the court) • Create new institutions	• Removal of the chief justice after annulling the 16th Amendment of the constitution.

Source: Author, based on Levitsky and Ziblatt (2018, 78).

The first stage of the process in Bangladesh under the incumbent AL was targeting the constitution. The 15th Amendment of the constitution passed in 2011, which removed the caretaker government (CTG) provision, and was intended to establish the dominance of the ruling Awami League. With the removal of the CTG provision the incumbent removed the uncertainty regarding election results. As mentioned earlier, all elections held under the incumbent in Bangladesh between 1973 and 1990 and in February 1996 delivered victory to the ruling party. The 15th Amendment made sure that the same could be repeated, as under the new stipulation elections would be overseen by the incumbent. The door for unchecked electoral fraud was opened through this new arrangement. The ruling party and its allies used a summary verdict of the Supreme Court delivered in May 2010 as a pretext to bring this change, despite objections of the members of civil society and opposition political parties. On May 10, 2011, the Supreme Court issued a verdict on a case challenging the constitutionality of the existing CTG system. The summary verdict stated that 'The Constitution (Thirteenth Amendment) Act, 1996 (Act 1 of 1996) is prospectively declared void and ultra vires of the Constitution.' But it also observed that, 'The election to the Tenth and the Eleventh Parliament may be held under the provisions of the above-mentioned Thirteenth Amendment' (Sarkar, 2011, 1). The verdict – the summary and the complete verdict made public 14 months later – did not unequivocally suggest a complete scrapping of the CTG system, yet the ruling party used it as a pretext. Interestingly, a 15-member parliamentary committee was set up in July 2010 to amend the constitution, specifically to examine the provision of the CTG. The BNP declined to join the committee and it became a committee with all ruling party members. Between July 21, 2010 and May 29, 2011, the committee met 27 times. In these meetings, the committee invited more than 100 people from various walks of life, including former chief justices, constitutional experts, editors, and leaders of civil society organizations. The overwhelming majority of them suggested amending but maintaining the CTG system. The committee's recommendation was to amend the provision until the final meeting with the prime minister, who unilaterally decided to annul the system (Riaz 2019, 143).

The 15th Amendment of the constitution removed the CTG system and stipulated that the parliamentary election would be held within 90 days prior to the completion of tenure (or within 90 days of the dissolution of parliament, if the parliament were dissolved before completion of its tenure). It was implied that the incumbents in the cabinet would continue to serve up to the time of the election, and that the parliament would continue to function. It also stipulated that an election would be held while the previously elected parliament remained effective, which is contrary to the level playing field necessary for ensuring an acceptable election and common practice of parliamentary systems around the world. It was a classic move to turn the country into a hegemonic electoral authoritarian regime, a regime that holds 'uncompetitive multiparty elections that are not free or fair' (Diamond 2002), where 'there is never any uncertainty in the outcome of national elections' (Roessler and Howard 2009), and which 'systematically … render elections instruments of authoritarian rule rather than

62   The Making of an Autocratic Regime

"instruments of democracy"' (Schedler 2006). An electoral authoritarian regime, to ensure its access to power, effectively strips the efficacy of elections. As such, the 15th Amendment of the Bangladeshi constitution was neither a response to the abuse of the caretaker system by the previous government nor the Supreme Court's verdict, but a way to make the elections ineffective.

The opposition parties, including the BNP, threatened to boycott the election if the CTG system was not restored (Economist 2011). The international community repeatedly called for ensuring an inclusive election, and a UN-brokered talk between the incumbent and BNP failed to yield any result (UN News 2012). The incumbent went ahead with the election, which was boycotted by all opposition parties. The result, therefore, was a forgone conclusion. Additionally, more than half of the 300-member parliament were elected unopposed, because the opposition parties didn't field any candidates (Ahmed 2014). Various features of the election – from number of parties participating to voter turnout to election of unopposed candidates (Figure 3.1) – not only bear the marks of an unusual election, but also show how the removal of the CTG has

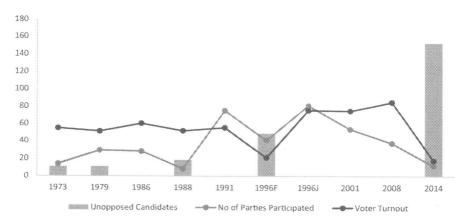

Figure 3.1 Bangladeshi Elections: Party Participation, Voter Turnout, and Unopposed Candidates, 1973–2014.

Notes:
(1) Parties participated: Among the 12 parties that participated in the 2014 election, 5 had less than three candidates (Khelafat Majlish: 2; Islamic Front: 1; Gonofront: 1; Tariquat Federation: 3; and Gonotontri Party: 1). Only 7 parties had more than 5 candidates and there were 6 parties with 10 or more candidates.
(2) Voter turnout: Official sources, including the Election Commission, claimed that the turnout was 39 percent. But this figure is contested by the local and international press, amid reports that ballots were stuffed by party activists, particularly in the afternoon as it became evident that the turnout would be too low. The *Guardian* reported that voter turnout was 10 percent, while others have suggested about 22 percent at best. It is worth noting that in 50 polling centers no votes were cast. Considering that the election was held for 147 seats, a 39 percent turnout is about 18 percent of the total number of eligible voters.

Sources: Compiled by the author based on information from the Election Commission and press reports

The Making of an Autocratic Regime   63

impacted the electoral landscape. For example, the number of parties partici-pating in the election was down to 12 from 38 in the previous election.

Although immediately after the election Sheikh Hasina hinted at a fresh poll ahead of schedule, she later reneged. With a new system in place, and the result of 2014, Bangladesh became a hegemonic authoritarian system under which the 2018 election became a stage-managed show. With the constitutional change completed the incumbent entered the second stage, the persecution of opposition leaders, particularly the BNP. By bringing frivolous charges against them and engaging them in court battles, the incumbent succeeded in weakening them. Along with the opposition, the incumbent targeted the media and civil society organizations. The most telling example of the persecution of the opposition is in the number of cases filed against the BNP chairperson and former prime minister, Khaleda Zia. Between 2012 and 2019, a staggering 36 cases were filed against her (The Business Standard 2020). During the period of caretaker government (2007–2008), several corruption cases were filed against Sheikh Hasina and Khaleda Zia. But they faced a different fate after Hasina came to power in 2009. By May 2010, all 15 cases against Sheikh Hasina – some filed during the BNP government in 2001–2006 and some filed by the CTG in 2007–2008 by the Anti-Corruption Commission – were dropped or quashed by courts (BBC 2010), while cases against Khaleda Zia remained active (*The Daily Star* 2018a). Khaleda Zia was sentenced to five years in prison by a special court in a February 2018 graft case (Rashid 2018). Her prison sentence was increased to ten years by the High Court in October 2018, an unprecedented event (*The Asian Age* 2018). Her son, Tarique Rahman, was also convicted on these graft charges (Aljazeera 2016). In the same month she was sen-tenced to seven years in another case.

Corruption is so endemic in Bangladesh, like many other developing coun-tries, that it was ranked the most corrupt country by Transparency Interna-tional for five years in 2000–2005. But as democracy eroded, the corruption became institutionalized as neopatrimonialism became pervasive (Islam 2013). In such a system, corruption serves various purposes, from buying friends to muzzling media. But in competitive authoritarian systems, anticorruption tends to be weaponized and used against political opposition. The persecution of opposition was very much on display when the government adopted harsh measures against the Jamaat-i-Islami soon after the International Crimes Tri-bunal was appointed in 2010 to try those who committed crimes against humanity in 1971 (Islam 2011). In addition to the change in the constitution, the government changed a law related to freedom of expression which was essen-tially designed to silence the critics: the law in question is the Information and Communication (ICT) Act. Although the Act was formulated in 2006, it was not applied until 2008. There was an amendment made in 2009, but the most significant and far-reaching changes were brought about in 2013. The amended law not only provided the power to law enforcement agencies to arrest someone without a warrant but also to detain him/her for an indefinite period. Article 57 of the ICT Act 2006 (as amended in 2013) stated that one can be charged for publishing materials which are 'false,' 'prejudicial to the state or person,' and/or

64 The Making of an Autocratic Regime

hurt 'religious beliefs' (*The Daily Star* 2015). None of those offenses were defined yet; the steep penalty for the violation – 14 years' imprisonment and a fine of a crore taka ($125,000) – was set. The Act, since 2013, became a tool for curtailing freedom of speech, for allegedly hurting religious sentiment, and criticizing the government. The International Commission of Jurists (ICJ) along with human rights groups and groups working for freedom of media described it as draconian. The ICJ stated, 'Provisions of the original ICT Act, particularly section 57, are also incompatible with Bangladesh's obligations under Article 19 of the International Covenant on Civil and Political Rights (ICCPR)' (ICJ 2013).

Soon after enacting the law, it was used against 'secularist' bloggers on the one hand, while clamping down on Islamist websites on the other. Human rights defenders were charged under the newly amended law. Article 57 has been the key in silencing the critics and gradually establishing complete control over cyberspace, resulting in the precipitous decline of freedom of expression since 2013 (Figure 3.2). Further legal and extralegal measures to muzzle the press and gag the dissenting voices were taken. Eminent journalists and editors, as well as newspapers, faced the wrath of the government and its supporters. Seventy-nine cases were filed against an editor (Sattar 2016) after the prime minister had spoken harshly against the editor (bdnews24 2016), another editor was incarcerated for years (BBC 2016) and was attacked at the court premises (Sagor 2018), the government forced businesses to stop advertising in two newspapers to deprive them of revenue (DW 2015), and a photojournalist was detained for months (Meixler 2018). In October 2018, months before the election, the government implemented a vaguely defined law with harsher punitive measures called the Digital Security Act 2018. The Digital Security Act criminalizes many forms of freedom of expression and imposes heavy fines and prison sentences for legitimate forms of dissent. It is incompatible with international law and standards and should be amended immediately,' said Dinushika Dissanayake, Deputy South Asia Director at Amnesty International

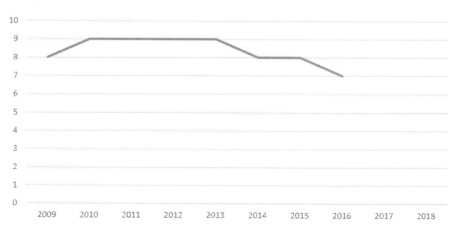

Figure 3.2 Freedom of Expression in Bangladesh, 2009–2018.
Source: Freedom House (n.d.)

in November 2018 (Amnesty International 2013). According to Freedom House, the scores of Bangladesh between 2009 and 2018 reveal the decline (Figure 3.2).

The government used all legal and extralegal measures to silence critics, weaken the opposition, and create a culture of fear. Human rights activists were systematically persecuted (DW 2015). The incidences of extrajudicial killings, particularly the so-called crossfire – a term euphemistically used to describe the killings by law enforcing agencies – and enforced disappearances increased and naturalized. In 2013, the year before the election, 329 people became victims of the violence. As for the enforced disappearances, which began in 2011, they began to spike in 2014, the election year (Figure 3.3).

The failed violent movement to halt the election by the BNP, and its alliance with the Islamist party Jamaat-i-Islami,[1] played into the hands of the ruling party. By then the regime began transmutating and structurally the election was designed to favor the incumbent. Notwithstanding the pre- and post-election violence (Riaz 2014a; Riaz 2014b; Riaz 2015), the 2014 election became a watershed moment in the history of the nation. Whether participation of the BNP would have made a difference has been discussed at length in subsequent years. It gained further currency after the BNP launched a movement on the anniversary of the election in 2015. But it was evident to analysts, even before the failed movement of the BNP, that the ruling party already had a game plan to decimate the BNP. Zafar Sobhan, for example, predicted in a commentary on January 1, 2015, that 'There can be only one.' Sobhan wrote:

> 2014 marked the end of the compact of co-existence that was forged between the AL and BNP at the end of the 1980s, and that has provided the pattern for the past quarter century of political life. … The game plan for the ruling AL is clear. … The AL plan for the coming year is therefore straightforward: Continue to squeeze the life out of the BNP.
>
> (Sobhan 2015)

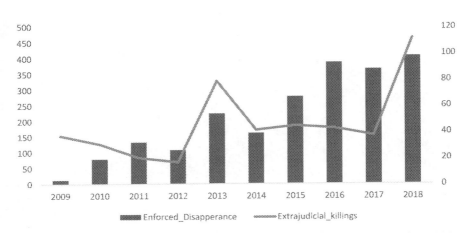

Figure 3.3 Enforced Disappearances and Extrajudicial Killings in Bangladesh, 2009–2018. Source: Odhikar (2019)

66 *The Making of an Autocratic Regime*

It was quite evident that after the 2014 election, the road was not leading to, but rather away from, democracy. The 2014 election produced a legislature that was completely under the control of the ruling party and the executive, with the Jatiya Party declared the 'official opposition,' and being a part of the cabinet, it became a *de facto* one-party state. This is also borne out by the data from Polity IV, particularly about political competitiveness (Figure 3.4).

Finally, in the third stage, control over various institutions, especially the court, has been imposed. In this case, the ruling party not only packed the court with its supporters, but also forced the chief justice out of the court and into exile. Subordination of the judicial arena is almost a prerequisite for the maintenance of the hybrid regime. Levitsky and Way argue that this is often done by means of bribery and extortion, and, if possible, by appointing and dismissing judges and officials (Levitsky and Way 2002, 52). According to Brown and Wise, institutions such as the Supreme Court or constitutional courts tend to function not only as arbiters of constitutionality and legal principles but also as advocates of the current regime (Brown and Wise 2004). The 16th Amendment of the Bangladesh constitution passed by parliament in September 2014, which has empowered parliament to impeach judges of the Supreme Court for incapability or misconduct, falls within this kind of effort. The insalubrious rhetoric of the ruling party leaders after it was struck down by the High Court (May 2016) and the Supreme Court (July 2016) is indicative of the mindset to establish complete control over the higher courts. This is what led to the 'resignation' of Chief Justice S.K. Sinha, who also left the country (*Dhaka Tribune* 2017). The chief justice, in his memoir published a year later, claimed that he was forced to resign and go into exile (Bergman 2018). Similarly, retaining the power of appointment, administration, and removal of lower court judges in the president's hands as opposed to the Supreme Court through the Bangladesh

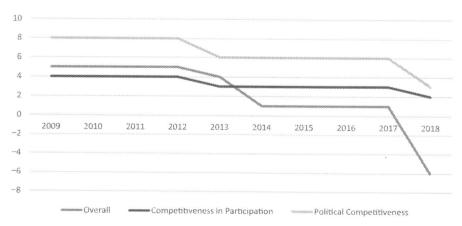

Figure 3.4 Democracy Score, Competitiveness in Participation, and Political Competition, 2009–2018.
Source: Polity IV (n.d.)

Judicial Service (Discipline) Rules 2017 contravenes the spirit of the separation of the executive and the judiciary (*The Daily Star* 2018b).

Despite various stages and specific actions at each stage, these are not mutually exclusive, and each stage is not a watertight compartment; rather, many actions overlap. Therefore, while the incumbent AL was focused to make the constitutional changes in 2011, persecution of opposition began, albeit in a limited scale, but with changes in the rules related to the next election, neutering the opposition became the primary target.

Beyond the Institutional Dimensions

Although the 'debilitation or elimination of the political institutions' is central to backsliding, it does not explain the process of how a country deviates from the path of democracy in its entirety. I argue that non-institutional measures are accompanied by, and in many instances proceeded by, ideational measures creating an environment that allows and legitimizes the undemocratic actions of the incumbent. Differences and contestation on various issues are not unique to Bangladesh, but they are increasingly portrayed as the source of epistemic insecurity – that is, the survival of the group is at stake. As such, a contrived 'us versus them' mentality and discourse have been inflamed in the past decade. Such discourse has proliferated with the encouragement of the incumbent on the one hand and by so-called Islamists on the other. This has created an unprecedented fissure, and it has undermined tolerance, a fundamental element of democracy.

The ideational effort of the ruling Awami League to undermine democracy became palpable in 2009–2010 when the supporters of the government insisted that development should precede democracy. The ruling party, since coming to power in 2009, underscored infrastructural development as a key to their economic agenda. It embarked on several large-scale infrastructure projects, often described as 'mega projects,' which have been touted as the marker of development and have the potential to change the livelihoods of the people of Bangladesh. These include the Padma Bridge and Roopur Nuclear Power Plant. It was argued by the supporters of the regime that development requires stability and continuity, which can only be achieved by continuation of the same party in power. By 2014, the central argument of the regime was that it is delivering an unprecedented economic growth measured by the GDP growth rate. Data belies this claim. Bangladesh's GDP began to grow in the 1990s when the country embarked on democratization. Data shows that, save one exception (2002), the GDP growth rate was above 4 percent and was in an upward trend despite alteration in power and bad governance (Figure 3.5).

Some of the pro-government intellectuals introduced the notion of 'democratic authoritarianism.' A false dichotomy between democracy and development was created to justify heavy-handed, often extrajudicial measures, of the government. The debate itself served as a source of legitimacy of the government and helped sway support of some people. Like many other countries

68   *The Making of an Autocratic Regime*

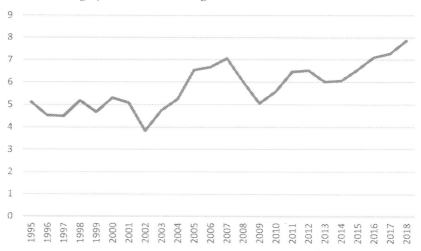

Figure 3.5 Bangladesh's GDP Growth Rate, 1996–2018.
Source: World Bank (n.d.)

where democratic backsliding has taken place in the past decade, the incumbent in Bangladesh has used 'patriotism' as a weapon to create schisms and used it as a legitimizing tool since it came into power in 2009. Since 2013, the country has witnessed efforts to accentuate this division using the term *muktijudhher chetona* (the spirit of liberation war) as a marker of that division. The concept, which literally means to uphold the ideals that underlined the 1971 war, has been used by the supporters of the ruling Awami League as an indicator of patriotism and unqualified support for the incumbent government. The 2013 grassroots movement demanding capital punishment for those who were convicted of crimes against humanity perpetrated during the 1971 war of independence was coopted by the ruling party (Zaman 2018). While the movement initially emerged spontaneously, the government soon coopted it and made the *muktijudhher chetona* as the battle cry. There is neither an agreed meaning to the term *muktijudhher chetona* and what it entails, nor is there a way to devise a common meaning for such a nebulous idea, yet it is used as a marker of identity and as an instrument to marginalize parties, groups, and individuals for their political positions. Criticism of the notion was portrayed as unpatriotic and almost treasonous. The movement, called *Gonojagorn Moncho*, gradually winded down but it created the environment for a non-inclusive election leading to the emergence of electoral authoritarianism.

Implications of the ideational element are not limited to a specific stage, although it started even before the institutional changes were made, yet it continues to serve as the source of legitimacy throughout the entire process of backsliding.

The 2018 Election and Beyond

As stipulated in the constitution, election was scheduled in December 2018 under the incumbent Awami League government headed by Sheikh Hasina. The BNP and the enfeebled opposition decided to participate in the election, making it the first participatory election in ten years. Ahead of the election, the Bangladesh Nationalist Party (BNP) joined an alliance called the Jatiya Oikya Front (JOF) under the leadership of Kamal Hossain, one of the framers of Bangladesh's original constitution. But as the election approached, fictitious cases were filed against opposition activists and general masses to create a climate of fear. The Election Commission, in many instances without any foundation, canceled the candidature of opposition nominees during the scrutiny. The appeal process against the decision led these candidates to courts, making it impossible for them to engage in a campaign. Opposition rallies were attacked by the ruling party activists while the members of the law enforcement agencies stood by as silent spectators.

On election day, polling booths were found to be under the control of the Bangladesh Awami League and its allies' supporters. Many voters found that their votes had been already cast. A BBC report showed that ballot boxes were stuffed the night before. In the following days it became evident that such incidents were not aberrations but a pattern throughout the country. What became clear through the election process was that the Election Commission, civil administration, law enforcement agencies, and the ruling party acted in unison to deliver a victory to the ruling party (for details, see Riaz 2019, 69–79). Such concerted actions were well planned through state capture. One analyst concluded:

> News coverage, reports from human rights organisations, confidential party documents leaked by journalists, and unusually candid public pronouncements by ruling party members, some of which went viral on social media ahead of the polls, revealed the government's elaborate plans for voter suppression, aggressive policing, systemic arrests and detentions of opposition activists – all with the singular objective of managing the election in the ruling party's favour.
>
> (Rabee 2019)

The extent of the manipulation and rigging in the voting led the *New York Times* editorial board to describe the election 'farcical' (*The New York Times* 2019). The Economist described the entire electoral process as 'transparently fraudulent' (Economist 2019). Although the result was a foregone conclusion, the scale of the incumbent's victory was astounding, to say the least: the AL and its allies had secured 289 of 300 seats (Table 3.3).

Emboldened by the election results and the clear demonstration that all the apparatuses were working in its favor, the incumbent's inclination towards its autocratic behavior became normal. Three sets of information are illustrative in

70 *The Making of an Autocratic Regime*

Table 3.3 Election Results 2018

Alliance	Party	Seats
Grand Alliance	Bangladesh Awami League	258
	Jatiya Party (Ershad)	22
	Workers Party of Bangladesh	3
	Jatiya Samajtantrik Dal	2
	Bikalpa Dhara Bangladesh	2
	Jatiya Party (Manju)	1
	Bangladesh Tariqat Federation	1
Jatiya Oikyo Front	Bangladesh Nationalist Party	6
	Gono Forum	2
Independents		3

Source: Bangladesh Election Commission.

this regard: the number of extrajudicial killings, the incidents of enforced disappearances, and the wanton use of the Digital Security Act 2018 (DSA). Between January 2019 and February 2022, there were at least 591 cases of extrajudicial killings involving law enforcement agencies. In 2019, 313 individuals became victims (Riaz 2022a). During the same period, 71 individuals became victims of enforced disappearance. Family, friends, and witnesses have alleged that they were picked up by plain-clothed members of law enforcement agencies. This has made the total number of individuals who faced this plight 593 since 2009 (Riaz 2022b). Although the DSA became a tool to silence the critics of the government since its introduction in October 2018, the government and the supporters of the ruling party began to use it wantonly in 2020. In June 2023, the law minister of the country acknowledged that 7,000 people had been accused under the law, although he did not provide any details about who are being accused, how many have been arrested, and how many are languishing in jails (*The Daily Star* 2023). According to a study published in January 2023, between October 2018 and August 2022, more than 29 percent of the accused were politicians and more than 27 percent were journalists (Riaz 2023). With laws like this and extra-legal measures, the government has succeeded in creating so much fear that online discourse is now severely muted (Shahid 2022).

Conclusion

Bangladesh's promising beginning towards democratization in 1991 has taken a wrong turn; the country had metamorphosed from an electoral democracy to an electoral hegemonic authoritarianism regime by 2014. Subsequently, the regime

The Making of an Autocratic Regime   71

has treaded the path of autocratization, and since 2019 has slid further towards becoming an autocracy. This chapter has described this pathway, especially the early stage of transformation, to understand how a democracy has descended into autocracy.

The initial pace of the transformation – from electoral democracy to competitive authoritarianism – was slow. But the pace accelerated after 2009 and was distinctly different from the gradual erosion of democracy in previous decades. In this instance, the incumbent embarked on a process that was intended to debilitate or eliminate political institutions that sustain an existing democracy. The pathway had three stages, changing the rules of governing, which include removal of the caretaker government in 2011, targeting the opposition and critics through incarceration, amending laws and legislating new laws such as the ICT Act in 2013, and the Digital Security Act of 2018, and targeting institutions such as the judiciary by expressing its displeasure of critical verdicts and the chief justice.

This process was institutionalized through two managed elections in 2014 and 2018, which produced *de facto* one-party parliaments, and allowed the concentration of power in the hands of the prime minister. Individualization of power is the key marker of an autocratic regime, and it is evident that Sheikh Hasina has amassed so much in her hands that she has been described as 'Asia's iron lady' (Economist 2023). As of writing the chapter in late November 2023, the country was heading to an election in January 2024. But the process leading to the election has already sealed a victory for Hasina and her party as major opposition parties have decided to boycott the election and are facing 'a violent autocratic crackdown' (Human Rights Watch 2023). In November 2023, Charlie Cambell, quoting the critics of Hasina, wrote in the newsweekly *Time* that 'January's vote is tantamount to a coronation and Hasina to a dictator' (Campbell 2023).

Note

1 The JI opposed the founding of Bangladesh during the war of independence in 1971. Some of its leaders have been convicted by the International Crimes Tribunal established by the AL in 2010, and five leaders have been executed between 2013 and 2015. The party has been deregistered by the Election Commission in 2013.

Bibliography

Ahmed, Farid. 2014. "Bangladesh ruling party wins elections marred by boycott, violence." *CNN*. January 6. https://www.cnn.com/2014/01/06/world/asia/bangladesh-elections/index.html. Accessed December 6, 2018.

Aljazeera. 2016. "Bangladesh: Tarique Rahman jailed for money laundering." July 21. https://www.aljazeera.com/news/2016/07/bangladesh-tarique-rahman-jailed-money-laundering-160721073133821.html. Accessed May 15, 2022.

Amnesty International. 2013. "Bangladesh: New Digital Security Act is attack on freedom of expression." November 12. https://www.amnesty.org/en/latest/news/2018/11/bangladesh-muzzling-dissent-online/. Accessed November 6, 2019.

72 The Making of an Autocratic Regime

Bakke, Elisabeth, and Nick Sitter. 2020. "The EU's *enfants terribles*: Democratic backsliding in Central Europe since 2010." *Perspectives on Politics*, 1–16. DOI:10.1017/S1537592720001292.

BBC. 2010. "Bangladesh drops leader Sheikh Hasina corruption case." May 30. https://www.bbc.com/news/10194392. Accessed November 2, 2019.

BBC. 2016. "Bangladesh opposition editor Mahmudur Rahman released." November 23. https://www.bbc.com/news/world-asia-38081334. Accessed March 15, 2020.

bdnews24. 2016. "Prothom Alo, Daily Star lied to have me arrested, PM Hasina says." February 29. https://bdnews24.com/bangladesh/2016/02/29/prothom-alo-daily-star-lied-to-have-me-arrested-pm-hasina-says Accessed January 17. Accessed November 15, 2023.

Bergman, David. 2018. "Bangladesh: Ex-chief justice alleges he was 'forced' to resign." September 28. https://www.aljazeera.com/news/2018/09/bangladesh-chief-justice-alleges-forced-resign-180927103453932.html. Accessed December 1, 2018.

Bermeo, Nancy. 2016. "On democratic backsliding." *Journal of Democracy* 12 (1): 5–19.

Blair, Harry. 2020. "Bangladesh paradox." *Journal of Democracy* 31 (4): 138–150.

Brown, Trevor L., and Charles R. Wise. 2004. "Constitutional courts and legislative-executive relations: The case of Ukraine." *Political Science Quarterly* 119 (1): 143–169.

BTI. 2022. *Transformation Index 2022: Governance in international comparison*. Gütersloh: Verlag Bertelsmann Stiftung.

Campbell, Charlie. 2023. "Sheikh Hasina and the future of democracy in Bangladesh." *Time*. November 2. https://time.com/6330463/bangladesh-sheikh-hasina-wazed-profile/. Accessed November 30, 2023.

Dhaka Tribune. 2017. "Sinha resigns as chief justice." November 11. https://www.dhakatribune.com/bangladesh/2017/11/11/chief-justice-sk-sinha-resigns/. Accessed December 26, 2019.

Diamond, Larry. 2002. "Thinking About Hybrid Regimes." *Journal of Democracy* 13 (2): 21–35.

DW. 2015. "Bangladesh blocks media ads, curbs press freedom." October 30. https://www.dw.com/en/bangladesh-blocks-media-ads-curbs-press-freedom/a-18816842. Accessed March 30, 2020.

Economist. 2011. "The opposition BNP threatens to boycott the 2014 election," July 14.

Economist. 2018. "Bangladesh's slide towards authoritarianism is accelerating." October 4. https://www.economist.com/asia/2018/10/04/bangladeshs-slide-towards-authoritarianism-is-accelerating. Accessed June 19, 2022.

Economist. 2019. "Obituary of a Democracy: Bangladesh." January 30. https://espresso.economist.com/0390aff9c68eeb7b64fbebe21c878de3. Accessed April 10, 2020. y system that emerged through the elections between 1991 and 2001, with an almost equal support base of these two parties â€" about 40Â percent of the popular vote (Riaz 2016) â€" made the system competitive and maintained an equilibrium. But the competition became increasingly vicious and the use of state power to persecute opponents through judicial and extrajudicial manners became the norm. P

Economist. 2023. "Sheikh Hasina is Asia's iron lady." May 24. https://www.economist.com/asia/2023/05/24/sheikh-hasina-is-asias-iron-lady. Accessed November 29, 2023.

Freedom House. n.d. "Freedom in the world: Aggregate and subcategory scores." https://freedomhouse.org/report/freedom-world#Data. Accessed May 16, 2024.

Freedom House. 2012. *Methodology*. https://freedomhouse.org/report/freedom-world-2012/methodology. Accessed January 17, 2019.

Freedom House. 2019. *Democracy in Retreat: Freedom in the world 2018*. Washington, DC: Freedom House.

The Making of an Autocratic Regime   73

Government of Bangladesh, Ministry of Law, Legislative and Parliamentary Affairs Division. n.d. "The Constitution of the People's Republic of Bangladesh." http://bdla ws.minlaw.gov.bd/act-details-367.html. Accessed June 6, 2020.

Hagerty, Devin T. 2007. "Bangladesh in 2006: Living in 'Interesting Times'." *Asian Survey* 47 (1): 105–112.

Hassan, Mirza. 2013. *Political Settlement Dynamics in a Limited-Access Order: The case of Bangladesh.* Working Paper, Manchester: ESID, 62. http://www.effective-states.org/wp -content/uploads/working_papers/final-pdfs/esid_wp_23_hassan.pdf. Accessed June 6, 2022.

Hossain, Akhand Akhtar. 2020. "Anatomy of creeping authoritarianism in Bangladesh: A historical analysis of some events that shaped the present state of Bangladesh's culture and politics." *Asian Journal of Political Science*, 28 (1): 13–39.

Hossain, Golam. 1995. "Bangladesh in 1995: Politics of intransigence." *Asian Survey* 36 (2): 196–203.

Human Rights Watch. 2023. "Bangladesh: Violent autocratic crackdown ahead of elections." November 26. https://www.hrw.org/news/2023/11/26/bangladesh-violent-a utocratic-crackdown-ahead-elections. Accessed November 27, 2023.

Huntington. Samuel. 1993. *The Third Wave: Democratization in the late twentieth century.* Norman: University of Oklahoma Press.

ICJ. 2013. *Bangladesh: Information and Communication Technology Act draconian assault on free expression.* https://www.icj.org/bangladesh-information-and-communication-technology-act-draconian-assault-on-free-expression/. Accessed November 3, 2019.

IDEA. 2022. "Global state of democracy: Forging social contract in a time of discontent." Stockholm: International Institute of Democracy and Electoral Assistance.

Islam, Mohammad Mozahidul. 2013. "The toxic politics of Bangladesh: A bipolar competitive neopatrimonial state." *Asian Journal of Political Science* 21 (2): 148–168.

Islam, Md Saidul. 2011. "'Minority Islam' in Muslim majority Bangladesh: The violent road to a new brand of secularism." *Journal of Muslim Minority Affairs* 31 (1): 125–141.

Kilinc, Faith Resul. 2017. "What we see in Venezuela is the faith of hybrid regimes." August 27. http://foreignpolicynews.org/2017/08/28/see-venezuela-faith-hybrid-regimes/ . Accessed December 10, 2018.

Levitsky, Steven, and Lucan A. Way. 2002. "Elections without democracy: The rise of competitive authoritarianism." *Journal of Democracy* 13 (2): 51–65.

Levitsky, Steven, and Daniel Ziblatt. 2018. *How Democracy Dies.* New York: Crown.

Maniruzzaman, Talukdar. 1992. "The fall of the military dictator: 1991 elections and the prospect of civilian rule in Bangladesh." *Pacific Affairs* 65 (2), 203–224.

Meixler, Eli. 2018. "'Journalism Is Under Threat.' Inside a Bangladeshi journalist's dangerous journey from photographer to prisoner." *Time.* December 30. https://time.com/ 5475494/shahidul-alam-bangladesh-journalist-person-of-the-year-2018/. Accessed March 12, 2020.

Molla, Gyasuddin. 2000. *Democratic Institution Building Process in Bangladesh: South Asian experience of a new model of a 'care-taker government' in a parliamentary framework.* Working Paper, No 3. Heidelberg: Department of Political Science, South Asia Institute, University of Heidelberg.

Montlake, Simon. 2007. "Bangladesh Army-backed government detains ex-prime minister." *Christian Science Monitor.* September 4, 1.

Mostofa, Shafi Md and D.B. Subedi. 2021. "Rise of competitive authoritarianism in Bangladesh." *Politics and Religion* 14 (3): 431–459.

74   *The Making of an Autocratic Regime*

Odhikar. 2019. "Total extra-judicial killings from 2001–2018." http://odhikar.org/wp-content/uploads/2019/08/Statistics_EJK_2001–2018.pdf. Accessed November 4, 2019.

Ottaway, Marina. 2003. *Democracy Challenged: The rise of semi-authoritarianism.* Washington, DC: Carnegie Endowment for International Peace.

Polity IV. n.d. "Annual Polity IV annual time series 1800–2018." Regime Authority Characteristics and Transitions Datasets, Center for Systemic Peace. https://www.systemicpeace.org/inscrdata.html.

Rabee, Safquat. 2019. "A deeper look at the Bangladesh election." Aljazeera English. January 2. https://www.aljazeera.com/opinions/2019/1/2/a-deeper-look-at-the-bangladesh-election, Accessed June 23, 2022.

Rashid, Muktadir. 2018. "Khaleda jailed for five years." *New Age.* February 9.

Riaz, Ali. 2010. "'Dynastic politics' and the political culture of Bangladesh." *Journal of International Relations* 8 (2).

Riaz, Ali. 2014a. "A crisis of democracy in Bangladesh." *Current History* 113 (762): 150–156.

Riaz, Ali. 2014b. "Bangladesh's failed election." *Journal of Democracy* 25 (2): 119–130.

Riaz, Ali. 2015. *The Troubled Democracy of Bangladesh: 'Muddling through' or 'a political settlement'?* Special Report, Institute of South Asian Studies, National University of Singapore, Heng Mui Keng Terrace, 17.

Riaz, Ali. 2016. *Bangladesh: A political history since independence.* London: I.B. Tauris.

Riaz, Ali. 2017. *Lived Islam and Islamism in Bangladesh.* Dhaka: Prothoma Prokashon.

Riaz, Ali. 2019. *Voting in Hybrid Regime: Explaining the 2018 Bangladeshi election.* Singapore: Palgrave Macmillan.

Riaz, Ali. 2022a. "Executions at will? Extrajudicial killing by state actors in Bangladesh." Dhaka: Centre for Governance Studies. March. https://cgs-bd.com/article/7048/Executions-at-Will–Extrajudicial-Killing-by-State-Actors-in-Bangladesh. Accessed May 15, 2023.

Riaz, Ali. 2022b. "Where are they? Enforced disappearances in Bangladesh." Dhaka: Centre for Governance Studies. March. https://cgs-bd.com/article/7880/Where-are-They–Enforced-Disappearances-in-Bangladesh. Accessed May 21, 2023.

Riaz, Ali. 2022c. "The unending nightmare: Impacts of Bangladesh's Digital Security Act 2018." Dhaka: Centre for Governance Studies. April. https://cgs-bd.com/article/8919/THE-UNENDING-NIGHTMARE–Impacts-of-Bangladesh%e2%80%99s-Digital-Security-Act-2018 Accessed April 5, 2022.

Riaz, Ali. 2023. "What's Happening? Trends and patterns of the use of the Digital Security Act 2018 in Bangladesh." January. Dhaka: Centre for Governance Studies.

Roessler, Philip and Marc Howard. 2009. "Post-Cold War political regimes: When do elections matter?" in *Democratization by Elections: A New Model of Transition*, ed. Lindberg, Staffan. Baltimore, MD: John Hopkins University Press, 101–127.

Sagor, Al Mamun. 2018. "Amar Desh's Mahmudur Rahman attacked in Kushtia." *Dhaka Tribune.* July 22. https://www.dhakatribune.com/bangladesh/nation/2018/07/22/chhatra-league-confines-amar-desh-editor-inside-court Accessed February 17, 2020.

Sarkar, Ashutosh. 2011. "Caretaker system declared illegal." *The Daily Star*, May 11, 1.

Sattar, Maher. 2016. "Bangladesh editor faces 79 Court cases after an unusual confession." *The New York Times*, March 27. https://www.nytimes.com/2016/03/28/world/asia/bangladesh-editor-faces-79-court-cases-after-saying-he-regrets-articles.html. Accessed March 5, 2020.

Savoia, Antonio and Niaz Md. Asadullah. 2019. "Bangladesh is booming, but slide towards authoritarianism could burst the bubble." *The Conversation*, 28 February. https://the

The Making of an Autocratic Regime   75

conversation.com/bangladesh-is-booming-but-slide-towards-authoritarianism-could-burst-the-bubble-112632. Accessed June 6, 2022.

Schaffer, Howard B. 2002. "Back and forth in Bangladesh." *Journal of Democracy* 13 (1): 76–83.

Schedler, Andreas. 2006. "The logic of electoral authoritarianism." In *Electoral Authoritarianism: The dynamics of unfree competition*, ed. Schedler, Andreas. Boulder, CO: Lynne Rienner, 1–24.

Shahid, Kunwar Khuldune. 2022. "Fear of arrest in Bangladesh is shutting down an entire nation's online discourse." *Daily Dot.* 19 June. https://www.dailydot.com/debug/bangladesh-digital-services-act-online-voices/. Accessed June 21, 2022.

Sobhan, Zafar. 2015. "There can be only one." January 1. https://www.dhakatribune.com/uncategorized/2015/01/01/there-can-be-only-one. Accessed June 2, 2018.

Strategic Forecast. 2016. "Bangladesh's descent into authoritarianism." May 31. https://worldview.stratfor.com/article/bangladeshs-descent-authoritarianism. Accessed July 12, 2018.

The Asian Age. 2018. "Khaleda Zia's jail term in corruption case doubled to 10 years." October 30.

The Business Standard. 2020. "Three dozen cases Khaleda Zia faces." February 8. https://tbsnews.net/bangladesh/corruption/three-dozen-cases-khaleda-zia-faces-42953. Accessed March 6, 2020.

The Daily Star. 2015. "Free speech vs section 57." August 22. https://www.thedailystar.net/frontpage/free-speech-vs-section-57-130591. Accessed September 5, 2019.

The Daily Star. 2018a. "34 cases against Khaleda." February 8. https://www.thedailystar.net/backpage/34-cases-against-khaleda-zia-bnp-chairperson-bangladesh-1531510. Accessed November 2, 2019.

The Daily Star. 2018b. "Lower courts' freedom undermined by 3 rules." January 2. https://www.thedailystar.net/frontpage/lower-courts-freedom-undermined-3-rules-1513600. Accessed December 27, 2018.

The Daily Star. 2018c. "August 21 attack: 'State-backed crime' punished." October 11. https://www.thedailystar.net/august-21-carnage/21-august-grenade-attack-verdict-tarique-rahman-awarded-life-1645090. Accessed January 7, 2019.

The Daily Star. 2023. "Over 7,000 cases under DSA: Law minister." June 5. https://www.thedailystar.net/news/bangladesh/crime-justice/news/over-7000-cases-under-dsa-law-minister-3338511.

The New York Times. 2019. "Bangladesh's farcical vote." January 14. https://www.nytimes.com/2019/01/14/opinion/editorials/bangladesh-election-sheikh-hasina.html. Accessed January 21, 2019.

UN News. 2012. "UN official calls for Bangladesh's next elections to be 'peaceful, inclusive and credible'." December 10.

V-Dem. 2019. *Democracy for All? V-Dem Annual Democracy Report 2018.* Gothenburg: Department of Political Science, University of Gothenburg.

Waldner, David and Ellen Lust. 2018. "Unwelcome change: Coming to terms with democratic backsliding." *Annual Review of Political Science* 21: 93–113.

World Bank. n.d.. *GDP Growth (annual %) – Bangladesh.* https://data.worldbank.org/indicator/NY.GDP.MKTP.KD.ZG?end=2018&locations=BD&start=1996. Accessed May 16, 2024.

Zaman, Fahmida. 2018. "Agencies of social movements: Experiences of Bangladesh's Shahbagh movement and Hefazat-e-Islam." *Journal of Asian and African Studies* 53 (3): 339–349.

4 Removals of Elected and Appointed Public Officials in Bhutan

Democratic Recession or Consolidation?

Sonam Kinga

Introduction

In the contemporary narrative of democratic recession, success stories from countries like Bhutan do not capture much media headlines or constitute evidence for counterarguments in academic discourse. A country of approximately 39,000 square kilometers and a population of about 700,000 may not grab attention or make an argument, but its geopolitical location as well as its being a constitutional democratic monarchy between two of the largest republics – India, which is a multi-party democracy and China which is a one-party state – make for an interesting case study. No less interesting is its unusual path to historic transition to parliamentary democracy (see below), which happened in 2006, the very year when democratic recession is said to have begun (Diamond, 2015, 14; Magen, 2015, 378).

Yet in the dominant academic construct of receding, regressing, retreating, eroding and backsliding of democracy, the distinct path of Bhutan's successful democratization first and now its consolidation is more a story on the margins. Even in South Asia, the contemporary developments in Sri Lanka and Pakistan only support the arguments of larger and widespread democratic recession aggravated by instabilities in Nepal, dynastic electoral regimes in Sri Lanka, Bangladesh and also in India even at the level of its states (Sinha, 2022).

The reasons for democratic recession are aplenty. The Freedom House Report of 2021 cites as causes the anti-democratic leaders and ruling parties with corrupt governance, the rise or deepening of autocracy or authoritarian regimes and stalling of the reform process (Csaky, 2021, 3–4). Breakdown of democracies due to coups, rigged elections, degradation of democratic process, promotion of alternatives by authoritarian regimes, financial crisis in the United States and European Union and democratic fragility of democracies to fulfil people's expectations (Amichai, 2015, 379–381) are also identified as causes. For Larry Diamond, bad governance without the rule of law and transparency are principal reasons (Diamond, 2015, 148). Transparency International highlights corruption as a major cause for weakness of democracies and warns that it worsens in newly democratized countries (Drapalova, 2019, 5). In highlighting many reasons as to how corruption can undermine the consolidation of

DOI: 10.4324/9781003261469-4

democracy, it points out that top politicians have strong incentives to cling to power by any means, avoid prosecution and enrich themselves (Pring and Vrushi, 2019). They wrote, "when corruption seeps into the democratic system, corrupt leaders may seek to prevent democratic checks and balances so that they can continue to remain in power unpunished."

Freedom House's country report is not always the best source of assessing the health and quality of democracy. It rated Bhutan as Partly Free in 2018, 2019 and 2020 with scores of 55, 58 and 61, respectively, out of 100. There are very important parameters of its assessment that are not only flawed but factually wrong. However, its observations concerning democratic transition and consolidation are noteworthy, and I will highlight a few of them here in relation to the topic of corruption and rule of law.

With the onset of democracy, it observes that Bhutan has made significant strides toward consolidating democracy and has held multiple credible elections and undergone transfers of power to opposition parties. It also notes how the monarch and royal family have retreated significantly from exerting political influence. On the question of free and fair elections, it gave Bhutan a score of 4/4. For fairness of laws and their impartial implementation, the score was 3/4. For the question of realistic opportunity for opposition to increase its support or gain power through elections, the score was 4/4. The scores were 3/4 each for safeguards against official corruption and strengthening of transparency. It observed that "the rule of law and due process has improved substantially in civil and criminal matters. In recent years, Bhutan's courts have functioned with a relatively high degree of effectiveness" (Freedom House, 2020).

Since the context of democratic recession or regression is not helpful in understanding the developments in Bhutan, I will situate it within the context of democratic consolidation. According to Schedler (1997, 1), a democracy can be deemed as consolidated if the probability of its breakdown is very low and it will survive for a long time. In the words of Linz and Stepan (1996, 2), democracy becomes "the only game in town" when no one seeks to undermine and overthrow it and when everyone commits to the idea of political changes or conflict resolution being done within the bounds of democratic norms and Constitution.

They identify five areas for a democracy to be qualified as consolidated. One, the existence of a vibrant civil society to articulate shared values and advance common interest of the members. Two, the existence of a political society consisting of institutions, structures and processes such as political parties, parliament, electoral laws, etc. to enable people to exercise legitimate power. Three, the rule of law, which is to hold democratic governments and the state apparatus accountable and tied to the principle of constitutionalism. Four, the existence of bureaucracy, which enjoys a monopoly on violence for the purpose of protecting the rights of citizens and providing basic services. And five, the presence of an economic society, which serves as the interlocutor or mediator between state and society, meaning that a set of rules and institutions must regulate the market (Linz and Stepan, 1996, 3–5).

For this study, I will focus only on one aspect, i.e. adherence to the rule of law, to illustrate the extent of democratic consolidation in Bhutan since its introduction 15 years ago. The context that I will use is the removals and resignations of very senior and highly positioned public officials who were either elected or appointed. Ranging from members of the cabinet, opposition party, parliament, judiciary, local government and civil service to the armed forces, Bhutan has witnessed resignations, removals, detentions and imprisonment. However, they have so far been disseminated by the media and internalized by the society as separate incidents without an academic approach that not only connects the dots of these developments on the socio-political landscape but also uses theorizing of democratic consolidation to frame the discussions.

I will discuss the various circumstances that led to these events, which were significant developments in the process of Bhutan's democratic consolidation. My argument is that they do not indicate a culture of political vendetta or arbitrary usage of state power to remove opposition or silence dissent. Intriguing as they appear and reflective perhaps of a certain character of democratic politics, I will argue that they attest to the political society's admirable commitment to due democratic process, rule of law, principle of transparency and accountability and indeed the expectation for the highest of moral and ethical conducts from elected leaders. In exposing corrupt or unethical practices, the media have played its part and due process of law has been followed in prosecution and defense of the accused leaders. The rule of law, which is fundamental to democratic process, has been upheld. This, I will argue, has been one of the main reasons for the success of consolidating Bhutan's nascent democracy. Owing to the contemporary and recent nature of these developments, I rely extensively on media reports. But first, it will be helpful to understand the nature and trajectory of democratic transition. Since I have written about it elsewhere extensively (Sonam Kinga, 2019), here I will only provide a brief overview.

Overview of Democratic Transition

In December 2006, His Majesty King Jigme Singye Wangchuck, the Fourth King of Bhutan, abdicated after a reign of 34 years. His abdication at the age 51 years was voluntary. He was at the height of his success as a modern and progressive king. There was no social unrest, economic crisis, political agitation or regional or internal pressure that triggered the abdication and demanded democracy. On the contrary, the people accepted democracy reluctantly and only at his behest (Varma, 2015). They were deeply worried about the unsettling effect it would have on a close-knit society and peaceful country especially in the context of perceived experience of democracy in neighboring countries. These have to do with corruption, nepotism, character assassination, party conflicts, strikes and communal disharmony leading to unstable governments.

Since the Fourth King initiated the drafting of the Constitution in 2001 by a broad-based and inclusive committee, the people knew that democracy was set

Removals of Elected and Appointed Public Officials in Bhutan 79

to come someday but did not expect him to abdicate. However, he made public his intention to abdicate in December 2005 and that the democratic transition would be led by a new king. The Constitution-drafting process included nation-wide consultations with the people. Both the King and the Crown Prince led the consultative process in all the 20 districts, which was preceded by the distribution of hard copies of the draft Constitution to every household in the country.

Meanwhile, important institutions such as the Election Commission and Anti-corruption Commission were set up in 2006. Private media were also given licenses in 2006. Political parties were being formed one after another. Finally, the parliamentary elections began in December 2007, with elections to the apolitical National Council first (hereafter Council) followed in March 2008 by elections of the party-based National Assembly (hereafter Assembly). Then in 2011, the nationwide local government elections were held.

Thus far, Bhutan has seen four rounds of parliamentary elections and three rounds of local government elections. In each parliamentary election (2008, 2013, 2018 and 2024), a new party has been elected to form the government, which serves a five-year term. Far greater numbers of new candidates have been elected in both the National Council and in local governments in comparison to re-election of incumbents.

The peaceful transition to democracy initiated by a young, popular and successful King against the wishes of a democracy-suspicious populace was unprecedented and historic in many ways. The common questions asked are how has this been possible and why the King took such a decision. I will highlight four important reasons.

First, a very telling aspect of Bhutan's monarchy is that it is a modern institution that was founded in 1907. It was neither based on the idea of "divine rights" nor was it a political institution forced upon the people by the founding monarch. Rather, it was a political outcome of a consensual contract or legal deed, which was signed among the King, members of the monastic community, leading public officials and those representing different communities of Bhutan. These democratic credentials, where the monarch and his successors were given consent by the people to govern, help to understand an aspect of the ideological basis of what I call Bhutan's "Contractual Monarchy" as opposed to the Euro-centric categorization of "absolute monarchy" based on divine rights.

Second, the monarchy has been the most progressive institution in Bhutan and indeed the agency for reforms and modernization. Monarchy is generally understood to be an archaic institution, very traditional and resistant to change, steeped in rituals, ceremonies and public spectacles and against democratization and empowerment of people. On the contrary, the Bhutanese monarchy has spearheaded not only socio-economic modernization but gradually and steadily engaged people in modern political institutions and popular decision-making processes. This leads us to the third point.

The transition to democracy in 2006 was not a sudden political decision. It was in fact a culmination of decades of political reforms, devolution of power and empowering of grassroots communities. Hence, we cannot isolate the

80   *Removals of Elected and Appointed Public Officials in Bhutan*

transition in 2006 from the preceding decades of democratization. It began in 1953, when the National Assembly was established by the Third King with the majority of members being elected representing different communities. Initially a conciliar body, it was given full legislative powers and also the authority to register a periodic vote of no confidence in the King. This too was initiated by the Third King himself. The idea of separation of powers was gradually introduced with the establishment of a High Court in 1965 and the cabinet in 1968. Between 1976 and 1992, the Fourth King established local development committees, which were distinct institutions, to encourage participation of local communities in making decisions concerning development activities. Twenty committees were set up at the district level and 198 at the county level, which later increased to 205. In 1999, the Fourth King stepped aside to be only the head of state. Full executive powers were devolved to a cabinet, which was elected for the first time by the National Assembly and was accountable to it. It had a five-year tenure. Under this system, two cabinets were elected, in 1999 and 2003. Thus, the kings had prepared the Bhutanese people in democratic norms, institutions and political processes for many decades. This ensured that democracy, although suspicious, was nonetheless not a stranger.

Finally, the King reasoned that democracy was best introduced in a time of great peace. The absence of internal conflict, foreign intervention and socio-economic crises ensures popular and widespread ownership of democracy as something domestic. Bhutan may never have such an opportunity to introduce democracy. For a small, developing and land-locked country surrounded by two giant neighbors, he said that political stability is paramount and democracy is a means towards strengthening it. People must also take responsibility and become active agents in the process of development and nation-building rather than being passive beneficiaries of projects on the margins. The monarchy has steered the nation through a century of modernization while preserving its sovereignty and independence. But the nation is every citizen's responsibility and democracy entrusts that responsibility along with the power it provides.

Resignation and Removal of Government Ministers

With this brief overview of the context, process and rationale of democratic transition, let me zoom in to the primary subject of this study. Lyonpo Sherub Gyeltshen,[1] the Home Minister, submitted his resignation on May 6, 2021 to the Speaker of the National Assembly after being in office for exactly two and half years. He was the Vice President of Druk Nyamrup Tshogpa (DNT), the political party which won the third general election in October 2018 and went on to form the government after securing 30 of the 47 seats in the two-party National Assembly. While his exit was not unexpected owing to his conviction in a corruption case on August 27, 2019, barely ten months into office, it became a major political milestone when it happened. Since Bhutan's historic transition to parliamentary democracy in December 2007, this was the first time a serving minister had resigned!

Removals of Elected and Appointed Public Officials in Bhutan 81

There were ministers in the two previous governments who had stepped aside (Chencho Dema, 2019), but the resignation of Lyonpo Sherub was one notch up. He not only resigned as minister but also as a Member of Parliament (MP) and as DNT's Vice President. A by-election had to be conducted soon after (see below). He was a distinguished and decorated public servant. He even served as the Justice of the High Court for three years from 2006.

What had led to his resignation? It concerned the insurance claim for his vehicle supposedly involved in an "accident." He had already retired from civil service. His last position was the Secretary of the Dzongkha Development Commission, which he joined after leaving the High Court. The 2018 election also had not taken place yet. The case is not complicated. On a journey from the town of Wangdi Phodrang to Thimphu on July 21, 2016, he stated that his vehicle was hit (Karma Chuki Namgyel, 2019). So, he took his car the following day to a workshop. There may not have been an intention then to claim insurance. But the notification letter sent later to the insurance company did claim an accident. However, the required procedures such as informing the police and insurance company and getting an assessment of the damages, etc. were not done. The receipts from an automobile workshop to adjust claims against supposed expenditure were found to be blanks. Repairs were also done by a different entity and not by the workshop which issued the receipt. This led to the fraudulent claim of Nu. 226,546. For this offence, deemed a petty misdemeanor, the Thimphu District Court convicted and sentenced him to two months in prison (Yangchen C. Rinzin, 2021a). Other officials of the insurance company were also convicted and sentenced.

In Bhutan's judicial system and process, cases are adjudicated by judges. There are no jury trials. So, conviction and sentencing happen simultaneously. Lyonpo Sherub was convicted and also sentenced simultaneously based on Section 311 of the Penal Code of Bhutan, which reads:

> A defendant shall be guilty of the offence of fraudulent obtaining of insurance, if the defendant presents a false statement as part of an application for commercial or personal insurance or as part of claim for payment on a commercial or personal insurance policy.
>
> (Royal Government of Bhutan, 2004, 55)

The question is what happens to elected public officials who are convicted and sentenced. Article 23.4.c of the Constitution states: "A person shall be disqualified as a candidate or a member holding an elective office under this Constitution, if the person is ... convicted for any criminal offence and sentenced to imprisonment" (Constitution of the Kingdom of Bhutan, 2008, 47).

The important point to note is that the offence has to be criminal, not civil, and the duration of imprisonment does not matter. This particular case was deemed a criminal offence and the sentence was two months' imprisonment. Was Lyonpo Sherub disqualified as a member based on the constitutional provision? Who is the legal authority to serve notice of disqualification? The Prime

82 *Removals of Elected and Appointed Public Officials in Bhutan*

Minister and Speaker are the legal authorities. But he was not disqualified or suspended. There are two reasons for not doing this. One, the appeal process is automatic in Bhutan's judicial process. A defendant can appeal to the next higher appellate court within ten days of conviction and sentencing. So, Lyonpon Sherub appealed immediately to the High Court citing various reasons. Two, there were precedents of ministers who were also not disqualified although they too were convicted and sentenced.

Even if he was disqualified and removed from office upon sentencing, he had to be reinstated if the sentence were reversed upon appeal. There is thus a legal tension between provision and practice. A former Chief Justice said that rather than disqualify or terminate the minister immediately, he should have been suspended and removed from Cabinet until the appeal process had been exhausted, and terminated only if the final court of appeal upheld the decision of the lower court. When the trial court convicts and sentences anyone, the person loses the constitutional guarantee or presumption of being innocent until proven guilty provided as a Fundamental Right in Article 7.16 (Personal communication, March 31, 2022). What legal provision permits suspension? Section 167 of the Anti-corruption Act empowers suspension of public servants, which include elected officials. Suspension can be effected either during the course of investigation or from the moment the person is charged until the outcome of the appeal process. For example, the Anti-corruption Commission (ACC) directed the insurance company to suspend its Chief Executive Officer and Executive Director on July 7, 2017 to investigate suspected fraud in a different case (Rinzin Wangchuk, 2017). The fact that the minister was not suspended despite the conviction and sentencing contrasts with suspension of local government officials, as I shall discuss subsequently.

The High Court upheld the lower court's judgment on October 9, 2020 (Tshering Palden, 2020). But the minister and others involved appealed to the larger bench of the High Court, which is a permissible judicial process. This bench also upheld on March 18, 2021 the earlier decisions (Yangchen C. Rinzin, 2021a). It was soon after, in April, that he tendered his resignation. The following Kuensel story reports his decision:

> Lyonpo Sherub Gyeltshen said that he decided to resign from the post himself without any external pressure because he wanted to show that in a democracy one should respect law and order and have faith in the law.
>
> "As a human being, I thought maybe the case was interpreted wrongly during the first verdict since it was based on only one judge but now about eight judges have studied the case and convicted," he said. "Then I should also think that maybe, I may be wrong and I was involved in enacting laws, it's not fair if I don't respect the same laws."
>
> (Yangchen C. Rinzin, 2021b)

While he had tendered his resignation, he had appealed to the Supreme Court on March 29, 2021 (Kinley Dem and Tshering Zam, 2022). And soon after, the

Removals of Elected and Appointed Public Officials in Bhutan   83

Supreme Court also upheld the decisions of the lower courts. Besides the constitutional provision cited above, the National Assembly Act of 2008 states "A member of the National Assembly shall be disqualified if the member: is convicted for any criminal offence and sentenced to imprisonment." Even if the minister stayed on, he would have been removed after the Supreme Court passed its judgment. Hence, he must have anticipated the Supreme Court's ruling and resigned before that came.

Let us now look at an earlier case of corruption involving two leaders of the first democratically elected government. On November 13, 2012, the ACC registered a case against the Speaker, Tshogpon Jigme Tshulthrim, and Home Minister, Lyonpo Minjur Dorji, in the Mongar District Court. This was four years into their term after their party, Druk Phuensum Tshogpa (DPT) won the first general elections in 2008. Both of them had served as the dzongda or district administrator of Mongar much earlier before they even resigned from civil service to contest the elections. The charges were criminal in nature and involved forgery, deceptive practices and official misconduct in the allotment of land at Gyalpozhing town. Among other beneficiaries, some senior ministers of the DPT government had also received land (*The Bhutanese*, 2012). In March 2013, the verdict came. Both of them were found guilty along with 14 other members of the Land Allotment Committee. Tshogpon Jigme was sentenced to two and half years of imprisonment while Lyonpo Minjur was sentenced to a year's imprisonment (*The Bhutanese*, 2013). They had just over four months of the remainder of their term in office. The ACC suspended the Speaker and Home Minister but the Office of Attorney General (OAG) filed a petition to the High Court to challenge the suspension. The High Court stayed the suspension order as it was deemed to be not within the purview and scope of the ACC Act of 2011, which came into effect on July 5, 2011. The court reasoned that the two leaders were charged under different laws, but the ACC viewed otherwise and appealed to the Supreme Court. "The general principle of retroactive or retrospective application of laws, and the canons of legislative construction presume that legislation is not intended to apply retroactively unless a particular provision or the language expressly makes it retroactive" (Minjur Dorji, 2012).

The ACC argued that its power to suspend public officials was included in the procedural part of the Act:

> In legal principle, procedural provisions of laws are applicable retrospectively unless it is otherwise stated. Substantive laws with penalty provisions are forward looking and are not applied retroactively. The accused were charged under the Thrimzhung Chenmo and the Penal Code of Bhutan 2004 and not under ACA 2011.
>
> (Anti-corruption Commission, 2012, 95–96)

Meanwhile, the convicts appealed to the High Court, which upheld, on May 16, 2013, the Mongar court's judgment. They further appealed to the Supreme Court which affirmed in July the earlier judgments. The appeal process and

84 *Removals of Elected and Appointed Public Officials in Bhutan*

time period enabled the convicted persons to stay in office until the completion of their tenure. They were neither suspended nor terminated despite the conviction and sentencing. The National Assembly dissolved on August 1, 2013 after completing its full tenure of five years. Because they were convicted, the two of them could not contest the parliamentary elections of 2013. Section 179 of the Election Act of Bhutan states that a person shall be disqualified as a candidate or a member holding an elective office under the Constitution, if he or she has been convicted for any criminal offence and sentenced to imprisonment.

Compare this with a development in India, the largest democracy. On July 10, 2013, India's Supreme Court removed a legal provision which did not disqualify a convicted lawmaker who had appealed to higher courts. In other words, a convicted lawmaker could now be disqualified (*IndiaTV*, 2013).

> The apex court in its judgment on July 10 had held that a person, who is in jail or in police custody, cannot contest election to legislative bodies, bringing to an end an era of under trial politicians fighting polls from behind bars.
>
> (*NDTV*, 2013)

The government submitted a plea to the Supreme Court to review it. The plea was dismissed. But the Indian parliament passed a law in September allowing those in prison to contest elections in a move that negated the court's order. It was passed after 15 minutes' discussion in the lower house. The upper house passed it on August 27, 2013 (*NDTV*, 2013).

In the United States, the Constitution does not prevent congressmen from holding office even after conviction unless it is a case of treason. In the Senate, a simple majority vote can be used to censure or criticize members, but to remove someone a two-thirds majority is needed. But there is no disqualification upon conviction (Bomboy, 2017). Even political candidates who have been imprisoned are not disqualified. Some candidates have used their past incarceration as a platform to campaign for criminal justice reform (Thompson, 2020). In Australia, different provinces have different laws where a ban on contesting elections is determined based on the nature of the crime or duration of sentences served after conviction. Conviction for treason is a life-long ban, but most bans are for the period when the person is serving sentences. Thereafter, anyone can generally re-contest (Holland, 2003).

Different countries seem to have different legal provisions concerning disqualification of political candidates or members of elective office when they are either charged or convicted for criminal offences. Bhutanese society has expressed no reservations against present legal provisions either during the period of parliamentary deliberations on the laws or in the aftermath of convictions and sentencing. Rather, they seem to be accepted as an important means of ethical filtering for candidates seeking leadership positions.

In January 2015, Lyonpo Rinzin Dorji of the People's Democratic Party (PDP), which won the second general elections in 2013, stepped aside from his responsibilities as the Foreign Minister after corruption charges were brought against him. It concerned alleged malpractices in the renovation of a temple called Lhakhang Karpo in the western district of Haa. The minister was serving then as the governor.

> He was accused of favouring LD Sawmill by awarding timber sawing works worth Nu 1.403M (million) without consulting the tender committee and paying the sawmill Nu 37.70 per cubic foot (cft). He was also charged for using the dzongkhag's DCM truck to transport his private timber from Haa to Thimphu.
>
> (Rinzin Wangchuk, 2015a)

OAG and ACC conducted the investigations. While the investigations were going on, he was not suspended. After these two agencies notified the government about the completion of investigations, the minister was given "authorized absence" until the case was resolved (Office of the Prime Minister and Cabinet, 2015).

After five months of trial, the minister was acquitted and both charges were dismissed. But the prosecutors appealed to the High Court, which reversed the decision of Haa court and sentenced him to a year in prison (Rinzin Wangchuk, 2015b). Then the defendants appealed to the Supreme Court, which overturned the High Court's ruling and acquitted the minister on July 28, 2016 (Rinzin Wangchuk, 2016). Even as the court proceedings and appeals were taking place, a government press release on July 20, 2015 stated that it had decided to appoint a new Foreign Minister. The incumbent Home Minister was appointed as the Foreign Minister and an MP, Dawa Gyetshen, was elevated as Home Minister (*The Bhutanese*, 2015). The government reasoned that the ministry could not be left vacant as the appeal process could go on for a long time (Tshering Palden, 2015). But it did not provide Lyonpo Rinzin any ministerial portfolio after he was acquitted as there was no ministerial position vacant then. He continued to serve as MP and completed his term.

Likewise, Labour Minister Lyonpo Ngeema Sangay Tshempo stepped aside in March 2015 when allegations of corruption were brought against him. But he resumed office in June after investigations were over. A year later, in March 2016, Education Minister Mingbo Dukpa stepped aside citing personal reasons. His resignation was not related to any corruption charges but more a concern over his health. He continued as MP.

Resignations and Removals of MPs

MPs have resigned, and one of the first to do so was Dasho Karma Ura. He was one of the five eminent persons appointed by His Majesty the King to the Council, one of the two chambers of parliament. This chamber has 25 members. The other 20 are directly elected by people of the 20 districts and cannot belong to any political party. After his appointment in 2008, he contested for the position of Chairperson. Winning the second maximum number of votes, he

86   *Removals of Elected and Appointed Public Officials in Bhutan*

served as the Deputy Chairperson but resigned in under a year due to health reasons. This was the only instance of an MP resigning from the Council. All other resignations came in the Assembly, and that too from DPT.

The first one was much earlier, in August 2013, when DPT's first President and Prime Minister resigned immediately after winning his constituency elections. He did not even take up his seat and resigned before the parliament convened (Bhutan Broadcasting Service, 2013a). His resignation letter was addressed to the Secretary General of the Assembly since the Speaker had not been elected yet. The only reason he gave in public about his resignation was to have a new president if the party was to remain strong rather than him lead the party for so long (Staff, 2013). In the by-election soon after, the DPT did retain its seat. This was the first parliamentary by-election and the only one in which the opposition retained its seat (Bhutan Broadcasting Service, 2013b).

The second MP to resign was the North Thimphu representative who had then served as a member of the opposition party for three years. MP Kinga Tshering of North Thimphu was one of the three opposition MPs elected in July 2013 as DPT's Vice President.[2] He resigned in 2016 to pursue studies at Harvard University (Tenzin Lamsang, 2016). He had applied for long-term leave to attend a program and had received a scholarship. He was initially given a week's leave to discuss possibilities of postponing the program and scholarship. When that did not come through, he applied for extension of the leave, which could not be granted because there are no legal provisions or rules that allow sitting MPs to go for long-term studies. So he resigned on August 22, 2016 (Tempa Wangdi, 2016). In the ensuing by-election, the North Thimphu constituency was won by a candidate of the ruling party PDP.

The next high-profile resignation was that of the opposition leader in June 2020, who was also the party's President (Subba, 2020). He had worked much earlier as a watershed specialist at the International Centre for Integrated Mountain Development (ICIMOD) based in Kathmandu, Nepal. When ICIMOD announced the position of the Director General, he must have applied for the post. On July 16, it announced that he was selected and his position would start from mid-October 2020. On its Facebook page, it posted: "We are excited to announce that our Board of Governors has selected a new Director General Dr Pema Gyamtsho who will take up the position at the retirement of our current Director General Dr David Molden in mid-October" (Business Bhutan, 2020).

He submitted his resignation to the Speaker of the Assembly on July 22 both as an MP and the opposition leader. DPT had three Vice Presidents; two were MPs and another one a party member. Dorji Wangdi, the MP for Panbang constituency, was elected on September 7 as the new opposition leader (Tshering Dendup, 2020). It may be pointed out that the other DPT Vice President had formed her own party earlier but dissolved it later and joined DPT. She did not win her seat from North Thimphu in 2018 and hence was not an MP. She too resigned from DPT a year later (Sonam Penjore, 2021). Soon after, in August 2021, its Secretary General, Phurba, also resigned, and a new one, Sonam Tashi, was appointed (Druk Phuensum Tshogpa, 2021). In a tragic incident, a well-known three-time DPT MP Choida Jamtsho passed away on April 18, 2021 owing to complications from food poisoning (Phurpa Lhamo, 2021). His demise was the first instance of death of a serving MP. In the subsequent by-election, DNT's Karma Dorji not only won but went on to become the immediate Minister for Labour and Human Resources.

The latest MP to resign was the representative of Khamdang-Ramjar constituency of Trashi Yangtse district. He was first detained on March 1, 2021 along with his brother, who was the mangmi or deputy gup of Khamdang Gewog or county of that district. The mangmi's three other sons were also detained. Except for the MP, the four others have been detained earlier as well but granted bail. They were detained with the MP again.

They were charged for illegal construction of a road in a sensitive border area near Arunachal Pradesh, India. The background story, captured in different news media, is summarized here (see Thinley Namgay, 2021). The mangmi's family started vegetable cultivation on a family-owned 15-acre piece of land at a place called Khosung, which was close to the international border. They applied for the district administration authority's approval to construct a road to the farm, which was denied owing to sensitivity of the area. They requested that they be allowed to use heavy machinery to help develop the farm, but that could not be approved as transporting it would result in land excavation, as the pathway is hilly and not a flat area. The MP also called the district administrator to help but it was denied owing to national security considerations. Despite this, the group marched the machine, which resulted in excavation of a road that was 233 meters long and 4.8 meters wide. Upon investigation, the district authority imposed a fine which the MP asked to have waived off. The decision to impose the fine was revoked as the case had a national security dimension. Then the police were asked to conduct an investigation. The MP asked them to treat it as a civil case, which obviously was not the case. So, he was detained along with the mangmi and his nephews. The district court denied him bail. "[The] Office of the Attorney General charged them for the commission of malicious mischief, breach of public order and tranquility, official misconduct, hindering prosecution and for violating Land Act, Environment Act and the Road Act" (*Kuensel*, 2021).

Upon trial, the MP was convicted and sentenced to five years in prison by the district court on August 14. The mangmi was sentenced to four years and three months while the others received three years and nine months (Thinley Namgay, 2021). All of them appealed to the High Court and then to the Supreme Court. Both upheld the judgment of the district court. Since the sentencing was consecutively for offences categorized "Misdemeanour" and "Petty Misdemenour," the defendants had the option to pay in lieu of imprisonment (Pema Seldon Tshering, 2021a). MP Kuenga resigned on November 15 after serving for three years. "The relieving order has been handed over to Kuenga Loday yesterday over a simple ceremony in the presence of the Cabinet Ministers, Leader of the Opposition, Members of the National Assembly, officials of the National Assembly Secretariat" (Staff Reporter, 2021a).

88 *Removals of Elected and Appointed Public Officials in Bhutan*

While the exit has been processed as a "resignation" and gracefully done through "a simple ceremony," the MP would have been removed by an order of the Speaker as is required by various legal provisions. His resignation is the first instance thus far where resignation took place only after the completion or exhaustion of the appeal process. In the by-election that followed on February 2, 2022, the ruling party's candidate Karma Gyeltshen won with 3,152 votes compared to DPT's Jigme Tashi, who secured 2,109 votes (Sonam Tshering, 2022).

Removal of Local Government Leaders

Mangmi Sangye Tempa of Khamdang Gewog was one of the many elected local government officials removed from office. In his case, there was no by-election as there was less than six months to go for his tenure to complete. This is as per the provision of the Local Government Act. He was elected in September 2016. It needs to be pointed out that the local governments in Bhutan are apolitical, like the Council. Members are all independents and cannot belong to political parties.

While the MP was not suspended despite criminal charges leveled against him in court, the mangmi was suspended. The suspension order stated that the OAG had informed the Department of Local Government of charges being registered against the mangmi in the Trashi Yangtse district court. Based on that, the governor of the district issued the suspension order on March 12, 2021. "Mangmi Sangye Tenpa is being suspended from his public position from today onwards till the completion of the court proceedings" (Thuje Tshering, 2021, translation mine).

On July 3, 2019, the gup of Bumdeling Gewog, also in the district of Trashi Yangtse, was detained for allegedly raping a 16-year-old girl, who was the daughter of a tshogpa or village representative, who served with the same gup in the gewog's local government. The girl's parents were away in the mountains to collect cordyceps, a lucrative source of cash income. Knowing of their absence, the gup visited the girl to present a new mobile phone he bought for her. In the process he raped her. The grandmother, with whom the victim shared the incident, informed the parents, who in turn reported to the police (Staff Reporter, 2019a). Later, he was sentenced to a 12 years in prison. The Deputy Thrizin of Trashi Yangtse Dzongkhag Tshogdu issued the termination letter on October 15, 2019 citing the order of the Department of Local Government as well as the verdict of the district court (Goenpo, 2019).

Soon after, a by-election was held to fill the vacancy created by his imprisonment. Gup Yeshi Dorji was elected in September 2019. Earlier, he worked as the clerk to the gup who was imprisoned. But this new gup was also sentenced to three years for forgery after about eight months in office. He was arrested in December 2019, three months after his election. He had obtained two different loans of Nu. 500,000 and Nu. 700,000 from a rural development bank by mortgaging the land of a farmer through forging of documents. The farmer had no idea of the forgery (Kelzang Wangchuk, 2019).

Removals of Elected and Appointed Public Officials in Bhutan 89

Like Mangmi Sangye, Gup Yeshi was also first suspended from his office on April 6, 2020. His suspension was effective from April 1 and was in force until the completion of legal processes. He was removed from office on May 26, 2020 (Thuje Tshering, 2020).

Although the by-election was scheduled to be conducted within three months of the gup's office falling vacant, it could not be done due to the onset of the COVID-19 pandemic. When it was held in November 2020, there was only a single candidate. Two other candidates were disqualified. One had criminal records and the other was a member of a political party (Neten Dorji, 2020). Both are grounds for disqualification to be candidates for local government. The lone candidate, Phub Thinley, won the by-election to serve for only about a year as the next local government elections were due the following year. When his tenure ended in November 2021 and elections were held, a different candidate, Mani Dorji, won (Chimmi Dema, 2021). Hence, Bumdeling Gewog had four gups in a little over five years. There were three gup elections within the single tenure of its local government, and a gup, serving for about a year.

In a protracted legal process, the county of Goshing Gewog in the central district of Zhemgang was without a gup for almost three years, which affected local governance and service to the people (Subba, 2021). The ACC investigated the case in 2016 after receiving complaints that the gup had embezzled funds meant for the construction of a road. Almost three years into his tenure, he was charged with embezzlement of public funds as well as solicitation, fraudulent claim and official misconduct. The sub-district (dungkhag) court of Panbang sentenced him to eight years in prison in 2019 and he was asked to pay back almost Nu. 3 million.

> The gup was found guilty of embezzling public funds from 2011 to 2015 by inflating the bills of Bhutan Oil Corporation (BOC) by colluding employees of the fuel depot in Gelephu for the purchase of petrol, oil and lubricants for excavators.
>
> (Staff Reporter, 2019b)

The gup appealed the decision and it was referred to the High Court instead of the district court because the newly appointed judge of the district court was his previous prosecutor. The judge declared a conflict of interest to try a person he had prosecuted when he worked as a prosecutor at the Office of Attorney General (Pema Seldon Tshering, 2021b). The High Court upheld the lower court's verdict.

There are three important points to be noted in this case. One, the gup was also the Chairperson or the Thrizin of the district local government known as Dzongkhag Tshogdu. His position as both the gup and Thrizin magnified the profile of the case. Two, the offence was committed before he was elected. And third, he was suspended in July 2018 (Subba, 2021). This was following the charges formally levelled against him. The ACC had forwarded the case to OAG in 2017 for prosecution after the completion of investigations (Pema

90   Removals of Elected and Appointed Public Officials in Bhutan

Samdrup, 2019a). The suspension of the gup after leveling formal charges contrasts with continuity in offices of the ministers and MP Kuenga. Until the High Court's ruling, the gup retained his position despite the suspension and received 50% of his salary. But it meant that Goshing Gewog had no gup and Zhemgang Dzongkhag Tshogdu had no Chairperson for almost three years (Pema Samdrup, 2019b).

An interesting case of removal of elected official concerned the Mangmi of Wangphu Gewog in Samdrup Jongkhar district. He owned a business license. A candidate to an elective office cannot hold an office or position of profit according to the electoral laws. If elected, his or her business can be construed as a conflict of interest with his or her position of authority and access to or control of public funds. Strangely, the Election Commission of Bhutan (ECB) seems to have known of his possession of the license but still permitted him to contest the local government elections in 2011. He was required to submit a letter of undertaking to the Returning Officer to transfer the license to his brother in the event he was elected. This was not just an oversight of the officer but a breach of the legal provision, which the Mangmi's contestant could have challenged. He did win the election but did not transfer the license ownership despite the undertaking.

The ECB repeated its breach of the laws by once again allowing him to re-contest the 2016 elections by making him sign yet another undertaking to transfer the license within 30 days. He won the re-election but did not transfer license ownership. Neither did the ECB follow up. Only when his license was used to bid for a contract work in 2019 did the tender committee realize that it was still with him. They reported to the election office and the case was referred to the High Court, which terminated him from his job although he had by then served almost two terms. The High Court also ordered the ECB to follow due diligence in conducting their duty (Kelzang Wangchuk, 2021).

A similar case cropped up in the Thrompon (mayor) election in the municipality of Phuntsholing. Only four major towns in Bhutan have municipal governments, the other three being the towns of Samdrup Jongkhar, Gelephu and Thimphu, the capital city. All other smaller towns elect a representative who serves as a member of the district local government or the Dzongkhag Tshogdu.

Thrompon Tsheten Dorji had completed one five-year term as Phuntsholing's mayor by 2015. He filed his candidature for re-election and was accepted by the ECB. There was only one other candidate, Uttar Rai. They were in the last days of their campaign with only two days left before the poll day. At that point, the ECB disqualified his candidature based on the fact that he owned a business license. He had the license when he contested in 2011 and was in possession of it throughout his first term. While he claimed that he gifted it to an employee, the ownership was not transferred. The last-minute transfer after ECB's decision did not help him (Subba, 2016). His misfortune did not end there. The ACC investigated the case and forwarded it to the OAG for prosecution, which forwarded the case to the Chhukha district court. He was accused of submitting false affidavits to the electoral authorities during the 2011 and 2015 elections (Bhutan Broadcasting Service, 2017).

The ECB's connivance and lack of due diligence was also expressed in another instance that saw a parliamentary debate. It made an announcement in 2014 stating that those who intended to take part in the local government elections in 2016 should transfer their census registry by December 31, 2014 to the constituency from which they wish to contest. Both the Constitution and electoral laws require a voter or a candidate to have at least one year of census registry in his or her constituency. The transfer of the census registry would not be necessary if someone was voting or contesting in the constituency where he or she is already registered. A serving gup Tshering Dorji of Drametse Gewog in Mongar transferred his registry to a neighboring gewog because his wife and children lived there (Tashi Phuntsho, 2015).

The moment he transferred his census registry to Ngatshang Gewog, he was no longer registered in Drametse Gewog. So, he had no legal basis to continue as its gup. But the ECB reportedly advised him to continue serving until the end of his tenure. This breached the provisions of both the Constitution and electoral laws. The Council took up the matter for deliberation. It called upon the government to take urgent and appropriate actions and conduct the by-elections immediately (Bhutan Broadcasting Service, 2015b). Based on this resolution, the Department of Local Government asked the gup to vacate his office by November 25, 2015. This was exactly one year after he had transferred his census registry (Tashi Phuntsho, 2015). This meant that he was allowed to continue in office for a year in Drametse despite being registered in Ngatshang. Due to this ill-advised connivance of the ECB, he also lost about seven months of office since his term was due for expiry in 2016. But because there were seven months of the tenure left, a by-election had to be conducted. Even then, three candidates filed their nominations. The winner, Rinzin, who secured 309 votes out of 640, served for about six months (*Kuensel*, 2015b).

The latest crime involving an elected local leader was the arrest, trial and conviction of Gup Namgyel Wangdi of Phongme Gewog in Trashigang district. He had an affair with a 14-year-old girl and impregnated her. He initially identified another person as the father and asked him to marry her. They started living together but the girl later confessed that the gup was the father. He did take steps to ensure the wellbeing of the victim and child's welfare. He also made financial compensation of Nu. 300,000 to the victim. But an affair with a minor including a sexual relationship is legally deemed rape even if the affair is consensual. On May 9, 2024, the court sentenced him to 11 years in prison and he was ordered to pay compensation of Nu. 225,000 (*Kuensel*, 2024).

Removal of Judges

One of the developments in Bhutan that made many headlines beyond Bhutan was the arrest and detention on February 16, 2021 of Justice Kuenley Tshering and Judge Yeshey Dorji. The former was the senior-most justice of the Supreme Court, and the latter the judge of the district court of Pema Gatshel. This followed the arrest earlier of a senior member of the armed forces,

92 *Removals of Elected and Appointed Public Officials in Bhutan*

Brigadier Thinley Tobgye, who served as commandant of the Royal Body Guards (RBG). This was in the context of an alleged conspiracy for Justice Kuenley to become the Chief Justice of the Supreme Court, Judge Yeshey to become either the Attorney General or Registrar General of the Supreme Court and Brigadier Thinley to become the Chief of the Army. The conspiracy was exposed following the arrest of a woman, Khandu Wangmo (Staff Reporter, 2021b).

The following story of the conspiracy is summarized from various news stories but primarily from an early investigative report by *The Bhutanese* (Tenzin Lamsang, 2021). All four had become friends over time. Khandu bore a personal grudge against the Chief of the Army, who had refused help for some personal issues. To defame and hurt him and his position, she first got Brigadier Thinley to obtain documents concerning procurement of military vehicles, which was intended to fabricate instances of corruption by the Army Chief. Besides their friendship and her personal charm, she succeeded in convincing the Brigadier about her concocted closeness with much higher authority through various deceptions. Impressing upon him first and then to others later about the support of higher authority in what she was doing, she drove the idea in him about blessings of higher authority to be the next Army Chief. She also induced him to loan her Nu. 6 million from the RBG fund, suggesting approval from higher authority and that the money would be refunded. He even gave her a military uniform with the insignia of a Brigadier's rank, his firearm and an official vehicle for her use.

In order to implicate the Army Chief, she had the Brigadier involve their common friend, Justice Kuenley, to formulate accusations of corruption and send it to the ACC. The impression given was that this would enhance his position of being the next Chief Justice. The allegation was that the local representative of the dealer to whom an order for supplies of vehicles was given was the Army Chief's nephew. The ACC had reviewed the complaint but found no basis to pursue it and hence closed the matter. Drangpon Yeshey was aware of the developments as he had married Khandu by then but did not report the conspiracy to anyone.

When Brigadier Thinley asked Khandu to pay back the money, their relationship soured. She persuaded her husband Judge Yeshey to take a loan for this purpose, saying that this would be reimbursed later as instructed by a higher authority. He applied for and received the loan by faking documents, but he soon realized he would not get back his money to pay the loan. This was part of the reason they divorced, and he subsequently filed a case against her. He won the case and got back his money. He then lodged a complaint with the police about Khandu's conspiracy and invoking names of higher authorities to legitimize her doings. Meanwhile, she resorted to writing and discreetly circulating highly seditious materials and attributing this to Judge Yeshey, his family members and an association of people from his village, all of whom had nothing to do with it. She misinformed the law enforcement agencies by accusing him of sedition.

Removals of Elected and Appointed Public Officials in Bhutan

Much earlier, Justice Kuenley had been a member of a panel to interview and select Khandu for a Chevening scholarship in the United Kingdom. Based on a text message supposedly from higher authority, he gave higher scores to Khandu, who was an applicant. While in the UK, she borrowed US $12,000 from a private person, Ms. Soth Toep. She returned to Bhutan without paying it back. A legal suit and prosecution against her in Bhutan was allegedly prevented by Justice Kuenley (Damchoe Pem, 2021).

The OAG soon charged them for various offences in the Thimphu district court. On July 23, 2021, they were convicted and sentenced to imprisonment. Khandu was given ten years and six months for various offences, and Brigadier Thinley 12 years and six months. Justice Kuenley was given five years for abetting of mutiny while Judge Yeshe also received five years for abetting of mutiny and larceny by deception (Tshering Zam, 2021). Except for Brigadier Thinley, the other three appealed to the High Court, which upheld the district court's judgment. They further appealed to the Supreme Court, which also upheld the lower court's judgment. Since Khandu was charged separately for sedition, she received an additional 21 years of imprisonment, taking the total sentence to 30 years. With the Supreme Court's ruling, the case came to a close on April 2, 2022 (Kinley Dem, 2022).

Even as they were in detention and trials were proceeding, Justice Kuenley was suspended by the Supreme Court based on constitutional provision and recommendation of the National Judicial Commission. Likewise, Judge Yeshey was suspended by the Judiciary Services Council (Tshering Palden and Tashi Dema, 2021). The position of Justice of the Supreme Court is a Constitutional Office, and holders of such office can only be removed through impeachment by parliament and then tried by the courts. But there is no impeachment law enacted yet.

The Council originated the Impeachment Bill in the summer session in 2019 and sent it to the National Assembly, which introduced it on January 16, 2020, but strangely it decided not to discuss it, citing vague objections. There is no legal option for either house not to discuss a bill which is passed by the other house. The Assembly's position that it will not discuss the bill passed by the Council undermined the very purpose of having a bi-cameral legislature. It was not in accordance with democratic principles and created dangerous precedence whereby the Council could simply refuse to discuss bills passed by the Assembly on any pretext. Based on a constitutional provision, the Council could have deemed the bill to have been passed at the end of the parliamentary session. While this would be legally correct, an important bill passed without even being discussed by one of the houses would not have enjoyed public confidence or support.

The Council nonetheless re-deliberated upon the bill. This was a new development in the legislative process since re-deliberation of bills can happen only if there are amendments or objections on contents arising from discussions of bills in the Assembly. The so-called "objections" on the bill that the Assembly sent to the Council were "reasons" for not discussing the Bills and not "objections or amendments" arising from the discussion of bills. So, there were no ground for re-deliberation. But to create spaces for dialogue and uphold democratic practices, the Council re-sent the bill to the Assembly, which asked the Council to withdraw it based on Legislative Rules of Procedure. It agreed to the withdrawal so that there could be an opportunity for re-introducing the bill. Otherwise, the bill would have been voted upon and without the Assembly's support, it would have been a "dead bill." The Council's attempt to have an Impeachment Act thus came to an end on March 4, 2020 (Samten Dolkar, 2020). Exactly a year later, Justice Kuenley was suspended, and trials proceeded without him being impeached. The trial could not be delayed merely because the Impeachment Act had not been enacted in the context of the gravity of the offences. Prosecutors from OAG argued that the provisions of the Constitution and relevant laws were reviewed and grounds for prosecution in the court were established even without introducing articles of impeachment in the parliament (Tshering Palden and Tashi Dema, 2021).

As the dust began to settle within the judiciary after the stormy affair of the removal of Justice Kuenley and Judge Yeshey, another storm soon engulfed it. On September 19, 2023, the Supreme Court removed two justices of the High Court: Justice Pema Rinzin and Justice Tshering Dorji. The government also removed Attorney General Lungten Dubgyur on September 9. All three of them were involved in a case which the Supreme Court deemed a "miscarriage of justice" and violation of the judicial code of conduct and the oath to uphold the Constitution.

In 2019, the son of the editor of the Dzongkha version of the national newspaper Kuensel was sentenced to five years in prison after a trial and conviction for trafficking in drugs. Another person involved in the crime was also sentenced. They appealed to the High Court. While the case was still sub judice, the editor, Attorney General and Justice Pema took an overnight trek to a monastery called Phajoding located high above Thimphu valley. Soon after their return, the High Court overturned the district court's sentence and converted the crime to a misdemeanor instead of a felony whereby the two defendants would be able to pay cash in lieu of imprisonment. But a complaint against this new sentencing was filed alleging collusion among the above persons. A special committee was constituted to determine the legitimacy of the allegation. They submitted a report to the Supreme Court, which directed the High Court to review the case. The Special Bench thus constituted indeed found that the two justices had caused a "grave miscarriage of justice" (Staff, 2023). How did this happen?

The two imprisoned persons were Thinlay Norbu and Tandin Penjor. In the case of Tandin Penjor, the two justices conducted a trial for two other persons: Kinga Gyeltshen and Kinlay Lhendrup. Earlier, they were alleged to have been involved in the same drug trafficking crime but the charges were dropped at pre-trial stage and even the prosecutors did not pursue the matter. Likewise, the justices also conducted a trial of another person called Jigme Samdrup who wasn't charged earlier. This was done to show that the 44 capsules of the drug called SP^+ were in the possession of four of them and not in the possession of Tandin Penjor alone. In other words, it would then be possible to argue that each of them possessed about 11 capsules each. The Narcotic Drugs Act does not deem it a felony if a defendant is in possession of fewer than 20 capsules. The intention was thus to overturn the sentence of felony by the district court for possession of 44 capsules by Tandin Penjor and reduce it to a misdemeanor so that he could walk out of prison by paying a fine instead of serving a prison sentence (Staff Reporter, 2023).

We need to explain why the Attorney General was removed. Normally, the Office of the Attorney General (OAG) appeals when a higher court reverses the judgment of the lower court for cases which it has prosecuted. Tandin Penjor was prosecuted by the OAG during the tenure of an earlier, different Attorney General. Attorney General Lungten Dubgyur was found to have directed his lawyers against appealing in this particular case. Both during the re-trial by the Special Bench and after its verdict to uphold the district court's judgment, Attorney General Lungten had tried to exert influence by sending text messages to a lawyer as well as a justice. Following a letter from the Chief Justice of the Supreme Court to the Prime Minister to take appropriate actions, the Attorney General was removed from office. Meanwhile, the editor had also resigned (Staff, 2023).

Removal of Government Secretaries

On December 12, 2014, a government press release announced that the Cabinet Secretary Penden Wangchuk, Foreign Secretary Yeshey Dorji and Economic Affairs Secretary Sonam Tshering were being surrendered to the Royal Civil Service Commission (RCSC) and that the institution of the Committee of Secretaries (CoS) was being discontinued with immediate effect. This was perceived as extreme action against the Secretaries and generated shockwaves and public discourse. The allegations against them were very serious and the government also called for an investigation.

ENERTIA, an Indian publication, had made allegations against Secretary Sonam. *ENERTIA* had organized a hydro power conclave in Bhutan on August 27, 2014. The Secretary informed it that the Economic Affairs Minister would not be able to attend. It may have felt snubbed. Retaliating, it published articles making corruption allegations by picking up information from a blog written by K.B. Wakhley, who worked with Secretary Sonam and was discharged dishonorably from civil service (Tenzin Lamsang, 2014).

It alleged that Bhutan Ventures Trading (BVT) had agreed to receive a commission of 1.5–1.8% for supplying electro-mechanical equipment from Bharat Heavy Electrical Limited (BHEL) to two hydropower projects in Bhutan. BVT was appointed by BHEL, which is not authorized to appoint agents (Bhutan Broadcasting Service, 2014a). The projects are overseen by the Ministry of Economic Affairs. The actual commission was later reported as 1.35% and the amount came to around Nu. 197.9 million. But BVT had claimed that it had received only Nu. 18.8 million. In 2019, BHEL terminated BVT as its agent (Tenzin Lamsang, 2022, 11).

CoS had discussed the allegations on four occasions but did not report to the Prime Minister or other ministers. Rather, it decided to request the Indian government's intervention and hence sent a letter signed by Secretary Yeshey without consulting or informing the Foreign Minister. The strongly worded letter came to the government's attention by accident a week after it was sent and ten weeks after CoS' decision. The government deemed CoS to have exceeded its mandate and the Secretaries to have breached important provisions of the Civil Service Act and Rules. Secretary Sonam was deemed to have mis-used CoS to discuss issues and take decisions concerning allegations against him by *ENERTIA*, Secretary Yeshey to have misrepresented the government by writing the letter without approval from Foreign Minister or Prime Minister and Secretary Penden to have kept away the information about discussions and decisions from the Prime Minister. The press release stated that the letter could have serious implications on Bhutan's foreign policy and relations with India (Office of the Prime Minister and Cabinet, 2014, 1–2).

The opposition party responded with its own press release asking the government to reinstate the Secretaries. It stated that the treatment was humiliating for such distinguished civil servants. It asked the RCSC to have the government explain how the Foreign Secretary's letter affects relations with India (Bhutan Broadcasting Service, 2014b). As the issue pressed on, the Prime Minister stated that the opposition party's position was meaningless and damaging (Bhutan Broadcasting Service, 2015a). The DNT, a party outside the parliament then, also issued a press release asking both the government and RCSC to facilitate quick justice and stated that there was a fundamental problem of trust between government and bureaucracy (Subba, 2015).

Then the RCSC issued its own press release on December 29, 2014, making it explicit that it cannot accept the "surrendering" of the Secretaries. It cited various legal provisions to convey to the government that civil servants can only be penalized after due administrative process and any such penalty for those in executive positions such as Secretaries can only be exercised by the RCSC. It asked the government to submit details and evidence of charges and decided that the Secretaries "will remain on authorized absence with benefits until the matter is resolved" (Royal Civil Service Commission, 2014, 2).

The government forwarded the evidence to the RCSC soon after charging the Secretaries with insubordination, breach of trust, withholding of information and violation of the Terms of Reference for CoS (Staff, 2015). The RCSC's investigation found that the issue originated with the minister's inability to attend the conclave and that Secretary Sonam had informed his minister about the course of action to be taken, including discussion in the CoS. However, there were procedural lapses and poor judgment despite their good faith. It pointed out that they should have sought approvals for a matter that was deemed to be of national importance and involved a foreign country. Its most important decision, communicated through a press release on February 28, 2015, was to reassign the Secretaries, since relieving them from civil service or having them continue in their earlier positions was not tenable (*Kuensel*, 2015a).

The government said it may not agree with the RCSC's decision but welcomed it (Sonam Pelden, 2015). Three days after that press release, Secretary Penden

Removals of Elected and Appointed Public Officials in Bhutan 97

superannuated on March 3. Secretary Sonam would have finished his five-year term by June 2016. Likewise, Secretary Yeshey would have completed his term in June 2017. They could not be re-appointed as Secretaries in other ministries since the government could have rejected their appointment (Tenzin Lamsang, 2015). The procedure for appointing Secretaries is for RCSC to submit a list of names to the Prime Minister, who finalizes the list and submits to His Majesty the King for formal appointment. Hence, it was highly likely that the Secretaries in whom the government had lost confidence and surrendered would be accepted. In the end, the two Secretaries were not reassigned. They were put on a waiting list, withdrawing their full emoluments, and separated from civil service when they completed their tenure as government secretaries.

Conclusion: Prevalence of Rule of Law

I have discussed various incidents of the removals and resignations of officials who were both elected and appointed in Bhutan's executive, legislature, judiciary, local governments and the bureaucracy since the introduction of parliamentary democracy in 2008. Each of these cases largely relates to corruption and abuse of functions. However, each was dealt with differently. Let me highlight key observations in each of them to draw some major conclusions.

Tshogpon Jigme, Lyonpo Minjur and Lyonpo Sherub were all accused of acts of corruption which were committed before they were elected. The fact that the anti-corruption laws nevertheless have the scope to prosecute them is an important consideration. It creates both social and political space for ethical leadership. In fact, the electoral laws prohibit anyone from contesting elections at the levels of local government or parliament if the person has been convicted and sentenced to imprisonment. While such legal provisions do not guarantee absolute ethical leadership, it provides an important minimum benchmark.

Tshogpon Jigme and Lyonpo Minjur were neither suspended nor removed even after sentencing and conviction. They used the time provided by the appeals process to complete their term. This is a significant dimension of legal enforcement that impacts ideas of ethical leadership. It is indeed a matter of right for those convicted to appeal. But once convicted by the trial court, public officials need to be suspended. While those at the ministerial positions were not suspended, we saw those at the local government's level being suspended, as was the case with Khamdang Mangmi Sangye Tenpa of Trashi Yangtse and Goshing Gup Sangay Lethro of Zhemgang.

> The Goshing gup's case has also raised questions about the lack of uniformity in the treatment of corruption cases. Those following corruption cases, including that of Home Minister Sherub Gyeltshen's, have questioned the uniformity in the application of laws and treatment of officials involved in corruption allegations.
>
> (Subba, 2021)

98   *Removals of Elected and Appointed Public Officials in Bhutan*

MP Kuenga was detained by the police but was not suspended by the Assembly. An important question concerns the authority to suspend officials after conviction and sentencing. Logically, the Prime Minister would have to suspend the ministers who would also be suspended by the Assembly Speaker since ministers are MPs in the first place. In the case of Mangmi Sangye and Gup Yeshi, the suspension orders were issued by the district's governor based on instructions of the Department of Local Government, but the termination order for Gup Yeshi was issued by Deputy Chairman of the Dzongkhag Tshogdu. Hence, there is a need to develop uniform application of laws concerning suspension and removals but also establishing clarity concerning authority to enforce them. A shared and common understanding as well as institutionalization of the practice have to be established whereby the appeals process after sentencing will not be used as opportunity to prolong stay in the office.

While there are such issues which need to be addressed, they do not dilute the quality of larger democratic norms and principles. While Tshogpon Jigme and Lyonpo Minjur completed their terms despite conviction and sentencing both by trial and appeals courts, they could not contest in the following elections. This again is due to the electoral laws provision that anyone sentenced for criminal offences cannot contest elections. The rule of law has been preserved. They also did not seek to amend this provision of the Election Act in order to make it possible for them to re-contest. Likewise, Lyonpo Sherub resigned after the High Court's ruling but before the Supreme Court's decision. MP Kuenga resigned after the Supreme Court's ruling. They also cannot re-contest future elections. But Lyonpo Rinzin was acquitted. Although he was not given his ministerial position by the government, he continued as MP and can re-contest future elections if he chooses to do so. But Gup Sangay, Gup Yeshi and Mangmi Sangye Tenpa cannot.

The fact that the senior-most justice of the Supreme Court and a judge were also convicted and sentenced along with the Brigadier impressed upon the public that the application of law is uniform irrespective of public positions. The Supreme Court demonstrated its commitment to uphold the judicial code of conduct and the oath of office for justices as administered in accordance with the constitutional requirement in its decision to remove the two justices of the High Court and recommend removal of the Attorney General. In the case of three secretaries, the RCSC upheld its constitutional mandate not to penalize civil servants without due administrative process. While the government surrendered them, the RCSC refused to accept this act of surrendering and put them on authorized leave during which investigations were conducted. The institution and mechanism of checks and balances ensured that there was no removal.

The resignations and removals of public officials from leadership positions, elected or appointed, generally indicate robust democratic institutions and processes that seek to prioritize the rule of law. The trigger for their resignations and removals has largely been conflict with laws. The application and enforcement of laws related to national security, corruption and other offences that

Removals of Elected and Appointed Public Officials in Bhutan 99

compelled resignations and required by-elections only show that elected leaders and senior officials are not above the law, and that fixing accountability on them is the hallmark of a young democracy consolidating its position.

We see that all the removals and resignations took place within the purview of electoral and corruption laws. Acts of corruption were not tolerated, electoral laws were uncompromised and the rule of law strengthened. The respect for the rule of law is fundamental to democracy, and even more so in the early years of democratic transition. This preserves public confidence in democratic institutions and processes.

Notes

1 In the first instance where a public official is introduced, I use his full name. Thereafter, I use his first name only with the official title preceding the name.
2 He was elected as the President of a new party called Druk Thuendrel Tshogpa, which contested the 2023 parliamentary elections but lost.

Bibliography

Anti-corruption Commission. 2012. *Annual Report 2012*. Thimphu: Anti-corruption Commission.

Bhutan Broadcasting Service. 2013a. "Former PM and DPT President submits resignation."August 5. Available from http://www.bbs.bt/news/?p=30110 (Accessed on December 9, 2021).

Bhutan Broadcasting Service. 2013b. "DPT's Dechen Zangmo wins Nanong-Shumar by-election." November 9. Available from http://www.bbs.bt/news/?p=33728 (Accessed on December 9, 2021).

Bhutan Broadcasting Service. 2014a. "Secretaries took unilateral decisions: Lyonpo Norbu Wangchuk." December 12. Available from http://www.bbs.bt/news/?p=47368 (Accessed on April 7, 2022).

Bhutan Broadcasting Service. 2014b. "Opposition asks government to reinstate 'surrendered' secretaries." December 18. Available from http://www.bbs.bt/news/?p=47512 (Accessed on April 7, 2022).

Bhutan Broadcasting Service. 2015a. "Opposition's stand on "surrendered" secretaries damaging: PM." March 6. Available from http://www.bbs.bt/news/?p=49162 (Accessed on April 7, 2022)

Bhutan Broadcasting Service. 2015b. "Take urgent and appropriate action against Dramedtse Gup: NC." November 20. Available from http://www.bbs.bt/news/?p=54663 (Accessed on April 5, 2022).

Bhutan Broadcasting Service. 2017. "Former Phuentshogling Thrompon charged with deception." October 18. Available from http://www.bbs.bt/news/?p=82722 (Accessed on April 4, 2022).

Bohland, James. 2022. "Is the decline of democracy inevitable?" January 31. Available from https://www.fairobserver.com/politics/james-bohland-decline-democracy-author itarianism-rise-far-right-news-12567/ (Accessed on July 7, 2022).

Bomboy, Scott. 2017. "Can a Senator serve in Congress after a conviction in court?" October 20. Available from https://constitutioncenter.org/blog/can-a-senator-serve-in-congress-after-a-conviction-in-court (Accessed on April 9, 2020).

100 Removals of Elected and Appointed Public Officials in Bhutan

Business Bhutan. 2020. "OL remains tight-lipped about resignation." July 29. Available from https://businessbhutan.bt/ol-remains-tight-lipped-about-resignation/ (Accessed on April 2, 2022).

Chencho Dema. 2019. "See top politicians struggling with past baggage." *Business Bhutan.* September 11. Available from https://businessbhutan.bt/top-politicians-struggling-with-past-baggage/ (Accessed on April 1, 2022).

Chimmi Dema. 2021. "Trashiyangtse elects four women for LG posts." *Kuensel.* December 28. Available from https://kuenselonline.com/trashiyangtse-elects-four-women-for-lg-posts/ (Accessed on April 3, 2022)

Chuki Namgyel. 2019. "Crisis for Govt as Home Minister is convicted for insurance fraud." *The Bhutanese.* August 31. Available from https://thebhutanese.bt/crisis-for-govt-as-home-minister-is-convicted-for-insurance-fraud/ (Accessed on April 7, 2022).

Constitution of the Kingdom of Bhutan. 2008. Available from https://www.nationalcouncil.bt/assets/uploads/docs/acts/2017/Constitution_of_Bhutan_2008.pdf (Accessed on April 11, 2022).

Csaky, Zselyke. 2021. *Nations in Transit 2021: The Antidemocratic Turn.* Washington, DC: Freedom House.

Damchoe Pem. 2021. *The Bhutanese.* "OAG files 23 charges against four defendants involved in the criminal conspiracy case." March 6. Available from https://thebhutanese.bt/oag-files-23-charges-against-four-defendants-involved-in-the-criminal-conspiracy-case/ (Accessed on April 7, 2022).

Diamond, Larry. 2015. "Facing up to the democratic recession." *Journal of Democracy*, Vol. 26, No. 1, 141–155.

Drapalova, Eliska. (2019). "Corruption and the crisis of democracy." Transparency International. March 6. Available from https://knowledgehub.transparency.org/assets/uploads/helpdesk/Corruption-and-Crisis-of-Democracy_2019.pdf (Accessed on April 10, 2022).

Druk Phuensum Tshogpa. 2021. "Sonam Tashi is Druk Phuensum Tshogpa's new Secretary General." August 31.

Freedom House. 2020. "Freedom in the World 2020: Bhutan." Available from https://freedomhouse.org/country/bhutan/freedom-world/2020 (Accessed on April 8, 2022).

Freedom House. 2021. "Freedom in the World 2021: Bhutan." Available from https://freedomhouse.org/country/bhutan/freedom-world/2021 (Accessed on May 16, 2024).

Goenpo. 2019. "Yangdzong/Tshogdu-01/2019–2020/4161." October 15. Trashi Yangtse: Dzongkhag Administration.

His Majesty the King. 2020. "Royal Kashos on civil service and education." Available from https://kuenselonline.com/royal-kashos-on-civil-service-and-education/ (Accessed on July 7, 2022).

Holland, Ian. 2003. "Crime and candidacy." March 24. Available from https://www.aph.gov.au/About_Parliament/Parliamentary_Departments/Parliamentary_Library/Publications_Archive/CIB/cib0203/03CIB22 (Accessed on April 9, 2022).

India TV. 2013. "MLAs, MPs convicted for 2 years or more cannot contest polls: historic Supreme Court verdict." July 10. Available from https://www.indiatvnews.com/news/india/mlas-mps-convicted-for-2-years-or-more-cannot-contest-polls-24871.html (Accessed on April 9, 2022).

Kelzang Wangchuk. 2019. "Newly elected Bumdeling gup arrested for forgery." *Kuensel.* December 14. Available from https://kuenselonline.com/newly-elected-bumdeling-gup-arrested-for-forgery/#:~:text=Police%20in%20Trashiyangtse%20detained%20the,election%20in%20September%20this%20year (Accessed on April 3, 2022).

Kelzang Wangchuk. 2021. "Wangphu Mangmi terminated for holding license." May 29. Available from https://kuenselonline.com/wangphu-mangmi-terminated-for-holding-license/ (Accessed on April 4, 2022).

Kinley Dem. 2022. "SC also finds Khandu Wangmo guilty of commissioning of criminal conspiracy." *BBS*. April 2. Available from http://www.bbs.bt/news/?p=167404 (Accessed on April 7, 2022).

Kinley Dem and Tshering Zam. 2021. "Home Minister appeals to Supreme Court against the Larger Bench's ruling." *BBS*. Available from http://www.bbs.bt/news/?p=146299 (Accessed on April 1, 2022).

Kuensel. 2015a. "Surrendered secretaries will be reassigned: RCSC." February 28. Available from https://kuenselonline.com/surrendered-secretaries-will-be-reassigned-rcsc-2/ (Accessed on April 7, 2022).

Kuensel. 2015b. "Drametse elects a new gup." December 31. Available from https://kuenselonline.com/drametse-elects-a-new-gup/ (Accessed on April 5, 2022).

Kuensel. 2021. "Khamdang-Ramjar MP Kuenga Loday detained." March 2. Available from https://kuenselonline.com/khamdang-ramjar-mp-kuenga-loday-detained/ (Accessed on April 3, 2022).

Kuensel. 2024. "Phongmey gup gets 11-year term in prison." May 11. Available from https://kuenselonline.com/phongmey-gup-gets-11-year-term-in-prison/ (Accessed on May 15, 2024).

Linz, Juan L. and Stepan, Alfred. 1996. "Towards consolidated democracies." *Journal of Democracy*, Vol. 7, No. 2, 14–33.

Magen, Amichai. 2015. "The democratic entitlement in an era of democratic recession." *Cambridge Journal of International and Comparative Law*, Vol. 4, No. 2, 368–387.

Minjur Dorji. 2012. "ACC suspension order quashed by High Court." *The Bhutanese*. November 30. Available from https://thebhutanese.bt/acc-suspension-order-quashed-by-high-court/ (Accessed on April 2, 2022).

NDTV. 2013. "Jailed politicians can contest elections as parliament amended law: Supreme Court." November 20. Available from https://www.ndtv.com/india-news/jailed-politicians-can-contest-elections-as-parliament-amended-law-supreme-court-541691 (Accessed on April 9, 2022).

Neten Dorji. 2020. "Only one candidate for Bumdeling's by-election for gup." *Kuensel*. November 5. Available from https://kuenselonline.com/only-one-candidate-for-bumdelings-bye-election-for-gup/ (Accessed on April 3, 2022).

Office of the Prime Minister and Cabinet. 2014. *Press Release*. December 12. Thimphu: Royal Government of Bhutan, Cabinet Secretariat.

Office of the Prime Minister and Cabinet. 2015. *Press Release*. Available from https://www.cabinet.gov.bt/the-government-has-been-notified-that-the-office-of-attorney-general-and-anti-corruption-commission-have-completed-the-investigation-on-alleged-malpractices-with-regard-to-the-renovation-of-lhakhang-k/ (Accessed on April 2, 2022).

Pema Samdrup. 2019a. "Goshing Gup sentenced to more than 10 years in prison." December 4. Available from http://www.bbs.bt/news/?p=124942 (Accessed on April 4, 2022).

Pema Samdrup. 2019b. "Goshing Gewog still without a gup." November 22. Available from http://www.bbs.bt/news/?p=124345 (Accessed on April 4, 2022).

Pema Seldon Tshering. 2021a. "Khamdang-Ramjar MP and five others appeal to the High Court." September 1. Available from http://www.bbs.bt/news/?p=156654 (Accessed on April 3, 2022).

102 *Removals of Elected and Appointed Public Officials in Bhutan*

Pema Seldon Tshering. 2021b. "Panbang Court sentences Goshing Gup to eight years in prison." November 3. Available from http://www.bbs.bt/news/?p=160123 (Accessed on April 4, 2022).

Phurpa Lhamo. 2021. "Ngalam MP dies after consuming a wild plant." *Kuensel*. April 20.

Pring, Coralie and Vrushi, Jon. 2019. "Tackling the crisis of democracy, promoting rule of law and fighting corruption." January 29. Available from https://www.transparency.org/en/news/tackling-crisis-of-democracy-promoting-rule-of-law-and-fighting-corruption (Accessed on April 8, 2022).

Rinzin Wangchuk. 2015a. "Foreign Minister acquitted in Lhakhang Karpo case." *Kuensel*. June 24. Available from https://kuenselonline.com/foreign-minister-acquitted-in-lhakhang-karpo-case/ (Accessed on April 2, 2022).

Rinzin Wangchuk. 2015b. "High Court convicts three in Lhakhang Karpo case." October 29. Available from https://kuenselonline.com/high-court-convicts-three-in-lhakhang-karpo-case/ (Accessed on April 2, 2022).

Rinzin Wangchuk. 2016. "SC exonerates former foreign minister and project manager." August 5. Available from https://kuenselonline.com/sc-exonerates-former-foreign-minister-and-project-manager/ (Accessed on April 2, 2022).

Rinzin Wangchuk. 2017. "ACC suspends top RICBL executives." July 8. Available from https://kuenselonline.com/acc-suspends-top-ricbl-executives/ (Accessed on April 1, 2022).

Royal Civil Service Commission. 2014. *Press Release*. December 29. Thimphu: RCSC, Royal Government of Bhutan.

Royal Government of Bhutan. 2004. *Penal Code of Bhutan*. Available at https://www.rbp.gov.bt/Forms/PCB%202004.pdf (Accessed on April 11, 2022).

Samten Dolkar. 2020. "National Council withdraws Impeachment Procedure Bill of Bhutan 2019." March 4. Available from http://www.bbs.bt/news/?p=129164 (Accessed on April 7, 2020).

Schedler, Andreas. 1997. "Expected stability: Defining and measuring democratic consolidation." *IHS Political Science Series Working Paper 50*.

Sinha, Arun. 2022. "Dynastic politics: BJP feeds the monster while claiming to spear it." *The Federal*. February 17. Available from https://thefederal.com/opinion/dynastic-politics-bjp-feeds-the-monster-while-claiming-to-spear-it/ (Accessed on April 8, 2022).

Sonam Kinga. 2019. *Democratic Transition in Bhutan: Political Contests as Moral Battles*. New Delhi and London: Routledge.

Sonam Pelden. 2015. "We may not agree but we respect RCSC's decision: PM." *Kuensel*. March 7. Available from https://kuenselonline.com/we-may-not-agree-but-we-respect-rcscs-decision-pm/ (Accessed on April 7, 2022).

Sonam Penjore. 2021. "Lily Wangchuk resigns from DPT." *Bhutan Times*. August 2.

Sonam Tshering. 2022. "The ruling party factor contributed to DNT's Karma Gyeltshen's win." *BBS*. February 5. Available from http://www.bbs.bt/news/?p=165413 (Accessed on April 3, 2022).

Staff. 2013. "JYT steps down." *The Bhutanese*. July 12. Available from https://thebhutanese.bt/jyt-steps-down/ (Accessed on April 2, 2022).

Staff. 2015. "Government forwards evidence and charges against three secretaries to RCSC." *The Bhutanese*. January 17. Available from https://thebhutanese.bt/government-forwards-evidences-and-charges-against-three-secretaries-to-rcsc/ (Accessed on April 7, 2022).

Staff. 2023. "Attorney General removed from office." *The Bhutanese*. September 9. Available from https://thebhutanese.bt/attorney-general-removed-from-office/ (Accessed on December 24, 2023).

Removals of Elected and Appointed Public Officials in Bhutan   103

Staff Reporter. 2019a. "Bumdeling gup detained for alleged rape of minor." *Kuensel*. July 15. Available from https://kuenselonline.com/bumdeling-gup-detained-for-alleged-rape-of-minor/ (Accessed on April 3, 2022).

Staff Reporter. 2019b. "Panbang court sentences Goshing gup and three others in corruption case." *Kuensel*. December 5. Available from https://kuenselonline.com/panbang-court-sentences-goshing-gup-and-three-others-in-corruption-case/ (Accessed on April 4, 2022).

Staff Reporter. 2021a. "Khamdang-Ramjar MP resigns." *Kuensel*. November 19. Available from https://kuenselonline.com/khamdang-ramjar-mp-resigns/ (Accessed on April 3, 2022).

Staff Reporter. 2021b. "Supreme Court justice and drangpon detained." *Kuensel*. February 17. Available from https://kuenselonline.com/supreme-court-justice-and-drangpon-detained/ (Accessed on April 7, 2022).

Staff Reporter. 2023. "SC removes two justices who were suspended in August." *Kuensel*. September 20. Available from https://kuenselonline.com/sc-removes-two-justices-who-were-suspended inaugust/#:~:text=Justice%20Pema%20Rinzin%20and%20Justice,of%20narcotic%20drugs%20and%20psychotropic (Accessed on December 25, 2023).

Subba, M.B. 2015. "Little trust between government and bureaucracy: DNT." *Kuensel*. January 10. Available from https://kuenselonline.com/little-trust-between-government-and-bureaucracy-dnt/ (Accessed on April 7, 2022).

Subba, M.B. 2016. "Former Phuentsholing thrompon disqualified." *Kuensel*. January 23. Available from https://kuenselonline.com/former-phuentsholing-thrompon-disqualified/ (Accessed on April 4, 2022).

Subba, M.B. 2020. "OL formally tenders resignation." *Kuensel*. July 29. Available from https://kuenselonline.com/ol-formally-tenders-resignation/ (Accessed on May 8, 2024).

Subba, M.B. 2021. "Goshing without gup for almost three years." *Kuensel*. March 4. Available from https://kuenselonline.com/goshing-without-gup-for-almost-three-years/ (Accessed on April 6, 2022).

Tashi Phuntsho. 2015. "Drametse gup vacates post." *Kuensel*. December 1. Available from https://kuenselonline.com/drametse-gup-vacates-post/ (Accessed on April 5, 2022).

Tempa Wangdi. 2016. "Opposition MP Kinga Tshering resigns." *Kuensel*. August 23. Available from https://kuenselonline.com/opposition-mp-kinga-tshering-resigns/ (Accessed on April 2, 2022).

Tenzin Lamsang. 2014. "The letter that got three secretaries to surrender." *The Bhutanese*. December 13. Available from https://thebhutanese.bt/the-letter-that-got-three-secretaries-to-surrender/ (Accessed on April 7, 2022).

Tenzin Lamsang. 2015. "Two Secretaries to be reassigned soon." *The Bhutanese*. August 15. Available from https://thebhutanese.bt/two-secretaries-to-be-reassigned-soon/ (Accessed on April 7, 2022).

Tenzin Lamsang. 2016. "Political quake as DPT's star MP puts up resignation." *The Bhutanese*. August 22.

Tenzin Lamsang. 2021. "The story behind the criminal conspiracy." *The Bhutanese*. February 21. Available from https://thebhutanese.bt/the-story-behind-the-criminal-conspiracy/ (Accessed on April 7, 2022).

Tenzin Lamsang. 2022. "BHEL and MHPA resolve issues amicably as two governments step in." *The Bhutanese*. April 9. Available from https://thebhutanese.bt/bhel-and-mhpa-resolve-issues-amicably-as-two-governments-step-in/ (Accessed on May 8, 2024).

The Bhutanese. 2012. "ACC files Gyelpozhing land case in Mongar Court." November 16. Available from http://thebhutanese.bt/acc-files-gyelpozhing-land-case-in-mongar-court/ (Accessed on April 2, 2022).

The Bhutanese. 2013. "Mongar court passes guilty verdict on Gyelpozhing land case." March 8. Available from https://thebhutanese.bt/mongar-court-passes-guilty-verdict-on-gyelpozhing-land-case/ (Accessed on April 2, 2022).

The Bhutanese. 2015. "Breaking news: Foreign Minister removed from cabinet." Facebook. July 21. Available from https://m.facebook.com/story.php?story_fbid=pfbid0Xh3eLcMg56tV5Mu66KXiBSJVm6AnqTawQttXKC788oWxpVyuSgVWhw9euTSC5TJNl&id=174895472616391&m_entjjjjstream_source=permalink&locale2=es_LA&__tn__=-R (Accessed on April 7, 2022).

Thinley Namgay. 2021. "Khamdang-Ramjar MP sentenced to five years in prison." *Kuensel.* August 14. Available from https://kuenselonline.com/khamdang-ramjar-mp-sentenced-to-five-years-in-prison/ (Accessed on April 3, 2022).

Thompson, Christie. 2020. "These political candidates are embracing their criminal records." June 23. Available from https://www.themarshallproject.org/2020/06/23/formerly-incarcerated-political-candidates (Accessed on April 9, 2022).

Thuje Tshering. 2020. *Termination Order.* Yangdzong/Tshogdu/01/2019-2020/1655. May 26. Trashi Yangtse: Dzongkhag Administration.

Thuje Tshering. 2021. *Suspension Order.* YangDzong/Tshogdu?04/2020-2021/6299. March 12. Trahi Yangtse: Dzongkhag Administration.

Tshering Dendup. 2020. "Panbang MP Dorji Wangdi is the new Opposition Leader." *BBS.* September 7. Available from http://www.bbs.bt/news/?p=136194 (Accessed on April 2, 2022)

Tshering Palden. 2015. "Why Govt. replaced the foreign minister." *Kuensel.* August 1. Available from https://kuenselonline.com/why-govt-replaced-the-foreign-minister/ (Accessed on April 2, 2022).

Tshering Palden. 2020. "High Court convicts Home Minister, others in fake insurance claim case." *Kuensel.* October 10. Available from https://kuenselonline.com/high-court-convicts-home-minister-others-in-fake-insurance-claim-case/ (Accessed on April 1, 2022).

Tshering Palden and Tashi Dema. 2021. "Supreme Court suspended Justice Kuenley Tshering and Drangpon Yeshey Dorji." *Kuensel.* March 12. Available from https://kuenselonline.com/supreme-court-suspended-justice-kuenley-tshering-and-drangpon-yeshey-dorji/ (Accessed on April 7, 2022).

Tshering Zam. 2021. "Criminal conspiracy case judgment – Thimphu District Court." *BBS.* July 23. Available from http://www.bbs.bt/news/?p=154332 (Accessed on April 7, 2022).

Varma, Pavan K. 2015. "How democracy took roots in Bhutan." *The Hindu.* April 1. Available from https://www.thehindu.com/opinion/columns/How-democracy-took-roots-in-Bhutan/articles56841853.ece (Accessed on December 29, 2022).

Yangchen C. Rinzin. 2021a. "HC's larger bench upholds lower court's judgment in Home Minister's case." *Kuensel.* March 19. Available from https://kuenselonline.com/hcs-larger-bench-upholds-lower-courts-judgment-in-home-ministers-case/ (Accessed on April 1, 2022).

Yangchen C. Rinzin. 2021b. "Home Minister resigned officially." *Kuensel.* May 7. Available from https://kuenselonline.com/home-minister-resigned-officially/ (Accessed on April 7, 2022).

5 Democracy in India: Continuities, Realignments, and Promises

Anup Shekhar Chakraborty

Introduction

In light of the extensive studies conducted by experts on democratization in South Asia, it is impossible to summarize a number of crucial empirical and theoretical insights in a single paragraph. However, a few facets warrant further investigation. South Asian analysts' preoccupation with political consolidation suggests a deep unease about democratization's teleology. Democracy preceded nation- and state-building, making challenges harder. The challenges of South Asian states, and particularly those of India, suggest that state and nationhood are necessary for effective democratization (Das Gupta, 1989; Diamond, 1989b; Diamond et al., 1990; Moore, 2017). Ram Madhav (2023, 11 March) noted that

> Ambedkar, in his address to the Constituent Assembly on November 25, 1949, pointed out that India was not ignorant of democracy, parliaments, or parliamentary procedure. The *Bhikshu Sanghas*, or Buddhist parliaments, were found to have followed all modern parliamentary practices. Though he used them in *Sangha* meetings, the Buddha must have adapted these parliamentary rules from the political assemblies of his time.

The Nehruvian state and its progeny appear to have managed the challenge of building a developing democracy while reconciling a plural conception of nationhood, even if it is bitterly contested in the peripheral regions, and if statehood and nationhood are seen as necessary prerequisites of effective democratization. Even if some readings suggest that a 'centralized state' is the secret to Indian democracy's success or that transitions' failures are due to the nation- and state-building, South Asian democratization and ideals differ from European ones (Mahalingam, 1967; Baker, 1976; Morris-Jones, 1971; Kohli, 1990, 2001; Jayal, 2001; Ganguly et al., 2007; Spencer, 2007; Doornbos & Kaviraj, 1999; Kaviraj, 2010; Corbridge & Harriss, 1999; Corbridge et al., 2005).

The issues of political consolidation that plague most South Asian states point to a more fundamental problem with post-transition democracy: its substantive nature and varied experience. Political decay, de-institutionalization,

DOI: 10.4324/9781003261469-5

106 *Democracy in India: Continuities, Realignments, and Promises*

mal-governance, institutionalized corruption, re-militarization, resource control and contest, nepotism, political silence, etc. explain post-transition regimes' fragility (Dahl, 1971, 1982; Blondel, 1972; Bollen, 1979; Bobbio, 1987; Das Gupta, 1989; Diamond, 1989a, 1989b, 1992; Diamond et al., 1990; Moore, 2017). Heller (2000) argues that constitutional design and class forces contribute to a 'virtuous cycle of democratization' in other Indian provinces and post-transition regimes in Bangladesh, Nepal and Pakistan (1988–1999). Heller argues that Kerala's case shows that a hierarchical, caste-ridden society can become a democratic society with associational life and class organizations. 'If democracy works better today in Kerala, it is because its citizens are active and organized and because horizontal associations prevail over vertical (clientelist) forms of association.' Over the last 50 years, conflict and social mobilization have created civil society, not elite engineering or regional culture. Kerala serves as a noteworthy anomaly in a region where substantial horizontal associations are absent even in the most effective democratic models.

South Asia's 'third wave' has been 'democratization from below' (Huntington, 1991) and the developments since 1989 have encouraged village-level political participation and decision-making. External pressure or anticipation of it has drastically changed local government, which had been largely dormant since decolonization. The 73rd Constitutional Amendment Act (1993) established *panchayati raj* (local self-government) in India's 800,000 villages, with delegated funds and reservations for backward classes/castes and women. Ironically, *panchayati raj*, meant to undermine the states and centralize power in New Delhi, has reshaped local democracy to include the excluded—women and the underprivileged (Sisodia et al., 2018; Kashyap, 2011; Aslam, 2007; Dreze & Sen, 2002). The 'democratization from below' has fostered a transparency and accountability culture that manifests in many forms of citizen activism, including local movements against corruption in development fund disbursement and growing demands to audit government programs. These movements are increasingly sponsored internationally, and some have influenced local policies. South Asian states' systemic transformation from below is most likely to be based on a growing culture of democratic accountability.

Social movements and activism, significantly since the early 1990s, have helped 'democratization from below' succeed. Social movements have taken over state-society discourse and organization as political parties have lost power. These movements vary greatly, from transformative to single-issue. Women's, environmental, and local movements often collaborate with multinational organizations and NGOs to bring their demands to the international stage. Some academics see the Hindu right as a social movement that seeks political power and long-term social change through Hindutva (Baird, 1981; Narain, 1993; Ghose, 1992; Gopal, 1991). Other revivalist or fundamentalist faith movements are similar (Smith, 1963; Das, 1992; Robinson, 1974; Roy, 1990). These movements' influence far outweighs their numbers. Social movements have avoided electoral politics, which have become the arena for 'representing and endorsing essentialized identities and institutionalizing them.'

Democracy in India: Continuities, Realignments, and Promises   107

Instead, they frequently articulate interests within the state's judicial-administrative apparatus because it is more receptive to interest rather than identity (Srivastava, 1992). It allows the state to negotiate the diversity of interests that perform a very different democratic function than party or electoral politics (Baker, 1976; Chandra, 2004; Michelutti, 2008; Witsoe, 2013; Palshikar et al., 2014). If institutional sclerosis seems to characterize most South Asian states, we are told that social resilience is where democratization is found. Social activism in South Asia provides a 'discursive space in which new and transformative meanings are constantly being generated,' even if it doesn't meet institutional significance. Social movements are vital to renewal and cohesion, and the best hope for lasting reform.

Within the region, contrary to much otherwise expert speculations owing to its abject pervasive poverty and illiteracy, the largest democracy began its march in October 1951 as the country held its first free and fair elections. It was a defining moment, as 'the country managed to laugh in the face of the academic insistence that there was a causal—perhaps even mathematical—link between economic development and political democracy' (Chowdhury & Keane, 2021: 5). Since then, India, with a brief interruption of the '1975 emergency,' has largely managed to stay on the democratic path in a way unprecedented among states freed from colonialism during the last century. Many other postcolonial states that won their independence in the twentieth century lapsed into dictatorship or military rule, but India made its 'tryst with destiny' as a torch bearer by abiding virtues of its model of pluralist liberal democracy. Since democracy was guaranteed now, its promises were inextricably linked to liberal democratic notions such as political participation, contestation, and, to a lesser extent, an independent media and judiciary. Once there was participation and contestation, it was reiterated that Indians would truly have a democratic life (Varshney, 2014). For most democratic theorists, competitive elections are considered to be a vital condition for the functioning of a democracy. In fact, 'no elections, no democracy' is a theoretical dictum of widespread acceptability. Since 1947, India has had 17 national and 389 (and counting) state elections. Other than a 21-month period of nationwide authoritarianism (June 1975–March 1977) and a few electoral suspensions in areas of unrest, elections have decided who will rule India and its states and, after 1992–1993, its local governments as well. This has been true even in the contemporary period of Modi-led BJP's rule since 2014. While the Modi-led BJP may not have lost an election nationally since coming to power, their electoral trajectory at state level elections underscores that the electoral principle of India's democracy remains intact. The free and fair regular elections in a competitive multiparty system with peaceful transfer of power between governments have been the hallmarks of the world's largest stable parliamentary democracy. Until a decade or two ago, democracy in India seemed to be doing well. Its institutions garnered respect from the general public. The Election Commission (EC), responsible for electoral oversight, had a long record of administering free and fair elections. The judiciary was also trusted to be impartial, especially at the higher levels and the Supreme Court. Media was regarded as free and stood for human rights. At the turn of the twenty-first century, India obtained fairly high scores for freedom of expression and the citizens had relatively easy access to alternative sources of information, according to the Varieties of Democracy (V-Dem) project (Ozturk, 2021). The Freedom in the World reports by Freedom House have rated India as Free for 20 consecutive years. However, with the specter of the global decline of democracy, as the growing body of literature underscores, with scholars adding new conceptual terminology like 'backsliding,' 'recession,' 'regression,' and 'erosion,' various experts have expressed a sense of sadness and despair at the trajectory of the world's largest democracy. According to Suhas Palshikar, 'today, all serious scholars of Indian politics would probably agree that something is wrong with India's democracy, even if the details of their analyses may vary' (Palshikar, 2021). The Bharatiya Janata Party (BJP), which is currently in power in India and is considered to be on the right of the political spectrum, has recently established a constitutional review commission to assess the 'Westminster model,' which has been interpreted by some as an attempt to move the country towards a presidential system. Democracies, it is argued, deserve some qualification—'people's democracies,' 'guided democracies,' 'liberal democracies,' 'illiberal democracies,' and 'authoritarian democracies.' In recent years, India has evolved from being labeled a 'conservative democracy' to a 'democratization of democracy' to an 'ethnic democracy.' The international media has been critical and human rights organizations have expressed serious concern about the recent democratic retreat. While Freedom House has downgraded India's status from 'Free' to 'Partly Free' on account of the country's weakening protection of civil liberties, the V-Dem Institute went a step further, saying 'the world's largest democracy has turned into an electoral autocracy' (*The Wire*, 2021). While Indian scholars have acknowledged that something is wrong with the current state of democracy, they also point towards the exaggeration of the decline of democracy. For example, Ashutosh Varshney suggests that to say India is not an electoral democracy is an overstretched claim because its record as an electoral democracy is far better than its record as a liberal democracy, and electoral vitality coexists with liberal deficits (Varshney, 2022). As Palshikar acknowledges, there is a crisis today in Indian democracy, but the long-term context is a growth of 'sub-democratic' politics (Palshikar, 2021). While it can be argued that despite numerous challenges faced by the world's largest democracy, there are certainly some underlying forces and developments that have taken place (and are taking place) in India that give reason for optimism.

Political Democratization to Social Democratization: India in Process 1947–2014

During the first few decades, when the 'congress system' was unopposed, socialist rhetoric from Jawaharlal Nehru and Indira Gandhi constantly threatened the constitutionally based democratic conservatism of the time. Nehru

Democracy in India: Continuities, Realignments, and Promises 109

(1947–1964) failed to liberate his party, the Indian National Congress, from prominent members wedded to long-held customs and perks. Only local leaders, former princely state rulers who became congressmen, and regional heavyweights with caste-panchayat patronage networks could win elections (Brecher, 1976; Ali, 1985; Brown, 1985; Chandra, 1993; Brass, 1994). This was the time when the Indian democracy was in its *Praja-Raja* (subject and rulers) phase. All of these notables were men belonging to the upper caste, who derived their social standing from traditional economies and political strategies. They utilised 'progressive' ideologies to establish the Planning Commission and implement a moderate nationalisation programme, which aimed to assert the authority of the state. This programme granted significant landholdings to large landowners and enhanced the financial clout of the business community. The Congress in order to win the elections in 1952, 1957, and 1962 was compelled to seek support of conservative notables who did not share Nehru's socialist views through a clientelist strategy. As a result, Nehru could not carry out the land reform that had been a central plank of his electoral platform (Harrison, 1960; Brass, 1994; Jayal & Mehta, 2010).

Indira Gandhi's progressive discourse as prime minister concluded similarly to her father's. After winning the 1971 elections on a populist platform that included lofty social promises—'*Garibi hatao*' (remove poverty)—Indira realized that she needed the backing of both local heavy hitters and Congress's conservatives if she wanted to be elected. Her opponents made fun of her by saying that her campaign slogan was '*Garibo ko hatao*' (get rid of the poor). They devised a unified anti-Indira slogan: '*Indira hatao*' (remove Indira). Under pressure from the opposition and the judiciary, she suspended democracy and declared a state of emergency between 1975 and 1977. Since the elections had been postponed indefinitely, she took advantage of the situation to redistribute more land (Gupte, 1992; Hart, 1976). Socially and politically, however, the declaration of the state of emergency was autocratic. The opposition, which assisted in toppling Mrs. Gandhi's government, established the Second Backward Classes Commission to assist the OBCs (Other Backward Class). In 1980, however, early elections were held, resulting in Indira Gandhi's return to the position of prime minister. She favored a growth strategy supported by the private sector over a genuine social agenda (Carras, 1979; Masani, 1976; Moraes, 1980). Following her assassination in 1984 by Khalistan secessionist groups (Nayar & Singh, 1984; Gupte, 1985; Kapur, 1987), her son Rajiv inherited this policy (Jain, 1992; Humbers, 1992; Seshan, 1993).

With Rajiv Gandhi's defeat in the late 1980s at the hands of the same coalition of opposition parties that had overthrown his mother in 1977, India's transition to democracy had officially begun (Bhattacharjee, 1992). This election had shaken the foundations of India's democracy. Emerging coalition governments sought to dismantle the *Praja-raja* (subject and rulers) *syndrome* that had allowed Hindu society's upper castes and classes (Brahman, Kayasth, Baniya) to rise to power under the conservative Congress. Their ultimate aim was to replace conservative democracies with liberal ones completely. The backward

110 *Democracy in India: Continuities, Realignments, and Promises*

castes and their '*Mandali*' ('collective of the marginals') began to control the social and economic spheres. After the Green Revolution of the 1960s, many farmers in this class could sell their surpluses and join the new affluent class (Eldridge, 1970; Dhanagare, 1983; Rudolph & Rudolph, 1984, 1987; Hardgrave & Kochanek, 1933).

The Janata Party, which held power from 1977 to 1980, and the Janata Dal, which ruled from 1989 to 1991, both advocated for the lower castes, particularly the OBCs. With B.P. Mandal at the helm, the Janata government established a new Backward Classes Commission in 1978. This group looked into OBC housing and suggested reforms. Due to their low educational attainment and inability to own land as tenant farmers or landless peasants, the Mandal Commission concluded that OBCs required a positive discrimination program. In 1990, the Janata Dal Party resurrected the initiative, and Prime Minister V.P. Singh implemented it. The Janata Dal Party was established in 1988 by merging the factions of the Janta Party, Lok Dal, Jan Morcha, and the INC (Jagjivan group). The Janta Party itself was formed by combining various political organizations during Indira Gandhi's 'emergency period.' This reform under V.P. Singh that reduced the number of public sector jobs—the most coveted before the 1991 economic liberalization—was met with immediate resistance from the upper castes, who even took to the streets in protest. The lower castes were outraged by the 'upper caste resistance' and they banded together to fight clientelism and support lower-caste parliamentary candidates. As a result, previously ignored, disregarded groups, such as those living in rural areas and having lower levels of education, emerged as a formidable political force (Chandra, 1993; Chanchreek & Prasad, 1993). As a direct result of the Janata Dal and its regional offshoots, the percentage of OBC MPs from the Hindi belt increased from 10 to 20 percent. The Hindi belt is the crucial battleground, accounting for 45 percent of Lok Sabha seats. Even after the Janata Dal Party disintegrated in the early 1990s, the democratic processes it had begun continued. Janata Dal initially initiated this dynamic. First, since clientelist mechanisms were no longer viable, all parties, including Congress, had to field several OBC candidates. Over half of the population comprised OBCs, making the new 'OBC vote' a force that could not be ignored. Second, Congress and lower-caste parties established new public policies to safeguard their interests. When Congress reinstated the 27 percent OBC quota in public universities in 2004, it infuriated the higher castes. These laws shielded the lower classes. The leap of the '*Mandali*' ('marginal classes collective') from the margins to the center officially inaugurated the era of Mandalization of Indian democracy (Kohli, 1990, 2001; Ganguly et al., 2007; Jayal, 2001; Spencer, 2007; Doornbost & Kaviraj, 1999; Kaviraj, 2010; Corbridge & Harriss, 1999, Corbridge et al., 2005).

P.V. Narasimha Rao took control of the Indian National Congress (INC) after the 'Babri Masjid demolition' (Narain, 1993; Ghose, 1992; Gopal, 1991) in March 1993 during the party's Surajkund session, in contrast to the Tirupati session in April 1992, when the Nehru-Indira Gandhi line of leadership was not questioned. Post-Babri, and with the assassination of Rajiv Gandhi, the

Democracy in India: Continuities, Realignments, and Promises 111

Congress under Rao attempted to resurrect the INC and reidentified the power of the name 'Gandhi' to rehaul its membership drive from village level (Serrakai, 2000). Women's participation in political leadership at all levels shifted in the late 1990s and early 2000s. Sonia Gandhi, Mayawati, Jayalalithaa, Sushma Swaraj, Meira Kumar, and Mamata Banerjee all gained widespread recognition.

The politicization of the Mandal (both the recommendations of the Mandal Commission's reports and the OBC aspirational consciousness) by then-Prime Minister V.P. Singh sparked a violent backlash among upper-caste youths. Anger among men of higher castes was channeled into the 'Kamandal' (a pot used by ascetics to hold holy water; a metaphor for Hindutva politics) political movement, and muscular Hindutva began to be identified with the BJP's *lohapursh* (Ironman) L.K. Advani and his Ratha-yatra and the Ram Janmabhoomi movement of the 1990s. Post-Babri Masjid, the BJP bridged the gap between the '*Mandal*' (backward caste cohorts) and the '*Kamandal*' (forward/upper caste cohorts) into a mutually compatible and workable electoral formula as evidenced by BSP (under Kansi Ram) and the BJP in Uttar Pradesh (UP); the Arya Samaj and the RSS-BJP's passageway to garner the support of the *Jats* (OBC cohort spread across northwest India). At times triumphant, at others unsuccessful, the BJP attempted to unite people based on their shared religious beliefs and social identities (Andersen & Damle, 1987; Jaffrelot, 1998, 2007). In UP at the time, the BJP put efforts into the political art of reimagining history, mythology, and religion to unite and mobilize Hindus from different castes and subcastes into a powerful voting bloc. In response to Janata Dal's *Mandal*, the BJP groomed a group of Dalit and other backward castes/class leaders at the grassroots level, beginning with Kalyan Singh and continuing with Uma Bharati and Narendra Modi after that. By the 2000s, the BJP had developed a strategy for electoral success based on reconciling *Mandal* (backward caste cohorts) and *Kamandal* (upper caste cohorts), two political ideologies that appear to be diametrically opposed at first glance.

Throughout the 1980s and 1990s, debates on secularism in India, as well as the concept of 'Indian secularism,' have given rise to new interpretations which question the notion of 'being secular.' For instance, the BJP and the Sangh Parivar have been insisting on a distinction between their own 'positive secularism' and the 'pseudo-secularism' of the Congress. According to them, 'positive secularism' stands for 'justice for all and discriminations against none.' At the same time, Congress's 'pseudo-secularism' vilifies Hindu categories and symbols while also pampering Muslim minority communities as 'vote banks' (Derrett, 1968; Pantham, 1997).

In theory, India's secular state is supposed to treat all religions equally. This neutrality, however, is not to be maintained through a complete lack of involvement in religious matters but rather through a 'fair' engagement with India's religiously diverse landscape. A shift from an equidistant to a principled distance model is needed, but all too often its actual political practice has involved actively balancing favors to various religious communities (Vanaik, 1997). Thus, there are ambiguities in the Indian context, and this has led scholars to

112 *Democracy in India: Continuities, Realignments, and Promises*

almost unequivocally conclude that secularism in India is in crisis (Nandy, 1992: 69–72; Madan, 1997; Smith, 1963; Nandy, 1998; Bhargava, 2000; Chandhoke, 1999, 2004).

It is interesting to note that the character of the Indian constitution was decisively shaped predominantly in response to the deteriorating Hindu-Muslim relations. The Indian State excluded religion on certain grounds, for example by refusing to allow separate electorates, reserved constituencies for different religious communities, reservations for jobs based on religious classification, and the organization of states based on religion. Studies on secularism and accommodations of diversities in India have failed to look into the cases beyond the caged perspectives of communalized Hindu-Muslim relations. The operation of religious politics in the northeast of India thus has remained 'uninteresting' or 'unimportant' for the intelligentsia from New Delhi and other metropolises. The age-old debate on secularism in India remains an important factor in contemporary Indian politics, just as it did in the past.

Modi, Modi-fications in the Age of the Marginals

Unlike his contemporaries and peers in India's corridors of power, Modi comes with no legacy or inheritance. Modi's rise, albeit in a party other than the Janata Dal, is a continuation of the rise of the marginals in Indian democracy. In fact, until recently, few people even knew he was a member of the marginalized Dalit community, and he rarely exploits his status as an outlier to make his point. As the new apostle of democracy, Modi comes from the working class—*aam aadmi* (commoner)—and not from a dynastic background. Experts have determined that Modi's leadership style is a presidential type. Modi has transformed the perception of the prime minister's office from an inaccessible office to someone easily reachable via message or telephone. His campaign techniques combine charisma with well-honed party machines and exude self-assurance and determination. The era of Modi has witnessed the calculated use of social media and technology to reach distant people and realign political connections via the technology-and-people interface. This *Manthan* (churning) of the Neo-Hindutva through Modi's pledge (*sankalp*) of 'Making India Great Again' relies on strategies that emphasize the significance of the shared heritages (*dharohar*) and ancient cultures *(prachinsabhyata)* of the people, culture, and ecosystem that foster the nation's sense of self-worth. Modi reinvoked Deendayal Upadhyay's mantra of being rooted in India's ethos, *antyodaya* (uplifting the poorest), *daridranarayan seva* (service to the poor), *Jan seva hi prabhuseva hai* (service to people is service to god), and has promoted vernacular languages, vernacular technology, and investment in India's glorious past, as illustrated by the use of historical anniversaries as project deadlines. Various grand schemes have been tied to historical events or landmarks, such as the 150th anniversary of Gandhi's birth (2019) and the 75th anniversary of independence (*Amritmahaotsav*) in 2022. *Modi hai to mumkinhai* (with Modi present, anything is conceivable) has become the mantra that sways the *Modi leher* (Modi wave) in the age of the marginals.

Social media and meme landscapes in South Asia reveal that Narendra Modi is also the most maligned public figure. Even though the opposition is deeply fragmented for many minor reasons, they are united in their desire to abuse Modi. Fascinating is the fact that Modi rarely responded to such personal attacks on social media platforms or in the ordinary course of parliamentary business. Instead, Modi responded to these insults and reacted appropriately, turning the abuse on its head by proudly announcing the hashtag '*Main Bhi Chowkidar*' (I too am a watchman) campaign for the 2019 Lok Sabha election on his Twitter profile (16 March 2019). This resonated with his mass as well as social media following. The '*chaiwallah*' (tea seller) tagline worked for Modi in 2014, while the '*kaamdaar*' (workaholic), and not the '*naamdaar*' (famous), tagline worked for Modi in 2019.

Likewise, Modi's brilliant connection with 'aspirational India' worked wonders in 2014, helped along by the discredited status of the UPA-II Government. Post-2014, Modi has unleashed a series of changes in reaching out to the people of India. Modi is the 'dream merchant' ('*sapno ka saudaagar*') of jobs and a shining economic future. Modi is an engaging leader: '*sab ka saath, sab ka vikaas*' (everyone's contribution, trust) for poverty elimination, not poverty alleviation. From 2014 to 2023, Modi systematically reinscribed the face of Hindutva under Atal Behari Vajpayee with his Modi-fied Hindutva version. Modi is the new apostle of Hindutva and democracy in India, carrying forward the ideas of *pitrubhoomi-punyabhoomi-karmabhoomi* (ancestral land, sacred land, land where one works) construct.

Neo-Hindutva in neoliberal times advocates for strategic recalibrations and accommodation of opposing viewpoints. As a continuation of global Hinduism/ global Hindutva, Neo-Hindutva seeks to patch up the crevices and voids that have opened up inside India's geographic limits. For instance, Hindutva in this age of neoliberalism and post-globalism has firmly distanced itself from the traditional Rashtriya Swayamsevak Sangh's (RSS) unwavering support for *swadeshi*, which refers to economic self-reliance and a muted advocacy for small traders and shopkeepers to welcome global capitalism with open arms. The catchphrase 'make in India' encapsulates this concept the best. The rise of China as a hyper-capitalist state and the self-proclaimed 'factory of the world' contrasts with the pressing need in India to create manufacturing jobs for the country's growing youth population. The animal spirit of turbocharged capitalism is also a good fit with the narrative of turbocharged nationalism that Modi and Shah have been pushing. The Making India Great Again (MIGA) mission of Modi 1.0 and Modi 2.0 has seen only limited influence from lobbies such as the Swadeshi Jagran Manch. During Vajpayee's tenure as prime minister, influential interest groups such as the Swadeshi Jagran Manch exerted great power.

Modi thus, while addressing the BJP's national council meeting in 2016, quoted Pandit Deendayal Upadhyaya: '*Musalmano ko na puraskruit karein, aur nahi unko tiraskruit karein, balki unka parishkaar karein. Musalmano ko na vote ki mandi ka maal, nahi koi ghrina ki vastusamjhe, useh apna samjhe*' (Don't reward Muslims, don't rebuke Muslims, reform them. Don't treat the

114 *Democracy in India: Continuities, Realignments, and Promises*

Muslims as mere vote banks, nor ostracize them, treat them as your kith and kin). Deendayal Upadhyay's message for bringing those in the margins to the center is the mantra of the BJP. 'Our government is committed to the welfare of the last person in the society' (BJP National Meet Session 2, 2016).

Unlike Atal Bihari Vajpayee, Modi cannot be accused of wearing a *mukhauta* (mask) to hide his agenda or of being the right prime minister in the wrong political party. Since 2014, when Amit Shah became president of the BJP, Modi has had the ideal alter ego to represent the ideological face, along with senior RSS ideologues and assorted loose-cannon personalities of the Sangh Parivar. This has allowed Modi to put the *vikaaspurush* (development/progressive man) face in the spotlight. This separation of duties has enabled Modi to keep his position as prime minister without being tarnished by the 'nasty party' stigma. Modi's strategic silence on the most toxic manifestations of Neo-Hindutva, such as the *Gaurakshak* (cow-vigilante) lynch gangs, during his first term indicated his political craft. By not openly condemning the cow-vigilante lynch gangs, Modi managed to maintain a delicate balance between appeasing his right-wing Hindu base and projecting a moderate image to the international community. This strategic silence allowed him to consolidate his power and focus on his economic and development agenda, while leaving the issue of religious extremism unaddressed.

Guru Golwalkar's call for 'the 1950 Constitution to be re-drafted to 'sweep away all autonomous and semi-autonomous states within Bharat,' 'bury for good all talk of a federal structure,' and 'establish Unitary form of Government' with the proclamation of 'One Country, One State, One Legislature, One Executive' has been quietly brought to the forefront of national debates by Hindutva in Modi's times. Modi's Neo-Hindutva, in its 1.0 and 2.0 iterations, is a universal sponge-cum-disinfectant that can purge (*shuddhikaran*) tainted opposition leaders who defect to the BJP. It's a more practical take on Hindutva's original political philosophy but maintains the same values and principles.

The emergence of the BJP as a major political force over the past four decades is one defining feature of Indian politics, while the proliferation of regional parties in many states of the Union is another (Andersen & Damle, 1987; Jaffrelot, 1998, 2007). Although the Congress's diminished influence no longer threatens the Neo-Hindutva's aim of pan-Indian dominance, the disparate collection of regional parties is, in the main, still a factor to deal with in their respective states.

In recognition of India's political evolution since the 1990s, the Neo-Hindutva adopted the 'cooperative federalism' mantra in 2014. The phrase is most commonly associated with Arun Jaitley's tenure as Finance Minister. Still, Modi has also used and echoed it in a broader context: 'Our diversity is our strength.' Vajpayee's two coalition governments (1998–1999 and 1999–2004), supported by regional parties, unquestionably provided a precedent for this development. Vajpayee never explicitly invoked federalism, but those arrangements were dictated by the needs of the BJP and its regional allies. In the era of Modi, the BJP no longer relies on regional parties for the survival of the central

Democracy in India: Continuities, Realignments, and Promises 115

government. Still, it celebrates the grand alliances and the spirit of 'cooperative federalism' that Vajpayee championed to combat the Congress and its allies.

At a BJP National Executive meeting in Bhubaneshwar in 2017, Amit Shah (with Modi at his side) declared that his job as party president would not be complete until the BJP dominated India 'from Panchayat to Parliament' and 'every state' of India had a BJP government (Mathew, 2017). This statement exemplifies the Neo-Hindutva movement's aspiration for pan-Indian political hegemony. The announcement was made while Shah was still riding high from the BJP's victory in the 2017 UP state election, so his tone was exaggerated, but the statement's underlying message was profound (Vyas, 2017).

In order for the BJP's state-based strategy to be successful, it needs to distance itself from its unitarist, anti-federal reputation. The BJP's dedication to an ideology centred around Hindu homogeneity disregards other identities and affiliations, necessitating the need for recalibration and readjustments. It must consider the unique circumstances of individual states and give due recognition to linguistic and other communitarian identities to incorporate them, along with others like caste, into the Hindu nationalist framework. This is the way forward to fulfill the founders' original vision in the current ecosystem. In his victory speech at the BJP office in New Delhi on the evening of 23 May 2019, Modi distilled a new coinage, '*NARA*' (the call), an acronym for converging the twin goals of 'national ambition and regional aspirations,' making the potent claim that the BJP represents both in equal measure and is the only party capable of bringing them about. Modi emphasized the new trend of *saralikaran* (ease of work) and reduced government regulation and the value of simple work by calling attention to the need to value and promote tasks that are often overlooked because of their perceived insignificance. With its roots in society's periphery, the BJP has made its way to the political mainstream by emphasizing the importance of the little things (Parliament Session, 2019).

During the ongoing Modi-era politics, the issues of Diversity & Inclusion (D&I) initiatives have taken centerstage. Whether engaging with politics, economics, leadership, development, or any other sphere, the themes of D&I take pivotal roles and give newer meanings to emerging global conversations. D&I are the mantras that allow individuals to step outside their comfort zones, challenge assumptions, learn and be inspired to work with driven purpose, and engage with each other with a sense of emotional connectedness. But what meanings or implications D&I take for themselves in the corridors of power politics would require investment and engagement. D&I, in the socio-political sphere, would bridge the gaps of gender, age, nationality, race, caste, and sexual orientation. D&I enhance a nation's effectiveness and stimulate innovation by broadening outlook, bettering understanding, improving communication, and providing a more incredible opportunity for team spirit. Taking clues from India's past and traversing current engagements in *sab ka saath, sab ka vikas, sab ka viswas, sab ka prayaas* (collective support, collective development/ development for all, collective trust, collective efforts), Modi's Neo-Hindutva braids together diversities and creates a pluriverse that works together as a unit

116 *Democracy in India: Continuities, Realignments, and Promises*

to manufacture an *Aatmanirbhar Bharat* (Self-reliant India) and soar to become *Viksit Bharat* (a developed nation with a US $30 trillion economy) by 2047. Modi's Neo-Hindutva *manthan* (churning) relies on the innovation South Asia experiences through the *jugaad* (hack, frugal innovation), bridging tradition with modernity, and the un-digitized with the digital.

Pandemic to Vaccine Diplomacy: *Neo-Sanjeevani*

Towards the closing months of 2019, when the deadly coronavirus or COVID-19 infected the world, India was engaged in altering its federal rhythm, oblivious of the threats of the seemingly small virus. On the political front, the monolith of exceptional leadership within the BJP came to be questioned with conflicting commands from the PMO (prime minister's office) and the home ministry on issues such as the NRC (National Register of Citizens) and Modi's weakening position in front of the surge of Amit Shah amidst the Delhi riot during Trump's 24–25 February 2020 visit. The tensions in the altering federal rhythm were furthered by the failure of the opposition parties and the left intelligentsia to cope with the issues of the CAA (Citizenship Amendment Act) and NRC (National Register of Citizens). Significant problems in the altering federal rhythm included the abolition of Article 370, and the triple *talaq*. Several experts linked the disgruntled-ness to religious bigotry, the political agenda of Hindutva, and the center's excesses. All these disturbed the federal rhythm and the reactions of a few states added to the dystopia (Chakraborty, 2020).

The pre-COVID-19 India navigated with the politics of accusations and counter-accusations of 'being anti-national,' 'saving democracy,' 'causing the Modi wave to wane,' scripting a counter-narrative to Modi (Vij, 2019; Jayal, 2019; Ellis-Petersen & Rahman, 2020). The contending and competing leaderships from across political parties and ideologies have attempted to manufacture a consensus among the fractured and disparate opposition through a *Mahagathbandhan* (grand alliance). *Bharat* (the often-used word for rural India) was in slumber in parts and partially awakened to issues of the agrarian economy, market, and indebtedness in other parts. India exhibited signs of dystopia when sweeping across traditional barriers, political leanings, institutional affiliations, and geographies. Everyday democracy before the arrival of the pandemic in India was marked by a strong conviction that 'everything is in order,' or something would be *jugaad* to mitigate the alien 'Chinese' virus. Social media across India was flooded with viral videos and narratives. These videos did little to inject a sense of caution and preparedness to combat the globetrotting virus's arrival in India. The English print media in India from December to March placed the pandemic on less critical pages (Chakraborty, 2020).

The first task in Modi's political juggernaut in his televised call for a *Janata* curfew on Sunday, 22 March 2020 was to build a sense of *Rashtra sadbhavana evam ekata* (national goodwill and unity) with Modi's charm as the pivot. This was followed by his announcement on 24 March 2020 of a complete nationwide lockdown for 21 days beginning on 25 March 2020 (Chakraborty, 2020).

Opposition leaders claimed that Modi, like the virus, was a threat to India, and that the opposition were trying to homogenize India while Modi and the BJP through Hindutva were acting as spreaders of hate and divisive politics. Protesters at the *Saheen Bagh* and mini *saheen baghs* across the states, as well as those participating in the *Kisan Andolan*, were projected as those who shared a desire to bring people together in the name of spreading messages of secularism, love, and tolerance. Overall, the PMO had a daunting task before Modi could regain control of the situation by announcing *Janata* curfew.

Modi deftly countered the criticisms of opposition parties and competing stalwarts of Indian democracy, proving once and for all that his hands are the ones pulling the puppet strings. Modi framed the 'nation clapping, blowing conches and beating drums' in honor of the *Corona Yoddhas* as an expression of 'gratitude' to the nurses, doctors, civilian police, municipal workers (*safai karamcharis*), unnamed civic volunteers, etc.

The pandemic highlighted the pervasiveness of ad hoc-ism and tokenism in the day-to-day operations of India's State, politics, and societies. The non-consensus on the closing/reopening of railways/train services while the continuation of air/flight services (*Vande Bharat* program) can be a point of discussion to drive forward the privileges of class concerns in decision-making and policy implementation (*The Wire*, 2020; Gupta, 2020). The questions relating to the migrants remained unaddressed.

In the midst of the World Health Organization's (WHO) shifting narrative on the 'virus' and the pandemic, India's vaccine diplomacy experienced its first real test. India's response to the global health crisis followed its tried-and-true protocols, with Indian doctors and nurses taking the helm (Jeffery, 1979; Brazelton, 2020). Modi turned the disadvantages posed to his leadership and government during the pandemic to his advantage by chanting the mantra of gratitude, *Vasudhaivakutumbakum*, treating neighboring countries as kin, and engaging in vaccine diplomacy. In times of global crisis, Modi engaged in some profound, thought-provoking ideas, sending medical aid as it had in the past to all nations regardless of their ideologies or political affiliations (Jeffery, 1979). The 'vaccine mission of India' became a global *Neo-sanjeevani* for humanity. Modi and Neo-Hindutva were quick to draw parallels between the mythological accounts of the Ramayana war and how Hanuman saved Laxmana (King Ram's brother) by bringing the healing herb *sanjeevani*. The India-made vaccine was labeled as India's *sanjeevani* for the entire world, not just Indians.

Vernacular Democratization and De-Colonialization: Detoxing the Nation

The term 'going vernacular' is used to describe a movement within Neo-Hindutva that, in modern India, reinterprets *being swadeshi* to emphasize an acceptance of diverse cultural practices and perspectives. Decolonization of ideas and knowledge, re-establishing faith in the region's dynamic political pluriverse, and the recovery of shared heritages that had been lost are some of

118　*Democracy in India: Continuities, Realignments, and Promises*

the goals of this project. Realigning the nation's gaze from the West to act in the multimodal gaze is a definitive worldview, as evident from the neighborhood first policy and the idea of extended neighborhood fashioned during the Modi era. This realignment of the nation's gaze was accomplished during Modi's tenure. Vernacularization of daily life and vernacularization of institutions are two interesting things that can occur when local ethnicities interact with novel political expressions and overarching templates of state/nation-building enterprise in South Asia (Michelutti, 2008). This can lead to interesting things happening in South Asia. Democracies have recognized the significance of vernacular speech in the post-global era, and this recognition has been couched in the language of 'going local.' Vernacular language has evolved into a politically charged expression of local identities. The degree to which individuals feel that they are part of a community has never been higher as a direct result of the above-mentioned factors and within the current phase of 'make in India' and 'think in India,' and there is a pervasive sense of 'localness.' During the 1970s, 1980s, and 1990s, linguistic exchange between previously isolated communities in the northeast were limited; post-2014 these opened up and became more fluid. This occurred despite the fact that racial tensions have been present in the region for many decades. We can examine the long history of the vernacular in the northeast region by using examples of colonial proselytism among certain ethnic groups.

Additionally, we can investigate the vernacularization and current trends of 'Modi-fications' from the post-colonial through the post-global era by looking at the lexicons and political jargons in circulation. Indian democracy is developing its lexicons and acronyms through vernacularization and extensive use of, and reference to, traditional practices of statecraft, governance, and people-centered administration. From *Aatmanirbhar Bharat* initiatives, to renaming spaces, places, and sites, and the refashioning of the corridors of power from Lutyens' Delhi to Central Vista are just a few examples of such 'Modi-fications.' Detoxifying the nation from its colonial baggage and the inherited intergenerational colonial mentality is the mantra that is being spun to reclaim India's lost glory. The mantra that is being chanted is that of *Making India Great Again (MIGA)*, and becoming the *Vishwa Guru*—the 'New Apostle for the world,' leading the way and being the beacon of salvation from the realms of lived physical democracies to spiritual ones and the call for global oneness (*Vasudhaivakutumbakum*).

Digital Democracy and Techno-Nationalism: Right-Wing in Its New *Avatar* (Incarnation)

In the age of Modi's Neo-Hindutva, 'everyday' digital and virtual interactions are (contested) sites of knowledge production and power. 'Virtual ethnography' enables us to gain insight into technology-mediated social interactions that could be used for political assertions and mobilizations. Scholars argue that a 'new' ethnography is needed because the internet is both a site for 'cultural

Democracy in India: Continuities, Realignments, and Promises 119

formations' and a 'cultural artifact' formed by the beliefs and assumptions of those who participate in the 'social world of the internet.'

Social media enables newer forms of political participation in demand and supply politics through Hacktivism, e-Participation, Government 2.0, and Memescape. Social media provides avenues to increase digital democracy interactions between the electorate and the political leadership across political parties in its myriad evolving forms. The ivory tower imagery of government and long-distance governance has been replaced by technologically savvy, 24/7, digitally connected government at the door of the electorate. Using virtual ethnography, the discussion in this sub-section of the chapter will unravel the evolving political vocabularies and electoral discourse in India post-2014. As a result, the media's role has shifted from facilitating rational public discourse and debate to shaping, constructing, and limiting public discourse to themes validated and approved by media corporations. Hence, the interconnection between a realm of public debate and individual participation has been fractured and transmuted into that of a sphere of political information and spectacle, in which citizens-consumers ingest and absorb entertainment and information passively. Thus, citizens-consumers are reduced to objects of news, information, and public affairs as they watch media presentations and discourses that shape public opinion.

In a socioeconomic setting where the poor face multiple barriers to accessing their entitlements and rights, such as a bureaucracy indifferent to the basic needs of the poor or multiple intermediaries who eat into their dues, digital service delivery solutions are warranted. Efficiency, the amount of time and money that recipients waste waiting in line, and the prevalence of confusion and corruption could all be reduced with the help of technological advancements. On the other hand, recent impromptu experiments in digital governance paint a very different picture, in which technology becomes yet another paradigm of subjugation, discipline, and exclusion, always to the detriment of the most defenseless members of society. The rise of networked governance and data-driven rule has led to a situation in which discretionary tasks formerly performed by humans are outsourced to machines, public services are privatized, and welfare is managed as effectively as possible.

An impending governance crisis seems likely in the Indian context, given the widespread problems with Aadhaar-based authentication and the shockwaves caused by the demonetization drive. Insights from the northeastern state of Mizoram demonstrate that the fate of the poor in rural areas and representative democracy itself are in jeopardy due to the interventions of extremist religious groups and groups with primal ties. For instance, in the northeastern state of Mizoram, a section of the population resisted digitizing themselves for the UID (Unique Identification Number)—'Aadhaar,' citing religious beliefs as outlined in the Book of Revelation of the Bible, which warned believers about the satanic code 666 (mark of the beast) (UNI, 2018). Due diligence, the necessary backhaul and infrastructure, and, most importantly, safeguards to ensure that the millions who live their lives unconnected and disenfranchised do not fall

120   *Democracy in India: Continuities, Realignments, and Promises*

through the cracks are essential to the success of top-down digitalization. Democratic accountability norms, rules, and practices are urgently needed in an institutional setting. In addition, it is crucial to assert the civic-public value of digital technologies so that information and fresh opportunities for collaboration can be used to strengthen local democracies and provide more power to ordinary people. For India to realize its potential as a 'digital India,' technology must be used to empower its citizens by increasing their ability to have their voices heard, increasing government transparency and accountability, and facilitating the 'right to be heard.'

Through the pandemic, India's democracy has seen an increase in digital footprints, which took the form of 'work from home,' 'education from home,' 'online shopping,' 'online payments,' and other similar activities. The cash-based economy in India was replaced with a cashless one. This digital wave, like the previous digital wave that introduced computerization during the times of Rajiv Gandhi, was met with stiff resistance from multiple sections, as well as the states and their Chief Ministers. In addition, the increase in the new mode of digital transactions and online presence has spawned a wave of 'online frauds,' 'digital honey-trapping,' phishing, digital scamming, identity theft—through SIM duplication, hacking social media accounts, etc.—and other illegal traps in the digital world of cybercrime activity. The development of digital landscapes has extended to the redesigning of urban and peri-urban spaces with a focus on diversity, inclusivity, and carbon footprint reduction in the form of 'smart cities.'

An increasingly significant part of the virtualization of the public sphere is the constant *manthan* (churning) of memes, viral videos, groups, and platforms in social media with political overtures and the combating of political ideologies. Modi redirected the focus of national political debates even in the digital spaces in this direction by voicing his concerns about the paradox of the absence or deliberate insufficiency of intra-party democracy among political parties in India. How are party leaders chosen democratically, and how is democracy implemented within political parties? Through technology-mediated outreach programs such as *Mann ki baat*, Modi stressed that newcomers should be encouraged to grow within party structures, decision-making processes, and democratic systems rather than just entrenched insiders. Among the many things that need more attention are the mechanisms for self-correction, the training of cadres, the incorporation of democratic values into fundamental principles, and the nurturing of emerging leadership. Modi has repeatedly expressed concern about the trend of dynastic politics in India's major political parties. Like other political parties, the BJP has dynasties at all levels of its leadership. However, what sets the BJP apart is that it does not converge into a single family when electing party presidents and ranks.

The delicate topic of tolerance for debate and dissent has been re-ignited by Modi even in the virtual spaces; for instance, through anthems for various protest movements such as the *shaheen bagh* movement, the CAA/CAB protest *andolan*, or the *Kisan andolan* (farmer's movement) that spilt over to become online *andolan* (online/virtual movement) and evolved into channels on YouTube such as *Aisi Taisi Democracy* with more than 151,000 subscribers (ATD, 2020, 2021).

Democracy in India: Continuities, Realignments, and Promises 121

The increasing digital and techno-nationalism in Neo-Hindutva times includes the virtualization of nationalism and patriotism (*Desh Bhakti*). The 'selfie-nationalism' that Neo-Hindutva has exploited includes taking a selfie after voting, the *Harghartiranga* (house to house 'Tricolour' national flag campaign), the 'selfie after vaccination,' and sharing photographs and the pursuit of revalidation through online circulation. Digital and techno-nationalism have given right-wing nationalism a new avatar. Prime ministerial hopefuls from opposition parties have been quick to point out the uneasiness in the realignments and express concern for the future of democracy. Interestingly their domestic policies and practices within their home states show no signs of caring about democratic principles.

An intriguing new trend that Modi's era has witnessed is the proliferation of virtual and digital political debates and the circulation of ideas. The internet is currently flooded with political memes, satire, and other humorous takes on current events. These memescapes, compiled in many different vernaculars, bring much-needed relief to India through humor and cross-cultural communication that transcends politics. While projected 'PM candidates' from different parties and popular leaders from various regions have expressed offense at political satire, cartoons, and caricatures, Narendra Modi has emphasized the importance of investing in humor to liven up the otherwise dull and tedious process of politics (PTI, 2017).

Revisiting the Tolerance Question

Since political parties are inherently divided, revisiting the question of tolerance is crucial. Unlike issue-specific advocacy groups, political parties focus on a wide range of topics, and within the same ideological framework, it is normal for members to hold slightly different views. This helps to explain why Congress has remained an umbrella party where different opinions coexist. The BJP and its umbrella organization, the Sangh Parivar, are coalitions of various groups that share a commitment to Hindutva but operate independently from one another. After 1967, Congress dispute resolution mechanisms began to be dismantled. Afterwards, it frequently lost elections because its candidates stopped engaging in compromise.

The BJP is not very different. Conflicts like the recent one involving Yashwant Sinha occur because people are afraid to discuss their differences openly, which leads to unpleasant incidents. Sinha and three other 'elders' wrote a joint letter in 2015 pointing to the vanishing of inner-party democracy; if a response mechanism had existed or been created at the time, a senior leader would not have felt the need to express his concerns publicly. Except for choosing the party president in a manner unconstrained by the rule of dynastic succession, the BJP's democratic processes are primarily ceremonial. The letter (2015) mentioned that a small group also selects the chief of influential people behind closed doors. One instructive reminder is how the opposition of L.K. Advani to Modi's nomination as the BJP's prime ministerial candidate was crushed. The

122 Democracy in India: Continuities, Realignments, and Promises

Election Commission is vigilant in protecting the independence granted to it by the constitution, resulting in a more representative electoral process. It's encouraging that Prime Minister Narendra Modi has raised the issue of weak or nonexistent party democracy. Because of this flaw, India can never develop into a true democracy, remaining instead a procedural one. Political parties continue to resemble oligarchies, despite a more representative electoral process and, with a few exceptions, a vigorous defense of the Election Commission's constitutionally mandated autonomy. Modi, on the other hand, has demonstrated excellent timing in raising his concerns. That would imply his perspective is limited to the process of party leadership elections. The BJP continues to exploit the dynasty scare campaign and paint the Congress as a party that values dynastic succession over internal democracy while portraying itself as non-dynastic and democratic. Yet the Congress is hardly the only political organization advocating for dynastic rule. The BJP, like most other political parties, has multiple dynasties at different tiers of leadership.

Furthermore, intra-party democracy cannot be solely evaluated by looking at the process by which the president is chosen. We must also examine the party candidate selection procedures that foster patronage networks. The allegations that electoral tickets are given to favorites or sold for money are commonplace. It is concerning how hazy and uncontrolled it is. All parties' use of the 'winnability' factor is profoundly undemocratic. Criminal histories are ignored, as are ideological and program commitments, and there is no regard for evidence of corruption. In this scenario, the party's 'High Command' has become 'higher,' and the party is seen as nothing more than a voting machine to win elections, so the democratic processes of choosing candidates are discouraged. Tickets are routinely given to defectors from other parties, a sign that party loyalty is less important than ideological and organizational loyalty. The call for more internal party democracy is not unique to Modi. The issue has been studied by numerous government committees and commissions, all of which have made recommendations.

The centrality of religion in societies in India and plural cosmology handed over through generations had evolved into a lived experience of 'temperaments of tolerance' quintessentially understood as 'sarva-dharma samabhava' (Singh, 1993; Larson, 2001). The Indian State is secular in the sense that its constitution guarantees full religious liberty to all individuals and groups and forbids discrimination against any citizen on grounds of only religion and caste (Smith, 1963; Tejani, 2008). It is just as well that it is not secular in the Western sense of complete separation between church and state, for the state reserves for itself the right to intervene in the interest of necessary social reforms in matters that customarily come under the purview of religion. The Indian constitution thus guarantees individual and corporate freedom of religion and citizenship rights, and the State is not constitutionally connected with any particular religion, nor does it deliberately seek to promote or interfere with it (Misra, 1996: 101–103).

Indian secularism subscribes to the Hindu philosophical tenet that all religion has elements of truth, and no religion can claim the monopoly on truth.

Democracy in India: Continuities, Realignments, and Promises 123

Hinduism has never put forth the claims that it alone is the true religion (Jingram, 1995: 35). The spirit of tolerance stems from this foundational understanding of secularism.

Gandhi and India: Yesterday, Today, Tomorrow

Gandhi and his phantom must be interrogated and located in India's nation-building program (Raghurmamraju, 2006; Rudolph & Rudolph, 2006; Lal, 2008). Gandhi's ghost haunts the whole horizon, making a simple question like 'Where do you not find Gandhi?' difficult to answer. Gandhi seems to be omnipresent, from currency to posters, picture frames in offices, government and non-government, Bollywood movies, nationalist songs, to naming of streets and roads. Interestingly even a simple pictorial reference to Gandhi changes the course and future of social movements in India. For example, on the first day of Anna Hazare's first phase of fast in Jantar Mantar, New Delhi, in April 2011, a Muslim leader objected mildly to the broad picture of *Bharat Mata* (Sarkar, 1987) iconography of Mother India loosely drawn from the Hindu Goddess *Durga* placed as a centerpiece and mentioned that the movement seemed inclined towards the right-wing Hindu *nationalist* faction—the RSS. The organizers of the Anna Hazare movement immediately replaced the controversial picture of *Bharat Mata* with that of a photograph of Mahatma Gandhi (Pandita & Gandhi, 2011). In short, Gandhi has become a convenient and effective consensus-building icon in post-colonial India, a brand in itself, attractive-emotive merchandise with an ever-ready market.

Media and films in part convey or reaffirm reality and play a crucial role in reproducing the same and becoming visual texts embedded with messages. People's perception of media content influences the way they understand the world and react to other people (Shrum, 1994: 50–73). Media largely remains a symbolic representation of power and its contesting strands in a given society (Curran & Gurevitch, 1991; Fairclough, 1995; Folkerts & Lacy, 2004; Rose, 2007; Goodwin & Whannel, 1992; Keane, 1991). In this politics of representation, vocality, and audibility, the media has realized the weight and effect of keeping alive the image of Gandhi in the minds of the *aamaadmi* (commoner) in India. Consequently, media, namely print, television (Wober & Gunter, 1988), cinema, and the 'new media' (internet and the virtual spaces, and also cell/mobile communications) (Castells, 2000) have systematically spun and re-spun the image of Gandhi both as 'Mahatma' and as 'Bapu' (Parekh, 2001; Mukherjee, 1993; Prabhu & Rao, 1967; Carter, 1995; Scharff, 2008; Byrne, 1988).

In contemporary India, 'Gandhi' comes in many forms, including staunch Gandhities with Gandhi caps, moderate Gandhites, affectionate Gandhites, inclined Gandhites, the Congress version of Gandhi, the BJP version, Kejriwal's Gandhi and Gandhigiri, pseudo-Gandhites, Gandhi of the rich, Gandhi of the poor, Gandhi of India, Gandhi of Bharat, and many others. In all the hues of 'Gandhi' projected publicly and made visible in contemporary India, a token lip service to Gandhi stands out. In short, having a mere pictorial reference to

124 *Democracy in India: Continuities, Realignments, and Promises*

'Gandhi' or just mentioning '*Gandhi ne bola tha* ...' ('Gandhi had said ...') provides authenticity sufficient to attract the attention not just of the multitude but also the state. In short, the name Gandhi exerts a significant influence on the target audience.

It is intriguing to reconsider the word or term 'Gandhigiri.' We frequently use Hindi terms like 'Goondagiri' and 'Dadagiri' (also 'Didigiri') to refer to the brutish force or tactics used by goons, anti-socials, thugs, and con artists. Consider Gandhian methods stylized in Bollywood and served to the audience through films that purport to re-invent Gandhi's teachings: 'Gandhi, the man, was once the message. In post-liberalization India, "Gandhigiri" is the message' (Ghosh & Babu, 2006).

To lie or use unfair means for a good/noble cause, for example, is considered equivalent to 'a thousand truths.' Similarly, acts modeled after Robin Hood— robbing the wealthy and distributing the loot to the poor—are viewed as religious, noble, and Gandhian in nature. However, Gandhian notions of 'means and ends' are obliterated in this Bollywood-inspired imagery. Gandhi believed that means were as sacred as ends (Kriplani, 1958: 81–85; Iyer, 1973). These reflect the specter of Gandhi that haunts India's nationalist fervor.

The emulation of cinematic Gandhigiri in everyday dissent or protest has taken a viral form across India. From presenting roses to opposition parties in parliament (Post Jagran, 2015), to offering roses to lawbreakers by police personnel (Daily Post, 2018), to bestowing roses and flowers upon doctors on strike (Rediff News, 2006), and to dispatching pink panties to misogynists (NDTV, 2009), to substituting the customary legal notices with flowers when pursuing bank loans from evaders (NDTV, 2018), the practice of Gandhigiri has manifested in various innovative and popular actions. However, the ideals of Gandhi seem to be selectively emulated. For instance, when the current BJP-led government at the center announced the *Swachh Bharat Mission*, the public were taken aback. The broom has symbolic connotations with the lower castes in South Asia and carries significant caste images. The *Swachh Bharat* campaign faced criticism in response to this association (Rediff News, 2017). Why would the upper castes and educated English-speaking elites engage in the act of sweeping with a 'broom'? (Rediff News 2016). Few of my respondents (during interviews in Darjeeling in 2015) mentioned, 'If we clean and sweep the offices and surroundings, what will the *jamadars* (sweeper caste) do? Why should we do the cleaning when we have *jamadars?*'

It took a while for the broom to become an attractive photographic 'prop' to grab the media's attention through hashtags, virtual contests, and viral challenges. Gandhigiri thus became exhibitionist in overdrive in a substantial deviation from Gandhi's teachings.

As a conclusion to my arguments, I would reiterate that the 'Gandhian world visions,' despite their widespread acclaim, remain highly controversial. It elicits numerous academic and non-academic mutterings ranging from total acceptance to strong rebuttal to an uncomfortable choked endorsement (Parekh, 2001: 111–126), as expressed in the popular adage: '*Majboorika Naam*

Democracy in India: Continuities, Realignments, and Promises 125

Mahatma Gandhi' (helplessness thy name is Mahatma Gandhi). In contemporary times in India, people have accepted Gandhi uncritically as a convenient and effective icon for consensus building in a fragmented and contested sociopolitical terrain. Whether we want it or not, Indians fall back on Gandhi, making Gandhi over the years in post-colonial India ephemeral, infallible, and godlike.

The wave of Gandhigiri has engulfed and encircled the Indian public while validating the Habermasian conception of the public sphere, where private individuals united to form a multitude whose 'public reason' would check state power, and where the public sphere consisted of organs of information and political debate like newspapers and journals. The Internet and social media—Facebook, Twitter, and YouTube—have expanded democratic participation and debates, making new public spaces for political intervention more likely. These spheres and spaces can revitalize democracy and spread critical and progressive ideas, but they also offer new opportunities for manipulation, social control, conservative propaganda, and human differences. These 'new public spheres' reflect 'cyberspace democracy' participation. 'New' media, like 'old,' create 'new public spheres and spaces for information, debate, and participation' (Gitlin, 1998: 168–175).

Although modern neo-Gandhian movements claim to be nonviolent and peaceful, their tactics reveal resentment and hostility towards the 'system.' The youth population that Gandhigiri seeks to mobilize and direct is largely unfamiliar with Gandhi's ideas and methods. In a nutshell, today's Indian youth misinterpret Gandhi's message and fail to place him in the context of India's rapidly changing social and political landscape. The potential longevity of 'brand Gandhi,' which is dependent on the maneuverings and 'media management' of the manipulative market, can be seen in the continuity and realignment of Gandhi's popular iconography in India. The BJP government has also made an effort to recognize and honor leaders who have been overshadowed by stalwarts, as well as tribal icons from India's northeastern regions who have played important roles in the national movement. This is demonstrated by the annual commemoration of Gandhi and Lal Bahadur Shastri's birthdays, as well as the honoring of tribal icons such as Birsa Munda and U Tirot Sing Syiem, and the centering of national leaders such as Sardar Patel and Subhas Chandra Bose. Critics see this as the BJP's attempt to appropriate historical figures, tribal icons, and Congress leaders from the freedom movement.

Some Closing Thoughts

India has progressed beyond the nascent stage of the complex interactive process of state formation from traditional to modern. State-society-governance-citizenship ghosts plague it, as they do most young democracies. Mis-governance, political senility, the normalization of *bhrastachar* (corruption), *dalals* (broker/middlemen), and *ghus* (bribery), and a vigilant political culture demanding detoxification from past corruption and misgovernance are all features of India's contemporary democratic political culture. The *Janata* (people)

126 *Democracy in India: Continuities, Realignments, and Promises*

did not exhibit any hostility or indifference towards the state and unstable, short-lived coalition governments in the 1990s, nor did any other experiments in statecraft begin during that time. It's puzzling how the *Janata* have managed to persevere and put up with political senility for so long. Rapidly overcoming the *Praja-raja syndrome* that plagued them, urban *Janata Janardans* (citizens) adopted a newfound vigilance and a penchant for video documentation. When will India's electorate become *Jagrukta Sachet Janata Janardan* (informed, mindful citizens)? Time alone will provide a response. The right wing has rethought the connection between the state, the nation, and the citizen. Two new *jugalbandi* (entwined duet) of 'we-ness' have been unleashed: one within the union of India; and the other in its neighborhood.

'We-ness' for India: *Choronkal ki batein, kal ki baatpurani, naedaur mein likhenge milke nayi kahani; Hum Hindustaani, Hum Hindustaani* (Forget the past. It's a bygone era. We will together write a new story in the new era. We Indians, We Indians). [Singer: Mukesh. Film: *Hum Hindustani* (1960). Music: Usha Khanna. Dir. Ram Mukherjee]

'We-ness' for the neighborhood: *Yeh dosti hum nahi todenge. Todenge dam magar tera saath na chorenge* (We will never break our friendship until our last breath. We will not leave each other). [Singers: Kishore Kumar and Manna Dey. Film: *Sholay* (1975). Music: R.D. Burman. Dir. Ramesh Sippy]

These choral expressions of 'we-ness' elicit a wide range of feelings, from appreciation to concern to friendship to ecological sensitivity to a sense of global interconnectedness as styled by Modi. The Neo-Hindutva and the mantra of a pluriversal *Atmanirbhar Bharat* seek to re-awaken India (*Bharat kapunar navnirman*) and detoxify itself from the three burdens of colonialism, inheritance-legacy, and entitlements; and invoke a sense of unrestrained, unconditional, unlimited penance-like service *tapa* (heat, energy) to collectively churn (*manthan*) an ode to the nation (*Ma Bharati*).

References

Ali, Tariq. 1985. *An Indian Dynasty: The Story of the Nehru-Gandhi Family.* New York: Putnam.

Andersen, Walter K. & Shridhar D. Damle. 1987. *The Brotherhood in Saffron: The Rashtriya Swayamsevak Sangh and Hindu Revivalism.* Boulder: Westview Press.

Aslam, M. 2007. *Panchayati Raj in India.* New Delhi: National Book Trust.

ATD. 2020. *Hum KaagazNahiDikhaayenge.* https://www.youtube.com/watch?v=AISW4 N6uGQA retrieved on 10 March 2023.

ATD. 2021. *Super Spreader Anthem.* https://www.youtube.com/watch?v=yaqaNsizl0w retrieved on 10 March 2023.

Baird, Robert. 1981. *Religion in Modern India.* New Delhi: Manohar.

Baker, Christopher J. 1976. *The Politics of South India, 1920–1937.* Cambridge: Cambridge University Press.

Bhargava, Rajeev. 2000. 'Is Secularism a Value in Itself?' pp.101–109, in Imtiaz Ahmad, Partha S. Ghosh, & Helmut Reifeld (eds.), *Pluralism and Equality, Values in Indian Society and Politics.* New Delhi: Sage Publications.

Democracy in India: Continuities, Realignments, and Promises 127

Bhattacharjee, Arun. 1992. *Rajiv Gandhi: Life and Message.* New Delhi: Ashish.

BJPNational MeetSession 2. 2016. https://www.dnaindia.com/india/report-bjp-nationa l-meet-session-2-watch-livestreaming-of-pm-modi-s-speech-2258561 retrieved 10 March 2023.

Blondel, Jean. 1972. *Comparing Political Systems.* New York: Praeger.

Bobbio, Norberte. 1987. *The Future of Democracy: A Defense of the Rules of the Game.* Minneapolis: University of Minnesota Press.

Bollen, Kenneth. 1979. 'Political Democracy and the Timing of Development.' *American Sociological Review* 44: 572–587.

Brass, Paul R. 1994. *The New Cambridge History of India, IV.1: The Politics of India since Independence.* Cambridge: Cambridge University Press.

Brazelton, Mary Augusta. 2020. 'Viral Reflections: Placing China in Global Health Histories.' *The Journal of Asian Studies* 79 (3) (August): 579–588. doi:10.1017/ S0021911820002284.

Brecher, Michael. 1976. *The Politics of Succession in India.* Westport: Greenwood.

Brown, Judith M. 1985. *Modern India: The Origins of an Asian Democracy.* New Delhi: Oxford University Press.

Byrne, Donn. 1988. *Mahatma Gandhi: The Man and His Message.* Hyderabad: Orient Longman.

Carras, Mary C. 1979. *Indira Gandhi in the Crucible of Leadership.* Boston: Beacon Press.

Carter, April. 1995. *Mahatma Gandhi: A Selected Bibliography.* Westport: Greenwood Publishing Group.

Castells, M. 2000. *The Rise of Network Society.* Oxford: Blackwell.

Chakraborty, Anup Shekhar. 2020. 'The Pandemic and Dystopia: Complicating the Coming of the Virus to India.' *Multidimensions Magazine*, 24 June. https://multidim ensionmagazine.com/2020/06/24/the-pandemic-and-dystopia-complicating-the-com ing-of-the-virus-to-india/ retrieved on 10 March 2023.

Chanchreek, K.L. & Saroj Prasad (eds.). 1993. *Crisis in India.* Delhi: H.K. Publishers.

Chandhoke, Neera. 1999. *Beyond Secularism: The Rights of Religious Minorities*, Delhi: Oxford University Press.

Chandhoke, Neera. 2004. 'Re-presenting the Secular Agenda for India,' pp. 53–58, in Mushirul Hasan (ed.), *Will Secular India Survive?*New Delhi: Imprint One.

Chandra, Bipan. 1993. *Essays on Contemporary India.* New Delhi: Har-Anand.

Chandra, Kanchan. 2004. *Why Ethnic Parties Succeed.* Cambridge: Cambridge University Press.

Chellaney, Brahma. 1993. *Nuclear Proliferation: The U.S.-Indian Conflict.* New Delhi: Orient Longman.

Chowdhury, D.R. & J. Keane. 2021. *To Kill a Democracy: India's Passage to Despotism.* Oxford: Oxford University Press.

Corbridge, Stuart & John Harriss. 1999. *Reinventing India: Liberalization, Hindu Nationalism and Popular Democracy.* Cambridge: Polity Press.

Corbridge, Stuart, Glyn Williams, Manoj Srivastava, & Rene Veron. 2005. *Seeing the State: Governance and Governmentality in India.* New York: Cambridge University Press.

Curran, James & Michael Gurevitch (eds.). 1991. *Mass Media and Society.* London: Edward Arnold.

Dahl, Robert. 1971. *Polyarchy: Participation and Opposition.* New Haven: Yale University Press.

Dahl, Robert. 1982. *Dilemmas of Pluralist Democracy.* New Haven: Yale University Press.

128 *Democracy in India: Continuities, Realignments, and Promises*

Daily Post. 2018. 'Gandhigiri by Police Officials: Lawbreakers Offered Roses to Wear Helmets in Future.' 28 March. https://dailypost.in/news/diaries/punjab-diary/gandhigir i-by-doraha-traffic-police-law-breakers-offered-rose-to-wear-helmets-in-future/ retrieved on 1 October 2018.

Das, Veena. 1992. *Mirrors of Violence: Communities, Riots, and Survivors in South Asia*. New Delhi: Oxford University Press.

Das Gupta, Jyotirindra. 1989. 'India: Democratic Becoming and Combined Development,' pp. 53–104, in L. Diamond, J. Linz, & S.M. Lipset (eds.), *Democracy in Developing Countries: Asia*. Boulder: Lynne Rienner.

Derrett, J. Duncan. 1968. *Religion, Law, and the State in India*. London: Faber.

Dhanagare, D.N. 1983. *Peasant Movements in India, 1920–1950*. New Delhi: Oxford University Press.

Diamond, Larry. 1989a. 'Beyond Authoritarianism and Totalitarianism: Strategies for Democratization.' *The Washington Quarterly* 12 (Winter): 141–163.

Diamond, Larry. 1989b. 'Introduction: Persistence, Erosion, Breakdown and Renewal,' pp. 1–52, in L. Diamond, J. Linz, & S.M. Lipset (eds.), *Democracy in Developing Countries: Asia*. Boulder: Lynne Rienner.

Diamond, Larry, Juan Linz, & Seymour Martin Lipset (eds.). 1990. *Politics in Developing Countries: Comparing Experiences with Democracy*. Boulder: Lynne Rienner.

Doornbos, M. & Sudipta Kaviraj. 1999. *Dynamics of State Formation: India & Europe Compared*. Delhi: Sage Publications.

Dreze, Jean & Amartya Sen. 2002. *India: Development & Participation*. New Delhi: Oxford University Press.

Eldridge, P.J. 1970. *The Politics of Foreign Aid in India*. New York: Schocken.

Ellis-Petersen, Hannah and Shaikh Azizur Rahman. 2020. 'Delhi's Muslims Despair of Justice after Police Implicated in Riots.' *The Guardian*. https://www.theguardian.com/world/2020/mar/16/delhis-muslims-despair-justice-police-implicated-hindu-riots retrieved 20 May 2020.

Fairclough, Norman. 1995. *Media Discourse*. London: Edward Arnold.

Folkerts, Jean & Stephen Lacy. 2004. *The Media in Your Life: An Introduction to Mass Communication*. New Delhi: Pearson Education.

Ganguly, Sumit, Larry Diamond, & Marc Plattner (eds.). 2007. *The State of India's Democracy*. Baltimore: Johns Hopkins University.

Ghose, S.K. 1992. *Politics of Violence: Dawn of a Dangerous Era*. Springfield: Nataraj.

Ghosh, Arunabha & Tapan Babu. 2006. 'Lage Raho Munna Bhai: Unravelling Brand "Gandhigiri".' *Economic & Political Weekly* (23–29 December): 5225–5227.

Gitlin, T. 1998. 'Public Sphere or Public Sphericules?' pp. 168–175, in T. Liebes & J. Curran (eds.), *Media, Ritual, Identity*. London: Routledge.

Goodwin, A. & G. Whannel (eds.). 1992. *Understanding Television*. London: Routledge.

Gopal, Sarvepalli. 1980. *Jawaharlal Nehru: An Anthology*. New Delhi: Oxford University Press.

Gopal, Sarvepalli (ed.). 1991. *Anatomy of a Confrontation: The Babri Masjid-Ramjanmabhumi Issue*. New Delhi: Viking.

Gupta, Shekhar. 2020. 'Vande Bharat vs Bharat ke bande: Can Narendra Modi Be Losing His Political Touch So Soon?' *The Print*. 9 May. https://theprint.in/national-interest/vande-bharat-vs-bharat-ke-bande-can-narendra-modi-be-losing-his-political-touch-so-soon/417506/ retrieved 20 May 2020.

Gupte, Pranay. 1985. *Vengeance: India after the Assassination of Indira Gandhi*. New York: Norton.

Democracy in India: Continuities, Realignments, and Promises   129

Gupte, Pranay. 1992. *Mother India: A Political Biography of Indira Gandhi*. New York: Scribner.

Hardgrave, Robert L., Jr. & Stanley A. Kochanek. 1993. *India: Government and Politics in a Developing Nation*. 5th edn. Fort Worth: Harcourt Brace Jovanovich.

Harrison, Selig S. 1960. *India: The Most Dangerous Decades*. Princeton: Princeton University Press.

Hart, Henry C. (ed.). 1976. *Indira Gandhi's India: A Political System Reappraised*. Boulder: Westview Press.

Heinsath, Charles. 1964. *Indian Nationalism and Hindu Social Reform*. Princeton: Princeton University Press.

Heller, Patrick. 2000. 'Degrees of Democracy: Some Comparative Lessons from India.' *World Politics* 52 (July): 484–519.

Hill, John L. (ed.). 1991. *The Congress and Indian Nationalism: Historical Perspectives*. Westwood: Riverdale.

Humbers, Philippe. 1992. *The Rajiv Gandhi Years: Sunshine and Shadows*. New Delhi: Vimot.

Huntington, Samuel P. 1991. 'Democracy's Third Wave.' *Journal of Democracy* 2 (2) (Spring): 12–34.

Iyer, R.N. 1973. *The Moral and Political Thought of Mahatma Gandhi*. New York: Oxford University Press.

Jaffrelot, Christophe & Sanjay Kumar (eds.). 2009. *Rise of the Plebeians? The Changing Face of Indian Legislative Assemblies*. New Delhi: Routledge.

Jaffrelot, Christophe. 2003. *India's Silent Revolution: The Rise of the Lower Castes in North India*. London: Hurst.

Jaffrelot, Christophe. 2007. *Hindu Nationalism: A Reader*. Princeton: Princeton University Press.

Jaffrelot, Christophe. 1998. *The Hindu Nationalist Movement in India*. Columbia: Columbia University Press.

Jai, Janak Raj & Rajiv Jai. 1999. *Political Trends: Revival of Two Party System in India: Ruling vs. Combined Opposition*. New Delhi: Regency Publications.

Jain, C.K. (ed.). 1992. *Rajiv Gandhi and Parliament*. New Delhi: CBS.

Jayakar, Pupul. 1992. *Indira Gandhi: A Biography*. New Delhi: Penguin.

Jayal, Niraja Gopal (ed.). 2001. *Democracy in India*. Delhi: Oxford University Press.

Jayal, Niraja Gopal. 2019. 'Faith-Based Citizenship: The Dangerous Path India is Choosing.' *India Forum*. 1 November. https://www.theindiaforum.in/article/faith-cri terion-citizenship retrieved 19 December 2019.

Jayal, Niraja Gopal & Pratap Bhanu Mehta. 2010. *The Oxford Companion to Politics in India*. Delhi: Oxford University Press.

Jeffrey, Robin (ed.). 1978. *People, Princes, and Paramount Power: Society and Politics in Indian Princely States*. New Delhi: Oxford University Press.

Jeffery, Roger. 1979. 'Recognizing India's Doctors: The Institutionalization of Medical Dependency, 1918–39." *Modern Asian Studies* 13 (2) (April): 302–326.

Jingram, Saral. 1995. *Secularism in India: A Reappraisal*. New Delhi: Har-Anand Publications.

Kapur, Rajiv. 1987. *Sikh Separatism: The Politics of Faith*. New Delhi: Vikas.

Kashyap, Subhash. 1969. *The Politics of Defection*. New Delhi: National Publishing House.

Kashyap, Subhash C. 2011. *Our Political System*. New Delhi: National Book Trust.

130 *Democracy in India: Continuities, Realignments, and Promises*

Kaviraj, Sudipta. 2010. *The Imaginary Institution of India: Politics and Ideas.* New Delhi: Permanent Black.

Kaviraj, Sudipta & Sunil Khilnani (eds.). 2001. *Civil Society: History and Possibilities.* Cambridge: Cambridge University Press.

Keane, J. 1991. *The Media and Democracy.* Cambridge: Polity Press.

Keay, John. 1992. *Democracy and Discontent: India's Growing Crisis of Governability.* Cambridge: Cambridge University Press.

Kohli, Atul. 1990. *Democracy and Discontent: India's Growing Crisis of Governability.* Cambridge: Cambridge University Press.

Kohli, Atul (ed.). 2001. *The Success of India's Democracy.* Cambridge: Cambridge University Press.

Kothari, Rajni. 1970. *Politics in India.* Boston: Little, Brown.

Kriplani, Krishna (ed.). 1958. *All Men Are Brothers: Life and Thoughts of Mahatma Gandhi as Told in His Own Words (Centennial Reprint 1869–1969).* Switzerland: UNESCO.

Lal, Vinay. 2008. 'The Gandhi Everyone Loves to Hate.' *Economic & Political Weekly* (4–11 October).

Larson, Gerald James. 2001. 'Introduction: The Secular State in a Religious Society,' pp. 1–14, in Gerald James Larson (ed.), *Religion and Personal Law in Secular India: A Call for Judgement.* Bloomington: Indiana University Press.

Madan, T.N. 1997. *Secularism and Fundamentalism in India: Modern Myths, Locked Minds.* New Delhi: Oxford University Press.

Madhav, Ram. 2023. 'Don't cry for democracy.' *The Indian Express.* 11 March. https://indianexpress.com/article/opinion/columns/ram-madhav-writes-dont-cry-for-democracy-8489918/ retrieved on 12 March 2023.

Mahalingam, T.V. 1967. *South Indian Polity.* Madras: University of Madras.

Mahapatra, Chintamani & Netajee Abhinandan (ed.). 2018. *India's Engagement with Extended Neighbourhood: Issues & Challenges.* Toronto: Roots Media.

Masani, Zaheer. 1976. *Indira Gandhi: A Biography.* Farmington: Brown.

Mathew, Liz. 2017. 'Amit Shah's target: Panchayat to Parliament, and every state. *The Indian Express.* 16 April. https://indianexpress.com/article/india/amit-shah-target-panchayat-to-parliament-and-ever-state-4614855/ retrieved on 10 March 2023.

Michelutti, Lucia. 2008. *The Vernacularization of Democracy: Politics, Caste and Religion in India.* New Delhi: Routledge.

Misra, R.S. 1996. *Hinduism and Secularism: A Critical Study.* New Delhi: Motilal Banarsidass.

Mohanty, Manoranjan. 2011. 'People's Movement and the Anna Upsurge.' *Economic & Political Weekly* 46 (38) (17–23 September): 16–19.

Moore, Alfred. 2017. *Critical Elitism: Deliberation, Democracy, and the Problem of Expertise.* Cambridge: Cambridge University Press.

Moraes, Dom. 1980. *Indira Gandhi.* Boston: Little, Brown.

Morris-Jones, W.H. 1971. *The Government and Politics of India.* London: Hutchinson.

Mukherjee, Rudrangshu (ed.). 1993. *The Penguin Gandhi Reader.* New Delhi: Penguin Books India.

Nanda, B.R. 1958. *Mahatma Gandhi.* Boston: Beacon Press.

Nandy, Ashis. 1992. 'The Politics of Secularism and the Recovery of Religious Tolerance,' pp. 69–72, in Veena Das (ed.), *Mirrors of Violence: Communities, Riots and Survivors in South Asia.* New Delhi: Oxford University Press.

Democracy in India: Continuities, Realignments, and Promises 131

Nandy, Ashis. 1998. 'The Politics of Secularism and the Recovery of Religious Toleration,' pp. 324–325, in Rajeev Bhargava (ed.), *Secularism and Its Critics*. New Delhi: Oxford University Press.

Nandy, Ashis. 2007. 'Closing the Debate on Secularism: A Personal Statement,' pp. 107–117, in Anuradha Dingwaney Needham & Rajeswari Sunder Rajan (eds.), *The Crisis of Secularism in India*. New Delhi: Permanent Black.

Narain, Harsh. 1993. *The Ayodhya Temple Mosque Dispute*. New Delhi: Penman.

Nayar, Kuldip & Kushwant Singh. 1984. *Tragedy of Punjab: Operation Bluestar and After*. New Delhi: Vision Books.

NDTV. 2009. 'Pink Chaddi Campaign.' 18 December. https://www.ndtv.com/photos/news/pink-chaddi-campaign-1793#photo-18320 retrieved on 1 October 2018.

NDTV. 2018. 'PNB Embraces Gandhigiri to Recover NPAs Amounting to 1,800 Crore Rupees.' April 21. https://www.ndtv.com/business/pnb-embraces-gandhigiri-to-recover-npas-amounting-to-1-800-crore-rupees-1840897 retrieved on 1 October 2018.

Noble, Allen G. & Ashok K. Dutt (eds.). 1982. *India: Cultural Patterns and Processes*. Boulder: Westview Press.

Nugent, Nicholas. 1991. *Rajiv Gandhi: Son of a Dynasty*. New Delhi: UBS.

Ozturk, O. 2021. 'Democratic Erosion in India: A Case Study.' *Democratic Erosion*. 5 February. https://www.democratic-erosion.com/2021/02/05/democratic-erosion-in-india-a-case-study/.

Palshikar, S. 2021. 'Understanding the Downslide of India's Democracy.' *The Indian Forum*. 5 May.

Palshikar, Suhas, K.C. Suri, & Yogendra Yadav (eds.). 2014. *Party Competition in Indian States: Electoral Politics in Post-Congress Polity*. New Delhi: Oxford University Press.

Pandita, Rahul & Jatin Gandhi. 2011. 'Spin Doctors: The Story of Their Experiments with Gandhi.' *OPEN* (5 September): 20–23.

Pantham, Thomas. 1997. 'Indian Secularism and Its Critics.' *The Review of Politics* 59 (3) (Summer): 523–524.

Parekh, Bhikhu. 2001. *Gandhi: A Very Short Introduction*. New York: Oxford University Press.

Park, Richard L. & Bruce Bueno de Mesquita. 1979. *India's Political System*. Englewood Cliffs: Prentice-Hall.

Parliament Session. 2019. 'PM Modi Says National Ambition with Regional Aspiration Is Our Mantra.' https://youtu.be/9rlmt9yBN5A retrieved on 10 March 2023.

Post Jagran. 2015. 'Gandhigiri in Lok Sabha: BJP MPs Offer Roses to Protesting Congress Parliamentarians.' 15 December. http://post.jagran.com/gandhigiri-in-lok-sabha-bjp-mps-offer-roses-to-protesting-Congress-parliamentarians-1450167195 retrieved on 1 October 2018.

Prabhu, R.K. & U.R. Rao. 1967. *The Mind of Mahatma Gandhi*. Ahmedabad: Navajivan Trust Navajivan Mudranalaya.

PTI. 2017. 'Humour, Satire "Best Healer", Need More of It in Daily Life, Says PM Narendra Modi.' 15 January. https://www.ndtv.com/india-news/homour-satire-best-healer-need-more-of-it-in-daily-life-says-pm-narendra-modi-1648958 retrieved on 10 March 2023.

Raghurmamraju, A. (ed.). 2006. *Debating Gandhi*. Delhi: Oxford University Press.

Rediff News. 2006. 'AIIMS Doctors Try Gandhigiri on Health Minister.' 11 October. http://www.rediff.com/news/2006/oct/11aiims.htm retrieved on 1 October 2018.

132 *Democracy in India: Continuities, Realignments, and Promises*

Rediff News. 2016. 'Is It Modi's Job to Get Indians to Be Clean?' 9 January. http://www. rediff.com/news/column/is-it-modis-job-to-get-indians-to-be-clean/20160109.htm retrieved on 1 October 2018.

Rediff News. 2017. 'UN Expert Finds Holes in Modi's Swachh Bharat Abhiyan.' 10 November. http://www.rediff.com/news/report/un-expert-finds-holes-in-modis-swa chh-bharat-abhiyan/20171110.htm retrieved on 1 October 2018.

Robinson, Francis. 1974. *Separatism among Indian Muslims: The Politics of the United Provinces' Muslims, 1860–1932*. Cambridge: Cambridge University Press.

Rose, Gillian. 2007. *Visual Methodologies: An Introduction to the Interpretation of Visual Materials*. Los Angeles: Sage Publications.

Roy, Asim. 1990. 'The Politics of India's Partition: The Revisionist Perspective.' *Modern Asian Studies* 24 (2) (April): 385–415.

Rudolph, Lloyd & Susanne Hoeber Rudolph. 1984. *The Modernity of Tradition: Political Development in India*. Chicago: Chicago University Press.

Rudolph, Lloyd & Susanne Hoeber Rudolph. 1987. *In Pursuit of Lakshmi: The Political Economy of the Indian State*. Chicago: Chicago University Press.

Rudolph, Lloyd & Susanne Hoeber Rudolph. 2006. *Postmodern Gandhi and Other Essays*. New Delhi: Oxford University Press.

Saksena, N.S. 1993. *India: Towards Anarchy, 1967–1992*. New Delhi: Abhinav.

Sarkar, Tanika. 1987. 'Nationalist Iconography: Image of Women in 19th Century Literature.' *Economic & Political Weekly* (21–27 November): 2011–2015.

Scharff, Anne. 2008. *Mahatma Gandhi: 20th Century Biographies*. Irvine: Saddleback Educational Publications.

Serrakai, Francis. 2000. 'Party Politics and Fragmented Leadership Dilemmas in Indian Politics,' pp. 195–125, in Francis Serrakai (ed.), *Leadership and Politics in Asia: People versus Government*. New Delhi: Dominant Publishers and Distributors.

Seshan, N.K. 1993. *With Three Prime Ministers: Nehru, Indira, and Rajiv*. New Delhi: Wiley-Eastern.

Shrum, L.J. 1994. 'Media Consumption and Perceptions of Social Reality: Effects and Underlying Processes,' Chapter 4, pp. 50–73, in Jennings Bryant & Mary Beth Oliver (eds.), *Media Effects: Advances in Theory and Research*. New York: Routledge.

Singh, Karan. 1993. *Essays on Hinduism*. New Delhi: Ratna Sagar Publication.

Sisodia, Yatindra Singh, Ashish Bhatt, & Tapas Kumar Dalapati (eds.). 2018. *Two Decades of Panchyat Raj in India*. Jaipur: Rawat Publications.

Sisson, Richard & Stanley Wolpert (eds.). 1988. *Congress and Indian Nationalism: The Pre-Independence Phase*. Berkeley: University of California Press.

Sitapati, Vinay. 2011. 'What Anna Hazare's Movement and India's New Middle Classes Say about Each Other.' *Economic & Political Weekly* 46 (30) (23–29 July): 39–44.

Smith, Donald E. 1963. *India as a Secular State*. Princeton: Princeton University Press.

Spencer, Jonathan. 2007. *Anthropology, Politics and the State: Democracy and Violence in South Asia*. New Delhi: Cambridge University Press.

Srivastava, Ramesh Chandra. 1992. *Judicial System in India*. Lucknow: Print House.

Stein, Burton (ed.). 1975. *Essays on South India*. Honolulu: University Press of Hawaii.

Tejani, Shabnum. 2008. *Indian Secularism: An Intellectual History 1890–1950*. Bloomington: Indiana University Press.

The Wire. 2020. 'Fact Check: No, the Centre Isn't Paying for Migrant Workers' Train Journeys Home.' 6 May. https://thewire.in/government/indian-railways-migrant-wor kers-fare retrieved 20 May 2020.

Democracy in India: Continuities, Realignments, and Promises   133

The Wire. 2021. 'India Is No Longer a Democracy but an "Electoral Autocracy": Swedish Institute.' 11 March. https://thewire.in/rights/india-no-longer-democracy-electoral-autocracy-v-dem-institute-report-bjp-narendra-modi.

UNI. 2018. 'Section of Mizoram Christians Sense the Biblical 666 on Aadhaar.' 24 March. http://www.uniindia.com/section-of-mizoram-christians-sense-the-biblical-666-on-aadhaar/states/news/1178438.html retrieved on 10 March 2023.

Vanaik, Achin. 1997. *Communalism Contested: Religion, Modernity and Secularization*. New Delhi: Vistar Publications.

Varshney, A. 2014. *Battles Half Won: India's Improbable Democracy*. New Delhi: Penguin.

Varshney, A. 2022. 'What Gives Indian Democracy Its Long Life? The Choices Elites Make.' *The Print*. 9 September. https://theprint.in/opinion/what-gives-indian-democracy-its-long-life-the-choices-elites-make/1122051/.

Vij, Shivam. 2019. 'Modi's Fear of Narrative Is Our Insurance Against His Excesses.' *The Print*. 29 July. https://theprint.in/opinion/modis-fear-of-narrative-is-our-insurance-against-his-excesses/269413/ retrieved 20 May 2020.

Vyas, Bhanu Priya. 2017. 'UP Election Results 2017—BJP Chief Amit Shah, in Victory Speech, Says PM Narendra Modi Most Popular Leader since Independence.' https://www.ndtv.com/india-news/up-election-results-2017-pm-narendra-modi-most-popular-leader-since-independence-says-amit-shah-vict-1668681 retrieved on 10 March 2023.

Witsoe, Jeffrey. 2013. *Democracy against Development: Lower-Caste Politics and Political Modernity in Postcolonial India*. Chicago: Chicago University Press.

Wober, M. & B. Gunter. 1988. *Television & Social Control*. Aldershot: Avebury.

Wolpert, Stanley. 1996. *Nehru: A Tryst with Destiny*. New York: Oxford University Press.

6 Democracy in the Maldives: Unpacking the "Democratization-Backsliding" Rollercoaster

Arshid Iqbal Dar and Aijaz Ashraf Wani

Introduction

In the middle of the Indian Ocean, a few kilometers below the Indian subcontinent, lies the small low-lying archipelagic Islamic nation of the Maldives. Being the smallest South Asian nation, in terms of land as well as population, the Maldives is one of the most geographically dispersed sovereign countries in the world. The country has 26 atolls and more than 1,000 islands that are only 180 square miles, but it is home to nearly 400,000 people. The islands are world-famous for their beauty, but their environment is very fragile, and vulnerable to sea level rise. The archipelago's 26 natural atolls are divided into 18 atolls and 3 island cities. Most of the islands are less than one square kilometer, and most of the people living on the islands are communities with a population of less than 1,000 people (Naseem, 2020: 125). Despite not being absolutely colonized, the country did become a British protectorate and remained as such from 1887 to 1965 (Musthaq, 2014: 164). The British had only strategic interests in the Maldives—they never administered it; neither did they send their missionaries there, nor even did they intervene during famine or conflict. However, the British carried every type of communication through their colonial office located in Sri Lanka. After gaining independence from Great Britain in 1965, and formally joining the United Nations as a sovereign state, the island nation became a republic in 1968. Apart from being one of the founding members of the South Asian Association for Regional Cooperation (SAARC), the Maldives is also a member of the Commonwealth of Nations, the Organisation of Islamic Cooperation (OIC), and the Non-Aligned Movement (Kumar, 2016: 1). As a tiny island nation, the chances of the Maldives ever being a major influential actor in international relations may appear slim; however, its geo-strategic allure makes it a significant nation to reckon with. Its geo-strategic importance stems from its location on the main sea line of communications (SLOC) across the Indian Ocean, carrying Suez Canal and Strait of Hormuz traffic to India, Southeast Asia, and East Asia. In addition, its islands stretch 500 miles from north to south and 80 miles from east to west, and there is a large Exclusive Economic Zone (EEZ) covering more than 325,000 square miles of key Indian Ocean property (Smith, 2020: 2).

DOI: 10.4324/9781003261469-6

Democracy in the Maldives 135

Apart from the geo-strategic allure that, in the past few years, has turned this small nation into a 'strategic darling' for major powers, it is usually in the news due to its fragile natural environment, mostly because of the rising sea level, climate change, and its internal politics. Beyond the image of being an idyllic tropical holiday and luxury honeymoon destination, the country is much more interesting than just being an Indian Ocean paradise. It has seen coups and countercoups, Islamic extremism has rapidly increased, and institutional corruption has been deeply ingrained. J.J. Robinson, a close observer of the Maldives, has described the country as a 'testbed for the world's current political, social, economic, religious and environmental maladies' (Robinson, 2015: xviii). Similarly, Azra Naseem, an expert on the Maldives, has argued that 'the small island nation is a microcosm of some of the world's most pressing problems, such as 'declining respect for human rights and international norms, and volatile religious militancy' (Naseem, 2015: 99). Consequently, if anything, the greatest causality has been the fledgling democratic process that began in 2008. As such, beyond the so-called serene surface narrative, the country is in the midst of a desperate fight for its political and democratic future. Hence, if the second decade of the 21st century has been a decade of 'testing democratic waters' in South Asia, the Maldives is no exception to this phenomenon. The trajectory of democratic transition from an authoritarian regime under Mamoon Abdul Gayoom (r. 1978–2008), to a semi-democratic polity under Mohamed Nasheed (r. 2008–2012), to falling further into Abdulla Yameen's (r. 2013–2018) authoritarian regime, and finally culminating in a budding/nascent democratic polity under Ibrahim Mohamed Solih (r. 2018–present), Maldives presents an interesting case study for students of democratic transitions and trajectories.

The question of democratic trajectory in the Maldives begs a serious scholarly consideration given the overall trend of 'liberal democracy's fading allure' (Plattner, 2017: 5–14). Apart from the world's renowned organizations, such as Freedom House, the Economist Intelligence Unit, and V-Dem, which have been documenting and alerting us to the global decline in democracy, today's scholars, political leaders, and commentators around the world also recognize its growing vulnerability. We live in times when not a single week passes without the publication of a new essay, newspaper column, or book calling attention to the perilous state of democracy (Plattner, 2017: 6–7). Additionally, the emergence of a plethora of new concepts like 'democratic backsliding', 'regression', and 'recession' underscore the current pessimism that has engulfed democracy. In the larger dynamic of Asia-Pacific in general and South Asia in particular, there is growing literature on the 'crisis of democracy' (Croissant and Haynes, 2021; Vaishnav, 2021; Riaz, 2021; Mukherjee, 2021); however, no such serious scholarly attention has been given to the Maldives. This chapter attempts to fill this void. It unpacks the democratic trajectory of the Maldives and uncovers the 'democratic backsliding' phenomenon. This is empirically as well as theoretically alluring. When the world was coming to terms with the decline of democracy or when democracy stopped expanding, the Maldivian tryst with

136 *Democracy in the Maldives*

democracy began. Even more surprisingly, the transition to democracy was more peaceful than had been the case with most of the post–Cold War transitions across the globe. Additionally, being a 100% Muslim state, the Maldivian case was that of a trend-setter as the ousting of a 30-year dictatorship was a precursor to the Arab Spring revolts that swept across the Middle East two years later. However, the democratic dawn would not last long, and after a brief honeymoon with democracy, the specter of backsliding came to haunt Maldivian democracy. The Maldivian case has much to offer as far as the backsliding literature is concerned, as it will help in opening 'Pandora's box' and revealing the vulnerabilities of a fledgling democracy. After all, the phenomenon of backsliding is considered to be more about the failure of new or emerging democracies to consolidate than the deconsolidation in long-standing democracies (Carothers and Press, 2022: 6). Following this introductory section, the chapter is divided into four sections. The first section briefly chalks out the pre-democratic trajectory and the basis for the transition towards a multiparty democracy in 2008. Within the theoretical paradigm of backsliding, the second section looks at the overall state of democracy under the subsequent regimes in the Maldives covering the period from 2008 to the present. The third section explores the causal factors that prevent the fledgling democracy from taking root in the Maldives by focusing on the endogenous as well as exogenous variables. The final section concludes the analysis and arguments.

From Autocracy to Democracy: An Overview

The story of the Maldives is a story of political transitions. It has oscillated to be either a republic or a monarchy. The country has witnessed bloodshed, intolerance, and autocratic rule. It has been aptly described as a republic in theory and monarchy in practice. The monarchs-turned-autocrats resorted to overwhelming centralization and did not allow the essential institutions of a democratic polity, like an independent legislature, judiciary, as well as political parties, to operate (Amir, 2011: 25–26). The Maldives' autocratic trajectory took a decisive turn in the 1978 presidential elections when Maumoon Abdul Gayoom became the president to rule the country for the next 30 years and earn the title of South Asia's longest serving authoritarian leader (Chandramohan, 2010).

An Islamic scholar, Gayoom grew up in Egypt and studied at Cairo's Al Azhar University, then a stronghold of radical Islamic ideas. Consequently, he modeled his governance after Hosni Mubarak's secular Islamic state and was tough on terrorism, drugs, and extremism. By doing this, Gayoom delineated himself with the West (Mulberry, 2012: 3). Moreover, he brought about considerable changes to religious practices in the Maldives. Through 'Dheenuge Magu' (Path of Religion), a weekly newsletter published by the president's office, he dispensed religious opinions and advice on almost all matters—from personal hygiene to good manners. As argued by Azra Naseem, 'as a dictator with complete control, Gayoom quelled all religious debate and demanded

Democracy in the Maldives 137

absolute conformity, much as Salafi actors do now, except for differences in the forms of Islam so enforced' (Naseem, 2020: 132). Notwithstanding the fact that Gaymoon came to power under the banner of liberal reforms, once in control, he very quickly set to consolidate his grip on power by forging a regime of loyalists. He placed his three brothers-in-law in the roles of chief governor of all the provinces, head of security and trade, and leader of the nation's only media, a radio station. Furthermore, one among them was also entrusted with the task of developing a rudimentary TV station into an instrument of the state (Mulberry, 2012: 2). For the next 20 years, Gayoom gradually built bulwarks around his position of power while chipping away at the budding Maldivian civil society. The nature of his reign has been aptly described as 'an iron-fisted rule, marred by corruption, nepotism, cronyism, and stifling of any political dissent' (*Economic & Political Weekly*, 2008: 7); or as 'an appetite towards autocracy, where no challenger was allowed in elections that were invariably manipulated'. Consequently, he won six consecutive elections unopposed. Various international human rights organizations accused Gayoom of employing terror tactics, including arbitrary arrests, detention without trial, torture, forced confessions, and even politically motivated killings against dissidents. Amnesty International and Reporters without Borders in particular labeled him as the 'predator of press freedom' (Nasheed, 2012a: 2). Gayoom survived three coups and one assassination attempt, resulting fundamentally from his oppressive rule and accumulation of personal wealth. In one of the reports from the national auditor of the Maldives, his personal spending was said to be 'out of control' (Mulberry, 2012: 3), as he exploited his power to live a lavish lifestyle and extend munificence to those around him. The assets that the report highlighted including $9.5 million spent on a luxury yacht from Germany, the purchase of 11 speed boats and 55 cars, including the country's only Mercedes-Benz. Furthermore, an estimated $17 million was spent to renovate the presidential palace and family houses (Saltmarsh, 2010: 1). Even his so-called rapid transformation of the economy towards luxury tourism would only benefit the wealthiest 1%, while the living conditions of most Maldivians were akin to those in sub-Saharan Africa (Shackle, 2008: 2). Thus, the rampant corruption along with the extreme exploitation and the resultant acute poverty buttressed the public grievance (Mulberry, 2012: 3).

The simmering dissent began to find expression throughout the 1980s and 1990s but was brutally repressed by Gayoom. Among the oppositional forces, Mohamed Nasheed played the catalytic role in helping the Maldivians to dream of a democratic future. Since Gayoom throughout his rule resisted the acknowledgment of any political parties, on the excuse that such opposition parties would have spoiled the Maldivian society's homogenous nature, Nasheed through his pamphlet Huku pressed for allowing their formation and registration. It was through Nasheed's pivotal role in exile in Britain that the Maldivian Democratic Party (MDP), the country's first political party, was formed in 2001 (Kumar, 2016: 2). The party played a crucial role in spearheading the anti-government movements that ultimately culminated in the

138 *Democracy in the Maldives*

democratic transition. The tipping point for popular anti-Gayoom protests was the brutal custodial killing of a teenager named Evan Naseem at Maafushi Prison in September 2003. Naseem's mother challenged authorities and publicly demonstrated her son's assaulted body in the Republic Square and thereby leading to riots (Robinson, 2015: 2). Despite Gayoom's orders of quelling the demonstrations and declaring an emergency, the anti-government wave kept coming. Furthermore, his rule was shaken by the infamous December 26, 2004 Indian Ocean tsunami, which further accentuated the economic downturn. The wreckage not only required unconditional instant humanitarian assistance but also necessitated a long-term and very comprehensive development package. As is well known the global financial institutions and donor agencies had long ago placed the condition of aid on 'good governance', which demanded political and economic liberalization. Faced with a domestic crisis and external conditionalities, Gayoom was concerned about having to loosen his grip on power (Musthaq, 2014: 166). Nasheed was able to capitalize on this growing public discontent. Being received by the public as a hero, he increased pressure on Gayoom and compelled him to open the political space. Due to mounting popular dissent, Gayoom announced a reform package, vowing to form a new constitution and set up a human rights commission, and allow political parties to operate (Human Rights Watch, 2018a). While Nasheed publicly declared the arrival of his MDP, the new constitution was ratified by Gayoom's administration in 2008. Consequently, the country witnessed its first multiparty presidential election, which took place on October 8, 2008. Seen by many as a referendum on Gayoom (Evans, 2008: 1), the 2008 elections were monitored by United Nations (UN) diplomatic missions along with Transparency Maldives, an influential nongovernmental organization (NGO). In what became the first ever relatively free and fair elections, Mohamed Nasheed of the MDP secured 54% of votes and defeated the long-serving autocrat Gayoom (*The Independent*, 2008). Thus Maldives finally witnessed the moonset of authoritarianism and the sunrise of democracy.

The new democratic constitution adopted just a month before the elections, guaranteeing rule of law and fundamental human rights, also brought the principle of separation of powers to Maldives for the first time. The legislative, executive, and the judicial powers were respectively delineated statutorily among *Majlis* (parliament), the presidency and judiciary. The new constitution, besides paying homage to religious tenets by declaring Islam as the state religion (*Economic & Political Weekly*, 2008: 7), also provided for the establishment of separate independent commissions to preserve judicial independence, conduct free and fair elections, check and fight corruption, and ensure an effective and competent civil service. It is pertinent to mention here that unlike the experience of most of the countries that democratized in the post–Cold War era in Africa and post-communist Eurasia and Latin America, the Maldives' transition to democracy and the road ahead was far from smooth. The following section outlines the rollercoaster ride of democracy in the Maldives from 2008 onwards.

Democracy in the Maldives 139

Democratization and Backsliding Rollercoaster: 2008 to Present

a) Democratic Dawn and Rising Challenges

President Nasheed, who for some became 'the Maldives' Obama' (Chandramohan, 2010) and for others 'the Maldives' Mandela' (*The Independent*, 2008) and above all Amnesty International's 'prisoner of conscience' (Naseem, 2015: 100), inherited a monumental task to repair the 30 years of authoritarian baggage and to democratize the country. Gayoom's dictatorship had, to use President Nasheed's words, 'bequeathed to the infant democracy a looted treasury, a ballooning budget deficit and a rotten judiciary' (Nasheed, 2012b). After assuming the presidency, Nasheed in his address promised, both to Maldivians and the international community, introduction of greater democracy and more freedom, including the freedom of expression (*The Independent*, 2008). Promising liberal democracy, Nasheed stated: 'my legacy is going to be introducing a modern, liberal form of democracy. That is the greatest legacy anyone can give' (*Hindustan Times*, 2008). Accordingly, many independent commissions, such as the Maldives Human Rights Commission, Judicial Service Commission, Media Council, Maldives Inland Revenue Authority, and Police Integrity Commission, were established. The first and foremost profound outcome of Nasheed's democratic consolidation was the individual freedom that people began to enjoy. Furthermore, political parties started to enjoy their political rights; the rule of law was upheld in society; a supportive democratic institutional framework was in place; and steady economic progress was attained (Naseem, 2015: 101). For the first time the Maldivian government showed openness to criticism, and reporters were able to investigate issues and bring these issues to public notice—something the country had never seen before. One of the most provocative cases brought to the public notice was the alleged use of public funds worth US $10 million by former autocrat Gayoom as loans to his family, friends, and cronies (Saltmarsh, 2010). However, what was unique about President Nasheed was his government's treatment of Gayoom, who during his tenure had forced the former into exile in Britain and Sri Lanka. Nasheed ruled out pursuing criminal charges against his rival and said, 'he will instead organize a pension and adequate security for him' (*The Independent*, 2008). Nasheed believed that:

> [the] test of our democracy will be how we treat him. I don't think we should be going for a witch-hunt and digging up the past. This is a happier day than ever in the history of the Maldives. The Maldives will change; it will have a peaceful government.
>
> (ibid.)

It was Nasheed's democratic consolidation that led the international watchdog Freedom House to enlist Maldives for the first time in its history as an 'electoral democracy' in 2010.

140 *Democracy in the Maldives*

However, this newly acquired 'status' did not hold for long and soon faced rough weather. As a result, the fledgling democracy again began to experience backsliding towards autocratic tendencies. Although the challenges to democratization or contributing factors for democratic backsliding in Maldives will be dealt with in a separate section, it is desirable to make some passing reference here. Even though Maldives made a transition to democracy, its political class 'did not give up their predatory behaviour and unprincipled politics' (Zahir, 2018). Despite Nasheed's attempts at democratization, by creating various independent institutions to impose necessary checks and balances, his government failed to remove the previous regimes' influence on many key state institutions (Naseem, 2015: 101.) Additionally, the new political parties, their leaders, parliamentarians, judges, and those who pump money into politics did not fully embrace democracy (Zahir, 2018). These smaller parties and the opposition led by Gayoom gained a majority in the *Majlis*, which hampered Nasheed's efforts at democratization as he found it increasingly difficult to implement various structural reforms (Bonofer, 2010: 440–441). These included an impasse on the drafting and passing of foundational laws such as the revised Penal Code, Code of Criminal Procedure, and Evidence Act (Dzenisevich, 2016: 1). Not surprisingly, therefore, the 2009 parliamentary election saw the reversal of the process, with the opposition led by former dictator Gayoom's Dhivehi Rayyithunge Party (DRP) securing a majority. Despite substantial reforms in police and military forces by Nasheed, the vital elements within these institutions remained loyal to Gayoom, as did most of the judiciary, which in August 2010 successfully repelled all the sweeping constitutional reforms initiated by Nasheed. Faced with such a conundrum, Nasheed himself took what came to be regarded as 'controversial' and undemocratic steps that further buttressed the backsliding process. For example, frustrated with all his attempts to affect judicial reforms through lawful channels like the *Majlis*, as well realizing that the independent institutions were being thwarted by opposing forces, his government detained Abdullah Mohamed, the chief judge of the Criminal Court, in January 2012. He was arrested by the Maldivian National Defence Force (MNDF), which had no authority to arrest, and was held without charges (Kumar, 2016: 39).

Furthermore, for Nasheed things got complicated by the increasing role of Islamists in politics who regarded democracy and Nasheed's efforts to strengthen it as un-Islamic (Naseem, 2015: 101). It was basically the anti-Islamic rhetoric that helped Gayoom loyalists to buttress the anti-Nasheed wave. Finally, on February 7, 2012, President Nasheed was forced to resign at 'gunpoint' in what came to be regarded as a 'bloodless coup' (Mulberry, 2012: 15), thereby shifting the fledgling democracy from intensive care unit (ICU) to ventilator. As argued by Azra Naseem, 'with the fall of Nasheed's government, the regime changed from a transitional democracy with elements of competitive authoritarianism to one of competitive authoritarianism headed towards full-scale autocracy' (Naseem, 2015: 102).

Democracy in the Maldives   141

b) Backsliding to Authoritarianism

Following the controversial removal of President Nasheed, his Vice President Mohamed Abdullah Waheed was sworn in as the new president within hours. However, Nasheed's MDP supporters protested over the nature of their leader's removal and demanded fresh elections. Due to mounting pressure from the opposition, Waheed was compelled to call for fresh elections. While initially it was declared that the elections would be held in July 2013, instead of their original scheduled date of October 2013, the elections were finally held on September 7, 2013. In the first round of what came to be characterized as the 'most controversial elections', Nasheed won 45.45% of votes; Abdulla Yameen Abdul Gayoom (Gayoom's half-brother) of the Progressive Party of Maldives (PPM) received 25.35% of votes; Qasim Ibrahim of the Jumhooree Gulhun Party received 24.07% of votes; and Waheed received 5.13% of votes (Commonwealth, 2013). With no clear majority, a second round runoff vote was held. A contest between Yameen and Nasheed was required under the constitution, with the runoff vote scheduled for September 27, 2013. However, despite the first round of elections being hailed as free and fair and consistent with international standards by international observers, the Supreme Court in a controversial move not just annulled them but also ordered an injunction against the scheduled second round and announced its indefinite postponement (Bhim, 2019: 256). The Supreme Court's move was not just unconstitutional but also an assault on the country's fragile democracy. This move further established the continuing influence of the old regime over the judiciary. As Musthaq has put it very succinctly:

> indeed, it is no stretch to say that Gayoom's PPM was able at every turn to use judges and police officers to foreclose the possibility of an MDP victory. By delaying a final vote until November 16, the antics of the Supreme Court and the police gave the Gayoom family time to hammer together a coalition that could beat the MDP.
>
> (Musthaq, 2014: 167)

There were also allegations that the Maldivian Police Service (MPS) was not cooperating with the Election Commission of Maldives (ECM) and was obstructing the election process. The police intervention in the election process came at a point when the police felt as if they were the leaders of this operation and even the head of the ECM needed authorization from the police commissioner to enter the security room (Bhim, 2019: 256). Moreover, even the election officers were instructed by the Supreme Court to sit within the limited compounds without a cell phone to evade charges of malpractice (ibid.). While there were pro-democracy, anti-Supreme Court, as well as law enforcement agency protests, they were violently put down by the police. Thus, there started yet another phase of authoritarianism in the Maldives.

142 *Democracy in the Maldives*

The Maldives' return to full-fledged authoritarian rule underlines the vulnerabilities of a fledgling democracy to backsliding driven by residues of the past. The long-dragged-out and chaotic process eventually ended on November 16, 2013 with a win for Yameen (who received 51% of votes) over Nasheed (who received 49%)—with a difference of just over 6,000 votes. The MDP initially disputed the results but, stating that he wanted to avoid any violence, Nasheed conceded the defeat to the coalition led by Yameen Abdul Gayoom (Khandekar, 2018). Immediately after his takeover, Yameen embraced authoritarianism and through his 'executive aggrandizement' he heightened the pace of the backsliding process. It was Yameen's hollowing out of various independent institutions of democracy that turned the Maldives into the new face of 'competitive authoritarianism' (Naseem, 2015: 102–103) and 'new despotism' (Zahir, 2018). Moreover, undermining the independence of the judiciary, Yameen expanded the use of broad and vaguely worded laws to arrest, intimidate, and imprison his critics. Notable among those controversial laws passed by Yameen include the Counterterrorism Law of 2015, which was widely used against opposition activists and politicians; the anti-defamation laws, used against the media and social media activists who criticize the president or his policies; and restrictions on assembly that prohibit or severely limit peaceful rallies and protests (Human Rights Watch, 2018a). Almost all the major political rivals to Yameen were imprisoned on different charges (Zahir, 2018). More specifically, the arrest of Nasheed and sentencing him to 13 years in prison, as well as the ill treatment of other dissident voices by Yameen, confirmed that the Maldivian nascent democracy was rapidly in retreat. The democratic backsliding received further impetus by Yameen's declaration of emergency on November 4, 2015, curbing fundamental freedoms, including right to privacy, freedom of assembly, freedom of movement, freedom from unlawful arrest, detention and imprisonment, and freedom from search and seizure without reasonable cause. The timing of the declaration of emergency was crucial as it came two days before a rally was planned by opposition forces on November 6, 2015 to protest against Yameen's 'unjust and autocratic rule' (Dzenisevich, 2016: 3). Yameen's PPM 'engaged in bribery, extortion, patronage and a whole range of other mechanisms of co-optation to ensure that all legislation it wants are passed with the required majority' (Naseem, 2015: 105), and hence the *Majlis* itself played a crucial role in turning the regime towards full-scale authoritarianism. Additionally, even the Yameen-led Election Commission announced that it would nullify any primary results in which the nominee failed to meet the qualifications for president, including those convicted of criminal offenses (Human Rights Watch, 2018b). Nasheed, who was convicted in 2015, stepped down as a presidential candidate. All this resulted in considerable international criticism of Yameen's authoritarianism. The EU warned of sanctions ranging from travel bans to asset freezes against those responsible for human rights violations and undermining the rule of law in Maldives (Reuters, 2018). Likewise, while expressing its concern over 'continued democratic backsliding', the United States warned of appropriate measures against those undermining fair electoral process and democracy (*The*

Indian Express, 2018). In India, even the possibility of an 'Operation Cactus 2.0' (Sharma, 2018) was widely debated amid Nasheed's request to intervene to end the political crises. Unsurprisingly, Yameen turned towards his so-called 'friendly nations' for support (*The Economic Times*, 2018). While Saudi Arabia supported his decision to impose the emergency, China shielded him by describing it as an internal matter of the Maldives and warned against any foreign intervention. It was because of this crucial support that Yameen could get away with his authoritarian and provocative activities.

Two crucial aspects of the Yameen regime that helped him sustain his rule and strengthened the authoritarian traits in Maldives are the growing Islamic radicalism and external influence, particularly that of China and Saudi Arabia—both autocratic polities themselves. Both of these aspects are discussed in detail later in the chapter. While challenges posed by Islamic radicalism to the democratization process in the Maldives are discussed separately, suffice to say it has been regarded as the corollary of Saudi Arabia's mounting influence in the country's domestic politics stimulated by Yameen. Similarly, the close alliance with China has allowed people like Yameen to evade the pressures from the international community regarding the upholding of the rule of law and democratic principles, which he regarded as foreign interference and undermining the Islamic faith. Yameen consciously sought to use China, which did not even have an embassy in the Maldives before 2012, to further his interests and strengthen his hold on power.

c) *The Return of Democracy: One Step Forward, Two Steps Back*

Despite a lot of pessimism, the September 2018 elections brought the Maldivian rollercoaster back to a democratic path. The opposition parties from across the Maldivian political spectrum formed a united front to oust the authoritarian government of Yameen. Senior member of parliament and the founding member of MDP, Ibrahim Mohamed Solih, was made the face of this opposition. They promised to bring transparency, accountability, and above all democracy back to the country (BBC News, 2018a). The day of September 23 proved to be a watershed moment in the Maldivian democratic trajectory, with citizens of the Islamic nation standing in long queues to vote in the presidential election. In what turned out to be the highest voter turnout in its history (around 90%), the Maldivians choose democracy over authoritarianism by voting Mohamed Solih into power and ousting Yameen (Ayres, 2018). If anything, the election results underscore that Maldivians want their country back on the path of democracy, not backsliding from it. It was a clear expression of the people's strong desire for democracy, that for a second time in a decade they had rejected a sectarian autocrat and favored a secular democrat. In his victory speech, Solih called the election results 'a moment of happiness, hope and history' (*The Indian Express*, 2018b). Surely for the supporters of liberal democracy, its unexpected resurrection in the Maldives and reversing of the half-decade backsliding gave them some reason to cheer (Robinson, 2019).

144 *Democracy in the Maldives*

Expressing his happiness at Yameen's defeat, the former president, Nasheed tweeted, 'Democracy is a historical inevitability' (Khandekar, 2018). While assuming power the Solih-led government promised to provide justice for unsolved murders and forcible disappearances, and also to recover the assets that were lost due to the biggest corruption scandal to hit the Maldives, and the money laundering that went along with it (Moosa and Abi-Habib, 2018).

However, President Solih inherited a mess and it was never going to be easy to undo the historical faults in the country's politics and its institutions. Not only had most of the Maldives' supposedly independent commissions and human rights institutions been gutted, corrupted, or compromised, but there were also decisions to be made about the future of Yameen's former allies, such as former Defense Minister Mohamed Nazim and tourism tycoon Gasim Ibrahim (Tiezzi, 2020). To put into practice the promise of democracy, the Solih government in November 2018 established the Commission on Deaths and Disappearances to investigate past attacks on activists and journalists. The commission chair Husnu Al Suood stated in January 2018 that 'extremist Islamist gangs had influence over police and criminal courts, and colluded to protect perpetrators and "fix" the outcome of trials' (Human Rights Watch, 2019). The commission in a few cases implicated police and politicians for shielding the perpetrators from prosecution. Following the MDP's resounding victory in the April 2019 parliamentary elections, hopes for democratic reforms and justice for past atrocities grew stronger. Subsequently, the government established a Prison-audit Commission, which issued a report detailing corruption, systemic abuse, and mistreatment throughout detention facilities in the Maldives. Furthermore, the Home Minister established a committee to oversee prison reform, reduce overcrowding, and implement the Prison-audit Commission's recommendations (Human Rights Watch, 2020). Given the MDP-controlled legislature, the Solih government in 2019 replaced all five judges of the Supreme Court, whose predecessors were criticized for judicial overreach and circumventing the constitution. Parliament also repealed the Anti-Defamation and Freedom of Expression Act (Monitor, 2019), which the previous government had used to levy heavy fines against media that published critical content concerning the president. The return of Nasheed to electoral politics from exile as the Speaker of Parliament provided further impetus to the process of democratization. He brought new energy to his role as speaker to repair the damage of both the Yameen era and the previous 40 years of dictatorship—with the brief interruption of his own presidency. The Solih-led government's initial efforts to revise anti-democratic laws and establish transitional justice mechanisms did help to repair the damage that the Yameen government had inflicted on the country's image internationally. The EU, United States, and India congratulated Maldives on its return to the 'path of democracy' (BBC News, 2018b). The Election Commission was credited with an improved and more impartial performance in its administration of the 2019 parliamentary elections and its preparations for the 2020 local council elections, earning praise from Commonwealth observers (The Commonwealth, 2019).

However, notwithstanding the nascent progress towards greater transparency, accountability, and good governance, the Solih government's public support started to fade as it failed to live up to its initial promises. The public trust was seriously undermined by Solih's unwillingness to investigate cases of corruption involving his political allies as well as the numerous corruption scandals that emerged during his government. Moreover, the selective approach to prosecute only Yameen for corruption charges while overlooking his former administration's beneficiaries came to be criticized as politically motivated (Ghafoor, 2023). His administration also rebuffed efforts to amend the undemocratic Freedom of Assembly Act from Yameen's tenure and continued to use it to block protests. Moreover, the passing of the controversial New Evidence Act, which allows courts to force journalists and media outlets to reveal their sources, seriously undermined press freedom in the country (Human Rights Watch, 2023). Consequently, due to this legislation Maldives dropped 15 places in the World Press Freedom Index (Human Rights Watch, 2022). The issue of Islamic radicalism in particular reversed the trajectory of initial efforts of democratization. The influence of Islamist extremist groups remained pervasive within the Solih government, police, and the judiciary. As Human Rights Watch aptly pointed out:

> Authorities bent to pressure from these groups, as well as from the Muslim fundamentalist Adhaalath Party—a member of the ruling coalition—by rolling back fundamental rights, including freedom of speech and assembly, and the rights of lesbian, gay, bisexual, and transgender (LGBT) people, and of women.
>
> (Human Rights Watch, 2023)

What is of particular concern here is that the government even shut down the most prominent human rights organization, the Maldivian Democracy Network (MDN), in response to complaints from religious leaders that it had insulted Islam (Human Rights Watch, 2020). So, the extremist groups continued to pose a threat to human rights defenders and activists whom they accused of being 'too secular', and to exert influence over the police courts, and other government institutions (Human Rights Watch, 2019). Moreover, the May 6, 2021 incident when the Speaker of Parliament Nasheed was wounded in an alleged terror attack near his residence in Male justified the concern of escalating radicalism (Moorthy, 2021: 2). Additionally, due to the internal divisions within the MDP driven by a rift between Solih and Nasheed, when the latter's loyalists formed a new breakaway party called the Democrats, the government attempted to delay its registration process. Furthermore, when the president of the Election Commission moved to expedite the registration process, he was subjected to a no-confidence motion, thereby politicizing the body and undermining its independence (Ghafoor, 2023).

While the latest presidential elections of September 2023 were comparatively competitive and peaceful, it does indicate that democracy even in its procedural

146 *Democracy in the Maldives*

form is at work in the Maldives. People made their choice and elected Dr. Mohamed Muizzu of the Progressive Party of Maldives. Despite the nominal assurance of governing the country as per the people's wishes, the post-2008 democratic trajectory provides a cautionary tale. No government until now has fully adhered to the democratic norms, and thus, only time will tell whether the new president will be able to break that trend.

Besieging Democracy in Maldives: Unpacking the Causes of Backsliding

In the aforementioned section, while analyzing the post-2008 democratic trajectory of the Maldives, the challenges that continue to hold back democracy or lead to its backsliding have been implicitly revealed. However, in this section an attempt is made to explicitly explore the causal variables that underpin the Maldivian nascent democracy's backsliding phenomenon. Based on the aforementioned analysis of democratic trajectory in the Maldives, the causal variables are divided into two categories based on their origin. These are the internal/indigenous and external/exogenous. As for domestic or indigenous causes, as the above analysis demonstrated, the Maldives' democratization has, among others, become the casualty of three interrelated challenges, namely the authoritarian residues, presidential hegemony and the resultant executive aggrandizement, and finally the Islamic radicalism. In the external or exogenous arena, democracy in the Maldives has been the victim of mounting influence of autocratic states, especially China and Saudi Arabia, which have greatly contributed to its backsliding.

a) Internal/Indigenous Causal Variables

i) Authoritarian Residues

One of the important causal variables that has and continues to undermine the Maldives' nascent democratization process is the residues of past authoritarianism or what President Nasheed has referred to as 'the dregs of dictatorship' (Nasheed, 2012b). Although Gayoom, who ruled with an iron-fist policy for almost 30 years, lost the first democratic elections, he still retained a strong support base in the country. During his rule he had patronized certain sections and powerful elites for three decades who continued to remain loyal to him even after his ousting. Having tasted the fruits of authoritarianism this section tried their best to subvert the process of democratization. Gayoom had also helped his loyalists infiltrate into powerful institutions, especially the security forces and the judiciary (Musthaq, 2014: 167), which helped him not only to crush opposition but also keep his influence intact even when he was no longer in power. Consequently, while attempting to consolidate democracy in the Maldives, Nasheed found his regime increasingly challenged by the constant opposition and conspiracies of the 'vestiges of dictatorship' of Gayoom. Even after setting up important institutions to democratize the country, Nasheed failed to wipe out the influence of the previous regime on many key state institutions. From the very beginning, the *Majlis*, controlled by Gayoom-led opposition, made it the weakest actor in the democratization process, as it blocked democratic reforms. Similarly, while trying to reform the judiciary, the lifeblood of any democracy, Nasheed found himself engaged in a herculean task. In 2010, the judiciary blocked sweeping reforms required by the new constitution (Naseem, 2015: 101) and instead favored the status quo. The judiciary was corrupt and incompetent and the chief justice of the Maldives' criminal court, Abdulla Mohamed, was seen by many as the prime example of this. Appointed during the Gayoom regime, Abdullah Mohamed was known for his repeated efforts to block corruption and embezzlement cases involving members of Gayoom's administration. Consequently, Nasheed sought the help of the Judicial Services Commission—the body responsible for monitoring the behavior of judges—to investigate Abdullah Mohamed's case, wherein he was found guilty. Ironically, the chief justice not only refused to cooperate with the investigation but also quashed his own arrest warrant. It was the consequence of this that there remained no formal procedure that could hold people like Abdullah Mohamed accountable. Nasheed finally ordered his arrest by the Maldives National Defence Force (Mulberry, 2012: 15). However, in a dramatic turn of events following the arrest, 'the former president's supporters', said Nasheed, 'protested in the streets, and police officers and army personnel loyal to the old government mutinied and forced me, at gunpoint, to resign' (Nasheed, 2012a). Pertinent to mention here is that the police force was led by rogue officers of the Special Operations Unit, once called 'Star Force', created and used by Gayoom to crush dissent. Even Nasheed's vice president, who would later be sworn in as the new president, had been part of the coup plan. The anti-Nasheed lobbies created by former authoritarian regime loyalists instead of letting the democratic transition go on, despite disagreements, sought to end his government by any means. Therefore, the brief democratic honeymoon that Maldives experienced under president Nasheed was brought to an untimely and tragic end by the dregs of past authoritarianism. In one of his write-ups published in the *New York Times* after he was forcibly ousted, President Nasheed lamented:

> dictatorships don't always die when the dictator leaves office. The wave of revolutions that toppled autocrats in Tunisia, Egypt, Libya and Yemen last year was certainly cause for hope. But the people of those countries should be aware that, long after the revolutions, powerful networks of regime loyalists can remain behind and can attempt to strangle their nascent democracies.
>
> (Nasheed, 2012b)

A few years later, the Foreign Affairs Minister of the Nasheed regime, Ahmed Naseem, would also open up about the coup by citing a similar reason. For him, the coup occurred because it is hard to get rid of a dictatorship, as 'its roots had penetrated society so much. Very often people who serve dictators

148 *Democracy in the Maldives*

have a lot of wealth, and are affluent. It's very difficult to get away from their grip' (Bhim, 2019: 176). The fragile political opening visible after Nasheed's rise to the presidency could not be sustained in that the old authoritarian elite was not ready to change.

Following his role in ending Nasheed's presidency, caretaker President Waheed worked simply as a proxy of the Gayoom loyalists as he stacked his administration with them. Gayoom's daughter was appointed as junior foreign minister; his lawyer was made attorney-general; his former spokesman was appointed as a cabinet minister; and the three former military and policemen at the forefront of the coup were made police chief, defense minister, and deputy home minister (Nasheed, 2012b). Additionally, Waheed's attempts at postponing the elections and helping Gayoom's PPM led by Abdullah Yameen, half-brother of Gayoom and one-time cabinet minister, win the election further substantiated the claim of the 'dregs of authoritarianism' hurting any fledgling democracy like the Maldives. The Maldivian trajectory can be a lesson for other countries experiencing nascent democratization. The lesson is to use Nasheed's words: 'the dictator can be removed in a day, but it can take years to stamp out the lingering remnants of his dictatorship' (Nasheed, 2012b). It is in this context that Robinson has aptly described the democratic trajectory of the Maldives as follows: '[The] Maldives observes the pageantry of democratic politics, but it is still very much in the latter stages of a bruising transition from decades of autocracy' (Tiezzi, 2020).

ii) Presidential Hegemony and Executive Aggrandizement

Following Nasheed's ousting, the Maldives' nascent democratic transition caused the phenomenon of 'presidential hegemony' and the consequent 'executive aggrandizement'. The caretaker president, or what can be referred as a 'proxy of Gayoom', Waheed undermined the transition to democracy by supporting the vested interests of the elite beneficiaries of the previous authoritarian regime. It was during Waheed's presidency that the Maldives began to experience 'presidential hegemony' post the 2008 democratic transition. Waheed undermined almost all of the democratic institutions and suppressed dissident voices. In fact, it was his presidential hegemony along with the vestiges of dictatorship that paved the way for Abdullah Yameen to win the 2013 presidential elections. As discussed above, President Yameen would become the crude personification of the phenomenon of 'presidential hegemony' and will probably go down in the Maldivian trajectory of democracy as the worst architect of executive aggrandizement. While veering off the path of democracy, he gradually took control of various institutions, hollowed them out, and made them subservient to his political agenda. The *Majlis* (parliament) was made entirely subordinate to the ruling party by Yameen and therefore came closer to what Steven Levitsky and Lucan A. Way characterize as 'competitive authoritarianism' (Levitsky and Way, 2020: 51–65). Yameen used the parliamentary majority to manipulate the *Majlis* in order to pass a number of restrictive, and often

Democracy in the Maldives 149

oppressive, laws and measures. Among these were the counter-terrorism laws, widely used against opposition activists and politicians; and anti-defamation and the 'Freedom of Expression Act', to curb the critical voices and place restrictions on assembly that prohibit or severely limit peaceful rallies and protests. While on the face of it most of these laws were passed legally through a parliamentary procedure, deeper analysis clearly reveals the use of blackmail, bribery, corruption, and coercion. To substantiate this argument one can refer to the controversial amendment made in 2013 to lower the minimum age of presidents and vice presidents from 35 to 30 years, and to cap the same at 65 years (Moorthy, 2015). The amendment was driven by Yameen's personal wish to have his Vice President Mohamed Jameel replaced by his close aide Ahmed Adeeb. However, since he was just 32 years of age and therefore not eligible for the job as per existing law, this amendment was brought forth. Yameen caused Jameel's impeachment and Adeeb was appointed in 2015 by an overwhelming majority. Additionally, through *Majlis*, Yameen, by making amendments to the Parliament's Standing Orders, restricted the rights of the opposition to participate in the legislative process. Only the ruling party was permitted to submit the taxation bills and the opposition was even denied the early-day motions and resolutions. Moreover, parliament could submit, debate, and vote on a bill in one sitting, thereby denying the opposition time to review the bills (Dzenisevich, 2016:11).

The judiciary has been one of the main victims of Yameen's presidential hegemony. He used his party's legislative majority to change the law regulating the composition of the country's top court. He managed to remove the chief justice and lower court judge, both of whom were against the annulling of the first round of the 2013 presidential elections. Through the *Majlis*, Yameen also induced the amending of the Judicature Act to reduce the strength of the Supreme Court bench from seven to five and hence effectively undermine the impartiality and independence of the judiciary. While criticizing Yameen's decisions as an 'assault on the independence of judiciary', the International Commission of Jurists regional director, Sam Zarifi, lamented that 'the Maldivian parliament and executive have effectively decapitated the country's judiciary and trampled on the fundamental principles of the rule of law and separation of powers' (International Commission of Jurists, 2014). Subsequently, Yameen used the fully controlled judiciary to weaken the opposition by imprisoning almost all his major political rivals on various charges. Those included former President Nasheed, his own half-brother (Gayoom), his own vice president (Ahmed Adeeb), the Adalat Party leader (Imran Abdullah), and the country's richest man, Gasim Ibrahim. Similarly, when his 'presidential hegemony' estranged his coalition partners and he lost their legislative majority, the courts and the elections body barred 12 opposition MPs from their seats (Zahir, 2018). In February 2015, the Maldives Criminal Court issued a warrant to Nasheed and he was physically dragged to court without permission to consult a lawyer. Subsequently, in March he was sentenced to 13 years in prison after being declared guilty of terrorism (Amnesty International, 2015). The

150   Democracy in the Maldives

Supreme Court repeatedly intervened in political affairs and apparently exceeded its constitutional authority to act according to the political interests of the ruling dispensation. Even when there was a slight deviation by the judiciary, Yameen would exercise his presidential hegemony to get the job done. For example, in September 2017, the government victimized lawyers by suspending the licenses of dissenters and the Maldives Supreme Court indefinitely suspended 54 lawyers who petitioned for independence and reform of the judiciary. Furthermore, in 2018, when the Supreme Court ordered the release of Yameen's political rivals, ruling that their trials had violated the constitution and international law and were 'politically motivated', the president denounced the ruling as illegal. To 'hold the judges accountable', as Yameen said, he announced the emergency to mount an 'all-out assault on democracy' (Human Rights Watch, 2018a). In February 2018, Yameen's military forces raided the Supreme Court and arrested two of its judges, including the chief justice. Subsequently, in March the *Majlis* without a quorum passed legislation that allowed the removal of judges once the Supreme Court has upheld their conviction. This was done regardless of the constitutional requirement that says, 'judges be removed through a two-thirds vote in the parliament after [they have been] found guilty of gross misconduct or incompetence by the Judicial Service Commission'. Both the judges were removed and imprisoned and Yameen appointed replacements in June 2018 (Freedom House, 2020).

The Election Commission was also politicized to allow various controversial interventions in the electoral process by Yameen. Shortly after becoming president, he used the Supreme Court to remove the Election Commission chief, Fuwad Thowfeek, and his deputy, Ahmed Fayaz Hassan, from office. Both of them were charged with contempt of court in a *suo motu* case related to their criticism of the Supreme Court's role in the November 2013 presidential elections (Moorthy, 2014). The dismissal of the Election Commission members was engineered to pave the way to make the independent Election Commission a subordinate of the ruling government. Afterwards, the Election Commission was utilized in such a way as to ensure that the ruling party had no meaningful opposition in the parliamentary elections. Additionally, as discussed earlier, amid the controversial emergency, in a bid to disqualify Nasheed the Election Commission announced that it would nullify any primary results in which the nominee failed to meet the qualifications for a presidential office as outlined in the 2008 constitution (Mallempatti, 2018). Since Article 109(f) of the constitution provides that the president cannot be sentenced to more than 12 months in prison for a criminal offense within the past three years and because Nasheed was sentenced to 13 years (*The Guardian*, 2015), he was automatically rendered ineligible. In effect, the commission left only President Yameen eligible to contest the elections.

Additionally, Yameen used his presidential hegemony and the consequent executive aggrandizement to choke the freedom of the press by arresting, intimidating, and even killing the anti-regime voices. Also, Yameen's allies reportedly forced public- and private-sector employees to refrain from participating in opposition protests or other political activities with threats of dismissal from

Democracy in the Maldives 151

service. Such workers were also forced to attend pro-government events. According to Thowfeek, the former Election Commissioner,

> people holding civil service or senior positions in government companies told me they were informed to become a member of the ruling party PPM or resign. Almost all the people belonging to independent institutions, civil service and government companies are required to attend PPM functions which have a strict attendance register.
>
> (Bhim, 2019: 191–192)

Consequently, in 2017, due to Yameen's silencing of dissent, Freedom House downgraded the Maldives' press freedom rating to 'Not Free' (Zahir, 2018). In hindsight, Yameenm, despite being an elected president, ruled purely as an autocrat and his actions resonated with that of dictatorships or autocracies. He became, to use the description of B. Rogers, 'the Robert Mugabe, perhaps even bordering on the Kim Jong Un, of Maldivian politics' (Rogers, 2016: 334). He utilized the parliament, security forces, judiciary, and 'independent' institutions to serve his own interests and prosecute political rivals in a crude manifestation of 'presidential hegemony' to hold the fledgling democracy back.

iii) Islamic Radicalism

Besides the deep-seated self-interest of the elite sections in preserving the authoritarian system in the Maldives, religious extremism has also posed a serious challenge to the democratization process in the country. Interestingly, it has been (mis) used by dictators to give sanctity to their rule. As briefly pointed out earlier, the downfall of Nasheed, which marked the end of the Maldives' brief honeymoon with democracy, was to a large extent an indication of the challenge posed by religious extremism, along with other forces. During his presidency Nasheed and his MDP openly took a liberal stance on religion. However, it is pertinent to mention that even though he was a champion of secular democracy, Nasheed joined hands with the Islamic radicals like the Adhaalath Party (AP), which takes its inspiration from Egypt's Muslim Brotherhood, to come to power. For their part, the AP joined Nasheed in order to influence his government's policy through Islamic Ministry. Consequently, under the influence of the AP, Nasheed replaced the Council of Islamic Affairs with the Ministry of Islamic Affairs, which was mostly controlled by the AP. The influence of the AP on Nasheed can also be seen in the fact that from 2008 to 2009, a number of proposals like outlawing places of worship for non-Muslims and banning the sale of alcohol were submitted in the *Majlis*. Fissures started to grow between Nasheed and the AP, as his original idea of separating religion from politics failed completely. Nasheed's emphasis on secular democracy and the AP's determination to make the Maldives a pure Islamic country clashed, culminating in the AP severing its ties with the MDP in 2011 (Sultana, 2015: 29). Consequently, the political rivals from the Islamist camp led by the AP unleashed a campaign against him by calling him '*laa-dheene*' (irreligious in

152   *Democracy in the Maldives*

Dhivehi). Democracy was denigrated as a concept imported by infidels and Nasheed was depicted as their 'Maldivian agent'. Being at the heart of an anti-Nasheed coalition, the AP played a crucial role in launching the 'defending Islam' campaign against Nasheed, who was accused of 'destroying Islam' (Musthaq, 2014: 168). His 'liberal stance' on Islam was portrayed as uprooting Islam altogether in favor of the Western ideals and culture of religious freedom. These messages were continuously circulated on the internet. Moreover, the AP organized rallies, with the biggest one on December 23, 2011 (ibid.), to mobilize the masses against what they called 'an infidel Nasheed'. Even his own former minister of Islamic Affairs vowed to see him defeated during the next election, and led rallies in which participants took an oath to defend Islam. Moreover, the Jumhooree Party (JP) leader Qasim Ibrahim repeatedly called for 'jihad' against the MDP government in order to save the country and its religion from Nasheed. Worse, Nasheed's Vice President Abdullah Waheed would refer to his supporters as 'holy warriors' and called his resignation as the 'will of Allah'. Additionally, a 30-page booklet accusing Nasheed and his MDP of undermining Islam and encouraging vice was published by the former presidential candidate and Attorney-General Hassan Saeed's Dhivehi Qaumee Party (DQP) (Musthaq, 2014: 169). The rising wave of radicalism can further be substantiated by the fact that when Nasheed was attacked for not being 'Muslim enough', his detractors celebrated, saying 'he had it coming' via messages posted on Facebook, Twitter, Telegram, and in the comments sections of newspapers (Markar, 2021).

The 'defending Islam' rhetoric played a pivotal role in the 2013 presidential elections that paved the way for Yameen. Throughout his presidency, Yameen kept the rhetoric of 'defending Islam' alive, using it regularly to shore up public support or denigrate the opposition. It was during Yameen's time that the Maldives moved very close to Saudi Arabia (the role of Saudi Arabia is discussed in a separate section), which resulted in the Wahhabi and Salafist ideologies beginning to dominate the religious discourse in the Maldives. Given the Maldivian legal system, which makes Islam the state religion and restricts religious freedom, as well as the aggressive rhetoric of Islamic NGOs and political parties, few are willing to openly express views contrary to this discourse. Moreover, as Azra Naseem points out, 'the Salafi belief in "progression through regression", however, is often in conflict with the aspirations and ideals of the democratic system of governance, making the interplay between religion and politics both tense and intense' (Naseem, 2020: 124). Yameen's policy of giving tacit support for and enabling radicalization to flourish with relative impunity had wider implications, as it steadily advanced and is changing the fabric of Maldivian society. Dissent, diversity, and richness of opinions as well as religious freedom are becoming its casualty. There has been an increase in flogging and the introduction of other Sharia punishments, a reduction of women's rights and role in society, and attacks against 'secular' and 'liberal-Islamic' groups and individuals (Dzenisevich, 2016). Since concepts like secularism and democracy are denounced as alien and incompatible with the Islamic way of life, this is directly threatening democracy and human rights, as well as putting those advocating these values at risk. The Salafi activist-challengers are strongly intruding in the non-governmental arena as well. Many prominent Salafi actors have their own NGOs, while many non-registered groups also operate news and educational websites. These are used for extending Da'wa and monitoring the conduct of citizens, both on- and offline, so that they don't digress from the righteous path of the al-salaf-al-sālihin. While there is nothing wrong in Da'wa per se, as it is a call for righteousness, there is a particular exclusivist brand of religion with political interests that these groups advocate. The most influential nongovernmental Salafi actor is Jamiyyath Salaf, which campaigned for abolishing the Maldivian Democracy Network (MDN), a local NGO working toward protection of human rights and democratic values. In September 2019, Salaf condemned the MDN Report as 'obvious proof of continuing efforts to wipe Islam from Maldivian territory and to establish a secular government' (Dzenisevich and Reddy, 2021), and demanded that the NGO be shut down. The rising tide of Islamic radicalism has in the recent past turned the Maldives into a breeding ground for pan-Islamic militant networks, such as Al-Qaeda and the Islamic State group. It is believed that an estimated 250 to 450 Maldivians left the islands to join the Middle East terror network. According to an estimate by the US State Department, the Maldives had emerged as the largest supplier of Islamic State (IS) operatives per capita (Bansal, 2023). The recruits included 61 men, who took their wives and children through Turkey to join IS camps in Syria. In 2019, the US government affirmed this link, earning the Maldives more notoriety. Washington identified Ahmed Ameen, a Maldivian, as the liaison between Maldivian fighters and IS operatives in Syria and Afghanistan (Markar, 2021). In September 2019, authorities also revealed that local terror cells connected to Al-Qaeda were responsible for at least three high-profile killings in the Maldives between 2012 and 2017. These included the killings of Afrasheem Ali, a parliamentarian and religious scholar; Yameen Rasheed, a liberal blogger; and journalist Ahmed Rilwan. IS-inspired attacks in the Maldives have also gained notoriety (Naseem, 2020: 131). In February 2020, after three foreigners were stabbed, a video message surfaced featuring three masked men, who claimed to be members of a Maldivian Islamic extremist group linked to IS, taking responsibility for the attack (Markar, 2021). The present government led by Solih might have again raised the hopes for a 'democratic resurrection', but incidents like the shutting down of the MDN (Dzenisevich and Reddy, 2021) and the May 6 bomb attack on Nasheed in the capital city of Maldives (Moorthy, 2021) underscore that democracy in Maldives is at risk of being hijacked by reactionary groups who oppose the democratization of the government.

b) The Tragedy of Authoritarian Leverage: China and Saudi Arabia as External Influences

Apart from the serious internal challenges, the trajectory of democratic backsliding in the Maldives also underscored the vulnerability of a nascent democracy falling prey to external authoritarian 'sharp power'. To explain this, we bring to the forefront the role of two authoritarian states who exert enormous

154 *Democracy in the Maldives*

influence on the tiny island nation of the Maldives and fuel the democratic backsliding process. These are China and Saudi Arabia. Both these states have pumped huge amounts of aid into the Maldives in the most recent decade and especially during the turbulent authoritarian regime of president Yameen. Given their indifference to democratic norms and values, their mounting influence has been counter-democratic and has in fact buttressed authoritarian tendencies. This is clear from their overwhelming support for Yameen.

China's overtures to the Maldives began during President Nasheed's time despite the fact that he publicly embraced the 'India first' policy. It was in 2009 that Maldives opened its embassy in China and in 2010 that Nasheed paid a visit to Beijing (Moorthy, 2010). However, given Nasheed's liberal democratic mindset, he made it clear that the Maldives was not going to play the China card, and that it was easier to deal with India than China. The role of China in Maldivian politics became more visible during the turbulent anti-Nasheed time. China opened its embassy in the Maldives in 2011 (Outlook, 2021) amid the escalating anti-Nasheed protests. Unsurprisingly, China's mounting influence in the Maldives and its authoritarian turn ran parallel. In the post-Nasheed period this influence was quite visible. Within a year of Yameen's presidency, Xi Jinping became the first Chinese premier to visit the Maldives. Xi's description of the China-Maldives relations as 'a model of equality and harmonious interaction between countries of different sizes' (Naseem, 2015: 110) makes it attractive for authoritarian leaders to bet on Beijing. The international condemnation for democratic backsliding led by Yameen further made him tilt towards the Chinese orbit. He visited Beijing in September 2014, securing a US $16 million grant, and would host Xi in the same month. The Maldives signed a 'free trade agreement' with China, along with nine other infrastructure agreements, and most importantly China secured Yameen's pledge to support and be part of the Belt and Road Initiative (Smith, 2020: 6). China's 'non-interference' policy or what can be referred to as 'domestic indifference' yielded better results in its employment of 'sharp power' to shield Yameen. Yameen frequently justified his tilt towards China as a means to meet the challenges of what he alleged as 'Western colonial powers' interference in Maldivian domestic politics' (Minivan News, 2014) that threaten the country's Islamic identity. For him, doing business with China didn't involve any such compulsion for the Maldives. To put it differently, the authoritarian Yameen found solace in China's authoritarian leverage, which didn't have the strings of so-called 'Western concepts' or 'Western notions' of human rights and principles of democracy attached to it. Capitalizing on this, China has made full use of its 'sharp power' to keep the Maldives fully under its sway. The Chinese Communist Party (CCP) patronized a section of the Maldivian government officials to 'burnish its image in the eyes of the Maldives' political and economic elites, as well as common citizens. Beijing has also been training Maldivian civil servants. In 2017 alone 300 civil servants visited China for professional training (Shullman, 2019: 61). Taking recourse to its 'public diplomacy', China back in 2013 donated 25,000 LED light bulbs across the country and worked with the Maldives' Ministry of Health to sponsor cataract operations (Minivan News, 2013).

While analyzing the strategy of Beijing in 13 countries, the US-based International Republican Institute (IRI) found that increasing dependence on China in target countries has negative repercussions for democracy (Shullman, 2019). The Maldives displays similar characteristics. Beijing's investment has reinforced authoritarian instincts. The big deals with China have been questionable and very controversial, with allegations of corruption, secrecy, and espionage. Most of those deals were made possible by undermining the constitution and other democratic institutions. Consider the 2015 decision by the Yameen-led *Majlis* to amend the constitution to allow foreign ownership of land. The fact that a process that normally would take weeks or months was concluded within just 48 hours, almost completely bypassing conventional channels of consultation and deliberation (Lim and Mukherjee, 2019: 509), justifies the claim of China's hand in the backsliding of Maldivian democracy. Likewise, the fast-tracked debate and legislative process to approve the 'Free Trade Agreement' (FTA) with China further demonstrates the negative consequences for the country's democratic trajectory. The parliamentary committee to study the FTA met behind closed doors and rushed through thousands of pages of FTA documents in just ten minutes. Moreover, the legislation was passed the following day with only 30 votes from the 'ruling party lawmakers in the 85-member legislature' in an unplanned meeting that the opposition MDP boycotted (*Maldives Independent*, 2017). In 2018 China also shielded Yameen's decision to impose the controversial emergency state amid the mounting international condemnation and possible intervention. It was because of Beijing's 'security umbrella' that Yameen could get away with his undemocratic moves. The role of deepening engagement with China in undermining the country's democratic and liberal institutions was also evident in Beijing's attempts in buttress Yameen's chances of re-election. Inaugurating the 'China-Maldives Friendship Bridge' even though the bridge was incomplete just before the 2018 presidential elections (Shullman, 2019: 61) demonstrated the full exercise of 'sharp power' by China to manipulate elections and hence drive the backsliding phenomenon. It will be very interesting to watch the future democratic trajectory of the country as the latest presidential elections (2023), which were described in media as a referendum on being either pro-China or pro-India (*The Guardian*, 2023), resulted in the most pro-China candidate, Mohamed Muizzu, elected as the new president.

Saudi Arabia's role in the Maldives' democratic backsliding can be determined from the fact that Riyadh's growing role in Malé's domestic politics has fueled anti-democratic rhetoric. As in the case with China, Yameen's authoritarian turn also ran parallel with his growing closeness with Saudi Arabia. The huge influx of Saudi aid and oil-rich investments in the 'heavenly Maldives' (Aruma, 2014) was robustly encouraged by Yameen. Keeping in mind Yameen's highest priority of protecting courtiers' 'Islamic identity', the Saudi Kingdom assumed the significance of a 'natural ally'. In March 2015, Yameen paid a state visit to Riyadh during which he acquired US $20 million for budget support, and secured Saudi pledges to invest in various development projects in the

156 *Democracy in the Maldives*

Maldives. In August 2015 Riyadh opened an embassy in Malé and since then the Crown Prince Mohammed bin Salman has been a frequent visitor. The religious underpinnings driving the Maldives-Saudi comradery were evident during Yameen's visit. He signed a joint communiqué pledging to 'fortify' bilateral relations in all sectors' for the purpose of 'accomplishing their common interests and providing support to the issues of the Muslim nation, while rejecting foreign interference in their internal affairs' (Minivan News, 2015). While entering into a formal agreement in Islamic affairs, Saudi Arabia pledged US $1.7 million in free aid for the development of 'world-class' mosques in various parts of the Maldives. It is also offering 150 scholarships for Maldivian students to study in the kingdom, and in May 2015 the Saudi Arabian Muslim Scholars Association pledged a grant of US $100, 000 to promote Islamic education in the island nation. The government signed a Memorandum of Understanding (MOU) with Saudi Arabia to 'maintain religious unity' in the Maldives (Naseem, 2020: 136). Moreover, apart from the two-fold increase in the number of Maldivian hajj pilgrims, Saudi Arabia also agreed to build a hotel exclusively for them in Mecca along with Saudi assistance 'in all works of establishing an Islamic University in the Maldives' (Naseem, 2015: 115). In 2016, Saudi Arabia also vowed to build a new national mosque, the nation's largest, in the capital city of Malé, named after King Salman (*Saudi Gazette*, 2021), which was opened to the public with the congregation of the Friday prayer on April 1, 2022.

Despite Yameen's insistence on non-interference in internal affairs and 'no strings attached' to the Saudi assistance (as was the case with Western aid, according to him), the fact remains that the Maldives has witnessed the flourishing of the Saudi-sponsored Wahhabi brand of Islam. While examining the linkage between Saudi aid and the spread of revolutionary Islamism in the Maldives, Azra Naseem points out that 'the Maldives provides a prime example of the spread of Wahhabism/Salafism, with the "acculturizing effect" of the erosion of an ethnic Islamic culture and its contributions to radical and violent religious ideologies' (Naseem, 2015: 116). Likewise, as Robinson has argued, 'the education system is being quietly radicalized and young Maldivians are increasingly indoctrinated by an imported Saudi Wahhabism completely alien to the country's historically moderate Islam' (Robinson, 2016: 224). As discussed in the section on Islamic radicalism, with the politicization of radical Islamic elements by Yameen to sustain his anti-Nasheed and in fact anti-democratic rhetoric, the Saudi patronage added fuel to the fire. Not just democracy itself, but even those who spoke of it were ruthlessly targeted and killed. This had a direct impact on the nascent democratic process in the country. Apart from various state and non-state actors associated with the growing radical Islamism, the country's media and school curricula have been saturated with messages of hate against 'nonbelievers', be they Maldivians or outsiders. Those who oppose this narrative and instead call for tolerance and human rights, and for the reduction of religious involvement in politics, are ridiculed and labeled as enemies of Islam (Markar, 2021). Apart from the 'acculturizing effect', harmful for political pluralism and other reforms, Saudi Arabia also openly encouraged Yameen's unbridled lurch towards authoritarianism. Saudi Arabia not only supported Yameen's declaration of emergency but also granted a US $160 million in aid to him, thereby strengthening his authoritarian moves.

Conclusion

The Maldives, despite being a low-lying small archipelago nation, has recently assumed much significance in media and academic circles. The country beyond the much-hyped holiday and honeymoon destination has much to offer to the growing literature on the 'Pandora's box' of democratic backsliding. The country witnessed a far-from-smooth transition to democracy in 2008 by removing Asia's longest serving dictator, Abdullah Gayoom. When most of the world was coming to terms with the 'declining allure of democracy', this small, entirely Islamic nation started as a trend-setter and served as a precursor to what would later become the much-famous 'Arab Spring'. However, the newly gained status of an 'electoral democracy' didn't go well and the brief Maldivian honeymoon with democracy ended tragically in 2012, when the country's pro-democracy and first democratically elected president Mohamed Nasheed was forced at 'gun-point' to resign. The resignation of Nasheed in what came to be characterized as a 'bloodless coup', if anything, underscores the perils of backsliding in a fledgling democracy. Following Nasheed, the country witnessed democratic backsliding under the caretaker Mohamed Waheed and the oppressive Yameen, who entered office as president in the controversial elections of 2013. If Nasheed were the Maldivian 'Obama' or 'Mandela', Yameen would become its Robert Mugabe or Kim Jong Un. The first tragedy that engulfed the nascent democracy and that would drive the backsliding process was what president Nasheed termed as the 'dregs of dictatorship'. The authoritarian loyalists would haunt Nasheed's efforts at democratization and would pave the way for the former autocrat Gayoom's half-brother Yameen to win the elections. Furthermore, the opposition led by the authoritarian residues under Gayoom utilized the growing Islamic radicalism to force Nasheed out of office. Throughout this period, Yameen adopted a policy of ambivalence towards Islamic radicals and in a way politicized them, which further undermined democratic prospects. However, the Maldivian democracy also became a casualty of the phenomenon of 'presidential hegemony' under Yameen and the subsequent 'executive aggrandizement'. Despite being an elected ruler, albeit controversially, Yameen hollowed out almost all the essential institutions of democracy and made them subservient. He exercised a quintessential presidential hegemony to attack the *Majlis* (parliament), judiciary, and the Election Commission to ensure no one challenged his autocratic rule. He jailed almost all dissident voices, including his half-brother Gayoom and the former president Nasheed. The backsliding trajectory of the Maldivian democracy also demonstrates the perils of 'autocratic sharp power'. The nascent democracy was exposed to the dangers of outside authoritarian temptations by President

158 *Democracy in the Maldives*

Yameen that served his own autocratic moves. China and Saudi Arabia's growing influence in the Maldives has anti-democratic consequences and therefore further buttressed the backsliding process. Even though the 2018 presidential elections were hailed as a triumph of democracy, and despite Mohamed Solih's initial attempts to set the country back on the path of democracy, the specter of backsliding returned. While the latest presidential elections of September 2023 were comparatively competitive and peaceful, this does not indicate that democracy even in its procedural form is at work in the Maldives. Notwithstanding the nominal assurances given by new President Mohamed Muizzu of governing the country as per the people's wishes, the post-2008 democratic trajectory provides a cautionary tale. No government until know has fully adhered to democratic norms. Until there is a rigorous effort to uphold the rule of law, respect the separation of powers, and uphold the principles of democracy, the Maldives' nascent democracy will continue to be vulnerable to the specter of backsliding. While much of the onus is on the people of the Maldives, as well as its ruling elite, to ensure that the principles of democracy are upheld, the international community also has a role to play in supporting the effort to ensure the Maldivian fledgling democracy takes off.

References

Amir, H. 2011. *Islamism and radicalism in the Maldives*. Naval Postgraduate School Monterey California Department of National Security Affairs.

Amnesty International. 2015. "Maldives: Former president Mohamed Nasheed ill-treated after arrest, denied medical treatment and legal representation". March 3, https://www.amnesty.org/en/documents/ASA29/1114/2015/en/.

Aruma, Fathimath. 2014. "President calls out for investments to 'heaven-like' Maldives". Haveeru Online. December 24.

Ayres, Alyssa. 2018. "Maldives halts democratic backsliding". Council on Foreign Relations. September 24.

Bansal, A. 2023. "Maldives: Choices and implications for India". Centre for Joint Warfare Studies. October 30.

BBC News. 2014. "Entire Maldives election commission sentenced". March 9, https://www.bbc.com/news/world-asia-26508259.

BBC News. 2018a. "Maldives election: Ibrahim Mohamed Solih claims victory". September 23, https://www.bbc.com/news/world-asia-45592375.

BBC News. 2018b. "Maldives election: Opposition defeats China-backed Abdulla Yameen". September 24, https://www.bbc.com/news/world-asia-45623126.

Bermeo, N. 2016. "On democratic backsliding". *Journal of Democracy*, Vol. 27, No. 1: 5–19.

Bhim, M. 2019. "Does electoral authoritarianism persist? A comparison of recent elections in Fiji, Seychelles, and Maldives", in J.I. Lahai (ed.), *Governance and political adaptation in fragile states*. London: Palgrave Macmillan, 243–270.

Bonofer, J.A. 2010. "The challenges of democracy in Maldives". *International Journal of South Asian Studies*, Vol. 3, No. 2: 433–449.

Carothers, T. and O'Donohue, A. eds. 2019. *Democracies divided: The global challenge of political polarization*. Washington: Brookings Institution Press.

Carothers, T. and Press, B. 2022. "Understanding and responding to global democratic backsliding". Carnegie Endowment for International Peace.

Chandramohan, Balaji. 2010. "Maldives struggling with infant democracy". *Open Democracy*, September 30.

Coppedge, M. 2017. "Eroding regimes: What, where, and when?" V-Dem Working Paper, November.

Croissant, A. and Haynes, J. 2021. "Democratic regression in Asia: Introduction". *Democratization*, Vol. 28, No. 1: 1–21.

Diamond, Larry. 2021. "Democratic regression in comparative perspective: scope, methods, and causes". *Democratization*, Vol. 28, No. 1: 22–42.

Dzenisevich, U. and Reddy, K. 2021. "Authoritarianism and radicalization undermine Maldivian Democracy". Commonwealth Human Rights Initiative. https://www.humanrightsinitiative.org/blog/authoritarianism-and-radicalisation-undermine-maldivian-democracy-a-chri-investigation-finds.

Dzenisevich, Uladzimir. 2016. "Searching for a lost democracy: A fact finding mission report on the Maldives". Commonwealth Human Rights Initiative. https://www.humanrightsinitiative.org/download/1456297508CHRI_Fact%20Finding%20Mission%20to%20the%20Maldives_2015-16.pdf.

Economic & Political Weekly. 2008. "Transition to multiparty democracy". November 22.

European Foundation for South Asian Studies. 2019. "The Maldives: Return of democracy and challenges ahead". January, https://www.efsas.org/The%20Maldives%20%20Return%20of%20democracy%20and%20challenges%20ahead.pdf.

Evans, Judith. 2008. "Maldives hold first multiparty presidential poll". Reuters, October 8.

Freedom House. 2020. "Maldives: Freedom in the world 2020". https://freedomhouse.org/country/maldives/freedom-world/2020.

Ghafoor, M. Abdul. (2023). "The past, present, and future of Maldivian democracy". *The Diplomat*, October 25.

Hindustan Times. 2008. "Maldives despot's record reign ends". October 30.

Human Rights Watch. 2018a. "'An all-out assault on democracy': Crushing dissent in the Maldives". https://www.hrw.org/report/2018/08/16/all-out-assault-democracy/crushing-dissent-maldives.

Human Rights Watch. 2018b. "Maldives: Opposition candidates barred from election". May 29, https://www.hrw.org/news/2018/05/29/maldives-opposition-candidates-barred-election.

Human Rights Watch. 2019. "Maldives: Human rights group shut down". October 11.

Human Rights Watch. 2020. "World report 2020: Maldives". https://www.hrw.org/world-report/2020/country-chapters/maldives#.

Human Rights Watch. 2022. "Maldives new 'evidence' law undermines media freedom". July 1, https://www.hrw.org/news/2022/07/01/maldives-new-evidence-law-undermines-media-freedom. Human Rights Watch. 2023. "World report 2023: Maldives: Events of 2022". https://www.hrw.org/world-report/2023/country-chapters/maldives.

International Commission of Jurists. 2014. "Maldives: Removal of Supreme Court judges an assault on independence of the judiciary". December 18, https://www.icj.org/maldives-removal-of-supreme-court-judges-an-assault-on-independence-of-the-judiciary/.

Khandekar, Omkar. 2018. "Maldives: Leap of freedom". *Open the Magazine*. October 3.

Kumar, Anand. 2016. *Multi-party democracy in Maldives and the emerging security environment in the Indian Ocean region*. New Delhi: Pentagon Press.

Levitsky, S. and Way, L.A. 2020. "The new competitive authoritarianism". *Journal of Democracy*, Vol. 31, No. 1: 51–65.

160 Democracy in the Maldives

Lim, D.J. and Mukherjee, R. 2019. "Hedging in South Asia: Balancing economic and security interests amid Sino-Indian competition". *International Relations of the Asia-Pacific*, Vol. 19, No. 3: 493–522.

Maldives Independent. 2017. "China-Maldives free trade deal rushed through parliament". November 30, https://maldivesindependent.com/politics/china-maldives-free-trade-deal-rushed-through-parliament-134382.

Mallempatti, Samatha. 2018. "Pre-presidential election developments in Maldives: Is free and fair elections possible under the present political conditions?" Indian Council of World Affairs. June 20, https://www.icwa.in/show_content.php?lang=1&level=3&ls_id=2436&lid=1838.

Maloney, C. 1976. "The Maldives: New stresses in an old nation". *Asian Survey*, Vol. 16, No. 7: 654–671.

Markar, M.M. 2021. "Murder attempt on Maldives ex-president reveals rising radicalism". *Nikkei Asia*. May 17, https://asia.nikkei.com/Politics/Murder-attempt-on-Maldives-ex-president-reveals-rising-radicalism.

Merkel, W. 2014. "Is capitalism compatible with democracy?" *Zeitschrift für vergleichende Politikwissenschaft*, Vol. 8, No. 2: 109–128.

Minivan News. 2013. "China donates 250,000 energy efficient LED lights to the Maldives". April 2, https://minivannewsarchive.com/news-in-brief/china-donates-250000-energy-efficient-led-lights-to-the-maldives-55587.

Minivan News. 2014. "President Yameen slams 'Western colonial powers,' declares foreign policy shift to East". November 11, https://minivannewsarchive.com/politics/president-yameen-slams-western-colonial-powers-declares-foreign-policy-shift-to-east-90937#sthash.NKgfKGS4.dpbs.

Minivan News. 2015. "Saudi Arabia assured loan assistance for airport development, says Dr Shainee". March 22, https://minivannewsarchive.com/politics/saudi-arabia-assured-loan-assistance-for-airport-development-says-dr-shainee-94244#sthash.aLter25C.dpbs.

Monitor. 2019. "Criminal defamation law repealed but those expressing critical views still at risk". January 30, https://monitor.civicus.org/updates/2019/01/30/criminal-defamation-law-repealed-those-expressing-critical-views-still-risk/.

Moorthy, N.S. 2010. "President Nasheed wrests the initiative". Observer Research Foundation. October 19, https://www.orfonline.org/research/president-nasheed-wrests-the-initiative/.

Moorthy, N.S. 2014. "Maldives: EC crisis ends, polls as scheduled". Observer Research Foundation. March 15, https://www.orfonline.org/research/maldives-ec-crisis-ends-polls-as-scheduled/.

Moorthy, N.S. 2015. "Maldives: Trivializing the presidency". Observer Research Foundation. January 3, https://www.orfonline.org/research/maldives-trivialising-the-presidency/.

Moorthy, N.S. 2021. "The Maldives: Is the attack on Nasheed a sign of escalating radicalism?". Observer Research Foundation. May 7, https://www.orfonline.org/expert-speak/the-maldives-is-the-attack-on-nasheed-a-sign-of-escalating-radicalism/.

Moosa, H. and Abi-Habib, M. 2018. "Fears of Maldives crisis ease after president concedes election loss". *The New York Times*. September 24, https://www.nytimes.com/2018/09/24/world/asia/maldives-presidential-election-ibrahim-mohamed-solih.html.

Mukherjee, C. 2021. *Democratic backsliding in South Asia: Is terrorism to blame?* NUPRI Working Paper. https://nupri.prp.usp.br/pdf/wp/NUPRI_Working_Paper_13.pdf.

Mulberry, M. 2012. "The Maldives—from dictatorship to democracy, and back?". *Non-Violent Conflict*. July, https://www.nonviolent-conflict.org/maldives-dictatorship-democracy-back/.

Democracy in the Maldives 161

Musthaq, Fathima. 2014. "Shifting tides in South Asia: Tumult in the Maldives". *Journal of Democracy*, Vol. 25, No. 2: 164–170.

Naseem, Azra. 2015. "The honeymoon is over: Maldives as a growing security threat in the Indian Ocean". *Irish Studies in International Affairs*, Vol. 26: 99–119.

Naseem, Azra. 2020. "Democracy and Salafism in the Maldives: A battle for the future", in Ali Riaz (ed.), *Religion and politics in South Asia*. London: Routledge, 124–140.

Nasheed, Mohamed. 2012a. "Trouble in paradise". *Foreign Policy*, March 1.

Nasheed, Mohamed. 2012b. "The Dregs of Dictatorship". *The New York Times*, February 8.

OHCHR. 2018. "Maldives state of emergency 'all-out assault on democracy'—Zeid". February 7, https://www.ohchr.org/EN/NewsEvents/Pages/DisplayNews.aspx?NewsID=22640&LangID=E.

Outlook. 2011. "SAARC Summit: China opens embassy in Maldives". November 8, https://www.outlookindia.com/newswire/story/saarc-summit-china-opens-embassy-in-maldives/740767.

Pérez-Liñán, A., Schmidt, N., and Vairo, D. 2019. "Presidential hegemony and democratic backsliding in Latin America, 1925–2016". *Democratization*, Vol. 26, No. 4: 606–625.

Plattner, M.F. 2017. "Liberal democracy's fading allure". *Journal of Democracy*, Vol. 28, No. 4: 5–14.

Ranjan, Amit. 2021. "Mohamed Nasheed attacked: Rise of Islamic radicalism in the Maldives". NUS Institute of South Asian Studies (ISAS). May 18.

Repucci, S. and Slipowitz, A. 2021. "Democracy under siege". Freedom House. March 9.

Reuters. 2018. "European Union warns of sanctions against Maldives rights violators". July 16, https://www.reuters.com/article/us-eu-maldives-idUSKBN1K61KA.

Riaz, A., 2021. "The pathway of democratic backsliding in Bangladesh". *Democratization*, Vol. 28, No. 1: 179–197.

Robinson, J.J. 2015. *The Maldives: Islamic republic, tropical autocracy*. London: C Hurst & Co Publishers.

Robinson, J.J. 2016. "The Maldives: What went wrong with the democracy experiment?" *The Round Table*, Vol. 105, No. 2: 223–225.

Robinson, J.J. 2018. "The Maldives' political soap opera won't end without judicial reform". *The Guardian*. February 7, https://www.theguardian.com/commentisfree/2018/feb/07/maldives-political-soap-opera-judicial-reform.

Robinson, J.J. 2019. "The Maldives' Games of Thrones". *The Diplomat*. January 1.

Rogers, B. 2016. "The Maldives: A threat to us all". *The Round Table*, Vol. 105, No. 3: 333–335.

Saltmarsh, Matthew. 2010. "Going after government looters". *The New York Times*, June 11.

Saudi Gazette. 2021. "Maldives' largest mosque named after King Salman set to open soon". September 1.

Shackle, Samira. 2008. "Democracy for Maldives". *The New Statesman*. October 30.

Sharma, Rajiv. 2018. "How the Maldives crisis developed, the China factor, and why Modi is unlikely to do a Rajiv Gandhi". *Money Control*. February 10, https://www.moneycontrol.com/news/opinion/how-the-maldives-crisis-developed-the-china-factor-and-why-modi-is-unlikely-to-do-a-rajiv-gandhi-2505235.html.

Shullman, David. 2019. "Chinese malign influence and the corrosion of democracy: An assessment of Chinese interference in thirteen key countries". International Republican Institute.

162 *Democracy in the Maldives*

Smith, Jeff M. 2020. "China and the Maldives: Lessons from the Indian Ocean's new battleground". Heritage Foundation Backgrounder. October 28.

Sultana, Gulbin. 2015. "An unholy alliance of politics and radical Islam in Maldives". MP-IDSA. November 20, https://idsa.in/idsanews/alliance-of-politics-and-radical-islam-in-maldives_201115.

The Commonwealth. 2013. "Reports of the Commonwealth observer groups—Maldives presidential election". September 7.

The Commonwealth. 2019. "Maldives parliamentary elections". April 6.

The Economic Times. 2018. "Maldives sends envoys to 'friendly nations', not to India". February 9, https://economictimes.indiatimes.com/news/politics-and-nation/maldives-sends-envoys-to-friendly-nations-not-to-india/articleshow/62835191.cms.

The Guardian. 2015. "Maldives ex-president Nasheed jailed for 13 years on terrorism charges". March 13, https://www.theguardian.com/world/2015/mar/13/maldives-ex-president-nasheed-jailed-13-years-terrorism-charges.

The Guardian. 2023. "Pro-China candidate Mohamed Muizzu wins Maldives presidency, upending relationship with India". October 1.

The Independent. 2008. "Asia's longest-serving ruler ousted in Maldives". October 29.

The Indian Express. 2018a. "Maldives' opposition presidential candidate Ibrahim Mohamed Solih claims victory". September 24, https://indianexpress.com/article/world/maldives-opposition-presidential-candidate-solih-claims-victory-5371161/.

The Indian Express. 2018b. "US expresses concern over continued democratic backsliding in Maldives". September 7, https://indianexpress.com/article/world/us-expresses-concern-over-continued-democratic-backsliding-in-maldives-5344968/.

The Wire. 2017. "Maldives parliament approves FTA with China—but with no opposition present". November 30.

Tiezzi, Shannon. 2020. "JJ Robinson on the Maldives' return to democracy". *The Diplomat*. November 1.

Vaishnav, M. 2021. "The decay of Indian democracy: Why India no longer ranks among the lands of the free". *Foreign Affairs*. March 18.

V-Dem. 2021. "Autocratization turns viral". https://www.v-dem.net/static/website/files/dr/dr_2021.pdf.

Walker, C. 2018. "What is 'sharp power'?" *Journal of Democracy*, Vol. 29, No. 3: 9–23.

Wehrey, F. 2015. "The authoritarian resurgence: Saudi Arabia's anxious autocrats". *Journal of Democracy*, Vol. 26, No. 2: 71–85.

Wike, R., Silver, L., and Castillo, A. 2019. "Many across the globe are dissatisfied with how democracy is working". Pew Research Center. April 29.

Wright, Oliver. 2014. "Islamic State: The Maldives—a recruiting paradise for jihadists". *The Independent*. September 14.

Zahir, Azim. 2018. "The Maldives: The rise and fall of a Muslim democracy". Al Jazeera. September 23.

7 Nepal's Tryst with Democracy: Internal Dynamics, External Influences

Abijit Sharma

Introduction

Despite ushering in a new era of democracy in 1951, Nepal's search for political stability and prosperity has remained elusive. Its seven-decade-long democratic journey has been characterized by political deadlocks, infighting among parties, frequent falls of governments and intrusive external interventions. As a result, governance remains poor, corruption is endemic and economic growth has consistently been anemic. The country has seen parliamentary democracy, an autocratic monarchical rule, a constitutional monarchy and now a federal system. But little change has been witnessed in terms of stability. Since 1951, the country has seen more than 50 different governments, none of which has completed its full term. When the decade-long insurgency ended in 2006 and subsequently promulgated a new constitution ushering in a federal structure, many expected revolutionary changes. However, five years later, the euphoria has gone, thanks to the growing feud among leaders and political parties. Much research and many discourses have taken place to comprehend Nepal's inability to secure a stable democracy. This chapter primarily places the focus on two factors – geopolitics and the country's pliant leadership. Given its strategic location, Nepal has turned out to be a battleground for its two neighbors – China and India – who openly flex their muscles and vie for influence (Bhatta, 2019). The latter has been prominent in the politics of Nepal for the past seven decades (Sharma, 2019), while Beijing's role has become prominent only in recent years (Upadhya, 2008). Post-2006, Western actors, through bilateral and multilateral aid agencies, have also been active (Bhatta, 2013). Nepali domestic politics has thus seen frequent intrusions from external actors, which have contributed to vested decision making, discord among the political parties and leaders and formations of splinter groups. This has subsequently made political stability elusive.

The chapter begins with a history of Nepal's tryst with democracy. The first section highlights the context in which democracy entered Nepal in 1951 and points out how historical signs of democratic regression in the country became visible as early as 1962 when the then King assumed executive power (Joshi & Rose, 2004/1966). While there were brief moments of euphoria, first in 1990

DOI: 10.4324/9781003261469-7

164 *Nepal's Tryst with Democracy*

when multi-party democracy returned and subsequently in 1991 when the general elections were held, the section discusses how these were short-lived. The next section talks about the continued regression of democracy at the turn of the century, which was characterized by a bloody insurgency until it ended in 2006. I have also attempted to characterize the nature of democratic regression in the country, noting that while democratic regression is often associated with populist authoritarianism, the case is different for Nepal. I argue that in Nepal, the problem is that of poor democratic consolidation (caused by the two factors mentioned earlier). I have tried to provide evidence of how poor democratic consolidation has led to various issues such as promissory coups, executive aggrandizement and weakening of horizontal accountability mechanisms. Then, one of the central arguments of this chapter, i.e., how geopolitical rivalry has disturbed Nepal's democratic journey, is taken up. I've started by discussing India's role in Nepali politics from 1951 (Rose, 1971), its relatively lax approach towards the Maoists (Sharma, 2019), its mediation role in bringing the Maoists to mainstream politics (Muni, 2012) and subsequently its support to Madhesi regional outfits (Jha, 2012) – all of which have been guided with the prime objective of maintaining its influence in the country. Nepal's northern neighbor, which has historically been less active in Nepali politics, has become more prominent post-2006, citing a number of instances, the most notable one being its role in bringing together two communist parties to formulate the country's biggest ever communist party (Mulmi, 2021). The section also delves briefly into how this geopolitical rivalry has been further complicated by the entry of Western actors (Bhatta, 2013). The chapter then raises the point that exogenous factors cannot work alone to derail a country's democratic process. While acknowledging the impact of geopolitics or foreign actors in Nepal's internal politics, it has also been pointed out that Nepal's pliant leadership has helped exogenous hands become successful in exerting influence. Pliant leadership coupled with other factors such as civil society have made Nepal a battleground for external actors (Tiwari, 2001). The chapter concludes by highlighting the need for Nepal's neighbors to understand that a stable and prosperous Nepal is more conducive to serve their national interests than an unstable Nepal. Needless to say, a large part of the responsibility lies with Nepali leadership. Until and unless the leadership sheds its docile nature, Nepal's democracy will never come of age.

Historical Overview of Democracy

Nepal had its first taste of democracy in 1951. The country had been ruled by an oligarchy (Rana family), with the King being a mere ceremonial head (Sharma, 2006/1986). Following the Revolution of 1950 and including a brief armed uprising by the Nepali Congress, the Ranas conceded defeat. Nepal's southern neighbor then helped broker a deal among the Ranas, the Nepali Congress and the King with the provision of an interim government, which was to set up the Constituent Assembly, promulgate a democratic constitution and

Nepal's Tryst with Democracy   165

hold elections for Nepal's first democratic government (Sharma, 2006/1986). However, what appeared to be a prosperous future for Nepal slowly began to go wrong. The period from 1951 to 1960 saw nine short-lived governments. There were no elections. Governments formed and fell, as political parties tussled while confronted by an increasingly assertive palace. The palace was active and involved in the making and unmaking of Prime Ministers (Joshi & Rose, 2004/1966). Following massive pressure, an election was finally held in 1959, nine years after the country had ushered in democracy. Nepal's first truly democratic government was formed in 1959 under the visionary Congress leader and statesman, B.P. Koirala. However, the euphoria was short-lived as an assertive and power-hungry palace could not foresee a democratic government progressing (Joshi & Rose, 2004/1966). Coupled with the King's jealousy for the Prime Minister's growing popularity, the King staged a coup in 1960, throwing out the elected government in just over a year (Chatterjee, 1977). Two years later, he introduced a new constitution, which promoted the party-less *Panchayat* system[1] and placed the monarch at the apex of power.

The period of 1962 to 1989 saw the continuation of the party-less *Panchayat* system, which, although the King had tried to portray it as people-centric and 'democratic', it wasn't (Baral, 1973). Only loyalists were selected to key positions. Political parties were banned. After more than two and half decades of the system, it started fragmenting as it was beset with corruption and scandals, and indeed the growing unity among opposing parliamentary parties (Thapa, 2005). Influenced to a large extent by the third wave of democratization that was engulfing Asia, the winter of 1989 witnessed the first 'People's Movement' to reinstate democracy. The *Panchayat* regime fell and a new era of democracy began in 1990. A new constitution drafted in 1990 turned Nepal into a constitutional monarchy and in 1991 general elections were held in which the Nepali Congress emerged victorious.

The new constitution, with limited powers for the assertive monarchy and a fresh election, did signal some level of stability for Nepal. Unfortunately, the period following 1990 is characterized, as with the period after 1951, by bitter infighting between parties, ego clashes among leaders and frequent changes of government (Brown, 1995). The turn of events was so quick that it was difficult to keep track; it was the beginning of a chaotic era of minority and coalition governments (Joshi & Rose, 2004/1966). Communist parties split one after another, while the royalist parties also fragmented and there was growing factionalism within the Nepali Congress, which almost tore the party in two. An election in 1991 gave the Nepali Congress the majority, but the then Prime Minister G.P. Koirala dissolved the parliament just three years later following internal dissension in his party. The mid-term elections gave the leftist United Marxist Leninist (UML) party an advantage and it formed a coalition government. Just about ten months later, the minority government collapsed following a motion of no-confidence. In 1995, a faction of the Nepali Congress formed a government. The lust for power among political leaders was so intense that by this time they had started discarding their ideological leanings (Brown, 1995).

166   *Nepal's Tryst with Democracy*

Democratic forces such as the Nepali Congress and the communist UML were forming coalitions with right-wing royalist parties that had sworn allegiance to the King. Parties that had ushered in democracy were willing to compromise everything in exchange for a short stint in power (Sharma, 2019).

Continued Breakdown of Democracy at the Turn of the Century

Nepali politics entered the new century by carrying the chaotic baggage of the past one. The restoration of democracy in 1990 had brought about a lot of elation in the country. It appeared that democratic erosion, which had begun after the King's authoritarian rule in the 1960s, had finally been reversed. However, the state of affairs changed only a little, even after 1990. In fact, democracy continued to suffer repeated and more severe blows (Thapa & Sharma, 2009). Although some stability seemed to have prevailed in 1999 when the country saw its fourth general elections and the formation of a government by the Nepali Congress, the internal bickering in the following year caused the fall of that government yet again. While parties continued to fight among themselves and bring down their own governments in Kathmandu, rural Nepal was burning a violent Maoist insurgency (Thapa & Sharma, 2009). The decade-long war, which ended only in 2006, cost the lives of over 17,000 Nepali citizens (Adhikari, 2019). Amidst all this chaos, two significant events occurred which changed the future course of Nepali democracy. First, in 2002, the then Prime Minister Sher Bahadur Deuba dissolved parliament with the support of the palace. He was then fired a few months later by King Gyanendra. Three years later the King staged what came to be known as a 'royal coup', citing incompetence of successive governments to provide a solution to the political stalemate. The King's move bore an eerie resemblance to what his father had done in the 1960s. However, unlike his father, the King's autocratic rule was short-lived this time around. In 2006, the country saw the 'Second People's Movement', which not only ended the King's rule but abolished the 240-year-old monarchy (Routledge, 2010).

In 2008, following the elections for the Constituent Assembly (CA), Nepal began the significant task of writing a new constitution (International Idea, 2015). The country also saw a Prime Minister from the Maoist Party, which had fought against the state for a decade and had only laid down its arms two years earlier (*The Hindu*, 2016). Despite a new party being at the helm and a relatively new political face as the head of government, the political culture remained unchanged. Nepali politics was unwilling to shed its old image. Just the following year, the Maoist government fell due to an issue involving a contentious decision of the Prime Minister.[2] Meanwhile, after multiple extensions, the term of the first elected CA ran out in 2012 without a constitution having been drafted. It was clear that for the political parties, constitution promulgation was the least of their worries (Dixit, 2012). In 2013, an election was held again for a second CA. This CA finally promulgated a constitution in 2015. Amidst all these developments, governments continued to form and fall in

Nepal's Tryst with Democracy   167

short periods. The new constitution transformed Nepal into a federal republic (Ghimire, 2015). A general election was held in 2017, the first in almost two decades. The local-level bodies, which were devoid of elected representatives for two decades due to the Maoist insurgency, were elected representatives – marking a new milestone for grassroots democracy (Al Jazeera, 2017b). However, five years later, little had changed. Despite high hopes of stability following the end of the Maoist insurgency, the introduction of a new administrative structure and a fresh election, the same cycle of political turmoil has continued to characterize Nepali politics. The country's development has taken a direct hit from all these events. Economic growth has remained sluggish for years now and the country relies heavily on remittances and foreign aid (Prasai, 2021). More worryingly, corruption remains endemic in the political system, as one can gauge from the 2020 ranking by Transparency International, which ranked Nepal 117th out of 180 countries in terms of corruption (Transparency International, 2020). Although the country saw another parliamentary election in 2022, which brought a new coalition government to power, Nepali people have slowly started losing hope that mainstream parties will ever lead the country along the path to political stability.

Explaining Nepal's Fledgling Democracy

Waldener and Lust define democratic backsliding as occurring not through a coup d'état or a random political development but a series of actions (Waldener & Lust, 2018). They further write that 'backsliding can make elections less competitive without entirely under-mining the electoral mechanism, restrict participation without explicitly abolishing norms of universal franchise and loosen constraints of accountability by eroding norms of answerability and punishment' (Waldener & Lust, 2018: 95). Bermeo sees a central role of the state in democratic backsliding, and writes that democratic backsliding refers to the state-led enfeeblement of the political institutions that sustain democracy (Bermeo, 2016). The extant literature on democratic backsliding largely blames the breakdown of democracy on populist authoritarian leaders. Explaining the trend, Larry Diamond writes that democratic backsliding since the turn of the century has been characterized by elected populist leaders neutering or taking over institutions that were set up to keep a check on them (Diamond, 2020). These include courts, prosecutors, legislatures, mass media, oversight and regulatory agencies and electoral administrations, which these authoritarians then have the liberty to deploy as weapons against opponents (Diamond, 2020). However, Nepal's case has been slightly different. The country hasn't really seen populist authoritarianism, like that of Narendra Modi in India or Mahindra Rajapaksa in Sri Lanka who have strangled democratic freedom in their respective countries (Dhume, 2019). Apart from the brief period from 2005 to 2006 when the King assumed a direct executive role, stifled civil liberties and imposed a state of emergency, citizens have always had the opportunity to exercise their basic rights. Nepal has also not reached the point at which it can be called an illiberal democracy. Although elections have not been held as regularly as they should have been, this is largely due to political disturbances rather than the meddling of a single strongman or party. Furthermore, none of the governments that have come up since 2000 have persecuted minorities or have leveled huge attacks on press freedom, like in neighboring Myanmar and Bangladesh, respectively (BBC News, 2020; Hassan, 2021).

Many theorists today claim that the most dramatic and far-reaching varieties of backsliding – coup d'états, executive coups by elected leaders and election related frauds – are on the decline compared to the past (Bermeo, 2016). But all these phenomena have always been alien to Nepal – before the turn of the century and after. Nepal has never seen a military coup d'état as in Pakistan, nor has it seen rigged elections at the hands of authoritarian leaders. Nepal scored 56 out of 100 in Freedom House's Freedom in the World Report 2021, being categorized as only 'Partly Free'. It has scored well on indicators for electoral process, political participation and pluralism, civil liberties, associational and organizational rights and personal autonomy and individual rights (Freedom House, 2021). Nepal's score was better than its South Asian counterparts Bangladesh (39), Pakistan (37), Maldives (40) and Afghanistan (27) (Freedom House, 2021). So, given the sui generis nature of Nepal's democratic trajectory, how can one explain Nepal's democratic journey? In Nepal, poor democratic consolidation has been the main problem throughout its democratic journey. Democratic consolidation is a process by which new democracies become strong enough to ensure that democratic breakdown is no longer likely (Gasiorowski & Power, 1998). The country has not been able to consolidate its democracy even seven decades after the onset of a democratic system. Despite its tryst with different political systems, regimes and parties, the country has a fledgling democracy due to the various exogenous and endogenous factors mentioned later in this chapter.

The fledgling democracy has paved the way for many other issues, for example, executive aggrandizement. In 2020, the then Prime Minister K.P. Oli, who had won the election mandate, displayed what Bermeo (2016) calls executive aggrandizement – a form of backsliding that occurs when elected executives gradually weaken checks on executive power, undertaking a series of changes that hamper democratic practices. Oli undertook moves such as bringing under his purview monitoring institutions such as the Department of Money Laundering Investigation, the National Investigation Department and the Department of Revenue Investigation; and more worryingly, he attempted to introduce a new media regulation bill, which was widely seen as the government's deliberate attempt to curb press freedom (Rai, 2020).

The consequences of poor democratic consolidation in Nepal have been grave. The figures speak for themselves: from 1951 to 2021, only five general fully democratic elections have been held with the participation of parliamentary parties. A total of six constitutions have been promulgated during this time. The most startling fact is that not even a single government has completed its full tenure of five years. Providing support to Crossaint and Diamond's

Nepal's Tryst with Democracy   169

claim that the decay of democracy seems to occur and tends to be more severe in poorer and less developed countries, Nepal is a case in point (Croissant and Diamond, 2020). Although Nepal has fared well in terms of electoral process and political pluralism in Freedom House's report, the extremely low scores in terms of functioning of government, transparency, the presence of safeguards against corruption and prevalence of due process in civil and criminal matters showcase Nepal's poor democratic practice (Freedom House, 2021). An example of how bad governance has plagued Nepal can be seen through the corruption that exists at the local level. Just a few years into the federal system, local governments are now recognized as the second most corrupt institutions in the country (Shrestha, 2019). Weak institutions and the rapacious nature of leadership have penetrated every aspect of decision making. In June 2020, the parliamentary Public Accounts Committee (PAC) opened a formal investigation into potential corruption over allegations that government officials procured essential medicines and health products at inflated prices, taking advantage of the Covid-19 pandemic (Pradhan, 2020). The question then is: what has led to this poor democratic consolidation? As hinted at earlier, there are both external and internal variables that underpin Nepal's failure in consolidating democracy, which are discussed in the proceeding sections.

Role of India: 'The Big Brother'

Nepal's two big neighbors have been at the heart of most of the big political developments in the country (Bhatta, 2013). Nestled between rising powerhouses China and India, the role of the latter has been more prominent if not overtly interfering. Sharing religious, cultural and economic ties, the relationship between Nepal and India is often compared to that of a 'small brother and big brother'. While this big brother has never really harbored interests of directly usurping its small brother's territory, it has always been adamant about being the most decisive force. Any decision taken in Kathmandu without the consultation of Delhi often infuriates it and results in serious consequences (Sharma, 2006). Ironically, Delhi played an instrumental role in ushering democracy into Nepal in 1950 when it brokered a deal among the Nepali Congress, the Rana family and the King that ended the century-old rule of the autocratic Rana family. Leo Rose writes that the 'decisive battle of Nepal's first democratic struggle was thus not really fought in the hills of Nepal but in the halls of New Delhi' (Rose, 1971: 194). However, India's move not only ushered in a democratic system, but also paved the way for it to become a decisive force in the largely isolated and impoverished Nepal. After all, Nepal's geopolitical situation forced it to be entirely dependent on India for trade, commerce and access to the sea. This allowed Delhi to play a manipulative role in Nepali politics to serve India's interests (Mishra, 2004). For the purpose of this chapter, three major political developments are highlighted to exemplify this 'manipulation' and explain how these have contributed to poor democratic consolidation in Nepal.

170   *Nepal's Tryst with Democracy*

The first one is India's role in the Maoist insurgency. During the peak of the Maoist insurgency, many suspected that the insurgents were closer to the country where their ideology came from. This was not true (Jha, 2012). Throughout Nepal's decade-long internal war, Beijing firmly distanced itself from the Maoists – even refusing to call them by their name. When King Gyanendra visited China in 2002, state media quoted Chinese President Jiang Zemin terming the Maoists as 'armed anti-government forces' (Pan, 2002). Support for the insurgents thus came not from communist China, but from democratic India (Mishra, 2004). While there is no denying the fact that the insurgency sprang up as a response to decades of marginalization of rural Nepal, it received considerable moral support from Nepal's southern neighbor. After the police launched a brutal offensive against Maoists from 1998, a considerable chunk of the Maoist leadership crossed the border. In fact, the party chairman Prachanda himself has recounted that he had spent a number of years in Indian cities when insurgency was at its peak in Nepal (Sharma, 2019: 99). Sharma writes that 'the headquarters of the Maoist Eastern Command were in Patna and Siliguri while those of the Western Command were in Gorakhpur and Lucknow' (ibid.). It is impossible to believe that these activities were being carried out so freely on Indian soil without the knowledge of Indian authorities.

Before 2006, the Indians denied supporting the Maoists. But a lot of literature since 2006 (when the Maoists joined mainstream politics) has provided evidence of support – which Indian intelligence officers and experts themselves have corroborated (Sharma, 2019; Jha, 2014; Muni, 2012). It was initially the intelligence agencies, particularly the Research and Analysis Wing (RAW) which started to engage with the insurgents (Jha, 2014). However, since 2002 they have made attempts to contact the political establishment, too. Nepal expert and an interlocuter between the Maoist and the Indian government, S.D. Muni writes that when the Maoists made the request to contact the Indian government in 2002, the Indian Prime Minister's Office had a 'hesitant but cautiously engaging response' (Muni, 2012: 320). Ironically, the insurgents were still recognized as 'terrorists' by the Indian government at that time. The question of why democratic India sympathized with the communist insurgents will be dealt with later in this chapter. However, before that, I will discuss another political development in Nepal where Delhi's role was instrumental. At no other time did the southern neighbor's role become more prominent in Nepali politics than in 2006, when it facilitated the forging of the '12 point agreement' (or popularly known as the Delhi agreement)[3] between an alliance of seven different Nepali parliamentary parties and the Maoists, who were all opposing the King (Jha, 2012). In 2009, in an interview with an international news agency, the then Indian External Affairs Minister described Delhi's facilitation role in 2006 and accepted that India had 'persuaded' the Maoists to participate in mainstream national politics and that the Maoists had 'listened to their advice' (Al Jazeera English, 2009). Although India had traditionally relied on the Nepali monarchy as its reliable partner, it had become disenchanted with King Gyanendra because of his disregard for constitutional monarchy and his

Nepal's Tryst with Democracy 171

'pro-China' rhetoric. Muni writes that 'India's support to the seven party alliances was directly correlated to the degree of defiance shown by King Gyanendra' (Muni, 2012; 326). For instance, as soon as the King secured arms from China in August 2005, 'India encouraged the Nepali Congress to adopt a resolution in support of democracy, which for the first time, did not include a reference to the constitutional monarchy' (ibid.).

Drafted in Delhi, with active participation of the Indian establishment, the 12-point agreement ultimately brought down the two-and-a-half-century-old monarchy in Nepal and turned the country into a federal republic. Needless to say, this was one of the turning points in Nepali history – something that would not have been possible without Delhi's hand. In what turned out to be one of the most public displays of India's engagement in Nepal, the frequent to-and-fro of Nepali leaders between Kathmandu and Delhi, the Indian ambassador's maneuvering in Kathmandu and the surfacing of the Indian Prime Minister's emissaries and Indian foreign secretary in the Kathmandu airport made it clear that India's role was much more than just a 'well-wishing neighbor' (Sharma, 2019).

If India's role during 2006 was prominent, its role in the aftermath of 2006 has been even more brazen and unrestrained. While India's role in ushering in democracy in its neighboring Nepal should be lauded, it also paved the way for Delhi's unabashed interference in the internal matters of the country. Following its decisive role in abolishing monarchy, Delhi started to micromanage even the smallest developments in Nepal. Moreover, it began to lend support to regional outfits – especially the Madhesi parties. For many decades, the leadership in Kathmandu had not been sensitive to the issues of Madhesh, the southern plains of Nepal. Capitalizing on this, Delhi began to support the Madhesi parties who claimed to be championing Madhesh's cause (Bhatta, 2013). Jha writes that India's objective of supporting Madhesh's cause was to create a 'reliable constituency of support within Nepal' (Jha, 2012: 345). As a result, in 2007–2010, 'Indian involvement in Madheshi mainstream politics – from determining its shape, influencing intra-party dynamics, backing certain actors and discouraging other and shaping agendas – increased sharply' (Jha, 2012: 347). Madhesi leaders themselves have accepted that India has used them at their convenience but never really pressured Kathmandu to give them rights (Jha, 2012). In 2015, using these very parties, the Narendra Modi government unofficially imposed a five-month-long economic blockade in Nepal to express its unhappiness over the constitution (Sharma, 2019).

But why would the world's largest democracy want to interfere in the internal affairs of another independent, sovereign and democratic nation? It is because India has always considered Nepal and other small South Asian countries as falling within its arc of influence. India's greatest concern in Nepal and all over South Asia in terms of its strategic, economic and political interests is the growing presence of China (Manuel, 2017). When Nepal's first democratically elected Prime Minister B.P. Koirala made attempts to build equal relations with Delhi and Beijing, he fell in the estimation of India (Malla, 1989). When

172   *Nepal's Tryst with Democracy*

King Birendra attempted to turn north for arms procurement for the army, Delhi was not happy. When King Gyanendra made attempts to bring China to South Asian Association for Regional Cooperation (SAARC) and betrayed Delhi on multiple occasions, the South Block didn't just topple his regime; it brought down the entire monarchy (Sharma, 2019). To serve its national interest and to continue to keep Nepal within its sphere of influence, India has thus adopted whatever means it deemed necessary. At times, it has taken lessons from its former colonial masters and adopted a 'divide and rule' policy, whereas at other times, it has helped forge alliances and give birth to new forces that it can control. Whatever the method, India finds its national interest much more important than democracy or the maintenance of cordial relations with a neighbor (Sharma, 2019). Sanjay Upadhyay writes that in Nepal, India is so focused on achieving its national interest that it has excluded taking any other factor into consideration (Upadhya, 2008). This has not just given rise to 'anti-Indian' sentiment in Nepal, but has turned out to be counter-productive for Delhi itself. Despite experts expressing their concern over India's Nepal policy, successive Indian governments, whether the Congress or the BJP, have failed to do away with the age-old 'colonial mindset'. Nepal's irritation at India's ongoing interference in Nepali politics became public in 2015 when a 'back off India' hashtag started trending spontaneously on social media after India imposed an unofficial blockade (BBC News, 2015).

The Steady Ascendance of Beijing

While India has featured heavily in the politics of Nepal for decades, China's appearance has become more prominent in the last decade and a half. Over the last decade, Beijing has become far more attentive to its South Asian periphery, taking into consideration political and security concerns and not just commercial interests (Pal, 2021). Its policy towards Nepal exemplifies this. While Beijing did take note of political developments in Nepal before 2006, it made sure not to be actively engaged. The aloofness caused by geographical division and, more importantly, the understanding that Nepal fell under the Indian arc of influence meant that Beijing did not want to be seen as an active player in Nepali politics. It never intended to change the status quo, which to a large extent earned itself a reputation for being the 'friendlier' and more benevolent neighbor. In reality, Beijing has been beneficent 'only when its own concerns have been addressed by Kathmandu' (Mulmi, 2021: xix). It always made sure to open its arms wide for leaders who wanted to play the 'China card'. This was exemplified by its actions such as signing an arms deal with King Gyanendra, who had fallen out with India and the cozying up to the Maoists after they had come to power and had fallen out with India.

Since the fall of the monarchy, Beijing's policy towards Nepal has been evolving gradually. It has been more active in Nepali politics – its interest being driven by economic as well as political ambitions (Mulmi, 2020). A few of the recent developments prove this. In 2017, Nepal became a signatory to Chinese the President's ambitious Belt and Road Initiative (BRI). A year earlier, it had also signed the Transit and Transport Agreement with China, which in principle ended Nepal's dependence on India for its supply chains (Haidar & Bhattacharjee, 2016). Reinforcing the rhetoric that China now attaches a higher degree of importance to Nepal, President Xi Jinping landed in Kathmandu in 2019, the first Chinese President to do so in two decades. It was clear that China was now much more than a 'card' that Nepali politicians used for bargaining with India. Beijing's primary interest in Nepal is its soft underbelly, Tibet, with whom Nepal shares a 1,400-km border. Nepal is home to at least 20,000 Tibetan refugees. Kathmandu upholds the one China policy, and apart from a few sporadic incidents has been able to keep a tight grip on the Tibetans, much to the delight of Beijing. Along with concerns regarding Tibet, China's interest in recent times also includes challenging Indian influence along with Western engagement (particularly the United States) (Mulmi, 2021). This ambition has had political repercussions. In order to bolster its investments as well as increase its influence, Beijing facilitated the merger of two big communist forces in the country in 2018 – the UML and the Maoists – to form Nepal's biggest communist party, the National Communist Party (NCP) (Giri, 2020). When rifts emerged in the party two years later, the Chinese ambassador reportedly met with top party leaders and urged them to stay united (Giri, 2020). As the party finally split, a team led by the Vice Minister of the International Department of the CCP, Guo Yezhou, met with President Bidya Devi Bhandari and UML leaders to avert the political crisis and forestall the party split (*The Himalayan Times*, 2020).

While Beijing might have helped forge a communist alliance, its intention isn't really establishing an 'ideological counterpart' in Nepal. As opposed to Delhi, Beijing adopts a very flexible approach when dealing with Kathmandu. It has never stuck to supporting just one actor in the country. It assesses the political environment in Kathmandu and courts the more 'popular' stakeholder and distances itself from 'unpopular' ones. In 2008, Beijing slowly cozied up to Maoists (the very party it had shunned years earlier) because it had emerged as the most popular party in the elections. Before the political landscape changed in Kathmandu, communist China had found a reliable ally in the monarchy. But once the People's Movement started gaining momentum and it sensed that the King was becoming unpopular, it slowly distanced itself from the palace.

As expected, Beijing has also harbored economic interests in its neighboring Himalayan nation. It overtook India as the biggest foreign direct investment (FDI) source for Nepal in 2014 (Krishnan, 2014). In the fiscal year 2020/21, it contributed to over 70% of total FDI Nepal had received. It was the sixth consecutive year China had led in terms of FDI pledges (Xinhua, 2021). China also has interest in Nepal's largely untapped hydropower sector. Currently, some of the major projects where Nepal has received assistance from China are the construction of the Pokhara International Regional Airport, a cross-border optical fiber link, and the upper Marsyangdi Hydropower Station. A railway network linking Kathmandu and Kerung has also featured in Kathmandu-

174 Nepal's Tryst with Democracy

Beijing talks. When completed, it is expected to facilitate Nepal's connectivity with the rest of the world through China's road network (Pal, 2021). In 2018, the Chinese and Nepalese governments and private firms signed agreements on eight projects – covering areas such as hydropower and the cement industry – designed to greatly boost the landlocked nation's infrastructure (Business Standard, 2018). China has also worked to send a higher number of tourists to Nepal every year. Between 2009 and 2019, Chinese arrivals increased from a little over 30,000 visitors to almost 170,000 visitors.

Geo-Political Rivalry

Nepal's case provides an interesting point in the discussion of fledgling democracy – the role of geopolitics. Given its strategic location, Nepal has turned out to be a battleground for its two neighbors, who now openly flex their muscles and vie for influence (Bhatta, 2019). India has been the traditional actor in the Nepali polity for decades. But since 2006, 'China's arrival in South Asia has altered the region's centre of gravity – a shift that will (and to a large extent, already has) have lasting reverberations on Nepal as well as its ties with India' (Upadhya, 2008: 245). The result has been frequent political changes, pliant leadership and, subsequently, a gradual erosion of democracy. The influx of other external actors, most notably the West after the ushering in of a new political environment in 2006, has made matters even more complicated (Bhatta, 2013). The exogenous forces have 'divided Nepali society along various fault-lines such as ethnic, religious, and regional' (Bhatta, 2013: 194).

There has not been a lot of research into the role of foreign actors, and more particularly a country's geopolitics, in how it contributes to strong democratic consolidation, and few resources are available. Most studies, however, do not treat a foreign actor as the sole contributing factor. Abraham Diskin, Hanna Diskin and Reuven Hazan, in their study of why democracies fail, found five crucial variables that are responsible for the collapse of democracy. One of them is foreign involvement, along with cleavages, a malfunctioning economy, unfavorable history and governmental instability (Diskin, Diskin & Hazan, 2005). However, they note that a single debilitating factor is highly unlikely to bring about democratic collapse and that the key to democratic demise is a combination of these variables (ibid.). Nepal perfectly exemplifies this situation. While foreign involvement is the overarching factor responsible for Nepal not being able to consolidate its democratic gains, the subsequent variables, which are a product of this overarching factor, including a malfunctioning economy, government instability and vested interest of the political leaders, have collectively contributed to the poor practice of democracy. The fact that foreign interventions can also lead to democratic failures was noted even by Robert Dahl in his seminal work *On Democracy*. He cited the Soviet interventions in Central and Eastern Europe and US interventions in Latin America as an example (Dahl, 1998). Although a direct kind of intervention like the ones Dahl was referring to is definitely less common these days, subtle interventions are still very common. Then again, Nepal's case also defies what Mark Gasiorowski and Timothy Power found in their paper – that the contagion effect of democratic neighbors increases the likelihood of consolidation (Gasiorowski & Power, 1998). Despite having the world's largest democracy as its neighbor, Nepal has not been able to accord maturity to its democracy. In fact, as mentioned earlier, both of Nepal's neighbors, democratic and autocratic, have placed their national interest above everything else. Indian interlocuters luring Nepali leaders with benefits are also not unheard of (Dixit, 2020). On the other hand, in 2019, the then Nepal Communist Party and the Chinese Communist Party jointly organized a symposium to discuss the 'Xi Jinping's thought' (with some even terming it as a 'training program'), which some quarters saw as a move by Beijing to make Nepali leaders pliable towards the north (Giri, 2019). Such maneuvers by the two neighbors have resulted in constant changes of government, stalled projects and weak political institutions.

While there is no doubt that both Beijing and Delhi's role in Nepal has been intrusive in nature, one should be careful while discussing Beijing's role. While explaining democratic backsliding, some commentators have concluded that the rise of China is a crucial factor in democratic backsliding in the world today. Walker writes that today's 'authoritarian' states – notably China and Russia – are using 'sharp power' to project their influence internationally, with the objectives of limiting free expression, spreading confusion and distorting the political environment within democracies (Walker, 2018). Croissant falls short of naming China as a direct 'cause' of democratic decline, but says that the growing influence of China's governing model is increasingly affecting the domestic politics of countries (Croissant, 2020). Diamond writes that Russian rage and Chinese ambition are two of the factors responsible for democratic backsliding, which in different ways have damaged and eroded the post–World War II, and especially the post–Cold War, hegemony of liberal values and institutions (Diamond, 2021). He further adds that in this new era of geopolitical competition, China along with Russia and Iran are actively working to promote their authoritarian values and to fan doubt and suspicion about democracy (Diamond, 2020). In Nepal's case, this argument is naïve. Although China has impacted the country's democratic journey by being as one of the geopolitical actors, it hasn't really harbored any interest in raising a communist party counterpart that intends to erode democratic values and propagate communist ideas. As mentioned earlier, China is best understood as 'opportunistic' in Nepal's context. Its interest, rather than promotion of its 'authoritarian' political ideology, is actually reaping benefits and ensuring no threat is posed in respect of Tibet. China has been working to increase its economic and political clout, but it has not made any attempts to spread authoritarian narratives about the dynamism and success of China as claimed by Diamond (2021). The fact that Beijing was a staunch supporter of the palace and the monarchy is its evidence.

176 Nepal's Tryst with Democracy

The Role of Endogenous Factors

While acknowledging the impact of geopolitics or foreign actors on Nepal's democracy, we also need to understand the role of endogenous factors. While agreeing that international factors can have an impact on democratic consolidation, theorists note that these factors work overwhelmingly through their influence on domestic factors – not in a standalone manner (Waldener & Lust, 2018). Indeed, simply blaming geopolitics for democratic erosion would be unfair in Nepal's context. Both of Nepal's neighbors have exploited the subservient nature of Nepali leaders and the volatile political situation to their advantage. Explaining Nepal's southern neighbors' interference in Nepal, Prashant Jha says, citing history, that India has never really 'acted in a vacuum' and that its moves have always depended on the context (Jha, 2012). When there is political consensus, Delhi has found it difficult to act against this consensus (Jha, 2012). Leading expert Devendra Raj Panday says that India prefers to play a game of divide and rule, with multiple power centers in Nepal competing for Indian support (Panday, 2012). India's strategy is facilitated by weak Nepali leadership that has little regard for its obligation towards domestic constituency (Panday, 2012). The case is similar with China.

The subservient nature of political leadership in Nepal has thus paved the way for geopolitics to play out and, subsequently, contribute to democratic erosion. Take for instance the startling fact that not one of the governments in Nepal that came after the introduction of democracy in 1950 has ever completed its full term. Nepal's governments are either brought down by opposition parties or, even worse, their own party members. In its seven-decade-long democratic journey, the country has seen almost 50 different governments. Leaders have always prioritized personal gain over national interest, which has allowed external factors to easily influence Nepal's national politics. Many leaders are known openly to be 'pro-China' or 'pro-India' in Kathmandu. The tendency of dependence on either neighbor for personal gain is quite common. When a certain leader finds his or personal interest being directly challenged by his fellow party member, he does not hesitate to form a splinter group, in many cases with support from either one of the neighbors.

International relations theories talk about how in global politics national interest is of the highest concern for every country (Walt, 1998). It is thus not uncommon for big countries to try and exert pressure on their smaller counterparts to increase their sphere of influence. But serious problems emerge when domestic leaders easily sell out to external actors. This leads to biased decision making, renders institutions weak and, more worryingly, generates a general disregard for the country's national interest. The role of political parties is absolutely crucial in sustaining democracy in a country (Dahal, 2016). However, the prolonged political transition in Nepal has so far signified that the mainstream parties lack the vision and ability to ensure proper governance and institutionalize and consolidate democratic gains (Aditya & Bhatta, 2016). Baral (2012) blames fractured ideological parties and lack of well-knit parties based

Nepal's Tryst with Democracy   177

on democratic values and norms for Nepal's 'democratic underdevelopment'. Indeed, personal gain has taken so much precedence that leaders have stopped paying attention to the institutionalization of parties. This has been a problem since the 1950s. Take for instance the Nepali Congress. The vanguard party of democracy in Nepal has suffered from factionalism from the very beginning (Khadka, 1993). In the early 1950s, it saw conflict between its two senior leaders B.P. Koirala and M.P. Koirala, leading the latter to form his own party. In the early 1990s, it saw conflict play out between senior leaders like G.P. Koirala and K.P. Bhattarai, as a result of which the government was displaced just three years after it had won a majority in the general elections (Thapa, 2005). In 2002, conflict between G.P. Koirala and Sher Bahadur Deuba led to the party splitting (Thapa, 2005). Communist parties have met a similar fate. The most startling of factionalism can be seen in *Madhesh*-based regional parties, where it is difficult to keep track of the number of times the parties have split and merged.

Nepali politics is replete with examples of political leadership taking decisions to favor the leadership in Delhi or Beijing for political gains. The role of external actors like India in Nepal is facilitated by Nepali leadership that does not care much about its responsibilities towards the domestic constituency (Panday, 2012). The awarding of infrastructure projects provides a case in point. China and India jostle for influence with aid and investment in infrastructure projects in Nepal. In 2017, the government of Sher Bahadur Deuba, known to be 'India-friendly', scrapped a US $2.5 billion deal made between a Chinese company and Nepal to build Nepal's largest hydropower project (Sharma, 2017). Four months earlier, it was the 'China-friendly' Maoist government that had awarded the contract to the Chinese Gezhouba company. But just when a controversy surrounding the opaque manner in which the bid was awarded to the Chinese company was about to subside, another 'China-friendly' Prime Minister K.P. Oli, who came into power in 2018, again reversed his predecessor's decision and asked the same company to build the hydropower project (Sharma, 2018). The problem, thus, for Nepal is its leaders' inability to maintain a neutral foreign policy balance (Bhatta, 2014). This has resulted in other problems that have directly or indirectly threatened the country's democracy. An example is the politicization of almost every sphere, most notably the bureaucracy. Since as early as the 1950s, the bureaucracy has been used as a political instrument by the ruling party or leaders (Khadka, 1993). Political patronage has continued even to this day. Many appointments are political, and in many instances bureaucrats who are close to the ruling party are appointed to higher positions. This has rendered the country's bureaucracy inefficient. Political leaders have sustained their power base through patronage, with systems established to reward party clients by granting licenses and awarding contracts, lucrative jobs, promotions, etc. (Bhatta, 2012).

Poor democratic consolidation has also resulted in the weakening of horizontal accountability mechanisms. Whether the system has institutionalized parties and agents of horizontal accountability determines to a large extent the quality of democracy in a country. This subsequently decides whether

178 Nepal's Tryst with Democracy

democracy in that country erodes or not (Diamond, 2021). A clear example of this can be seen in the country's judiciary. Political interference in the judiciary became blatant in 2013 when the sitting Chief Justice was asked to take up the role of the country's new Prime Minister and lead a caretaker government to hold elections. The move was a 'compromise solution' put together by the political leaders who were unable to agree on a political candidate for the job (Sharma, 2013). Although he did not participate in court hearings while heading the government, the Chief Justice retained his judicial position – creating a highly unusual atmosphere in the country. A more serious case of tainted judiciary came to light as late as 2021, when the sitting Chief Justice was found to have made politically motivated decisions in favor of political gains[4] (*The Kathmandu Post*, 2021). In 2017, the country's first female Chief Justice, Sushila Karki, faced an impeachment motion after she lawfully ruled against the choice of Police Chief proposed by the ruling Maoist and Nepali Congress parties (Al Jazeera, 2017a). The parties filed the impeachment motion because they were harboring personal animosity against her. Thanks to poor horizontal accountability mechanisms, the culture of impunity has been a permanent feature of the Nepali polity. The corruption at the executive level has spilled over, not just to the judiciary but even to other bodies – for instance, the counter-corruption agencies. In 2017, the Supreme Court disqualified the chief of the Commission for Investigation of Abuse of Authority (CIAA) as he did not hold the 'high moral character' required to lead the CIAA and did not meet the criteria set to head the constitutional body (Pyakurel, 2017). The chief was earlier found to have engaged in 'witch hunts' and had used the agency as a personal tool to settle scores with political actors and civil society leaders who disliked him. The decision exposed how arbitrarily heads of constitutional bodies are appointed in the country (Dahal, 2017).

Not just political parties and leaders, but Nepali civil society has been equally responsible for weakening the country's democracy. Rather than becoming the watchdogs of democracy, they have contributed to its erosion. Civil society members have a tendency of making way for foreign power to play a greater role in Nepal's internal affairs for their vested interests (Tiwari, 2001). Nepal's strategic location has tempted international powers to create leverage at the political and elite civil society level who, in turn, facilitate external influences (Bhatta, 2014). Tolstrup (2013) identifies civil society actors as one of the gatekeepers 'that hold the capacity to facilitate or constrain relationships with external actors' (Tolstrup, 2013: 725). Many civil society members, most notably nongovernmental organizations (NGOs), community-based organizations (CBOs) and a handful of prominent experts, are thus in many cases taken into confidence by bilateral and multilateral aid agencies through development projects and other lucrative offers to advance their agenda (Bhatta, 2013). These trends have weakened the institutional basis of democracy.

Whither Democracy?

Theories to explain democratic backsliding are still emerging. Waldener and Lust say that whatever theoretical debates exist – centered on the causes of democratic transitions, democratic breakdowns, authoritarian resilience, and democratic consolidation – remain unresolved (Waldener & Lust, 2018). The issue becomes more complex when trying to explain democratic erosion in the South Asian context. Although countries in the region might share some level of cultural similarity, the political systems of the South Asian countries are completely different from each other. Nepal has not seen democratic backsliding at the hands of populist authoritarians (like Narendra Modi in India), nor has it seen military coups (like in Pakistan). It does not really have prominent polarizing leaders (as in Bangladesh) who have contributed to democratic backsliding, nor has the state persecuted minorities (as in Myanmar). Nepal's issue is its geopolitics coupled with domestic leadership. Both exogenous and endogenous factors have played the role of poor democratic consolidation in the country. As a result, despite the seven decades of its democratic journey, the country has been unable to consolidate its democratic gains.

Ironically, despite being a fragile democracy, Nepal has been able to avoid a complete democratic breakdown. This makes Nepal a case of what Ginsburg and Huq define as a 'near miss'. Ginsburg and Huq define a near miss for democracy as a case in which a country, initially, experiences deterioration in the quality of well-functioning democratic institutions, without fully sliding into authoritarianism, but then, within a timeframe of a few years, at least partially recovers its high-quality democracy (Ginsburg & Huq, 2018). Although Nepal hasn't really recovered a 'high-quality democracy', neither has it remained in a slump. While analyzing democratic recession in Asia, Croissant and Diamond find that countries such as Nepal, the Philippines, Thailand, Sri Lanka and Bangladesh have indeed gone through more than one democratic erosion and made 'quick comebacks' (Croissant and Diamond, 2020). In the context of the ambitions of the two rising superpowers, and given Nepal's seven decades of fragile democracy, a question arises: will Nepal ever be able to enjoy a full-fledged quality democracy? For a poor, small, landlocked country like Nepal, surrounded by giant neighbors, is there a possibility for leaders and institutions to seek support from its neighbors and still act 'independently'? Can small nations like Nepal really resist foreign meddling and become a consolidated democracy? The question is difficult to answer. Indian Prime Minister Atal Bihari Vajpayee, referring to India's relationship with Pakistan, once said, 'You can change your friends, but not your neighbors'. Sandwiched between India and China, Nepal can do very little to avoid the interference of its two gigantic neighbors. However, external actors need to respect Nepal's sovereignty and independence and refrain from overtly engaging in its domestic issues, simply to keep the country under their spheres of influence. It is common in international relations for big nations to exert their influence on smaller neighbors to increase their clout. But excessive intervention will turn out to be

180 *Nepal's Tryst with Democracy*

counter-productive for these big nations. Interventions have been positive at times, for instance, India's role in ushering in democracy in the country multiple times. But the role it has played in the aftermath has not been particularly positive. Nepal's two neighbors need to understand especially that a stable and prosperous Nepal will serve their national interest better rather than an unstable one.

Needless to say, a large part of the responsibility lies with Nepal's leadership. Until and unless the leadership sheds its docile nature, Nepal's democracy will never come of age. It is imperative for leaders to put their personal interests aside and give preference to national interests, as the precedence of personal interest over national interest has been one of the major factors for Nepal's poor democratic consolidation. It is unfortunate that despite being situated in such a strategic position between China and India, the country has been unable to leverage the potential benefit. With tremendous scope for economic development, leaders need to understand that a prosperous Nepal would produce a win-win for everyone – its neighbors, the country's political parties, the leaders themselves and, of course, the people.

Notes

1 The *Panchayat* system was a four-tier structure with 4,000 village assemblies, 75 district assemblies and 14 zone assemblies ending in the *Rastriya Panchayat* (National Parliament). Though people could elect their representatives, the *Panchayat* system was based on the absolute power of the monarchy, with the King as sole authority over all governmental institutions, including the Cabinet and the Parliament.
2 The Prime Minister Prachanda resigned after the country's President overruled his decision to dismiss the then Army Chief. Prachanda termed the president's interference 'unconstitutional' while many saw Prachanda's dismissal of the Army Chief as a political move.
3 The 12-point understanding was reached between seven different parliamentary parties and the Maoists in Delhi and was made in the context of King Gyanendra's 'royal coup'. The parties pledged to work towards 'democracy, peace, prosperity and social advancement and ending autocratic monarchy'. Through the agreement, the CPN Maoist made clear their commitment to institutionalise the values of a competitive multi-party system.
4 It was largely believed that Chief Justice Cholendra Sumsher Rana sought his share in the Cabinet as part of the quid pro quo with the Sher Bahadur Deuba government which had come into power after a decision made by his bench ousted the government of CPN UML headed by KP Oli.

Bibliography

Adhikari, D. (2019). Nepal: 13 years after civil war ends, victims await justice. *Anadolu Agency*. https://www.aa.com.tr/en/asia-pacific/nepal-13-years-after-civil-war-ends-victims-await-justice/1530499#
Aditya, A. & Bhatta, C.D. (2016). *The Role of Political Parties in Deepening Democracy in Nepal: A Study of Party Image, Issues at Stake and Agenda Building*. Kathmandu: Friedrich Ebert Stiftung.

Nepal's Tryst with Democracy 181

Al Jazeera. (2017a, 1 May). Nepal: Chief justice Sushila Karki suspended. https://www.aljazeera.com/news/2017/5/1/nepal-chief-justice-sushila-karki-suspended (Accessed on 12 October).

Al Jazeera. (2017b, 14 May). Nepal votes in first local elections in 20 years. https://www.aljazeera.com/news/2017/5/14/nepal-votes-in-first-local-elections-in-20-years

Al Jazeera (2021, 11 January). Nepal: Pro-monarchy protesters clash with police in Kathmandu. https://www.aljazeera.com/news/2021/1/11/thousands-in-nepal-demand-return-of-centuries-old-monarchy

Al Jazeera English. (2009, 28 January). *Riz Khan – An Interview: Pranab Mukherjee – 27 Jan 09 – Part 2* (Video). YouTube. https://www.youtube.com/watch?v=UZUiX70SeGw

Baral, L.S. (1971). Nepal's apprenticeship in democracy 1951–1960. *India Quarterly*, 27 (3), 185–202. http://www.jstor.org/stable/45069804

Baral, L.S. (1973). The first Panchayat elections in Nepal, 1962–1963: The emergence of a new political generation. *International Studies*, 12(3), 462–477. https://doi.org/10.1177/002088177301200304

Baral, L.R. (2012). *Nepal – Nation-State in the Wilderness: Managing State, Democracy and Geopolitics*. New Delhi: Sage India.

BBC News. (2015, 23 September). Nepal constitution: Mind your own business, media tell India. https://www.bbc.com/news/world-asia-india-34333265

BBC News. (2020, 23 January). Myanmar Rohingya: What you need to know about the crisis. https://www.bbc.com/news/world-asia-41566561

Bermeo, N. (2016). On democratic backsliding. *Journal of Democracy*, 27(1), 5–19. https://doi.org/10.1353/jod.2016.0012

Bhatta, C.D. (2012). Reflections on Nepal's peace process (international policy analysis). https://library.fes.de/pdf-files/iez/08936-20120228.pdf

Bhatta, C.D. (2013). External influence and challenges of state-building in Nepal. *Asian Journal of Political Science*, 21(2), 169–188. doi:10.1080/02185377.2013.823800

Bhatta, C.D. (2014). Antinomies of Democracy and Peace in Nepal. In P. Upadhyaya & S. Kumar (Eds.), *Peace and Conflict: The South Asian Experience* (pp. 177–199). New Delhi: Cambridge University Press. https://doi.org/10.1017/9789384463076

Bhatta, C.D. (2019). Emerging powers, soft power, and future of regional cooperation in South Asia. *Asian Journal of Political Science*, 27(1), 1–16. doi:10.1080/02185377.2018.1557062

Brown, T.L. (1995). *The Challenge to Democracy in Nepal* (1st edn.). London: Routledge. https://doi.org/10.4324/9780203419649

Business Standard. (2018, 20 June). China, Nepal ink 8 pacts in major infrastructure projects. https://www.business-standard.com/article/pti-stories/china-nepal-ink-8-pacts-in-major-infrastructure-projects-118062000407_1.html

Chatterjee, B. (1977). *Nepal's Experiment with Democracy*. New Delhi: Ankur Publishing House.

Croissant, A. (2020) *The Struggle for Democracy in Asia – Regression, Resilience, Revival*. Bertelsmann Stiftung Asia Policy Brief. http://aei.pitt.edu/103242/

Croissant, A. & Diamond, L. (2020). Reflections on democratic backsliding in Asia: An introduction. *Global Asia*, 15(1), 6–13. https://www.globalasia.org/v15no1/cover/introduction-reflections-on-democratic-backsliding-in-asia_aurel-croissantlarry-diamond

Croissant, A. & Haynes, J. (2021). Democratic regression in Asia: Introduction. *Democratization*, 28(1), 1–21. https://doi.org/10.1080/13510347.2020.1851203

182 *Nepal's Tryst with Democracy*

Dahal, B. (2017, 13–19 January). The end of Karkistocracy. *Nepali Times*. http://archive. nepalitimes.com/regular-columns/Legalese/the-end-of-karkistocracy,827 (Accessed on 14 October).

Dahal, D.R. (2016). The Role of Political Parties in Deepening Democracy in Nepal. In C.D. Bhatta & A. Aditya (Eds.), *The Role of Political Parties in Deepening Democracy in Nepal* (pp. 115–144). Kathmandu: Friedrich Ebert Stiftung.

Dahl, R.A. (1998). *On Democracy*. New Haven: Yale University Press.

Dhume, S. (2019, 28 November). In South Asia, democracy loses and Beijing wins. *The Wall Street Journal*. https://www.wsj.com/articles/in-south-asia-democracy-loses-and-beijing-wins-11574967252 (Accessed on 12 February).

Diamond, L. (2020). Breaking out of the democratic slump. *Journal of Democracy*, 31(1), 36–50. http://dx.doi.org/10.1353/jod.2020.0003

Diamond, L. (2021). Democratic regression in comparative perspective: Scope, methods, and causes. *Democratization*, 28(1), 22–42. https://doi.org/10.1080/13510347.2020.1807517

Diskin, A., Diskin, H. & Hazan, R.Y. (2005). Why democracies collapse: The reasons for democratic failure and success. *International Political Science Review/Revue Internationale de Science Politique*, 26(3), 291–309. http://www.jstor.org/stable/30039034

Dixit, K.M. (2012). The life and death of the Constituent Assembly of Nepal. *Economic and Political Weekly*, 47(31), 35–41. http://www.jstor.org/stable/23251625

Dixit, K.M. (2020, 7 November). New Delhi's new dealings in Nepal. *Nepali Times*. https://nepalitimes.com/here-now/new-delhi-s-new-dealings-in-nepal

Freedom House. (2021). *Freedom in the World 2021 – Nepal*. https://freedomhouse.org/country/nepal/freedom-world/2021 (Accessed on 20 October).

Gasiorowski, M.J. & Power, T.J. (1998). The structural determinants of democratic consolidation: Evidence from the third world. *Comparative Political Studies*, 31(6). 740–771. https://doi.org/10.1177%2F0010414098031006003

Ghimire, B. (2015, 21 September). Constitution promulgated. *The Kathmandu Post*. https://kathmandupost.com/miscellaneous/2015/09/21/constitution-promulgated

Ginsburg, T. & Huq, A. (2018). Democracy's near misses. *Journal of Democracy*, 29(4), 16–30. https://doi.org/10.1353/jod.2018.0059

Giri, A. (2019, 24 September). Training programme on Xi Jinping Thought raises concern among opposition leaders. *The Kathmandu Post*. https://kathmandupost.com/national/2019/09/24/training-programme-on-xi-jinping-thought-raises-concern-among-opposition-leaders

Giri, A. (2020, 2 May). In a series of meetings, Chinese envoy calls for unity among ruling party members. *The Kathmandu Post*. https://kathmandupost.com/politics/2020/05/02/in-a-series-of-meetings-chinese-envoy-calls-for-unity-among-ruling-party-members

Haidar, S. & Bhattacharjee, K. (2016, 21 March). Nepal seals agreement on transit rights through China. *The Hindu*. https://www.thehindu.com/news/international/nepal-inks-transit-treaty-with-china-to-have-first-rail-link/article8381195.ece

Hassan, A.M. (2021, 27 May). Bangladesh journalist's arrest highlights growing curbs on press freedom. *The Diplomat*. https://thediplomat.com/2021/05/bangladesh-journalists-arrest-highlights-growing-curbs-on-press-freedom/

International Idea. (2015). *Nepal's Constitution Building Process: 2006–2015. Progress, Challenges, and Contributions of International Community*. https://www.idea.int/sites/default/files/publications/nepals-constitution-building-process-2006-2015.pdf

Jha, P. (2012). A Nepali Perspective on International Involvement in Nepal. In S. Einsiedel, D. Malone & S. Pradhan (Eds.), *Nepal in Transition: From People's War to*

Nepal's Tryst with Democracy 183

Fragile Peace (pp. 332–358). Cambridge: Cambridge University Press. doi:10.1017/CBO9781139021869.016

Jha, P. (2014). *Battles of the New Republic: A Contemporary History of Nepal*. New Delhi: Aleph Book Company.

Joshi, B.L. & Rose, L.E. (2004). *Democratic Innovations in Nepal: A Case Study of Political Acculturation*. Kathmandu: Mandala Book Point.

Khadka, N. (1993). Democracy and development in Nepal: Prospects and challenges. *Pacific Affairs*, 66(1), 44–71. https://doi.org/10.2307/2760015

Krishnan, A. (2014, 26 January). China is largest FDI source for Nepal, overtakes India. *The Hindu*. https://www.thehindu.com/news/international/world/china-is-largest-fdi-source-for-nepal-overtakes-india/article5618081.ece

Malla, K.P. (1989). *Nepal: Perspectives on Continuity and Change*. Kathmandu: Tribhuvan Univ. Centre for Nepal and Asian Studies.

Manuel, A. (2017). *This Brave New World: India, China and the United States*. New York: Simon & Schuster.

Mishra, R. (2004). India's role in Nepal's Maoist insurgency. *Asian Survey*, 44(5), 627–646. https://doi.org/10.1525/as.2004.44.5.627

Mulmi, A.R. (2020, 6 August). What does China want from Nepal? *The Kathmandu Post*. https://kathmandupost.com/columns/2020/08/06/what-does-china-want-from-nepal

Mulmi, A.R. (2021). *All Roads Lead North*. Chennai: Context.

Muni, S. (2012). Bringing the Maoists Down from the Hills: India's Role. In S. Einsiedel, D. Malone & S. Pradhan (Eds.), *Nepal in Transition: From People's War to Fragile Peace* (pp. 313–331). Cambridge: Cambridge University Press. doi:10.1017/CBO9781139021869.015

Pal, D. (2021). China's influence in South Asia: Vulnerabilities and resilience in four countries. Carnegie Endowment for International Peace. https://carnegieendowment.org/2021/10/13/china-s-influence-in-south-asia-vulnerabilities-and-resilience-in-four-countries-pub-85552

Pan, P. (2002, 14 July). China backs Nepal over Maoist rebels. *The Washington Post*. https://www.washingtonpost.com/archive/politics/2002/07/14/china-backs-nepal-over-maoist-rebels/23df97dc-2534-4bce-ac90-518dc6b6811f/ (Accessed on 30 October).

Panday, D.R. (2012). The Legacy of Nepal's Failed Development. In S. Einsiedel, D. Malone & S. Pradhan (Eds.), *Nepal in Transition: From People's War to Fragile Peace* (pp. 81–128). Cambridge: Cambridge University Press. doi:10.1017/CBO9781139021869.005

Pradhan, T.R. (2020, 23 June). Public Accounts Committee begins investigation into Omni Group's procurement of medical supplies. *The Kathmandu Post*. https://tkpo.st/2NywGQB (Accessed on 25 November).

Prasai, S. (2021, 22 August). Remittance hits Rs 961 billion, an all-time high in the time of Covid-19. *The Kathmandu Post*. https://kathmandupost.com/money/2021/08/22/remittance-hits-rs961-billion-an-all-time-high-in-the-time-of-covid-19 (Accessed on 7 February).

Pyakurel, D. (2017, 8 January). Supreme Court removes Lok Man Singh Karki from CIAA. *The Himalayan Times*. https://thehimalayantimes.com/nepal/supreme-court-disqualifies-lok-man-singh-karki-for-ciaa-chief

Rai, D. (2020, 3 July). How Oli destroyed Nepal's democratic machinery to serve his own ends. *The Record Nepal*. https://www.recordnepal.com/how-oli-destroyed-nepals-democratic-machinery-to-serve-his-own-ends (Accessed on 12 October).

184 *Nepal's Tryst with Democracy*

Rose, L.E. (1963). Nepal's experiment with traditional democracy. *Pacific Affairs*, 36(1), 16–31. https://doi.org/10.2307/2754771

Rose, L.E. (1971). *Nepal: Strategy for Survival*. Berkeley: University of California Press.

Routledge, P. (2010). Nineteen days in April: Urban protest and democracy in Nepal. *Urban Studies*, 47(6), 1279–1299. http://www.jstor.org/stable/43079913

Sharma, G. (2013, 14 March). Chief justice to lead Nepal's interim government to elections. *Reuters*. https://www.reuters.com/article/nepal-politics-government-idINDEE92C0GW201 30313 (Accessed on 10 October).

Sharma, G. (2017, 13 November). Nepal scraps $2.5 bln hydropower plant deal with Chinese company. *Reuters*. https://www.reuters.com/article/nepal-china-hydrop ower-idUSL3N1NJ3HD

Sharma, G. (2018, 23 September). Nepal restores $2.5 billion hydropower plant contract to Chinese firm. *Reuters*. https://www.reuters.com/article/us-china-nepal-hydrop ower-idUSKCN1M30CZ

Sharma, J. (2006). *Nepal: Struggle for Existence*. Kathmandu: CommInc ICT Private Limited.

Sharma, S. (2019). *Nepal Nexus: An Inside Account of the Maoists, Durbar and New Delhi*. Haryana: Penguin Random House India.

Shrestha, P.M. (2019, 31 January). Corruption rampant in local governments: Anti-graft body. *The Kathmandu Post*. https://kathmandupost.com/valley/2019/01/31/corruption-rampant-in-local-governments-anti-graft-body

Thapa, M. (2005). *Forget Kathmandu*. Delhi: Penguin Books India.

Thapa, G. & Sharma, J. (2009). From insurgency to democracy: The challenges of peace and democracy-building in Nepal. *International Political Science Review*, 30(2), 205–219. doi:10.2307/25652899

The Himalayan Times. (2020, 28 December). Chinese delegation led by Guo Yezhou lands in Nepal. https://thehimalayantimes.com/nepal/chinese-delegation-led-by-guo-yezhou-lands-in-nepal (Accessed on 10 November).

The Hindu. (2016, 3 August). Prachanda is new Nepal PM. https://www.thehindu.com/news/international/Prachanda-is-new-Nepal-PM/article14549333.ece (Accessed on 20 January).

The Kathmandu Post. (2021, 23 October). What is the controversy about Chief Justice Rana? https://kathmandupost.com/national/2021/10/26/what-is-the-controversy-about-chief-justice-rana (Accessed on 10 October).

Tiwari, S.P. (2021, 18 January). Nepal-China relations: Beware the dragon (Part I). *The Annapurna Express*. https://theannapurnaexpress.com/news/nepal-china-relations-beware-the-dragon-part-i-2980

Transparency International. (2020). *Corruption Perceptions Index 2020*. https://www.transparency.org/en/cpi/2020 (Accessed on 7 February).

Upadhya, S. (2008). *The Raj Lives: India in Nepal*. New Delhi: Vitasta Publishing.

Waldener, D. & Lust, E. (2018). Unwelcome change: Coming to terms with democratic backsliding. *Annual Review of Political Science*, 21, 93–113. https://doi.org/10.1146/annurev-polisci-050517-114628

Walker, C. (2018). What is 'sharp power'? *Journal of Democracy*, 29(3), 9–23. doi:10.1353/jod.2018.0041

Walt, S.M. (1998). International relations: One world, many theories. *Foreign Policy*, 110, 29–46. https://doi.org/10.2307/1149275

Xinhua. (2021, 21 July). China remains largest source of FDI for Nepal for 6 consecutive years. http://www.xinhuanet.com/english/asiapacific/2021-07/21/c_1310075557.htm

8 Democratization in Pakistan and Its Challenges

Mariam Mufti and Kazma Chaudhry

Introduction

Pakistan's relationship with democracy has been uneven and circuitous. Since independence in 1947, it has careened between periods of rule by democratically elected civilian politicians and military-led dictatorships. Adding to this instability has been the ratification of three constitutions in 1956, 1962 and 1973 that have swayed the country's institutional set-up from presidential to parliamentary. Pakistan embarked on its most recent transition to democracy when it held a founding election in 2008. Five years later, an elected, civilian government completed a full term in office and peacefully transferred power for the first time. In 2018, this was repeated. However, the dismissal of Imran Khan's government by a no-confidence vote in 2022 and the subsequent delay in elections—finally held in 2024 amid blatant pre-poll rigging—dashed all hopes that Pakistan had made enough gains to start consolidating a procedural democracy. The reality is that Pakistan continues to be ranked as a 'Partially Free' regime on the Freedom House index.

In this chapter, we make the argument that despite multi-party competition and regular elections, Pakistan persists as a hybrid regime rather than progressing towards democracy due to advantages enjoyed by the individual or collective actors who take advantage of the regime's ambiguous nature to achieve their preferred political goals. In other words, those who maintain the regime have no incentive for progressing towards democracy. We highlight several such actors that have played a role in the development of a hybrid regime in Pakistan to protect their interests. First, British colonizers implemented viceregalism in territories that eventually became Pakistan, which entrenched a strong military-bureaucratic establishment and weak representative institutions. Second, the Pakistani military has directly interfered in Pakistan's politics and undermined democracy through the imposition of martial law. Third, the political elite, which due to their short-term mindset, have failed to institutionalize and strengthen political parties to be a viable alternative to the dominant military-bureaucratic establishment. And fourth, international actors, in particular the United States, have aided and abetted non-democratic forces in Pakistan both economically and militarily. Given recent events in Pakistan's politics, we

DOI: 10.4324/9781003261469-8

186 *Democratization in Pakistan and Its Challenges*

question if there is a fifth actor in the form of the judiciary that might also be hindering democracy. Following this brief introduction, the chapter is divided into seven sections, including the conclusion. The next section theorizes Pakistan as a hybrid state and is followed by a discussion of each of the actors and how they have undermined democracy in Pakistan. The final section concludes the analysis and arguments with a word on looking ahead.

Theorizing Pakistan as a Hybrid Regime

Pakistan has been described as a 'hegemonic electoral authoritarian regime' (Diamond, 2002); a 'hybrid regime' transitioning towards authoritarianism (Morlino, 2009); or a 'tutelary democracy' (Levitsky and Way, 2010). This proliferation of descriptors for Pakistan's regime type is not surprising because since its inception Pakistan has fluctuated between periods when it has been purely authoritarian (1958–1962; 1969–1971; 1971–1973; 1977–1985; 1999–2002), periods when it has appeared to be transitioning towards authoritarianism (1962–1970; 2002–2008) and periods when it has attempted to make a transition towards democracy (1973–1977; 1988–1999; 2008–present).

Since 2008, most indices that measure regime type have treated Pakistan as a democracy. General Pervez Musharraf stepped down as the Chief of Army Staff in November 2007 and in August 2008 as the president of Pakistan. The election in 2008, although held under the auspices of a military-led regime, was seen as a founding election that set off a transition to democracy. In 2013, for the first time in Pakistan's history, a civilian government transferred power to another elected civilian government after completing a full term in office. Compared to previous elections, the 2013 election was undoubtedly an improvement and international observers lauded the extension of universal suffrage to the Federally Administrative Tribal Areas (FATA), the fact that political parties were placed on a level playing field to campaign and the fact that the Election Commission of Pakistan had made a greater effort to fairly administer the election. Nonetheless, on polling day irregularities in a number of constituencies raised concerns about electoral rigging; so much so that opposition parties repeatedly called for the resignation of Prime Minister Nawaz Sharif on charges of systematic manipulation of electoral results (Mufti, 2014). The 2018 election was watched very closely because it was expected to set the country on the path of democratic consolidation. It represented an uninterrupted continuation of the democratic process (European Union Election Observation Mission, 2018). However, the results of this election were also questioned by scholars who claimed that the military had worked behind the scenes to remove the incumbent government, with a more pliant party leadership under Imran Khan (Javid and Mufti, 2022; Siddiqa, 2020). Six years later (in 2024), Pakistan headed back to the polls. However, the electoral process has been marred by a brazen military campaign to decimate Pakistan Tehrik-e-Insaaf (PTI) in favor of its preferred candidate. The sentencing of Khan to over 30 years in prison, disqualification of PTI's candidates, denying the party its election symbol and

Democratization in Pakistan and Its Challenges 187

harassment of party activists has led voters to conclude that this was not an election but a 'selection'.

Adeney (2017) argues that although Pakistan has embarked on a period of democratization it is not yet a procedural electoral democracy. Using the 'fallacy of electoralism', she argues that free and fair elections, alternation of power and the growing power of opposition political parties are not enough to warrant the label of democracy. This is because it is impossible to ignore the illiberal aspects of Pakistan's regime such as the tutelary dominance enjoyed by the military and the lack of respect for political rights. Therefore, by acknowledging regime heterogeneity, Adeney suggests that Pakistan is still a hybrid regime, one that is located in the political continuum between democracy and non-democracy.

Apart from the dubiousness of election results, the military continues to retain tutelary control of Pakistan's politics. Although the military has taken a back seat, it continues to oversee issues of national security, in particular foreign policy towards India and dealing with religious militant organizations, and compelling the civilian political elite to conform to the military's policy preferences. The military also rejects any interference in matters pertaining to its internal organization, such as appointments and promotions of personnel, which is usually the prerogative of the civilian political elite. And finally, the military has continued to maintain its relevance by skillfully discrediting politicians each time it has seized political power through a coup, or by indirectly backing the president or a weak opposition to undermine a governing political party (see Shah, 2016).

A third aspect of Pakistan's regime hybridity is the lack of respect for political rights. Adeney (2017) documents the limits on press freedom imposed by the military, which systematically likes to maintain control of the prevailing narrative to benefit the military as an institution (Agha, 2017). Moreover, the rule of law, an essential requirement for a state to uphold its constitution and the civil and political liberties of its citizens, is also wanting. Access to quick and efficacious justice is a major problem that is further exacerbated by the judicial activism of a politicized Supreme Court, which is gradually positioning itself to be the arbiter of the tussle between the political elite and the military-bureaucracy (Qureshi, 2022).

The burgeoning literature on hybrid regimes, has tended to classify these regimes on the basis of electoral competition (Schedler, 2006; Levitsky and Way, 2010; Lindberg, 2009). However, hinging the classification of hybrid regimes on the basis of electoral competition on a uni-dimensional spectrum anchored by liberal democracy on the one end and closed authoritarianism on the other is problematic. For one, the role of elections in democracies and authoritarian regimes is significantly different. In the former, elections are held for legitimate elite succession; while in the latter elections serve as an instrument of elite management (Gandhi and Lust-Okar, 2009). To not pay attention to both the 'quality' and the 'meaning' of elections ignores that a political regime may be hybrid in other ways besides the competitiveness of an election (Gilbert and Mohseni, 2011). Therefore, a multi-dimensional conception of

188 *Democratization in Pakistan and Its Challenges*

hybridity using a configurative approach that can account for competitiveness, tutelary interference and civil liberties more effectively captures the complexity of a political regime. It is impossible to deny the advances that Pakistan has made since 2008 to democratize, and yet by adopting a multi-dimensional perspective we can see clearly that the coexistence of democratic elite succession and authoritarian rule-making aimed at maintaining the structural incentives of key political actors in Pakistan keeps the regime locked in a hybrid state.

Two approaches—structuralist and voluntarist—have been predominantly used to explain democratic transition in the literature. Structural approaches view the 'identities and interests of individual actors as defined by positions within social structures' (Mahoney and Snyder, 1999: 5). Therefore, the decision to democratize is a socially grounded response. On the other hand, voluntarist approaches emphasize 'ongoing interactions among purposeful actors' (ibid.: 5). By de-emphasizing social structures, the focus is on individual politicians at all levels of government and their incentives to democratize. Certainly, in Pakistan, the lack of democratization can be explained by examining structural factors, particularly the social and economic prerequisites of democracy (Lipset, 1994)—high levels of income, emergence of a middle class, high quality of education and civic culture. Pakistan's struggling economy, rapid urbanization and vulnerability to the forces of globalization are all worthy of further examination to understand why democracy has not taken root.

However, in this chapter, we have privileged a voluntarist, actor-centered approach to explain Pakistan's lack of democratization. The definition of a political regime entails both behavioral and institutional dimensions. A political regime is the set of formal and informal rules that identifies the powerholders and regulates their appointment to political office. It also determines the relationship between the rulers and the ruled and the relationships that might exist among the various powerholders. Negotiations among the elites to access and perpetuate themselves in power may cause shifts in the balance of power that underpins the regime. Hence, examining the actions of political actors is integral to the understanding of a regime (Mufti, 2018). And although both formal and informal institutions are important contextual factors limiting the actions of the political actors, we must acknowledge that the institutional setting is constructed by the actors themselves.

Legacy of the British Raj

British colonial administration was designed to meet the goals of the British in the various regions of the Indian subcontinent. The territories that eventually formed Pakistan were viewed as having immense strategic importance as the buffer against the threat of Soviet expansion from Central Asia. Consequently, the British emphasized law and order, political stability and militarization rather than popular representation, thereby bequeathing to Pakistan 'over-developed' administrative and military institutions (Alavi, 1983) that were reflective of a more autocratic tradition (also known as *viceregalism*) of rule as

Democratization in Pakistan and Its Challenges   189

compared to the rest of India (Sayeed, 1968; Waseem, 1989). Three features of the viceregal system of colonial administration had significant consequences for Pakistan's post-independence political trajectory.

First, NWFP (Northwest Frontier Province) and Punjab were governed as *non-regulation* provinces unlike Bengal, Bombay and Madras, which were regulation provinces. In the former, all political powers—executive, magisterial and judicial—were concentrated in the hands of the Deputy Commissioner who was an appointed officer of the Indian Civil Service—the bureaucratic arm of British India that was directly answerable to the Viceroy. The Deputy Commissioner could dispense justice and dole out patronage at his discretion to maintain law and order and elicit loyalty from colonial subjects. Unlike in the regulation provinces, the rights and obligations of citizens were not defined, breeding paternalism and hindering the growth of a political consciousness.

Second, the British preferred to establish consent instead of using coercion with the local population to build loyalty and facilitate a state of self-surveillance to avoid civil unrest. This was done by winning the support of large landowners, tribal leaders or *pirs* who were well respected in their community by granting them political pensions, honorary titles, cash, land and access to local administrative and judicial powers (Talbot, 1998: 60). By allowing this administrative influence to be passed on from father to son, the British centralized political control within particular families such as the Daultanas, Tiwanas and Legharis in Punjab; the Khuhros, Pagaros and Jatois in Sindh; the Bilours, Hotis and Khattaks in KP; and the Mengals, Bugtis and Jamalis in Balochistan, to name a few (Pattan Development Organization, 2006). The co-optation of the local landed elite severely diminished political institutionalization in the region, and instead encouraged an informal political system based on patrilineal inheritance and kinship networks rather than electoral representation, and reinforced a culture of clientelism and patronage. Peasants instead of turning to elected representatives for their needs relied on rural elites and Deputy Commissioners. This would later prove to be a significant obstacle in the development and progression of a strong middle class in Pakistan, which some scholars contend to be a key prerequisite for democratic transition and progression (Oldenburg, 2010: 193).

Third, the imperative to protect the Empire from Soviet expansion led to the deployment of troops from the British Indian Army that lent coercive power to the office of the Deputy Commissioner. Infrastructural developments were undertaken to sustain and facilitate the efficient mobilization of troops (Talbot, 1998, 54–57). The proximity to the so-called martial races in Punjab and NWFP led to a shift in military recruitment from Bihar and Awadh. By the 1920s, soldiers from Punjab, NWFP and Nepal formed 84% of the British Indian Army, and almost 30% of the soldiers at the time of World War II consisted of Punjabi Muslims alone (Lieven, 2011: 331). For their services, the British rewarded retired Punjabi soldiers with land grants, namely in the new canal colonies in Sindh. The British land-grant system was intended largely to provide a loyal and reliable source of recruitment of native Viceroy's Commissioned

190 *Democratization in Pakistan and Its Challenges*

Officers, who constituted the backbone of the British Indian Army and served as an essential link between the officer cadre and ordinary soldiers (ibid.: 332–333). This entrenchment of a paternalistic bureaucracy with wide discretionary powers, the personalization of authority in the hands of a dynastic rural elite and the militarization of the local indigenous population at the expense of representative political institutions was starkly demonstrated in the nationalist movement for an independent Pakistan led by the All-India Muslim League. The League was unable to mobilize grassroots support in Muslim-majority regions of NWFP, Punjab and Sindh, despite the Islamic appeal of demanding a separate homeland for Muslims, and it failed miserably in the 1937 elections. Furthermore, the leadership of the League belonged to Muslim-minority provinces in India and did not have a political base in the regions that later became Pakistan. As a result, the Muslim League relied on the well-entrenched rural leadership created by the British to muster constituency support in elections leading up to independence (see Tudor, 2014). After Partition, it was in the interest of this rural class to perpetuate itself by holding on to the levers of power and influence that had been given to it under the British. The stage that is therefore set for Pakistan's journey as an independent country is one with a powerful military and bureaucracy, weak politicians and a system of patronage to keep the country functioning.

The Military

Separated by an antagonistic India, Pakistan was made up of West Pakistan and East Pakistan (which later seceded to emerge as Bangladesh in 1971). It has always been deeply fearful of India's intentions towards its territorial integrity. The onset of conflict between the two countries over Kashmir, and further exacerbated by irredentist Pushtun claims in Pakistan's Northwest, further fueled this suspicion. Moreover, in the immediate aftermath of Partition, the fledgling state of Pakistan had to contend with a lack of economic resources (Talbot, 1998), popular grassroots support for the Muslim League (Tudor, 2014) and national unity (Jaffrelot, 2005). These factors fostered the mentality of a security state, 'distrustful of its own people, heavily reliant on intelligence services and ultimately dependent on the army to hold the country together' (Lieven, 2011: 127). As state survival and security became synonymized, the military legitimized its role as the pre-eminent guardian of Pakistan's national interest—to defend against India, defend Islam and defend the country against the ineptitude and corruption of the political elite (Cohen, 2006).

Rizvi (2003) lists four clusters of factors to explain the decline of civilian institutions and the ascendency of the military ultimately resulting in military coups in 1958, 1969, 1977 and 1999. Soon after independence, the death of Muhammad Ali Jinnah in 1948 and the assassination of Prime Minister Liaqat Ali Khan in 1951 plunged the newly independent state into a *crisis of leadership*. The Muslim League failed to transition from a nationalist movement to a national political party and quickly fragmented into splinter groups clustered around heavyweight politicians who lacked the incentive to establish democratic conventions (Waseem, 1989). The bureaucracy, bolstered by the military, stepped into this leadership void to deal with issues of governance, economy and security. In stark contrast to the disarray in the party system, the military stood out as a highly *professional and cohesive organization*. The military's self-confidence and organizational strength has been further reified by strategic alliances with *international actors* such as the United States, China and Saudi Arabia, which have provided training, technology and arms transfers. More importantly, wider Pakistani society sees the military as being disciplined, educated, progressive and the sole institution that adequately functions in Pakistan (Lieven, 2011: 305–306). Lastly, *civil-military relations are imbalanced*. Elected politicians have failed to assert their primacy over the military and restrict it to the professional domain. This, coupled with the failure of democratic institutions to cope with the challenges of governance and threats to security, have reinforced the perception of senior military commanders that their intervention in politics was justified.

However, despite the weakness of democratic institutions in Pakistan, the military has not been able to ignore them either. Increasing domestic and international pressures have required the military to maintain a democratic façade and seek legitimacy through the electoral process. Kennedy (2006) very cleverly explains how three military regimes—under Field Marshal Ayub Khan (1958–1968), General Ziaul Haq (1977–1988) and General Pervez Musharraf (1999–2008)—undertook a series of steps to establish this legitimacy.

First, martial law was justified by each of these regimes on the pretext of inefficient governance by corrupt and venal politicians. Ayub Khan blamed Pakistan's problems on parliamentary democracy and the lack of consensus among politicians. Ziaul Haq's Operation Fair Play questioned if 'Western-style democracy' was suitable for Pakistan. Musharraf evoked Nawaz Sharif's corruption to target a government which had dared challenged the military's institutional interests.

Second, all opposition to martial law was eliminated; that is, the parliament was dissolved and all the remnants of the previous regime were removed from office. Ayub Khan enacted executive orders giving former politicians the option to either stand trial for misconduct or withdraw from public life. Ziaul Haq eliminated all opposition by arresting incumbent Prime Minister Zulfikar Bhutto and charging him with conspiracy to murder. Musharraf similarly decapitated the leadership of PML-N (Pakistan Muslim League-Nawaz) by charging Nawaz Sharif with conspiracy to hijack a Pakistan International Airlines flight. Sharif was found guilty and exiled to Saudi Arabia

Third, martial law administrations entrenched themselves into the political system by seeking judicial sanction. They introduced a series of constitutional amendments designed to shift the fulcrum of power from prime minister to president, an office assumed by the military leader. Ayub Khan promulgated the Laws (Continuance in Force) Order that abrogated the 1956 constitution and replaced it with a new constitution in 1962 that introduced semi-presidential

192 *Democratization in Pakistan and Its Challenges*

Basic Democracy. Ziaul Haq similarly passed the Revival of Constitution Order of 1985 that substantially amended the 1973 Constitution to increase the powers of the president under Article 58 section 2b (also known as the Eighth Amendment). Musharraf similarly promulgated the Provisional Constitution Order of 1999 followed by the Legal Framework Order of 2002, establishing himself as the president for five years, and restoring the powers of the president that existed during the Zia era. During the period from 1988 to 1999, these powers were used to dismiss four elected governments midterm (Zia dismissed Junejo in 1988; Ghulam Ishaq Khan dismissed Benazir Bhutto in 1990 and Nawaz Sharif in 1993; and Farooq Ahmed Khan Leghari dismissed Benazir Bhutto in 1996). The most devastating impact of this so-called 58 2(b) system was the politics of confrontation between the governing and opposition political parties that were exploited by the president and army to perpetuate their dominance even after the military returned to the barracks. Under this constitutional amendment the president had the ultimate authority to dismiss the prime minister and his cabinet, while the army could manage politics indirectly by forcing the hand of the president to act in line with their agenda.

Fourth, as military governments made plans for constitutional reform, they actively pursued legitimacy through elected legislative assemblies. The military-bureaucratic nexus from 1958 to 1970 prioritized local over national politics through decentralization initiatives (Aslam, 2019); and non-partisan over partisan elections to hinder the development of genuine political competition. However, in 1970 Pakistan held its first general election, nearly a quarter of a century after independence. This last step warrants the recruitment of the political elite to fill the vacuum in political leadership and act as a conduit between the non-elected military government in the center and the rest of society. The elected legislative assemblies further create the perception of representative governance. By holding elections, a dyarchical sharing of powers between an elected prime minister and a president (in all three cases the Chief of Army Staff) was established. In all three regimes, the latter goal was achieved by entrusting legislators to act as patrons of their constituencies by providing material gain (developmental works), personal gain (employment, postings and transfers) or access to justice by dealing with local police on behalf of voters instead of legislation and oversight. This expectation was encouraged by the state, following a policy of providing legislators with equal-access, federal, constituency-development funds (CDF), a program that ran from 1988–2013 (Malik, 2019). This distribution of state patronage through legislators has had the adverse effect of turning parliament into an institution that rubber-stamps executive decisions. The logic of clientelism has become entrenched as the primary way citizen-state linkages are maintained, encouraging voters to hold elected representatives accountable for personalist service delivery and not law-making.

Since 2008, the military has receded into the barracks and has not directly interfered in politics, which has allowed a democratic transition to commence in Pakistan. It has also not contested political reforms designed to curb its political dominance, such as the Charter of Democracy in 2006, the abolition of the National Security Council (NSC) in 2009 or the passage of the Eighteenth Constitutional Amendment in 2010. Nonetheless, the military has continued to enhance its corporate autonomy and limit any civilian interference in its institutional prerogatives (Shah, 2016). In this post-2008 era, the military's modus operandi has moved away from direct intervention in politics. Instead, it prefers to exercise its influence in the background. During this period, the military purposefully prioritized its integrity as a professional institution that is trained, well equipped and combat-ready. Its strategies have been far more passive, but certainly not any less effective at retaining the tutelage of the military.

First, the military has evaded any attempts at executive accountability or parliamentary oversight. It has limited elected leaders from interfering in the process of appointments and promotions; the oversight of the defense budget by the parliamentary standing committee on defense; and the administration of military affairs by the Ministry of Defense. The military also continues to maintain a supralegal status in Pakistan and operates outside the purview of civilian law with almost complete impunity (see Shah, 2016).

Second, the military has zero tolerance for any civilian interference in the making of foreign policy, particularly towards India. The military leads with a 'Kashmir first' policy in its dealings with India, which implies that normalization of tensions with India is not possible unless the issue of Kashmir is resolved (Shah, 2016). Therefore, any attempt by the Pakistan People's Party (PPP), Pakistan Tehrik-e-Insaaf (PTI) or PML-N governments to negotiate peace or normalize trade has been met with resistance or threats to their survival in office, forcing civilian regimes to backtrack on their pursuit of an independent foreign policy (Clary, 2020). The military is similarly hawkish in its pursuit of 'strategic depth' on Pakistan's western border and its policy towards Afghanistan. To this end, the military exercises exclusive control of intelligence and counterintelligence through Inter-services Intelligence (ISI), which is constitutionally bound to report to the prime minister.

Third, the military has expanded its role in society as an economic actor—in the agriculture, services and manufacturing sectors. Apart from receiving the second-largest budgetary allocation (after debt servicing) towards defense, the military is also generating revenue from commercial ventures in fertilizer and cement production, real estate, security and education. Siddiqa (2007) describes the three-tiered 'milbus' comprising small-to-medium-sized enterprises using pension funds and often hiring retired military officers to run them. She explains that the military's economic involvement is to ensure its survival in a socio-political context led by civilian actors who are seen as incompetent.

Fourth, the military aspires to control the national narrative in order to solidify its significance to Pakistan's security and well-being. It does this by overemphasizing external threats, through self-glorification; presenting itself as the only credible guarantor of state survival; and amplifying the ineptitude and corruption of the political elite (Siddiqa, 2017: 61). To keep up with the growth of a liberalized media, the military has expanded the ISPR (Inter-services Public Relations) to surveil electronic and print media (Shah, 2016). It has attempted

194 *Democratization in Pakistan and Its Challenges*

to shape public opinion about the military through soft tactics such as active dissemination of exclusive news stories, producing TV serials to enhance its image, engaging academia and think tanks and the more coercive tactics of the ISI's Information Management Wing, which is known to have intimidated and blackmailed journalists or facilitated extrajudicial disappearances to instill fear.

Finally, and perhaps most damaging to democracy, is the infiltration of political parties by finding willing, pro-military collaborators to serve its interests. Siddiqa (2020) argues that the military is a 'king-maker'—central to the electoral process, which although competitive is also managed and rigged to advantage the military. In 2018, having tried the PPP and PML-N, the PTI emerged as the chosen party. Javid and Mufti (2022) document the strategies used by the military to tilt the elections in favor of the PTI, including

> the selective accountability of PML-N's leadership, coercing the media to support an anti-PML-N and pro-PTI narrative, forcing PML-N politicians to defect to rival parties and gerrymandering to produce a more favourable electoral map on the basis of the 2017 census.
>
> (ibid.: 71)

In 2024, the tables were turned, and this time the military's heavy-handedness was directed against Imran Khan in favor of Nawaz Sharif for reasons explained in the next section. The military used every tactic in its playbook to sideline the PTI, including the incarceration of party activists, coercing PTI members to defect to other political parties or to step away from politics, disqualifying Khan from elected office through judicial intervention, co-opting the opposition and hampering PTI's electoral campaign.

Despite this persecution, Imran Khan's popularity soared and his bold attacks against the military's reputation, its institutional integrity and support for corrupt politicians have truly challenged the national narrative spun by the latter. Further weakening the military's public image is the latest election result, in which PTI-backed independent candidates won the largest number of seats in the National Assembly. Perhaps for the first time, the military has underestimated how much Khan's anti-establishment rhetoric has resonated with voters and the widespread disillusionment, particularly amongst the youth, with the political system and the military's role within it. For an institution that prides itself on its operational mindset, professionalism and combat-readiness, the military has important existential questions to answer pertaining to its role in Pakistan's politics.

Indirect and direct military intervention in politics has created a vicious cycle of regime hybridity that is hard to break from—the weakness of the political parties in a clientelist polity gives the military a point of entry into the political system, which it exploits to weaken the political parties further. The resulting short-sightedness of political parties hinders their ability to exercise civilian primacy over the military, thus preventing democratic progress.

Weakly Institutionalized Political Parties

Schattschneider (1942) states, 'political parties created democracy and modern democracy is unthinkable save in terms of parties'. Yet in Pakistan, weakly institutionalized political parties due to their myopic understanding of their political responsibilities have placed a lasting strain on democracy. This behavior must be understood in the wider political context in Pakistan. Political parties have had to contend with an unstable political environment. Unbalanced civil-military relations, rampant constitutional engineering and confrontational relations between president and prime minister have shaped the incentive structures of individual politicians—be they in the opposition or the government—to treat their role in parliament to provide patronage to their constituency instead of shaping national policy.

Since 1988, political competition in Pakistan has been dominated by PPP and PML-led alliances (including the PML-N and Pakistan Muslim League-Quaid (PML-Q)) as control of the government has alternated between these two parties. From 1988 to 2013, these two parties have comprised 70% of the vote share and 68% of the seat share in the National Assembly. In 2018, PTI—a relatively new player in Pakistan's electoral politics—broke the two-party grip to win the election with a 32% vote share. Together, PML-N, PPP and PTI are thought of as 'mainstream parties' (Mufti et al, 2020). These parties contest elections nationally and attempt to appeal across the social divides of ethnicity and religion. Counterintuitively, however, the electoral success of these parties does not positively correlate with their organizational capacity. The need for survival has deterred political parties from investing in party organization or membership development, leading to low levels of professionalization among party cadres and party identification among voters. PPP, PML-N and PTI have also tended to be highly centralized organizations with decision-making resting largely in the hands of the party leaders who are known to only consult their inner circle of advisors. Moreover, except for the PTI, there are no intra-party elections, with dynasticism being the mode of elite succession in the PPP and PML-N. This tendency towards centralization has encouraged politicians to cultivate relations only with the party leader to advance their career instead of strengthening local party organization (Waseem and Mufti, 2012).

In contrast to the larger political parties, ethnic parties such as the Awami National Party (ANP) Mutahida Qaumi Movement (MQM) and Baloch nationalist parties and religious political parties such as Jamiat-Ulema-e-Islam (JUI-F) and Jamaat-e-Islami (JI) have typically contested elections from their ethnically defined, geographical strongholds and are not burdened by the need to be nationally representative. These smaller parties tend to maintain robust party organizations. They contest safe seats only where voters have strong partisan identification with the parties, sharply increasing the importance of their party label. Although these political parties are small and have very low seat shares in parliament, they have spatially concentrated voting blocs, which make them relevant as coalition partners in the formation of both provincial and national governments.

196 *Democratization in Pakistan and Its Challenges*

The weak party organizations of the three main political parties—PPP, PML-N and PTI—should not disguise the importance of these parties, because by winning elections they gain control of state resources, which in a clientelist polity makes them the primary route to political power. The visibility of local party organizations increases dramatically during elections, suggesting that the most important function of these parties is to operate as platforms for 'potential winners and not potential interests' (Waseem, 2002: 13). As the gatekeepers of political careers, the task of recruitment and candidate selection prior to an election rests largely with political parties. All three parties have relied on charismatic and 'electable' candidates. Electability is determined by a candidate's 'ability to finance their electoral campaign, maximize their personal vote shares by mobilizing kinship networks and to establish direct links with voters through the delivery of patronage' (Mufti and Jalalzai, 2021: 115). This emphasis on wealth and social status reveals that political parties seek candidates who can win elections with minimal support from a party's organizational infrastructure. Consequently, mainstream parties in Pakistan are dependent on self-sufficient politicians to advertise the party label instead of the politicians being dependent on the right party ticket to win the election, making it a candidate-centered political system. Individual politicians act more as autonomous entrepreneurs than as members of a political party. Since the party does not finance the campaign either, politicians are beholden to their own resources and constituents for re-election and can therefore switch to another party without incurring any significant costs.

The party leadership's inability to impose party discipline on its candidates is hugely detrimental to the party's electability and legislative agenda. It also results in a highly volatile party system. During the 1990s—the short democratic interregnum between the military regimes of Generals Ziaul Haq and Musharraf—Pedersen's (1979) index of electoral volatility (the net change resulting from individual vote transfers from one election to the next) was about 17.5. From 1997 to 2008, which witnessed the Musharraf regime and yet another democratic transition, electoral volatility increased, reaching a peak of nearly 40% in 2013 (Zhirnov and Mufti, 2019). Two factors explain this volatility in the party system: repeated party factionalization and party-switching.

Political parties, starting with the Muslim League, have historically been prone to splintering into factions led by heavyweight politicians whose political ambitions fly against the centralization of political parties and the lack of intra-party democracy. The dominance of political power by dynastic party leaders such as the Bhutto family in PPP and the Sharifs in PML-N explains why party members might defect in order to acquire the top political offices in the country. Another aspect of this is that party indiscipline has been routinely exploited by the military to splinter political parties by sowing seeds of distrust among its members.

The Muslim League has been described as a 'party for hire' (Siddiqa, 2020: 226). Pro-military Muslim Leaguers were co-opted by Ayub Khan to form the Convention Muslim League. Later in the 1980s, the military-bureaucracy axis

Democratization in Pakistan and Its Challenges   197

helped to cobble together a nine-party alliance (IJI—Islami Jamhoori Ittehad) to rein in the popularity of PPP. IJI split up in 1993 over its leadership with Nawaz Sharif—a protégé of Ziaul Haq's military regime—emerging as the leader of the party. Nawaz Sharif's faction PML-N proved to be the stronger and more dominant force, winning in 1993 and in a landslide victory in 1997. In the aftermath of the bloodless coup by General Pervez Musharraf in 1999 and the subsequent exile of Nawaz Sharif, a large number of party members defected from the PML-N to form the PML-Q. In the 2002 election, PML-Q, with Musharraf's patronage, emerged as the strongest party in the National Assembly. Meanwhile, PPP party leader Benazir Bhutto was also in self-exile during the 2002 election. Despite allegations of poll-rigging hurting the main opposition parties in favor of the pro-Musharraf parties, PPP performed quite well, securing 81 seats. But in the aftermath of the election a forward bloc of 10 members from PPP defected (facilitated by Musharraf) to join the PML-Q.

Party-switching prior to elections has been a relatively widespread phenomenon in Pakistan, with Qadri (2014) estimating that 19% of all candidates switched from one party to another in all the elections held between 1990 and 2008. About 60% of these were candidates who had ranked among the top three in their constituencies in the preceding elections. According to the Free and Fair Election Network (FAFEN), party-switching reached a historic peak in 2018, with 248 politicians at the national and provincial level switching parties between January and May 2018. Of these, 92 joined the PTI, followed by 48 switching to the PPP and 29 opting for the PML-N (Free and Fair Election Network , 2018). Zhirnov and Mufti (2019) have shown that party-switching is rife due to high electoral volatility and low party identification. As the PML-N, PPP and PTI compete to recruit electable candidates, they attempt to outdo the other's promise of patronage and privileges in exchange for electoral support. Javid and Mufti (2020) explain that across successive electoral cycles this weakens party structures and strengthens tendencies that prompt party-switching in the first place, namely a lack of investment in party organization, which results in the inability to attract voters and, therefore, dependence on electable candidates. Moreover, by accepting a party-switcher, parties send a signal to their own members that they are undervalued, creating even more dissension in the ranks.

Both party factionalization and party-switching are symptomatic of party weakness. In parliament, party indiscipline undercuts the ruling party's legislative agenda and makes it vulnerable to manipulation by the military and opposition parties in a crisis of legitimacy. This especially holds true for the 1990s, when instead of holding the government accountable through oversight procedures or presenting the public with an alternative set of policies, opposition parties chose to support the president's initiative, backed by the army, to dissolve the National Assembly using Article 58 2(b). This undermined democracy because it abruptly interrupted electoral cycles and limited voter choice by creating a perverse set of incentives that gave opposition parties an anti-incumbency advantage in a largely two-party system (Mufti, 2015).

198   *Democratization in Pakistan and Its Challenges*

More recently, the no-confidence motion against Prime Minister Imran Khan was also emblematic of party indiscipline and of opposition parties actively attempting to destabilize a sitting government. First, it is no coincidence that Imran Khan had become increasingly vulnerable to criticism and attacks from a united opposition led by the PDM (Pakistan Democratic Movement), as the military withdrew its support and distanced itself from Khan's politics. The rift between Imran Khan and the military widened as Khan asserted his civilian authority in the appointment of the ISI chief—a direct impingement of the military's institutional interests. Moreover, Khan's desire for a more independent foreign policy, which ostensibly has led him to cozy up with Russia and China and drift away from the United States, was viewed with much disapproval. Although the military repeatedly asserted that it was neutral in this vote of no-confidence, its obvious displeasure with the PTI government emboldened the opposition. Second, PTI's strategy to rely on so-called electable politicians to win key constituencies in 2018 also backfired. PTI accommodated politicians who defected from other political parties to contest on PTI's ticket. As the no-confidence motion drew near, PTI was unable to hold the party together as dissenting members promised to back the opposition (see Mufti, 2022).

The results of the election in 2024 will also prove to be a major test of party discipline. Since the PTI was denied the use of its electoral symbol, the bat, many of the party ticketholders contested as independent candidates. Nearly a hundred PTI-backed independent candidates won the largest seat share in the lower house. However, independent candidates cannot form a government. It remains to be seen if these candidates succumb to the pressure of defecting and joining other political parties or remain loyal to Imran Khan.

Finally, it is also important to examine party behavior in opposition. Historically, opposition parties have derailed government attempts to pass important legislation. This explains why rescinding the Eighth Amendment to restore parliamentary sovereignty took more than two decades from its enactment. Instead of using means of debate and deliberation, opposition parties have resorted to fiery rhetoric that has often degenerated into inappropriate behavior unbecoming of the country's elected representatives. Outside parliament, opposition parties have indulged in street agitation, mobilizing mass support through rallies, long marches, sit-ins or wheel-jam strikes to protest against the government policies and actions (Mufti, 2014). PTI's four-month-long *dharna* (sit-in) in 2014 demanded an inquiry into electoral rigging and the resignation of Prime Minister Nawaz Sharif on account of it. Irreconcilable differences between the two parties brought the army back into politics. Although not constitutionally empowered to do so, Army Chief General Raheel Sharif was compelled to step in and mediate between the PTI and PML-N as attempts at negotiation repeatedly failed and the protests became violent (Arif and Shah, 2015). Once again, the army projected itself as a 'referee and the only institution concerned with the national interest, rising above the disputes of power hungry politicians' (Jaffrelot, 2014).

Opposition parties, just like ruling parties, have been shaped by the prevalent exigencies of the political system. Mufti (2014) explains that ruling parties enter office on a defensive footing and are unable to ensure the rights of an opposition to exist. Moreover, in a clientelist polity, being in the opposition means not having access to state resources, creating an urgent need to return to power and increase local influence within the constituency.

This logic of clientelism permeates through all levels of political life. Party leaders have used patronage to control the party machinery and to win the support of party members. They cement the loyalty of party workers by doling out patronage in the form of houses, plots of urban land and public sector jobs. During elections, parties mobilize public opinion through charismatic leadership or the promise of material incentives to voters for electoral support. Citizens do not adhere to parties for ideology but for instrumental reasons that often lead to immediate material gain. Once elected, clientelism does not necessitate that governing parties actually follow up on their policy platforms. In fact, ruling parties use development funds as both a lure and a punishment to elicit credible commitments from its legislators. Clientelist politics does help to win elections, and a system based on private exchanges and trading favors does win political support. However, it does not create legitimacy, discrediting the very notion of democracy (see Javid, 2019). The most insidious incentive to engage in clientelist practices is that the exchange of resources between state agencies and private business can make politicians—and their friends and family—wealthy. Hence, patronage politics breeds corruption and nepotism that obviously takes its toll on the moral fabric of society but, more to the point, has a deleterious impact on democracy.

The International Community

In the previous sections, we have highlighted key domestic actors that have undermined the growth and stabilization of democracy in Pakistan. This section demonstrates how external actors, namely the United States and its geostrategic endeavors in the region—particularly Soviet containment and the War on Terror—has led to collaboration with the Pakistani military, further shifting the civil-military balance away from the political elites and strengthening the military's position within the polity. The United States-Pakistan alliance began shortly after independence in the mid-1950s, coinciding with the Cold War. At the time, Washington preferred Pakistan over India because its location bordering the Middle East made it an important geostrategic anchor for assuming control of the world's petroleum resources and for maintaining Afghanistan as a buffer against southward Soviet expansion. While Pakistan readily allied itself with the United States due to its need for security assistance against the perceived threat from India, the United States has been less certain of its ally. Pakistan's political instability and authoritarian tendencies defied its democracy promotion agenda. Washington has condemned each of Pakistan's military coups, but they have also purposefully collaborated with all military governments and overlooked the lack of democracy.

200   *Democratization in Pakistan and Its Challenges*

In the early years of the Cold War, the United States employed a strategy of propping up General Ayub Khan by providing generous military and economic assistance that spurred his 'decade of development'. The 1970s saw a cooling-off period as US President Carter initiated a 'moralistic' foreign policy aimed at limiting nuclear proliferation in South Asia and imposed sanctions after Pakistan reportedly attempted to enrich weapons-grade uranium. These sanctions were short-lived due to the Soviet invasion of Afghanistan in 1979 and Pakistan became a frontline state. Once again, Pakistan received an exorbitant amount of foreign aid in exchange for its cooperation. The Pressler Amendment—which prohibited such military assistance to countries developing nuclear explosives— was ignored to deliver this aid.

In 1990, with the end of the Cold War and Soviet withdrawal from Afghanistan, US strategic interests in Pakistan lapsed. Pakistan's domestic political instability and hostile relationship with India formed the justification for a drastic modification in US foreign policy. Relations continued to deteriorate when Pakistan tested nuclear weapons in 1998 and General Pervez Musharraf imposed martial law in 1999. But in the aftermath of 9/11, the United States turned a blind eye to nuclearization and lack of democracy, and once again Pakistan was enlisted to abet the US-led War on Terror and support counter-insurgency efforts in Afghanistan. For its continued cooperation, Pakistan received foreign aid, the bulk of which was in the form of foreign military financing aimed at counter-terrorism. This brief account highlights that American foreign policy has often had contradictory aims and goals characterized by maintaining the status quo yet demanding to see change (Mufti, 2012). The United States shored up three military regimes under Generals Ayub, Zia and Musharraf because they met its national security needs. But these large sums of money in the form of direct military aid have undermined democracy in Pakistan in significant ways.

First, the timing of US aid has significantly boosted the military's institutional power and prestige within Pakistan and played an important role in shaping the military's professional and political profile in the polity, as well as increasing its legitimacy. For example, US economic aid helped Ayub Khan boost Pakistan's GDP and attract much-needed foreign direct investment, and it similarly helped Musharraf solve Pakistan's economic problems in the early 2000s. These economic initiatives enhanced popular support for these regimes (Oldenburg, 2010: 165).

Second, the United States helped the Pakistani military substantially enhance its capacity and expertise. It was able to advance and replicate the training it received in fighting America's proxy war in Afghanistan against India in Kashmir. The exploitation of India as an existential threat and the waging of a 'jihad' against it has served to augment the military's image as 'martyrs' willing to sacrifice themselves in the name of Pakistan's territorial integrity and Islamic ideology (Fair, 2011: 587). The acquisition of modern technology and organizational skills through direct military-to-military transfers from the United States has inadvertently pitted a confident military against political institutions in the domestic context.

Democratization in Pakistan and Its Challenges   201

Third, and perhaps the most significant, is that the long-term flow of economic and military assistance has made Pakistan aid-dependent, undermined democratic accountability and slowed down institutional development. Successive Pakistani governments, whether civilian- or military-led, have bet on the country's critical geostrategic location and its nuclear status that the international community will rescue it in times of economic distress. Starting from the 1980s, World Bank and International Monetary Fund financing has helped to plug fiscal deficits and debt burdens. In return, the IMF has tied strict conditionalities and austerity measures to aid, which instead of being tailored to Pakistan's unique socio-political context have met the needs and incentives of external donors. Certainly, US endorsement of these bailouts in line with its national security agenda has reinforced the perception of Pakistan's geostrategic importance and disincentivized the ruling elite from developing sustainable economic institutions that foster growth (Burki and Naseemullah, 2016).

Since the end of the War on Terror, and Pakistan's reduced importance to US national security, Pakistan has increasingly turned to authoritarian states such as China and Saudi Arabia for economic aid. Pakistan has recently signed a $2.3 billion loan facility agreement with China and received $3 billion from Saudi Arabia to help its cash-strapped economy in the wake of depleting foreign exchange reserves. These, of course, are short-term fixes to keep the country economically afloat, but in the long term the consequences are devastating. For one, Pakistan is caught in a debt trap and deeply dependent on two authoritarian states for survival. China is Pakistan's largest arms supplier, while Saudi Arabia is its largest petroleum supplier. Doing business with authoritarian states, with their own nefarious foreign policies, limits Pakistan's agency and ability to have relations with Western democracies.

A Fifth Actor—the Judiciary?

This chapter has endeavored to describe Pakistan as a hybrid regime in which political power is contested and negotiated between the military on the one hand, and the political parties on the other. The judiciary, therefore, finds itself in a unique position—as the arbiter of political conflicts as both military and political elite seek an ally to perpetuate their positions of power. Historically, the judiciary played the role of a 'rubber-stamp institution' (Oldenburg, 2016) legitimizing the military's political interventions starting with Ayub Khan's first martial law in 1958; then Chief Justice Muhammad Munir validated the coup and abrogation of the constitution using the doctrine of state necessity. Subsequently the same doctrine legitimized Ziaul Haq and Musharraf's military regimes and provided institutional cover for bans on political activity, suspension of fundamental rights and erosion of legislative superiority.

In 2007, the judiciary broke away from the pattern of collaborating with the military by asserting its judicial autonomy. However, the judicial activism of Chief Justice Iftikhar Muhammad Chaudhry to hear cases that questioned the military's political prerogatives crossed a red line. Musharraf's response was to

202 Democratization in Pakistan and Its Challenges

unconstitutionally oust Chaudhry and force him to resign. This triggered the Lawyer's Movement (2007–2009), which together with high court judges, bar associations, political parties and civil society actors demanded the reinstatement of the Chief Justice, the restoration of the Supreme Court's rights and the ousting of Musharraf (Shafqat, 2018). This was a key turning point, as scholars argued that the Lawyer's Movement symbolized a more assertive judiciary. However, Qureishi (2020) argues that opposition to military rule in 2008 certainly did not imply support for the supremacy of political parties and parliament. In the democratic interregnum from 1988 to 1997, the Supreme Court weighed in on the constitutionality of presidential dissolutions of the National Assembly under Article 58 2(b). The Court also contradicted itself in the interpretation of the law by rejecting the president's power to dismiss the Assembly in the case of Muslim League governments (1988 and 1993), but in the case of the PPP governments (1990 and 1997) it upheld presidential powers. The inconsistencies in the Supreme Court's decisions by pointing to the 'institutional interlinkages' (ibid.: 237) between the Muslim League politicians—most of whom had entered politics during Zia's regime—the military and the judiciary. In the case of the PPP, the military's opposition and distrust of the party dissuaded the judiciary from being lenient (ibid.: 248–249).

More recently, the judiciary has demonstrated its disdain for political parties and their elected leaders by ousting two prime ministers. Although Pakistan has held three elections every five years since 2008, no prime minister has been able to complete a full five-year term in office. Both the hearings against former Prime Ministers Yusuf Reza Gillani, Nawaz Sharif and now Imran Khan have established the Supreme Court's willingness to address corruption as a malaise in the political fabric of the country. Gillani was ousted from power under contempt of court charges because he refused to write a letter to Swiss authorities to reopen corruption cases against PPP party leader Asif Ali Zardari. While Nawaz Sharif was removed from office under Article 62 based on a misdeclaration of assets, he was found to be neither *sadiq* (truthful) nor *ameen* (trustworthy); but more importantly, he was disqualified from electoral politics arbitrarily without the right of appeal on charges that had nothing to do with the allegations in the Panama Papers leak. Imran Khan has been sentenced to over 30 years in prison on a series of charges pertaining to the mishandling of state gifts in the Toshakhana case; conspiracy under the Official Secrets Act; and for marrying his third wife illegitimately.

These recent cases reinforce two characteristic features of the current Supreme Court. First, the Supreme Court will not shy away from using its powers under Article 184(3) to exercise judicial activism and dismiss a sitting prime minister. Second, the judiciary still considers the military's institutional interests when making its decisions. For example, the inclusion of military intelligence agencies on the Joint Investigative Team that led the probe deeper into the financial misdeeds of the Sharif family signaled a lack of trust in civilian institutions to conduct a sound investigation (Husain, 2017). Beyond purging electoral politics of parliamentarians who do not fulfill 'vague standards of morality and sagacity' (Qureishi, 2020: 247) as stated in Articles 62 and 63, which ultimately hurt the PML-N and benefited the PTI in the 2018 election, the Supreme Court is encroaching on parliamentary prerogatives. In its quest for autonomy and supremacy, the judiciary can inadvertently tip the balance of power by overregulating party politics and intervening in parliamentary crises. The no-confidence motion against Imran Khan has led the Supreme Court to weigh in on political disputes that should have been resolved within parliament. The most egregious case of this is the recent judgment on the anti-defection clause contained in Article 63-A of the constitution and the question of whether the votes of defecting legislators ought to be counted in a no-confidence motion and whether defectors ought to be disqualified from electoral politics. In a controversial ruling, the Court invalidated the vote of defecting legislators. The verdict issued by the Court has been criticized by legal scholars as going beyond the provision of the law and rewriting the constitution. But more crucially, this verdict is the main cause of controversy over the election of the Chief Minister in Pakistan's most populous province of Punjab. The recent consensus among the judiciary that it must redress issues of governance that the government and military have ignored has led to populist judicial actions that have made it harder for elected governments to deliver. Moreover, its willingness to hear cases that require the courts to mediate the horizontal institutional linkages between the military and political elites has the potential to undermine the judiciary's credibility.

Looking Ahead

The analysis in this chapter makes three important contributions: First, Pakistan's political regime is described as a hybrid regime transitioning towards democracy. It is hindered in this transition by the weakness of political actors, the tutelary dominance of the military and the growing influence of the judiciary. Second, we employ an actor-centered approach to provide a systemic explanation for the lack of democracy in Pakistan. We focus on the consequences of elite actions and incentives for the make-up of the political regime. In doing this, we emphasize that the current hybrid dispensation is meeting the immediate needs of the main political actors, because of which there is no pressing desire for democracy. Third, for democracy to take root and consolidate in Pakistan, the actor-centered approach would prescribe changing the incentive structures so that all relevant elites believe that 'democracy is the only game in town' (Linz and Stepan, 1996: 5).

In concluding this chapter, it is important to recognize the limitations of the actor-centered approach to describe Pakistan's democratic transition, for the challenges are immensely complex. Structural factors, particularly the flailing economy, poor governance and a growing population demanding social services, make democracy an expensive proposition that a country with burgeoning fiscal deficits can ill afford. The lack of national integrity, unbalanced center-province relations and Islamist extremism threaten political stability and

204 *Democratization in Pakistan and Its Challenges*

an elected government's mandate. Certainly, the voluntarist approach would recommend that for democracy to flourish the political and military elites should firmly commit to democratic norms. But this kind of top-down explanation removes agency from ordinary citizens and voters to demand democracy. And therefore, given the unexpected results of the 2024 election, the actor-centered approach, instead of taking a necessarily elite focus, should also examine grassroots initiatives, the media and civil society and potential drivers of change.

Bibliography

Adeney, K. 2017. "How to understand Pakistan's hybrid regime: the importance of a multidimensional continuum". *Democratization*, 24(1): 119–137.

Alavi, Hamza. 1983. "Class and State" in *Pakistan: The Roots of Dictatorship*, edited by H. Gardezi and J. Rashid. London: Zed Press.

Arif, Bushra and Aqil Shah. 2015. "Pakistan in 2014: Democracy under the Military's Shadow." *Asian Survey*, 55(1): 48–59.

Aslam, Ghazia. 2019. "Decentralization reforms in dictatorial regimes as a survival strategy: evidence from Pakistan." *International Political Science Review*, 40(1): 126–142.

Burki, Shahid Javed and Adnan Naseemullah. 2016. "Pakistan's Economy: Domestic Dissent and Foreign Reliance" in *Pakistan at the Crossroads: Domestic Dynamics and External Pressures*, edited by Christophe Jaffrelot, 165–187. Gurgaon: Random House India.

Clary, Christopher. 2020. "Parties and Foreign Policy in Pakistan" in *Pakistan's Political Parties: Surviving between Dictatorship and Democracy*, edited by Mariam Mufti, Niloufer Siddiqui and Sahar Shafqat, 253–271. Washington, DC: Georgetown University Press.

Cohen, Stephen P. 2006. *The Idea of Pakistan*. Washington, DC: Brookings Institution Press.

Diamond, Larry. 2002. "Thinking about hybrid regimes". *Journal of Democracy*, 13(1): 21–35.

European Union Election Observation Mission. 2018. *Pakistan: General Elections Final Report*. https://www.eeas.europa.eu/sites/default/files/final_report_pakistan_2018_english_1.pdf.

Free and Fair Election Network. 2018. *Preliminary 2018 Election Observation Report*. Islamabad: FAFEN.

Fair, Christine. 2011. "Why the Pakistan army is here to stay: Prospects for civilian governance". *International Affairs*, 87(3): 571–588.

Gandhi, J. and Lust-Okar, E. 2009. "Elections under authoritarianism". *Annual Review of Political Science*, 12: 403–422.

Gilbert, L. and Mohseni, P. 2011. "Beyond authoritarianism: The conceptualization of hybrid regimes". *Studies in Comparative International Development*, 46: 270–297.

Husain, Waris. 2017. "Nawaz Sharif and the Panama Papers Judgement in Pakistan". *The Diplomat*, April 25.

Jaffrelot, Christophe. 2005. *Pakistan: Nationalism without a Nation*. Lahore: Vanguard Press.

Jaffrelot, Christophe. 2014. "Going back to Rawalpindi". *The Indian Express*. September 13.

Javid, Hassan. 2019. "Democracy and Patronage in Pakistan" in *New Perspectives on Pakistan's Political Economy: State, Class and Social Change*, edited by Matthew McCartney and S. Akbar Zaidi, 216–241. Cambridge: Cambridge University Press.

Javid, Hassan and Mariam Mufti. 2020 "Candidate-Party Linkages: Why Do Candidates Stick with Losing Parties?" in *Pakistan's Political Parties: Surviving between Dictatorship and Democracy*, edited by Mariam Mufti, Niloufer Siddiqui and Sahar Shafqat, 144–161. Washington, DC: Georgetown University Press.

Javid, Hassan and Mariam Mufti. 2022. "Electoral manipulation or astute electoral strategy? Explaining the results of Pakistan's 2018 Election". *Asian Affairs: An American Review*, 49(2): 65–87.

Kennedy, Charles H. 2006. "A User's Guide to Guided Democracy: Musharraf and the Pakistani Military Governance Paradigm" in *Pakistan 2005*, edited by Charles H. Kennedy and Cynthia Botteron, 120–158. Oxford: Oxford University Press.

Lieven, Anatole. 2011. *Pakistan: A Hard Country*. London: Penguin Books.

Levitsky, Steven and Lucan Way. 2010. *Competitive Authoritarianism: Hybrid Regimes after the Cold War*. New York: Cambridge University Press.

Lindberg, S. 2009. *Democratization by Elections: A New Mode of Transition*. Baltimore: Johns Hopkins University Press.

Linz, Juan and Alfred Stepan. 1996. *Problems of Democratic Transition and Consolidation: Southern Europe, South America and Post-Communist Europe*. Baltimore: Johns Hopkins University.

Lipset, Seymour M. 1994. "The social requisites of democracy revisited". *American Sociological Review*, 59(1): 1–22.

Mahoney, James and Richard Snyder. 1999. "Rethinking agency and structure in the study of regime change". *Studies in Comparative International Development*, 34(3): 3–32.

Malik, Rabia. 2019. "(A)political constituency development funds: Evidence from Pakistan". *British Journal of Political Science*, 1–18. doi:10.1017/S0007123419000541

Morlino, Leonard. 2009. "Are there hybrid regimes? Or are they just an optical illusion?" *European Political Science Review*, 1(2): 273–296.

Mufti, Mariam. 2012. "The Impact of Pakistan's Domestic Affairs on the Making of US Foreign Policy" in *Pakistan: The US, Geopolitics and Grand Strategies*, edited by Julian Schofield and Usama Butt, 64–86. London: Pluto Press.

Mufti, Mariam. 2014. "Divided we rule". *The Herald*.

Mufti, Mariam. 2015. "The Years of a Failed Democratic Transition 1988–1997" in *The History of Pakistan*, edited by Roger D. Long, 633–679. Karachi: Oxford University Press.

Mufti, Mariam. 2018. "What do we know about hybrid regimes after two decades of scholarship?" *Politics and Governance*, 6(2), 112–119.

Mufti, Mariam. 2022. "Pakistan's crisis of legitimacy". *Australian Outlook*. https://www.internationalaffairs.org.au/australianoutlook/pakistans-crisis-of-legitimacy/.

Mufti, Mariam and Farida Jalalzai. 2021. "The importance of gender quotas in patriarchal and clientelistic polities: The Case of Pakistan". *Journal of Women, Politics & Policy*, 42(2), 107–123.

Mufti, M., S. Shafqat and N. Siddiqui (Eds.). 2020. *Pakistan's Political Parties: Surviving Between Dictatorship and Democracy*. Washington, DC: Georgetown University Press.

Oldenburg, Philip. 2010. *India, Pakistan, and Democracy: Solving the Puzzle of Divergent Paths*. London: Routledge.

Oldenburg, Philip. 2016. "The Judiciary as a Political Actor" in *Pakistan at the Crossroads: Domestic Dynamics and External Pressures*, edited by Christophe Jaffrelot, 89–120. Gurgaon: Random House India.

Pattan Development Organization. 2006. *Understanding the Role of Political Dynasties: Local Government Election 2005*. Islamabad: Pattan Development Organization.

206 Democratization in Pakistan and Its Challenges

Pedersen, Mogens N. 1979. "The dynamics of European party systems: Changing patterns of electoral volatility". *European Journal of Political Research*, 7(1): 1–26.

Qadri, Rida. 2014. "Jumping ship: The story of party switching in Pakistan". Institute for Development and Economic Alternatives Working Paper.

Qureishi, Yasser. 2020. "Judicial Politics in a Hybrid Democracy" in *Pakistan's Political Parties: Against All Odds*, edited by Mariam Mufti, Niloufer Siddiqui and Sahar Shafqat, 235–252. Washington, DC: Georgetown University Press.

Qureishi, Yasser. 2022. *Politics at the Bench: The Pakistani Judiciary's Ambitions and Interventions*. Washington, DC: Carnegie Endowment for International Peace.

Rizvi, Hassan Askari. 2003. *Military, State and Society in Pakistan*. Lahore: Sang-e-Meel Publications.

Sayeed, Khalid Bin. 1968. *Pakistan: The Formative Phase 1957–1948*. 2nd edn. Karachi: Oxford University Press.

Schattschneider, E.E. 1942. *Party Government*. New York: Farrar and Rinehart.

Schedler, Andreas. 2006. *Electoral Authoritarianism: Dynamics of Unfair Competition*. Boulder: Lynne Rienner Publishers.

Shafqat, Sahar. 2018. "Civil society and the lawyers' movement of Pakistan". *Law and Social Inquiry*, 43(3): 889–914.

Shah, Aqil. 2016. "The Military and Democracy" in *Pakistan at the Crossroads: Domestic Dynamics and External Pressures*, edited by Christophe Jaffrelot, 23–61. Gurgaon: Random House India.

Siddiqa, Ayesha. 2007. *Military INC: Inside Pakistan's Military Economy*. London: Pluto Press.

Siddiqa, Ayesha. 2017. "Mapping the Establishment" in *Pakistan's Democratic Transition*, edited by Ishtiaq Ahmed and Adnan Rafiq, 53–72. London: Routledge.

Siddiqa, Ayesha. 2020. "The King-maker: The Military and Pakistan's Political Parties" in *Pakistan's Political Parties: Surviving between Dictatorship and Democracy*, edited by Mariam Mufti, Niloufer Siddiqui and Sahar Shafqat, 215–234. Washington, DC: Georgetown University Press.

Talbot, Ian. 1998. *Pakistan: A Modern History*. London: C. Hurst and Co.

Tudor, Maya. 2014. *The Promise of Power*. Cambridge: Cambridge University Press.

Waseem, Mohammad. 1989. *Politics and the State in Pakistan*. Lahore: Progressive Publishers.

Waseem, Mohammad. 2002. *Electoral Reform in Pakistan*. Islamabad: Friedrich-Ebert-Stiftung.

Waseem, Mohammad and Mariam Mufti. 2012. *Political Parties in Pakistan: Organization and Power Structure*. Islamabad: Asia Foundation.

Zhirnov, Andrei and Mariam Mufti. 2019. "Electoral constraints on inter-party mobility of candidates: The case of Pakistan". *Comparative Politics*, 51(4): 519–554.

9 Constitutional Amendments (2001–2022) and Democracy in Sri Lanka

Nadarajah Pushparajah and Malini Balamayuran

Introduction

The island of Sri Lanka with its multicultural population is one of the oldest democracies in South Asia. The island nation's performance as a democracy proved to be relatively good (much like that of India) from the time of independence until the 1970s. After that period, the centralization of political power through new constitutions and various amendments led to a gradual decline in the quality of democracy. Through two constitution-making endeavors, followed by numerous amendments, successive governments of Sri Lanka consolidated power at the center. The major theme was to institutionalize an ethnocentric policy, while relegating the minorities to a second-class status. The current constitution, adopted in 1978, contributed greatly towards centralizing the power of the executive president and had the deleterious effect of weakening parliament and politicizing most of the governing institutions. To reduce the risks associated with centralized presidential power and the consequent politicization of government departments, Sri Lanka enacted five different constitutional amendments under different regimes from the year 2000. These amendments differed in their democratic characteristics, with some emphasizing democratic principles and others exhibiting undemocratic traits. Unfortunately, full implementation of the progressive amendments never materialized, whereas the implementation of retrogressive amendments contributed to a worrisome trend of backsliding in Sri Lanka.

The existing literature on constitutional scholarship reveals that frequent tampering with constitutions can potentially lead to instability in a democratic system. However, efforts of the government led by the People's Alliance, which ascended to power in 1994, proved significant as it adopted the progressive 17th Amendment in 2001 to eliminate 'politicization' and promote good governance based on democratic principles.[1] This amendment sought to curtail the executive president's power to interfere in the appointments, promotions and transfers of officials within public institutions and in certain other matters. It also reduced the presidential term limits to two. Later, when President Mahinda Rajapaksa was re-elected in 2010 on the strength of his military defeat of the Liberation Tigers of Tamil Eelam (LTTE) in May 2009, he introduced the 18th

DOI: 10.4324/9781003261469-9

Amendment, which removed presidential term limits and replaced the Constitutional Council with a Parliamentary Council. The 18th Amendment facilitated nepotism, corruption and politicization of the 'rule of law' foundations. Rajapaksa's regime was heading towards authoritarianism and patronage-driven autocracy. Therefore, it undermined the democratization of post-war Sri Lanka to a serious degree. However, this democratic backsliding was partially reversed by the Sirisena-Wickremesinghe duo's National Unity Government, which adopted the 19th Amendment to the Constitution in 2015. Its objective was to prevent corruption and ensure a non-dynastic leadership for the country. Therefore, it re-introduced the two-term presidential limit and restored the Constitutional Council, which was originally introduced as part of the 17th Amendment in 2001 to approve the appointment of persons by the president to the independent commissions and other 'rule of law' institutions. The 19th Amendment also enhanced the power of the prime minister and parliament at the expense of the president. This amendment put in motion a trend in reversing undemocratic provisions of the law and was therefore regarded as the most democratic and progressive amendment to the 1978 Constitution. After the next change of government, Gotabaya Rajapaksa's regime introduced the 20th Amendment in 2020, which again brought in some provisions that were introduced in the 18th Amendment, while annulling the 19th Amendment. However, within two years of being elected, the government of Gotabaya Rajapaksa was confronted by a dire economic crisis. This in turn led to a political crisis, which finally resulted in the ousting of the president from the office he had served in from 2019. The amendments continued, with the government of newly appointed President Ranil Wickremesinghe enacting the 21st Amendment in October 2022. While the 21st Amendment repealed the 20th Amendment and restored most of the reforms introduced under the 19th Amendment, some of its important provisions were left out. This again demonstrates only a partial restoration of democratic reforms.

Theoretical aspects of democratic backsliding and their many ramifications were given due consideration in the first chapter of this volume. However, for the purpose of this chapter, it is imperative to indicate the nexus between constitutional amendments and democratic process. Indeed, the practice of making constitutional amendments seems to be a double-edged sword in the context of the democratic process. On the one hand, progressive political leaders of a particular government may amend the constitution to rectify any existing shortcomings and strengthen democratic institutions and culture. On the other hand, another leader, his ruling political party, and allies may bring constitutional amendments mainly for the benefit of the party and the incumbent, and therefore contribute to democratic backsliding. This is the case in Sri Lankan politics, too. While acknowledging the different interpretations of democratic backsliding and constitutional amendments, this chapter restricts its analysis to how such amendments made by elected officials have compromised and even seriously undermined the qualities associated with democratic governance in Sri Lanka since the year 2000.

Constitutional Amendments (2001–2022) and Democracy in Sri Lanka 209

This qualitative study largely utilizes secondary sources of data from scholarly articles, books, reports, and news websites, and focuses on the five constitutional amendments made after 2000. It explains how governments have exploited these to consolidate their own political power rather than to strengthen democracy, enhance stability and improve social well-being in the country. The authors believe that it is vital to gain an understanding of the process of constitutional amendments because there are many useful lessons to be drawn from the previous failed attempts at reform that did little to strengthen democracy. Doing so would offer an opportunity to avoid repeating the same mistakes in future. To this end, this chapter is divided into three major descriptive and analytical sections: the first section examines analytically the brief history of post-independent constitutional changes in Sri Lanka. The second section details the democratic traits of the 17th, 19th, and 21st Amendments, which together played an essential role in shaping the nation's democratic evolution. The third section offers a detailed examination of the undemocratic features of the 18th and 20th Amendments, which contributed significantly to democratic backsliding in Sri Lanka. Finally, the conclusion offers some strategies to strengthen the process of constitution-making in postwar Sri Lanka.

Post-Independent Constitutional Order in Sri Lanka: A Brief History

The political system of Sri Lanka was influenced greatly by the colonizers, especially the British, from whom Sri Lanka gained independence in 1948. However, Sri Lanka continued to be part of the Commonwealth of the Empire until it was proclaimed as an independent republic by the first Republican Constitution of 1972. Although the Soulbury Constitution of 1947 was drafted by the British, it was recognized as the official constitution of Sri Lanka until the adoption of the 1972 Republican Constitution. Due to the legacy of British colonization, Sri Lanka had a Westminster-style parliamentary government, which was upheld by the republican constitution. In 1978 however, a second republican constitution was promulgated, replacing the 1972 Constitution. This new constitution introduced the executive presidential system that borrowed from both French and American models of governance. Whereas the 1972 Constitution was enacted by the Sri Lanka Freedom Party (SLFP), the 1978 Constitution was introduced by the United National Party (UNP). These two major political parties kept taking turns forming governments in post-independence Sri Lanka until 2019.[2]

Despite expectations, both post-independence constitutions, namely the first and second republican constitutions, did nothing to promote democracy. Both constitutions contributed equally to democratic backsliding as each one concentrated power in one institution – the 1972 Constitution concentrated power in the National State Assembly (the legislature), while the 1978 Constitution concentrated power in the executive presidency. There were a couple of reasons behind the move to introduce the executive presidential system in the 1978

Constitution: firstly, to effectively execute the free-market economic policy adopted in 1977, and secondly, to successfully deal with the Tamil and Sinhalese insurgencies in Sri Lanka. Both reasons were used to justify the expansion of the power of the executive president in the 1978 Constitution. In practice though, the executive presidency came to be used as an instrument to erode liberal democracy in Sri Lanka (DeVotta, 2020). The power of the executive presidency led to a democratic backsliding as there were inadequate safeguards to prevent the abuse of power, which was exacerbated by the immunity of the president. The executive powers under the 1978 Constitution allowed the president, *inter alia*, to dissolve the parliament at any time except during the first year after a general election. Moreover, the president could prorogue parliament without justification (Article 70(1)(a) of the Constitution), revoke ministerial portfolios, and make key appointments (Article 44). As provided in Article 33, the president also has the power to appoint judges of the Supreme Court and enjoy immunity from prosecution in any court or tribunal for both official and personal conduct. Apart from these powers, the president wielded enormous clout during a time of emergency in that he/she could promulgate regulations that would override the laws of parliament (Article 155). It is interesting to note that Sri Lanka was ruled under a state of emergency for more than three decades during the period of civil war. While there is an impeachment mechanism to remove the president, it requires a two-thirds majority in parliament on three separate occasions followed by a ruling of the Supreme Court about the misconduct of the president (Article 38). Therefore, in practice, implementing this procedure is almost impossible. According to the original Constitution of 1978, the president is a figure of great authority and influence.

The 1978 Constitution allows amendments to be made to it or even get it repealed, but this requires a two-thirds (2/3) majority in parliament. However, any changes to certain provisions, such as the name of the state, the unitary status of the country, sovereignty, design of national flag and anthem, and the status of Buddhism need to be approved by a two-thirds majority in parliament, followed by a national referendum (Article 83). Where the amendment process to the 1978 Constitution is concerned, it is noteworthy that this process was not inclusive; rather it was exclusive. Notably, amendments have been made by both parties, the SLFP and UNP. Most of the amendments were made soon after a regime change as the executive and his/her ruling party and/or alliance wanted to implement their own political agendas. The 1978 Constitution has been amended 21 times to date. Among those amendments, the 13th, 17th, 18th, 19th, 20th, and 21st Amendments were key amendments as they amounted to major revisions of the original Constitution of 1978. The 13th Amendment was made on November 14, 1987, while the other five amendments were enacted after 2000. The 13th Amendment is considered one of the most important amendments to the constitution as it addresses some of the concerns of the Tamil minority. This includes the conferring of official status recognizing the parity of the Tamil language with the Sinhalese language and the establishment of the North-East Provincial Council to fulfill, at least partially, the aspirations

Constitutional Amendments (2001–2022) and Democracy in Sri Lanka   211

of Tamils in Sri Lanka. It is necessary to highlight here that India proved to be a huge influence in the enactment of the 13th Amendment, as it was a result of the Indo-Lanka Accord of 1987. In general, the reforms introduced by the 17th, 18th, 19th, 20th, and 21st Amendments focus on the restriction or expansion of presidential powers, especially those relating to the appointment of public officers to a number of higher government institutions and independent commissions. The following two sections deal extensively with the amendments implemented after 2000.

The 17th, 19th, and 21st Amendments

From a broad perspective, the 17th, 19th, and 21st Amendments are seen as constructive and progressive measures as these amendments contained crucial provisions to strengthen democratic governance in Sri Lanka. These amendments primarily aimed to curb the potential abuse of the president's power and depoliticize the island's public service. The other amendments made to the 1978 Constitution in the past—except for the 13th amendment—significantly enlarged the powers of the executive presidential system. Scholars and experts in the field express the view that a formidable challenge involved in amending the 1978 Constitution is the inherent strength of the executive presidential system, which resists any attempts to reduce its power. Therefore, complete success may not be possible in pruning those powers, yet these amendments offer a mechanism to exert some control.

Again, the question that remains unaddressed is whether the changes that resulted from amending the constitution can be secured from the president's intervention. This is important because there were no provisions in either the 1972 or 1978 Constitutions to uphold the independence of public service institutions. Due to the lack of any safeguards the public service, independent commissions, and other institutions proved vulnerable to excessive political interference. As provided in Article 5 of the Fifth Republican Constitution of France, the president is required to ensure the proper functioning of public institutions. In Sri Lanka, however, such safeguards were not included, and so the proper functioning of public institutions was not upheld. To rectify those defects, these three amendments were enacted to limit the president's power and depoliticize the public service sector of the country. Under the provisions, the Constitutional Council, Independent Commissions, Right to Information Act, and various other measures were introduced to allow the public institutions to retain control over their own affairs. The next section delves into these matters to provide an in-depth understanding of how they work.

Constitutional Council

The concept of the Constitutional Council was first introduced in the governance system of Sri Lanka through the 17th Amendment. Its main objective was to depoliticize public service. As per the 17th Amendment, the ten-member

212 *Constitutional Amendments (2001–2022) and Democracy in Sri Lanka*

Constitutional Council must include the prime minister, the speaker, leader of the opposition, one person appointed by the president, five persons appointed by the president on the recommendations of both the prime minister and the leader of the opposition (made in consultation with the leaders of parties in parliament, with three of the appointees representing minority interests), and one person nominated with the agreement of a majority of members of parliament who do not belong to either the party of the prime minister or party of the leader of opposition. It is important to note that the people nominated for the last three categories must be persons of eminence and integrity, who have distinguished themselves in public life and are not members of any political party (Article 41 A). The quorum of the Council is six (Article 41 E(3)). According to Article 41 B(1) of the 17th Amendment, the members and Chairmen of the independent commissions are to be selected by the Constitutional Council and appointed by the president.

In 2010, the 18th Amendment replaced the Constitutional Council with the Parliamentary Council. In 2015, the 19th Amendment restored the Constitutional Council to prevent the politicization of independent commissions and ensure accountability. Under the 19th Amendment, the ten members of the Constitutional Council included the speaker, the prime minister, leader of opposition, one member of parliament nominated by the president, two members of parliament appointed by the president on the recommendation of both prime minister and leader of the opposition, one member of parliament nominated by political parties not headed by the prime minister or leader of the opposition, and three unelected individuals (persons of eminence and integrity who have distinguished themselves in public or professional life, who do not belong to any political party) jointly nominated by the prime minister and the leader of opposition (Article 41 A). The Constitutional Council outlined in the 21st Amendment follows very closely the provisions of the 19th Amendment.

The Constitutional Councils outlined by these three amendments (17th, 19th, and 21st) aimed to curtail the unfettered powers of the executive president. On the one hand, the Constitutional Council has no say in the appointment of the heads of independent commissions by the president, but on the other hand, presidential appointments to other high positions, such as the Chief Justice and judges of the Supreme Court, president and judges of the Court of Appeal, members of the Judicial Service Commission (except its chairman), Attorney General, Inspector General of Police, Auditor General, Parliamentary Commissioner for Administration (or Ombudsman), and Secretary General of Parliament, need to be approved by the Constitutional Council once the president proposes their names. This is in accordance with Article 41 C(1) of the 17th, 19th, and 21st Amendments. Such an arrangement has some control over the president's powers to appoint persons to the higher positions. Complete implementation of these provisions places some restrictions on the president in making appointments to the 'rule of law' and other important institutions, thereby facilitating a conducive democratic environment by putting a stop to the Sri Lankan political culture of interference by the president in matters of governance.

Constitutional Amendments (2001–2022) and Democracy in Sri Lanka   213

However, in practice, these amendments were challenged by the presidents who were the principal architects of these endeavors. Former President Chandrika Kumaratunga undermined and violated the provisions of the 17th Amendment. In March 2003, President Chandrika Kumaratunga refused to appoint a nominee proposed by the Constitutional Council as Chairman of the Elections Commission, as in her opinion he would not act impartially. This is regarded as a failure of the 17th Amendment. When this infraction on the part of the president was challenged in a court by the Public Interest Law Foundation (under Article 41 B), the court rejected the petition, citing the 'blanket immunity' conferred on the president under Article 35 of the constitution (*Public Interest Law Foundation v. the Attorney-General*, Application No: 1396/2003). The crisis further intensified when the Constitutional Council's first term expired in March 2005 and no new appointments were made to it. Several factors, such as vested political interests, structural flaws in the 17th Amendment relating to the appointment mechanism, and the court's failure to provide an unambiguous legal precedent to break the political deadlock contributed to this crisis. Accordingly, this crisis led the president to make appointments to the independent commissions without obtaining the approval of the Constitutional Council, which amounted to repeated violations of the provisions of the 17th Amendment (Jayakody, 2011). This is how the executive president failed to abide by the provisions of the 17th Amendment and this omission seriously undermined the functioning of many public institutions, contributing to the declining quality of democracy.

In comparison, the provisions relating to the Constitutional Council under the 19th Amendment were better drafted. The architects of the 19th Amendment took into consideration the structural flaws of the 17th Amendment and spelt out the provisions more strictly to avoid this type of crisis. According to Article 41 A(6) of the 19th Amendment, the president shall, within 14 days of receiving a written communication specifying the nominations made under Article 41 A(1)(e)–(f) (i.e., the four members of parliament and the three eminent persons), make the necessary appointments to the Constitutional Council. If the president fails to do so, the persons nominated shall be deemed to have been appointed as members of the Constitutional Council, with effect from the date of expiry of 14 days. Yet, the 21st Amendment backtracks somewhat and only retains the provision that 'The President shall, within fourteen days of the receipt of a written communication specifying the nominations made under subparagraphs (e) and (f) of paragraph (1), make the necessary appointments' (Article 41 A(6)). In fact, the 21st Amendment has omitted the provision in the 19th Amendment that stipulates, 'In the event of the President failing to make the necessary appointments within such period of fourteen days, the persons nominated shall be deemed to have been appointed as members of the Council, with effect from the date of expiry of such period' (Article 41 A(6)).

In brief, the measures relating to the appointment of the Constitutional Council in the 19th Amendment had the potential to foster democratic governance in Sri Lanka. However, the prevailing powerful executive presidential

214 *Constitutional Amendments (2001–2022) and Democracy in Sri Lanka*

system, established by the original 1978 Constitution, prevented the proper implementation of this measure. If the provisions relating to the Constitutional Council in the 19th Amendment had been carried over intact to the 21st Amendment, it could have played a crucial role in strengthening democracy in Sri Lanka.

Governance Reforms

Both democratization and democratic backsliding tend to take place gradually and do not occur suddenly. A process of democratization creates an environment conducive to the formation of a free, participatory, and less authoritarian society. The system of governance plays a pivotal role in the democratization process. The present presidential system, as per the 1978 Constitution, centralizes power in the hands of a single individual, viz 'the president', and this prevents the effective operation of the checks and balances within the various branches of government. Beginning in the 1990s, there have been repeated attempts to abolish the executive presidential system and establish a parliamentary system of governance. However, none of these attempts were successful in eliminating the presidential system; instead, some of the elected leaders focused on concentrating power in their hands once they assumed office as president. The 17th Amendment provided some measures to balance the powers of the president with the 'rule of law' institutions. This has been the starting point of the reformists who wished to make progress in reforming the presidency.

Yet the 19th Amendment went beyond the 17th Amendment in terms of restructuring governance (Welikala, 2019). The major reforms introduced by the 19th Amendment include: a) reduction of the terms of president and parliament from six years to five; and 2) reinstatement of the two-term limit for the president, which was removed under the 18th Amendment (Articles 30(2), 31(2), and 62(2)). Further, the president lacked the power to dissolve the parliament before the completion of four and a half years of the term. However, the dissolution could still be executed if parliament passed a resolution with a two-thirds majority (Article 70(1)). It is important to note that the 1978 Constitution and 17th Amendment had allowed the president to dissolve parliament before the expiration of one year if parliament by resolution requests the president to dissolve it (Article 70(1)(a)). As per the 21st Amendment, the president possesses the power to dissolve parliament before the expiration of two years and six months if parliament by resolution requests the president to do so. Of these three amendments, the 19th Amendment has more democratic features than the other two.

To reduce the authority of the position held by the president, the 19th Amendment strengthened the office of the prime minister within the executive branch. As outlined in the 19th Amendment, although the president appoints the prime minister, he no longer retains the power to remove him/her from the position (Article 46(2)). The prime minister is only subject to the approval and confidence of the parliament. However, the president does have the ability to

Constitutional Amendments (2001–2022) and Democracy in Sri Lanka 215

dismiss other ministers on the advice of the prime minister. The appointment of cabinet ministers is also done in accordance with the advice of the prime minister (Article 43(2), 44(1), 45(1), and 46(3)(a). The immunity of the president was also slightly reduced by allowing the Supreme Court to exercise its fundamental rights jurisdiction over the official acts of the president (Article 35). Therefore, it has been argued that the 19th Amendment has changed the character of the regime and turned it into a 'much more democratic model of "premier-presidential" or "semi-presidentialism" system' (Welikala, 2019: 606), which upholds democratic culture and enhances the separation of powers.

However, the 19th Amendment was also blatantly violated by former President Maithripala Sirisena who was one of the key actors in bringing constitutional reform. Since 2015, the Sri Lankan political landscape experienced poor governance due to the uncoordinated actions between the president and the prime minister, who came from different parties, the SLFP and UNP. Therefore, they had deep-seated political and ideological differences between them. These differences along with the personality conflict between two executives, president and prime minister, led to a constitutional crisis. The mounting differences of opinion between the two eventually led to the constitutional coup on October 26, 2018 in direct violation of the 19th Amendment to the constitution. This constitutional crisis occurred due to the removal of Prime Minister Ranil Wickremesinghe from his position. Although President Maithripala Sirisena appointed Mahinda Rajapaksa in his stead as the prime minister, Wickremesinghe did not lose confidence in parliament. Then, following his failure to secure a majority for Mahinda Rajapaksa in parliament on November 9, 2018, President Maithripala Sirisena attempted to dissolve parliament. According to the 19th Amendment, the president lacks the power to remove the prime minister, who still retains the confidence of parliament. Another constraint was that the president could not dissolve parliament until the expiration of four and a half years, except through a vote by members of parliament with a two-thirds majority. Eventually, the crisis and unconstitutional acts of the president ended in December 2018 for two reasons: firstly, Mahinda Rajapaksa failed to obtain a majority in the parliament, and secondly, both the Court of Appeal and the Supreme Court deemed the acts of the president unconstitutional (Welikala, 2019: 607). The restoration of constitutionality was in fact made possible by the 19th Amendment. But even after the end of the constitutional crisis, policy differences between the president and prime minister deepened. This dispute had a bad impact on some institutions that came under the purview of the president, and this included national security. The tussle for power made the operation of independent commissions impossible. Although the 19th Amendment incorporated several measures to curtail the authority of the president, some of these measures were not fully implemented.

Other Elements of Democratization

The 19th Amendment repealed the 'Urgent bill' procedure (Article 122) and required all bills to be gazetted 14 days prior to the legislative process (Article

78(1)). Yet, as per the 20th Amendment, 'Every Bill should be published in the Gazette at least seven days before it is placed on the Order Paper of Parliament' (Article 78(1)). Furthermore, the number of cabinet ministers was reduced to 20 and other ministers were also reduced in number (Article 46(1)). However, there is a possibility that the incumbent government could increase the number of cabinet ministers if the first and second largest parties represented in parliament formed a government through an Act of Parliament (Article 46(4) and (5)). The unnecessary enlargement of the cabinet is one of the issues embedded in the culture of Sri Lankan politics, though it lacks any real justification. The cabinet size is increased in representative politics merely to sustain the government. Therefore, imposing limits on the number of ministers would enhance rational policymaking and accountability as well as reduce the culture of patronage politics.

To prevent extreme politicization of the law enforcement institutions, the amendment set the age limit for the Attorney General and Inspector General of Police at 60 when they retire from their position (Article 61 E(2)). Another salient feature of this amendment is the annexure of the Right to Information Act in the section on fundamental rights, which makes this provision judicially enforceable for the first time since the 1978 Constitution was promulgated (Article 14 A). This right enforces accountability and transparency on the part of the government by virtue of the citizens' right to gain access to information. Therefore, it is evident that the 19th Amendment sought to some extent to equalize the balance of power between the three organs of government. In contrast to this, the 17th and 21st Amendments were limited in their intent to bolster democratic principles in the post-Aragalaya context.

The 18th and 20th Amendments

The end of 30 years of armed conflict between the government of Sri Lanka and the LTTE was regarded as providing a window of opportunity to unite the divided people through a reconciliation process and democratic reforms. However, the government did not make use of this opportunity. Instead, a coalition government led by the United People's Freedom Alliance (UPFA) took further steps to oppress the ethnic minorities, including the Sri Lankan Tamils and Muslims.[3] Sri Lankan constitutionalism also turned authoritarian from 2010 due to many changes in the rules of the game, as the objective was to favor and strengthen the ruling family to have absolute power over the Sri Lankan political system. The 18th Amendment is the constitutional amendment that came to be widely regarded as the first major reform made to the 1978 Constitution.

Considering the rapid rise of the Rajapaksa family and its deep involvement in every area of Sri Lankan politics, it can be said that the 18th Amendment played a big part in this. The Rajapaksa regime had been working on a political agenda since the end of the civil war in May 2009 to strengthen the position of the president and his brothers, especially Basil Rajapaksa, Gotabaya Rajapaksa, and Chamal Rajapaksa. Rajapaksa family members occupied very important

Constitutional Amendments (2001–2022) and Democracy in Sri Lanka 217

posts in the government. Basil Rajapaksa was the Minister of Economic Development while Gotabaya Rajapaksa was the head of the security apparatus. Chamal Rajapaksa soon followed as the speaker of parliament. In addition to President Mahinda Rajapaksa, his son Namal Rajapaksa served as a first-time parliamentarian and was often considered as the Crown Prince in the Rajapaksa dynasty. The intention of the architects behind the 18th Amendment was to prepare the groundwork for perpetuating the rule of the Rajapaksa dynasty in Sri Lankan politics (Saravanamuttu, 2011). The Rajapaksa regime was heading towards an authoritarian and patronage-driven autocracy. Therefore, it seriously challenged the democratization of post-war Sri Lanka.

The process of pushing through the 18th Amendment was also undemocratic in the sense that it was brought as an 'urgent bill' within ten days without much public consultation or discussion. But it was upheld as 'a matter of national urgency' aimed at rebuilding post-war Sri Lanka. For that purpose, the government carried out several one-sided public campaigns to present the 18th Amendment as an urgent bill. The government stated that the existing 17th Amendment was 'ineffective and impractical'. Further, it claimed that the restriction on the power of the president to appoint whoever he wanted was inappropriate in the presidential system as the president had the right to do so (Groundviews, 2010). Therefore, the government asserted that the 18th Amendment would rectify the shortcomings of the 17th Amendment that gave rise to the constitutional crisis. The amendment would also strengthen the powers of office of the president, so that the public service could be streamlined and made more efficient (Jayakody, 2011). To ensure the required two-thirds majority in parliament to pass the 18th Amendment, the Rajapaksa government offered half a million dollars as a bribe to each of several opposition MPs to win them over to their side (DeVotta, 2014). Put briefly, the amendment to the constitution was made without adhering to the proper procedures and without considering the real issues the country was facing after the armed conflict.

When examining the 20th Amendment, it becomes evident that its primary objective was to bring changes to the constitutional provisions introduced by the 19th Amendment. In particular, the Central Bank bond scam, constitutional crisis of 2018, and mishandling of the Easter Sunday terrorist attacks of 2019 by the National Unity government led by Ranil Wickremesinghe and Maithripala Sirisena collectively undermined the governance structure introduced by the 19th Amendment. The Rajapaksa family exploited these failures and polarized the nation by inculcating the nationalistic sentiment among the majority community. The promises made by Gotabaya Rajapaksa won over the mainly Sinhala Buddhist people who ensured his victory at the presidential election by a large margin. It is in some contexts true that people often endorse the undemocratic activities of incumbent leaders, thereby lowering the quality of democracy. Following the landslide victory of President Gotabaya Rajapaksa, politicians from the Sri Lanka Podujana Peramuna (SLPP) also called for parliamentary elections in the hope it would enable the government to effectively deal with the economic crisis and Covid-19 pandemic. At the parliamentary

218 Constitutional Amendments (2001–2022) and Democracy in Sri Lanka

elections held on August 5, 2020, the coalition led by President Gotabaya Rajapaksa secured a two-thirds majority, soon after which it initiated the process of drafting the 20th Amendment. The 20th Amendment was then passed on October 22, 2020 in parliament.

This latest amendment repealed the key provisions of the 19th Amendment except for three clauses, specifically the reduction of the term of office of the president and parliament from six to five years, a two-term limit on the office of the president, and the incorporation of the Right to Information Act. Other than these provisions, the 20th Amendment re-introduced the same provisions that were part of the 18th Amendment. Thus, these two changes facilitated the erosion of democratic institutions due to the centralization of power in the hands of one clan, the extended Rajapaksa family.

In brief, retrogressive amendments such as the 18th and 20th Amendments contained provisions that facilitated the process of institutionalized democratic backsliding. Among the provisions, the aggrandizement of the powers of the president will be explained further by describing measures like the Parliamentary Council and two-term limit for a detailed understanding.

Parliamentary Council

Both the 18th and 20th Amendments introduced the Parliamentary Council by repealing the Constitutional Council introduced by the 17th and 19th Amendments. Hence, both the 18th and 20th Amendments made major changes in institutions to ensure unfettered power to the executive presidency. The Parliamentary Council comprised five members, which included the prime minister, speaker, leader of the opposition, one member of parliament nominated by the prime minister and one member of parliament nominated by the leader of opposition (Article 41 A). The president simply sought non-binding observation from the Parliamentary Council when he wished to make appointments to the independent commissions. Therefore, the president is free to make the appointment even after receiving any unfavorable observations. Once the president seeks the observation from the Parliamentary Council, it must forward that within one week. Failing to do so will grant sole discretion to the president to proceed with the appointments (Article 41 A(8)). Therefore, this process can never serve as an effective mechanism to maintain any checks or balances on the executive presidency. Membership was not given to anyone outside of parliament, as only members of parliament could serve in the Council. This meant that meaningful consultation with other political parties in connection with the appointment process was very limited.

Removal of the Two-Term Limit

Attempts by the incumbent president or prime minister to remove the constitutionally mandated term is not exceptional. Recent examples show that authoritarian leaders such as Russian President Vladimir Putin and Chinese

Constitutional Amendments (2001–2022) and Democracy in Sri Lanka 219

President Xi Jinping removed term limits. Additionally, countries such as Azerbaijan, Bolivia, and Iraq have followed suit. A recent study by a group of scholars (Versteeg et al., 2020) reveals that 'Globally, no fewer than one-third of the incumbents who reached the end of their prescribed terms pursued some strategy to remain in office' and 'About two-thirds of them attempted to amend the constitution' through the formal procedure to remove the term limit (p. 173).

In Sri Lanka, President Mahinda Rajapaksa used the two-thirds majority he had in parliament to pass legislation to change term limits. Indeed, as mentioned above, the executive presidential system introduced by the 1978 Constitution is regarded as one of the most powerful of such systems in the world. However, the term limit was one of the restrictions placed on the president by this constitution. The 18th Amendment removed this two-term limit (Article 32(2)) and made the executive president's power even greater than that in the original Constitution of 1978. The president, therefore, can seek re-election any number of times. 'The purpose of imposing limitation on the term of office is to discourage a "personality cult" based version of democracy' (Jayakody, 2011: 50). Yet, President Rajapaksa wanted to extend his stay in office by making constitutional amendments to validate his personal rule. This type of constitutional tampering undermines the democratic framework and political culture of the country. However, the term limit was restored through the 19th Amendment to the constitution, and it has remained intact in the 20th Amendment as well.

Undemocratic Elements

In Sri Lanka, the centralization of power occurs through presidential aggrandizement where the incumbent president endeavors to concentrate the power in his hands through constitutional means. The 18th and 20th Amendments serve as examples that illustrate how presidents try to centralize power in their hands by eliminating the restrictions imposed by the 17th and 19th Amendments. When that happens, independent commissions such as the Elections Commission, Public Service Commission, National Police Commission, Human Rights Commission of Sri Lanka, etc. fall under the authority of the president (Article 41 A). Then it becomes impossible for the Elections Commission to put an end to the abuse of state resources, such as state media, for the purpose of promoting electoral campaigns. Both the 17th and 19th Amendments allowed the incumbent Election Commissioner to regulate the election campaign to ensure free and fair elections. Thus, a key pillar of democracy was put into a tight corner under the 18th and 20th Amendments.

In addition, it was exclusively at the discretion of the president to appoint the Attorney General, judges of the Supreme Court, and judges of the Court of Appeal. The president could appoint and remove superior court judges and senior judges without any consultation or following any legally established criteria (Article 41 A). Hence, there was the strong likelihood that the president would only pick judges who would go along with his political will and interest when making appointments to the higher 'rule of law' institutions. That is, the selection of judges would not be based purely on merit. Whenever the president felt displeased with a judgment, he could remove the judge from his position. For example, soon after the controversial impeachment of Chief Justice Shirani Bandaranayake, who was the first woman Chief Justice, President Rajapaksa removed her from the Supreme Court in January 2013 and appointed Mohan Peiris as Chief Justice in the same month (on January 15). It is important to note that both the Supreme Court and Court of Appeal had requested parliament to abandon the impeachment process, yet this was not heeded. This is a blatant example of how the 18th Amendment facilitated the undermining of constitutionality and democracy in the country.

In 2020, President Gotabaya Rajapaksa followed in the footsteps of his brother Mahinda by introducing the 20th Amendment. President Gotabaya went even beyond his brother in consolidating and centralizing power by removing all established constitutional restrictions. He militarized almost all the sectors of governance and undermined the democratically elected parliament and other institutions. The president carried out various activities by appointing various presidential task forces and commissions. These ad hoc bodies were created by the president without any consultation. Consequently, the foundational principles of constitutional democracy, centered on 'consent' and 'constraints', became largely destabilized. The removal of oversight and all restrictions then allowed unlimited rule by one person (Welikala, 2020).

The constitutional status given to the prime minister under the 19th Amendment was removed under the 20th Amendment so that he was no longer a political executive of the country. The president was also eligible to hold a ministerial portfolio (Article 43 (2)) and the restrictions on the size of the cabinet under the 19th Amendment were jettisoned so that the government could increase the size of the cabinet and the number of other ministers according to the will of the president (Article 44 (1)). The president could appoint and dismiss the prime minister and other ministers at his own discretion (Articles 43(3) and 47(2)). This again encouraged the patronage and loyalty politics in and out of parliament and the president was even able to buy politicians from the opposition to pass whatever law he wanted in parliament with a two-thirds majority.

Another key democratic provision that was removed from the 19th Amendment was the dissolution power of the president. The 20th Amendment gave the president power to dissolve parliament entirely at his own discretion, any time after two and half years had passed from the date of its first meeting (Article 70(1)(a)). By granting such discretion to the president over parliament, the amendment weakened the authority of the latter to restrict the abuse of power by the former. In addition to the weakness in respect of political accountability, the removal of legal accountability by the president in the 20th Amendment is another backsliding provision. According to the 20th Amendment, 'In the case of any person who holds office as President of the Republic of Sri Lanka, no civil or criminal proceedings shall be instituted or pursued against the said President in respect of anything done or omitted to be done by him,

Constitutional Amendments (2001–2022) and Democracy in Sri Lanka 221

either in his official or private capacity' (Article 35(1)). However, the 19th Amendment allows the Supreme Court to exercise jurisdiction over the official acts of the president when it amounts to fundamental rights violations (Article 35(1)). To some extent, it is an effort to cultivate the culture of accountability by the president. Compared to this, the 20th Amendment puts the president beyond the reach of the rule of law of the country and this challenges the rule of law. It has been suggested that 'weak rule of law is an "indicator" of trouble for democracy' (Diamond, 2021: 33).

In brief, both the 18th and 20th Amendments undermine democratic norms, including such aspects as power-sharing and accountability, while encouraging a sense of impunity. Both amendments showed scant regard for the principle of depoliticization of institutions and commissions. Comparatively, these two amendments exhibit more undemocratic characteristics than the 17th, 19th, and 21st amendments.

Conclusion

The constitutional amendments introduced after the year 2000 presented a diverse range of characteristics. While some were of a progressive nature so essential for fostering democracy, others clearly exhibited retrogressive and undemocratic features. However, the progressive amendments also suffered some drawbacks when they were invoked to promote and uphold democratic values, principles, traditions, and institutions in the country. Effective implementation of those amendments was frequently undermined by political leaders who exploited the amendments to advance their own political agendas during their tenure. Consequently, full implementation of the progressive amendments became unattainable due to political interventions, while the retrogressive amendments ultimately led the country to face severe economic and political crises. This chapter concludes that the process of amending the 1978 Constitution was carried out exclusively through parliamentary procedures. Furthermore, attempts to implement the amendments were hindered by the authoritarian nature of the executive presidential system. Any amendments that attempt to minimize the powers the president holds under the 1978 Constitution could lead to political stagnation. Therefore, this chapter has proposed that, considering the severe political and economic crises faced by the country, a new constitution that calls for broader participation, rather than one based on the agenda of a ruling political party, is essential—if real change is to be brought about in post-war Sri Lanka.

Notes

1 The People's Alliance (PA), which was formed by former President Chandrika Bandaranaike Kumaratunga in 1994, was dissolved in 2004.
2 Both were the oldest and most popular political parties in Sri Lanka. The UNP was formed in 1946, while the SLFP was founded in 1951 as an offshoot of the UNP.

222   *Constitutional Amendments (2001–2022) and Democracy in Sri Lanka*

Differences between UNP leader Ranil Wickremesinghe and deputy leader Sajith Premadasa in the run-up to the presidential election in 2019 were revealed during the 2020 parliamentary election, when the rebel party *Samagi Jana Balawegaya* (SJB) under the leadership of Sajith Premadasa won 54 seats, while the UNP secured just 1 national list seat. At the same time, the *Sri Lanka Podujana Peramuna* (SLPP), which originated from the SLFP, won both the presidential and parliamentary elections held in 2019 and 2020, respectively.
3 The United People's Freedom Alliance (UPFA) was formed by the SLFP and *Janatha Vimukthi Peramuna* (JVP) through a memorandum of understanding in 2004.

References

DeVotta, N. (2014). Parties, political decay, and democratic regression in Sri Lanka. *Commonwealth & Comparative Politics*, 52(1), 139–165. https://doi.org/10.1080/14662043.2013.867692.

DeVotta, N. (2020). Knocked down, getting back up: Sri Lanka's battered democracy. *Global Asia*, 15(1). Retrieved January 21, 2022, from https://www.globalasia.org/v15no1/cover/knocked-down-getting-back-up-sri-lankas-battered-democracy_neil-devotta.

Groundviews. (2010, September 2). *The 18th Amendment to the Constitution: Process and Substance*. Groundviews. https://groundviews.org/2010/09/02/the-18th-amendment-to-the-constitution-process-and-substance/.

Jayakody, A. (2011). The 18th amendment and the consolidation of executive power. In R. Edrisinha and A. Jayakody (Eds), pp. 23–59. *The Eighteenth Amendment to the Constitution: Substance and Process*. Centre for Policy Alternative.

Saravanamuttu, P. (2011). The 18th amendment: Political culture and consequences. In In R.Edrisinha and A. Jayakody (Eds), pp. 13–22. *The Eighteenth Amendment to the Constitution: Substance and Process*. Centre for Policy Alternative.

Versteeg, M., Horley, T., Meng, A., Guim, M., and Guirguis, M. (2020). The law and politics of presidential term limit evasion. *Columbia Law Review*, 120(1), 173–248.

Welikala, A. (2019). Constitutional reforms in Sri Lanka—more drift? *The Round Table*, 108(6), 605–612. https://doi.org/10.1080/00358533.2019.1687964.

Welikala, A. (2020, September 22). *Some Reflections on the Twentieth Amendment Bill*. Sri Lanka Brief. https://srilankabrief.org/some-reflections-on-the-twentieth-amendment-bill-asanga-welikala/.

Index

A

aamaadmi (commoner) (India), 123

Aatmanirbhar Bharat (Self-reliant India)
  initiatives, 118
  manufacture, 116

Abdullah, Imran, 149

absolute monarchy, 79

accountability
  approach (Bangladesh), 54
  semblance, removal, 58
  subnational level (Afghanistan),
    38–40

Adeeb, Ahmed, 149

Adhaalath Party (AP), Islamic radicals, 151

adults, inclusion (democratic process
  criterion), 4

Advani, L.K., 111, 121

Afghanistan

  Asia Foundation Survey, centralization
    issue, 44
  authority, centralization, 31
  Central Elections Commission,
    elimination, 44
  centralized governance system, failure, 35
  Citizens' Charter, impact, 40–41
  civil society (mobilization/participation),
    reasons (absence), 43
  community development councils
    (CDCs), creation/nonfunction, 40
  conflict-affected state, 34
  constitutions, false promise, 31
  creative energy, harnessing (inability), 32
  democracy/accountability (subnational
    level), 38–40
  democratic buy-in, concentration
    (Kabul), 42–44
  democratization project, 35
  District Stability Teams (DSTs),
    impact, 41

  elected provincial councils, creation,
    38–39
  failure, belief, 32
  inclusivity, absence (concerns), 45
  Independent Directorate for Local
    Governance (IDLG), 39
  Independent Elections Commission
    (IEC), 34, 38
  liberal state-building efforts, 44
  Ministry of Women's Affairs,
    elimination, 44
  Municipal Election Committees,
    creation, 39
  National Assembly, corrupt
    elections, 31
  National Assembly, houses
    (elimination), 44
  national-level politics, 33, 35–37
  oligopoly, approach, 43
  parallel structures, creation, 41
  parliamentary elections, importance, 44
  political power, concentration, 33–35
  political power, concentration (Kabul), 32
  power, distribution/sharing
    (unwillingness), 45–46
  programs, ineffectiveness/waste, 41
  provincial council members, citizen
    confidence (absence), 39
  Provincial Reconstruction Teams
    (PRTs), impact, 41
  reform proposals, indications, 43
  state, absence, 32
  state-created parallel structures,
    40–42
  Taliban rule, consequences, 44–45
  wealth, concentration, 43

Afghanistan democracy
  consequences, 40–42
  problems, 24

224 *Index*

provincial level, 38
vacuum, 35
Afghanistan Research and Evaluation Unit
(AREU), analysis, 42–43
Afghan Republic, collapse, 31–32
agenda, control (democratic process
criterion), 4
Aisi Taisi Democracy (India), 120
Al-Qaeda, impact, 153
ameen (trustworthy), 202
Ameen, Ahmed, 153
Amritmahaotsav (independence)
(India), 112
andolan online/virtual movement
(India), 120
andolan protest (India), 120
Anti-corruption Commission (ACC)
(Bhutan)
impact, 82
purview/scope, 83
setup, 79
antyodaya (uplifting the poorest)
(India), 112
Arab Spring, 157
Argentina, dictatorships (repression/vio-
lence), 10
Asey, Tamim, 43
Asia Foundation Survey, centralization
issue, 44
Asian democratization, 12–15
Asian pro-democracy movements,
backbone, 13
Asian values, 12
associational freedom/pluralism (liberal
democracy component), 6
authoritarianism, 10
democracy, alteration, 14
digital authoritarianism, phenomenon, 59
pace, acceleration, 51–52
resurgent authoritarianism, 16–17
authoritarian systems, legitimacy
problems, 11
autocracies
deepening, 76–77
power, 17
autocratic regime, making
(Bangladesh), 51
autocratization, reverse wave, 15
Autrocraization Turns Viral (V-Dem
Democracy Report), 16
Avatar (Incarnation) (India), 118–121
Awami League, ideational effort, 67
Awami National Party (ANP)
(Pakistan), 195

B
Babri Masjid demolition (India), 110–111
backsliding, 19–20
peculiarity, 20
Backward Classes Commission, Janata
establishment (India), 110
Balamayuran, Malini, 26, 207
Bangladesh
16th Amendment, passage (impact),
66–67
accountability, approach, 54
authoritarian categorization, 51–52
authoritarian regime, description, 51
autocratic regime, making, 51
Awami League, ideational effort, 67
background, 53–57
caretaker government (CTG),
annulment, 52
caretaker government (CTG),
incorporation, 55–56
caretaker government (CTG) provision
(removal), 15th Amendment
(impact), 61–62
competitive multiparty elections,
absence, 61–62
Constitution (Thirteenth Amendment)
Act (1996), impact, 61
corruption, Transparency International
ranking, 63–64
critics (silencing), legal/extralegal
measures (usage), 65
crossfire, incidences, 65
democracy, fragility, 52
democracy, score, 66
democratic era, entry, 52
democratic transition, overview, 78–80
Digital Security Act (2018), harshness,
64–65, 70
election (1991), 52–53
election (2018), 69–70
election (2007), machinations
(influence), 57
election (2018) results, **70**
electoral authoritarian regime,
impact, 62
electoral democracy, beginning/erosion
(1991–2001), 54–56
enforced disappearances, 65
expression, freedom, 64
extrajudicial killings, incidences, 65, 65
first-past-the-post (FPTP) system,
basis, 53
GDP growth rate (1996–2018), *68*
Gonojagorn Moncho, impact, 68

Index   225

Hartals (general strikes), 57
hegemonic authoritarian regime, 52
Information and Communication (ICT)
  Act, condemnation, 63–64
institutional dimensions extension,
  67–68
institutions, control, 66–67
Jamaat-i-Islami, persecution, 63–64
Jatiya Party, official opposition
  declaration, 66
mega projects, 67
military rule (1972–1990), 53
moderate autocracy, description, 51
monopolistic partyarchal governance,
  establishment, 56
muktijudhher chetona (spirit of
  liberation war), term (usage), 68
neopatrimonialism, pervasiveness,
  63–64
one-party populist authoritarian
  state, 53
opposition party candidates, absence,
  62–63
Padma Bridge (mega project), 67
parliament, importance (loss), 55–56
participation, competitiveness, 66
partisan control, 56
partyarchy, 56
political competition, 66
political culture, intolerance, 56
polling booths, Bangladesh Awami
  League control, 69
power transition, 55–56
prime ministerial system, creation,
  55–56
promissory coup, 52–53
pseudo-civilian military government,
  deposition, 53
Roopur Nuclear Power Plant (mega
  project), 67
semi-authoritarianism, 56
two-party system, emergence, 56–57
voter suppression plans, 69
Bangladesh Awami League (AL)
  BNP, coexistence, 65
  loss (1991), 55
  promises, 54
  victory, 57
Bangladesh, democratic backsliding,
  51, 52
  model, **60**
  process, 58–59
  sequences (2009–2018), 59–68
  stages, framework, 57–59

Bangladesh, elections
  farce, description, 69–70
  legitimacy, undermining, 55
  victory, ensuring, 57
Bangladesh. elections
  party participation/voter turnout/candi-
    dates (1973–2014), 62
Bangladesh Judicial Service (Discipline)
  Rules, impact, 67
Bangladesh Nationalist Party (BNP)
  14th Amendment, passage, 56
  AL, co-existence, 65
  cover-up, 57
  election boycott, threat, 62–63
  Jamaat-i-Islami, alliance, 65
  Jatiya Oikya Front (JOF), alliance, 69
  promises, 54
  victory (1991), 55
Basic Democracy (Pakistan), 192
Belarus, political parties (Lukashenko
  regime ban), 58
Belt and Road Initiative (BRI), 173
Berlin Wall, fall, 11
Bermeo, Nancy, 20, 51, 167, 168
Bertelsmann Transformation Index
  (BTI), 16
Bhandari, Bidhya Devi, 24, 173
Bharat (rural India), 116
Bharat Heavy Electrical Limited (BHEL),
  allegations, 95–96
Bharati, Uma, 111
Bharatiya Janata Party (BJP) (India)
  democratic processes, 121–122
  Hindu homogeneity, BJP dedication, 115
  National Executive meeting (2017), 115
  power, 108, 172
  rule, 107–108
Bharat Mata (India), 123
Bhasin, Madhavi, 14, 15
Bhattarai, K.P., 177
bhrastachar (corruption) (India), 125–126
Bhutan
  Anti-corruption Commission (ACC),
    impact, 82
  Anti-corruption Commission (ACC),
    purview/scope, 83
  Anti-corruption Commission (ACC),
    setup, 79
  bill, objections, 93–94
  Committee of Secretaries (CoS),
    discontinuation, 95–96
  conspiracy, 92
  Constitution, drafting (2001), 78–79
  Contractual Monarchy, 79

226 Index

corruption cases, 83–85
corruption, Freedom House Report
   (2021), 76
country report (Freedom House), 77
Dasho Karma Ura, resignation, 85–86
Dawa Gyetshen, political elevation, 85
democracy, acceptance, 78
democracy, transition, 79–80
democratic consolidation, context, 77
democratic consolidation, efforts, 77
democratic recession/consolidation,
   question, 76
democratization, 76
description, 76
Dorji Wangdi, election, 86
Druk Nyamrup Tshogpa (DNT),
   80–81, 96
Druk Nyamrup Tshogpa (DNT),
   election win (2008), 83
Druk Nyamrup Tshogpa (DNT),
   resignations, 86
elected/appointed public officials,
   removal, 76
Election Act, Section 179, 84
Election Commission of Bhutan (ECB),
   legal breaches, 90–91
Election Commission, setup, 79
Environment Act, violation, 87
Fourth King, impact, 80
Fundamental Right, Article 7.16, 82
Goshing Gup Sangay Lethro,
   suspension, 97
government ministers, resignation/
   removal, 80–85
government secretaries, removal, 95–97
gup case, appeal, 89–90
Gup Namgyel Wangdi, arrest/trial/con-
   viction, 91
gup of Bumdeling Gewog, detention, 88
gup, suspension, 90
Impeachment Act, 94
Jigme Samdrup, trial, 94–95
judges, removal, 91–95
judicial system/process, case
   adjudication, 81
Karma Gyeltshen, election win, 88
Khamdang Mangmi Sangye Tenpa,
   suspension, 97
Khamdang-Ramjar representative,
   resignation, 87
Khandu Wangmo, arrest, 92
Kinga Gyeltshen, trial, 94–95
Kinga Tshering, resignation, 86
Kinlay Lhendrup, imprisonment, 94–95

Kuenley Tshering, arrest/detention,
   91–94
Land Act, violation, 87
Land Allotment Committee members,
   guilty verdict, 83
Lhakhang Karpo temple, renovation, 85
local government elections, 79
local government leaders, removal,
   88–91
Lungten Dubgyur, removal, 94–95
Lyonpo Minjur Dorji (corruption case),
   83–85, 97
Lyonpo Ngeema sangay Tshempo,
   resignation, 85
Lyonpo Rinzin, acquittal, 98
Lyonpo Sherub Gyeltshen (resignation
   process), 80–83, 97, 98
malpractice investigation, 85
Mangmi of Wangphu Gewog, removal, 90
Mangmi Sangye Tempa, removal, 88
Mani Dorji, election win, 89
monarchy, founding/basis, 79
MPs, resignations/removals, 85–86
National Assembly Act (2008), 83
National Assembly, dissolution, 84
National Assembly, elections, 79
National Assembly, establishment, 80
National Council, elections, 79
parliamentary elections, 79
Pema Gyamtsho (Director General
   selection), 86
Pema Rinzin, removal, 94
Penal Code, Section 311 (impact), 81
Penden Wangchuk, surrender, 95
People's Democratic Party (PDP), 84–85
Road Act, violation, 87
road, illegal construction (Arunachal
   Pradesh), 87
Royal Civil Service Commission
   (RCSC), impact, 95–97
rule of law, prevalence, 97–99
secretaries, surrender, 95–97
Sonam Tshering, surrender, 95–96
Tandin Penjor, imprisonment, 94
Thinlay Norbu, imprisonment, 94–95
Thinley Tobgye, arrest, 91–93
Third King, impact, 80
Thrompon Tsheten Dorji, candidacy
   disqualification, 90
Tshering Dorji, legal breach/removal,
   91, 94
Tshogpon Jigme Tshulthrim
   (corruption case), 83–85, 97
Uttar Rai, candidacy, 90

Index   227

Wangchuck, Jigme Singye (abdication), 78
Yeshey Dorji, arrest/detention/surrender, 91–96
Yeshi Dorji, election/arrest, 88–89
Bhutan Ventures Trading (BVT), allegations, 95–96
Bhutto, Benazir
  assassination, 15
  dismissal, 192
  self-exile, 197
biased decision making, 176–177
Bose, Subhas Chandra, 125
British Raj
  consent, establishment, 189
  empire, protection, 189–190
  legacy, 188–190

C
Cambodia, Hun Sen regime (opposition party ban), 58–59
caretaker government (CTG) (Bangladesh)
  annulment, 52
  incorporation, 55–56
  provision (removal), 15th Amendment (impact), 61–62
Carter, Jimmy, 200
caste-panchayat patronage networks (India), 109
Catholic Church, liberalization, 11
Central Asia, Soviet expansion (threat), 188–189
Central Elections Commission, elimination, 44
centralized governance system, failure, 35
chaiwallah (tea seller) tagline (India), 113
Chakraborty, Anup Shekhar, 25, 105
Charter of Democracy (2006) (Pakistan), 192
Chaudhry, Iftikhar Muhammad, 201–202
Chaudhry, Kazma, 26, 185
China (Beijing)
  ascendance, 172–174
  authoritarian state, 175
  Belt and Road Initiative (BRI), 173
  dependence, increase (IRI study), 155
  endogenous factors, role, 176–178
  external influence, 153–157
  governing model, 175
  impact, 163
  King Gyanendra visit, 170, 172
  opportunism, 175
  pro-China rhetoric, 171
China-Maldives Friendship Bridge, inauguration, 155

Chinese Communist Party (CCP) patronization, 154
Choida Jamtsho, death, 87
citizens
  ongoing channels (liberal democracy component), 6
  political equality (liberal democracy component), 6
Citizen's Charter (donor project), 35
Citizens' Charter, impact, 40–41
Citizenship Amendment Act (CAA), 116
civic square, creation, 33
civilian authoritarianism, 13–14
civil society organizations, silencing, 58–59
clientelism, logic, 199
Cold War, 199–200
Collier, David, 1
Commission for Investigation of Abuse of Authority (CIAA), 178
Committee of Secretaries (CoS), discontinuation (Bhutan), 95–96
Communism, opposition, 5
communist ideologies, rise, 9
community-based organizations (CBOs), impact, 178
community development councils (CDCs), creation/nonfunction, 40
conceptual toolkit, recapitulation, 18–22
Confucianism, 10
consolidated democracy, qualifications, 77
constituency-development funds (CDFs) (Pakistan), 192
Constitution (Thirteenth Amendment) Act (1996), impact, 61
Constitutional Amendment Act (1993) (India), 106
Constitutional Council (Sri Lanka) concept, 211–214
Contractual Monarchy (Bhutan), 79
Coppedge, Michael, 20
coup d'états, 168
COVID-19 pandemic
  "blessing in disguise," 23
COVID-19 pandemic onset, 89
Crick, Bernard, 1
critics (silencing), legal/extralegal measures (Bangladesh usage), 65
Croissant, Aurel, 11
crossfire, incidences (Bangladesh), 65
cultural groups, prohibition (liberal democracy component), 6
culturally guided democracy, 15
Czechoslovakia democracy, Soviet pressure, 9–10

228 *Index*

D

Dahl, Robert, 4, 5, 174–175
Dar, Arshid Iqbal, 1, 134
Dasho Karma Ura, resignation (Bhutan), 85–86
Da'wa, extension, 153
Dawa Gyetshen, political elevation (Bhutan), 85
Deendayal Upadhyaya, Pandit, 113–114
deliberative democracy, 4
democracy
  analysis (Dahl), 5
  authoritarianism, alteration, 14
  consequences (Afghanistan), 40–42
  consolidated democracy, qualifications, 77
  decline, 2
  deliberative democracy, 4
  denial, 31
  digital democracy (India), 118–121
  electoral democracy, 7
  fourth wave, 15
  fragility (Bangladesh), 51
  global decline, 21–22, 108
  global triumph, 14
  illiberal democracy, 7
  interrupted democracy, 14
  large-scale democracy, application, 4–5
  liberal democracy, 2
  liberalism, connection, 5
  Maldives, 134
  polyarchal democracy, 4–5
  process-oriented approach, 4
  quality, decline, 19
  realist model, 3–4
  slow death, 17
  subnational level (Afghanistan), 38–40
  substantive democracy, 3
  tutelary democracy (Pakistan), 186–188
  understanding, 1–7
  weakening, 17–18
democratic advances, achievement, 22
democratic backsliding, 17, 19
  Bangladesh, 51
  Bangladeshi model, **60**
  Freedom House analysis, 58–59
  model, **59**
  process, 58
  sequences (Bangladesh) (2009–2018), 59–68
  stages, 58
  stages, framework (Bangladesh), 57–68
  theoretical aspects, 208
democratic bastion states, 22

democratic buy-in, concentration (Kabul), 42–44
democratic decline, facets, 18–22
democratic decoupling, 17
Democratic Design (Saward), 1
democratic erosion, 17, 20
  rational responses, 21
democratic failure, 18
democratic fragility, 76–77
democratic institutions, disassembly, 20
democratic legality, defense, 52–53
democratic process, criteria, 4
democratic recession, 17, 76
  reasons, 76–77
democratic regression, 17, 18
  reverse process, 18
democratic reversal, 9
democratic system, temporary suspension, 14
democratization
  backsliding (Maldives), 134–136, 139–146
  Bhutan, 76
  factors, 10–11
  fourth wave, 16
  open-ended process, complexity, 8
  process, 8
  process, unfolding, 8–9
  second wave, 10
  socio-economic prerequisites, 11
  Third Wave, 10–12, 15
  trajectory, 14
  transformation, 10
  virtuous cycle, 106
  waves metaphor, 7–10
demonstration effects (snowballing), 11
DeSouza, Peter R., 14
Deuba, Sher Bahadur, 177
dharna (sit-in) (PTI), 198
dharohar (shared heritages), 112
Dheenuge Magu (Path of Religion), 136–137
Diamond, Larry, 1, 2, 5, 14, 18–19, 22, 76, 167
dictatorships, continuation, 147
digital authoritarianism, phenomenon, 59
digital democracy (India), 118–121
digital honey-trapping, 120
digital nationalism (India), 121
digital scamming, 121
Digital Security Act (2018) (Bangladesh), harshness, 64–65, 70
Dissanayake, Dinushika, 64
District Stability Teams (DSTs), impact, 41

Diversity & Inclusion (D&I) initiatives (India), 115–116
Dorji Wangdi, election (Bhutan), 86
Druk Nyamrup Tshogpa (DNT) (Bhutan), 80–81, 96
  election win (2008), 83
  resignations, 86

E
economic boom, expectations, 11
Economist Intelligence Unit, 16
effective participation (democratic process criterion), 4
Eighteenth Constitutional Amendment (2010) (Pakistan), 193
Election Commission (EC) (India)
  electoral oversight responsibility, 107–108
  vigilance, 121–122
Election Commission members, dismissal, 150, 151
Election Commission of Bhutan (ECB), legal breaches, 90–91
elections, procedural approach, 4
electoral authoritarian regime, impact (Bangladesh), 62
electoral democracy, 7
  abusiveness, 14
  beginning/erosion (1991–2001) (Bangladesh), 54–56
  characteristics, 54
  indicators, V-Dem identification, 54
electoral outcomes, uncertainty (liberal democracy component), 6
enforced disappearances (Bangladesh), 65
enlightening understanding (democratic process criterion), 4
Environment Act, violation (Bhutan), 87
e-Participation, 119
Erdmann, Gero, 18
erosion, metaphor, 20
Ershad, H.M., 53
ethnic groups, prohibition (liberal democracy component), 6
European Union
  financial crisis, 76–77
  policies, change, 11
Exclusive Economic Zone (EEZ), 134
executive coups, 168
executive power, constraint (liberal democracy component), 6
extrajudicial killings, incidences (Bangladesh), 65, 65

F
Fascism, opposition, 5
fascist ideologies, rise, 9
Federally Administrative Tribal Areas (FATA), universal suffrage (extension), 186
first-past-the-post (FPTP) system, basis, 53
food relief program (dastarkhan-e milli) (Afghanistan), 37
foreign direct investment (FDI), 173–174
formal democratic institutions, perceptions, 56
Free and Fair Election Network (FAFEN), party-switching study, 197
freedom, erosion, 17–18
Freedom House, 6, 16
  backsliding analysis, 58–59
  country report, 77
  criteria, 7
  database, 10
  Freedom in the World Report 2021, 168
Freedom House Index, 23
Freedom House Report (2021), 76
Freedom in the World (Freedom House), 22
Free Trade Agreement (FTA), approval, 155
Fukuyama, Francis, 11, 15
fundamentalist faith movements, impact (India), 106–107

G
Gandhigiri, emulation (India), 124
Gandhi, Indira
  progressive discourse, 109
  socialist rhetoric, 108–109
Gandhi, Rajiv
  assassination, 110–111
  defeat, 109–110
Gandhi, Sonia, 111
Gandhi, term (usage), 123–124
Garibi hatao (remove poverty), Gandhi social promise, 109
Garibo ko hatao (get rid of the poor), Gandhi social promise, 109
Gasiorowski, Mark, 175
Gaurakshak (cow-vigilante), 114
Gayoom, Mamoon Abdul, 135–138, 146–149
  proxy, 148
geopolitical proximity, 21
Ghani, Ashraf, 23, 36, 39
  food relief program (dastarkhan-e milli), 37
Gillani, Yusuf Reza, 202
global democracy, high watermark, 16

230 *Index*

global democratic pessimism, 18
global democratic revolution, 10
global freedom, threat, 22
global organizations, policies (change), 11
global politics national interest, international
 relations theories, 176–177
Golwalkar, Guru, 114
Gonojagorn Moncho, impact, 68
Goshing Gup Sangay Lethro, suspension
 (Bhutan), 97
Government 2.0, 119
government legitimacy, creation, 33
government ministers, resignation/removal
 (Bhutan), 80–85
government secretaries, removal (Bhutan),
 95–97
Green Revolution (India), 110
Grugel, Jean, 5
guarantees, erosion, 17–18
Guatemala, dictatorships (repression/vio-
 lence), 10
Guo Yezhou, 173
Gup Namgyel Wangdi, arrest/trial/convic-
 tion (Bhutan), 91
gup of Bumdeling Gewog, detention
 (Bhutan), 88
Gutmann, Amy, 4

H
Hacktivism, 119
Haq, Ziaul, 196
 legitimization, 201
 military regime, 197
 Operation Fair Play, 191
Hartals (general strikes) (Bangladesh), 57
Hartmann, Hauke, 16
Hasina, Sheikh, 23, 55, 56
 poll, reneging, 63
 removal, idea, 57
Hassan, Ahmed Fayaz, 150
Haynes, Jeffrey, 11
Hazare, Anna, 123
Helmand Province, political seats
 (reservation), 37
High Command, elevation (India), 122
Hindu homogeneity, BJP dedication, 115
Hindu-Muslim relations, deterioration, 112
Hossain, Kamal, 69
How Democracy Dies (Levitsky/Ziblatt), 52
Hungary democracy, Soviet pressure, 9–10
Hun Sen regime, opposition party ban
 (Cambodia), 58
Huntington, Samuel P., 8–10
hybrid regime (Pakistan), 185–188

I
Ibrahim, Gasim, 149
identity theft, 120
Ikenberry, John, 9
illiberal democracy, 7
Impeachment Act (Bhutan), 94
inclusivity, absence (concerns)
 (Afghanistan), 45
In Defense of Politics (Crick), 1
Independent Directorate for Local
 Governance (IDLG), 39
Independent Elections Commission
 (IEC), 38
 voting station setup, avoidance, 34
India
 12 point agreement, 170–171
 aamaadmi (commoner), 123
 Aatmanirbhar Bharat (Self-reliant
  India), initiatives, 118
 Aatmanirbhar Bharat (Self-reliant
  India), manufacture, 116
 Aisi Taisi Democracy, 120
 Amritmahaotsav (independence), 112
 andolan (online/virtual movement), 120
 antyodaya (uplifting the poorest), 112
 Avatar (Incarnation), 118–121
 Babri Masjid demotion, 110–111
 Backward Classes Commission, Janata
  establishment, 110
 Bharat (rural India), 116
 Bharatiya Janata Party (BJP), power, 108
 Bharatiya Janata Party (BJP), rule,
  107–108
 Bharat Mata, 123
 bhrastachar (corruption), 125–126
 cash-based economy, replacement, 120
 caste-panchayat patronage networks, 109
 chaiwallah (tea seller) tagline, 113
 Citizenship Amendment Act (CAA), 116
 Congress, pseudo-secularism, 111
 Constitutional Amendment Act
  (1993), 106
 convicted lawmaker, political
  disqualification, 84
 data-driven rule, 119
 de-colonization, 117–118
 democratization from below, 106
 democratization, virtuous cycle, 106
 detoxing, 117–118
 dharohar (shared heritages), 112
 digital democracy, 118–121
 digital nationalism, 121
 Diversity & Inclusion (D&I) initiatives,
  115–116

Index   231

Election Commission (EC), 107–108, 121–122
fundamentalist faith movements, impact, 106–107
Gandhigiri, emulation, 124
Gandhi, Mahatma, 123–125
Garibi hatao (remove poverty), Gandhi social promise, 109
Garibo ko hatao (get rid of the poor), Gandhi social promise, 109
Gaurakshak (cow-vigilante), 114
governance crisis, 119–120
Green Revolution, 110
High Command, elevation, 122
Hindu homogeneity, BJP dedication, 115
Indira Hatao (remove Indira), 109
inner-party democracy, disappearance, 121–122
institutions/daily life, vernacularization, 118
jamadars (sweeper caste), 124
Janata curfew/impact, 116–117, 125–126
Janata Dal party, rule, 110
Janata Party, power, 110
Jan seva hi prabhuseva hai (service to people is service to god), 112
jugaad, 116
kaamdaar (workaholic) tagline, 113
Kamandal (forward/upper caste cohorts), gap, 111
Kisan andolan (farmer's movement), 120
Kisan Angolan participation, 117
localness, 118
Mahagathbandhan (grand alliance), 116
Main Bhi Chowkidar (I too am a watchman), 113
Majboorika Naam Mahatma Gandhir (helplessness thy name is Mahatma Gandhi), 124–125
Making India Great Again (MIGA) mission, 113, 118
Mandal (backward caste cohorts), gap, 111
Mandali (collective of the marginals), 110
Mann ki baat, 120
Manthan (churning), 112, 116
Modi-fications, 112–116, 118
Modi hai to mumkinhai (with Modi present, anything is conceivable), 112
Modi, impact, 112–116
Modi leher (Modi wave), 112
national faction, impact, 123
National Register of Citizens (NRC), 116

Nehruvian state, impact, 105
Neo-Hindutva, 118–119
Neo-sanjeevani, 117
Other Backward Classes (OBCs), assistance/impact, 109–111
panchayati raj (local self-government), establishment, 106
Planning Commission, establishment, 109
political consolidation, problems, 105–106
political democratization (1947–2014), 108–112
positive secularism, 111
prachinsabhyata (ancient cultures), 112
Praja-raja (subject and rulers) syndrome, impact, 109–110
Prara-raja syndrome, 126
pro-China/pro-India stances, 176
pro-China rhetoric, 171
public sphere, virtualization, 121
Ram Janmabhoomi movement, 111
Rashtra sadbhavana evam ekata (national goodwill and unity), 116
Rashtriya Swayamsevak Sangh (RSS), support (distance), 113
Ratha-yatra movement, 111
religions, equal treatment (problems), 111–112
revivalist movements, impact, 106–107
role, 169–172
Saheen Bagh protestors, 117
Sangh Parivar (BJP umbrella organization), 121
sankalp (Modi pledge), 112
sapno ka saudaagar (dream merchant), 113
sarva-dharma samabhava (temperaments of tolerance), 122
Second Backward Classes Commission, establishment, 109
secularism, 122–123
shuddhikaran (purge), 114
social democratization (1947–2014), 108–112
social movements, impact, 106–107
Swachh Bharat Mission, announcement, 124
swadeshi, 117–118
Swadeshi Jagran Manch, power, 113
techno-nationalism, 118–121
tolerance questions, revisiting, 121–123
'tryst with destiny,' 107
upper caste resistance, lower caste outrage, 110
vaccine diplomacy, 116–117

232   Index

Vande Bharat program, 117
Vasudhaivakutumbakam (mantra of gratitude), 117
vernacular democratization, 117–118
vikaaspurush (development/progressive man), Modi (relationship), 114
Vishwa Guru, 118
India democracy
continuities/realignments/promises, 105
initiation, 107
process, 25
suspension, 109
Indian National Congress (INC), 110–111
liberation (Nehru failure), 109
merger, 110
Indian secularism, concept, 111
Indira Hatao (remove Indira), 109
Indo-Lanka Accord (1987), 211
Information and Communication (ICT) Act (Bangladesh), condemnation, 63–64
Information Management Wing (ISI), 194
inner-party democracy, disappearance (India), 121–122
institutions, control (Bangladesh), 66–67
International Centre for Integrated Mountain Development (ICIMOD) (Nepal), 86
International Commission of Jurists (ICJ), impact, 63–64
International Covenant on Civil and Political Rights (ICCPR), ICT Act (incompatibility), 64
international inducements, rational responses, 21
International Monetary Fund, financing, 201
international relations theories, 176–177
International Republican Institute (IRI), China dependence impact, 155
interrupted democracy, 14
Islam
defense, rhetoric, 152–153
Wahhabi version, 156
Islamic radicalism, 145
Islamic Republic of Afghanistan, 33
Islamic State group, impact, 153
Islami Jamhoori Ittehad (IJI) alliance (Pakistan), 197

J
Jaitley, Arun, 114
Jamaat-e-Islami (JI) (Pakistan), 195
Jamaat-i-Islami
BNP, alliance, 65

persecution (Bangladesh), 63–64
jamadars (sweeper caste) (India), 124
Jameel, Mohamed, 149
Jamiat-Ulema-e-Islam (JUI-F) (Pakistan), 195
Janata
curfew, 116–117
perseverance, 126
Janata Dal party, rule (India), 110, 111
Janata Party (India)
merger, 110
power, 110
Jan Morcha party, merger (India), 110
Jan seva hi prabhuseva hai (service to people is service to god) (India), 112
Jantar Mantar, 123
Jatiya Oikya Front (JOF), BNP alliance, 69
Jatiya Party, official opposition declaration (Bangladesh), 66
Jiang Zemin, 170
Jigme Samdrup, trial (Bhutan), 94–95
Jirga, Wolesi, 37
Joint Investigative Team (Pakistan), 202–203
judges, removal (Bhutan), 91–95
Judicature Act, amendment (Maldives), 149
Judicial Service Commission, misconduct/incompetence, 150

K
kaamdaar (workaholic) tagline (India), 113
Kabul. *see* Afghanistan
Kaldor, Mary, 3
Kamandal (forward/upper caste cohorts), gap, 111
Karki, Sushila, 178
Karma Gyeltshen, election win (Bhutan), 88
Karzai, Hamid, 39
Khamdang Mangmi Sangye Tenpa, suspension (Bhutan), 97
Khamdang-Ramjar representative, resignation (Bhutan), 87
Khan, Abdur Rahman, 36
Khan, Ayub, 191
co-optation, 196–197
Khandu Wangmo, arrest (Bhutan), 92
Khan, Imran, 23–24, 202
loyalty, 198
military, impact, 194
military, rift, 198
no-confidence vote, 185, 198

Index   233

party leadership, 186–187
popularity, 194
Khan, Liaqat Ali (assassination), 190–191
Kim Jong Un, 151
Kinga Gyeltshen, trial (Bhutan), 94–95
Kinga, Sonam, 25, 76
Kinga Tshering, resignation (Bhutan), 86
King Gyanendra, China visit, 170, 172
Kinlay Lhendrup, imprisonment (Bhutan),
  94–95
Kisan andolan (farmer's movement)
  (India), 120
Kisan Angolan participation, 117
Kneuer, Marianne, 18, 20
Koriala, B.P., 165, 171–172, 177
Kuenley Tshering, arrest/detention
  (Bhutan), 91–94
Kumaratunga, Chandrika, 213
Kurzman, Charles, 8

L
Laebens, Melis G., 21
Land Act, violation (Bhutan), 87
Land Allotment Committee members,
  guilty verdict (Bhutan), 83
large-scale democracy, application, 4–5
Lawyer's Movement, 202
leadership, crisis (Pakistan), 190–191
Leghari, Farooq Ahmed Khan, 192
Levitsky, Steven, 1, 52, 148
Lhakhang Karpo temple, renovation
  (Bhutan), 85
liberal autocracy, reverse phenomenon, 7
liberal democracy, 2
  components, 6
  defensiveness, 16
  embedded capitalism, marriage
    (challenge), 17
  expansion, 9
  global decline, 15–18
  triumph, 11
  version, 5
liberalism, democracy (connection), 5
liberal state-building efforts, 44
Liberation Tigers of Tamil Eelam (LTTE)
  conflict, 216
  military defeat, 207–208
local government leaders, Bhutan removal,
  88–91
Lok Dal party, merger (India), 110
Lührmann, Anna, 21
Lungten Dubgyur, removal (Bhutan),
  94–95
Lust, Ellen, 19

Lyonpo Minjur Dorji (corruption case),
  83–85, 97
Lyonpo Ngeema sangay Tshempo,
  resignation (Bhutan), 85
Lyonpo Rinzin, acquittal (Bhutan), 98
Lyonpo Sherub Gyeltshen (resignation
  process) (Bhutan), 80–83, 97, 98

M
Maafushi Prison, Naseem (murder), 138
Madhesh issues (Nepal), 171
Mahagathbandhan (grand alliance)
  (India), 116
Main Bhi Chowkidar (I too am a
  watchman) (India), 113
Majboorika Naam Mahatma Gandhir
  (helplessness thy name is Mahatma
  Gandhi), 124–125
Majlis, usage, 149, 150
Making India Great Again (MIGA)
  mission, 113, 118
Maldives
  authoritarianism, 147–148
  authoritarian leverage, tragedy, 153–157
  authoritarian residues, 146–148
  autocracy, transition, 136–138
  China, external influence, 153–157
  China, overtures, 154
  Chinese Communist Party (CCP)
    patronization, 154
  civil society, 137
  Da'wa, extension, 153
  democratic constitution, adoption, 138
  democratic trajectory, question, 135
  democratization, 148
  democratization backsliding, 134–136,
    139–146
  Dheenuge Magu (Path of Religion),
    136–137
  dissent, 137–138
  Election Commission members,
    dismissal, 150
  executive aggrandizement, 148–151
  geo-strategic allure, 135
  internal/indigenous causal variables,
    146–153
  Islamic radicalism, 151–153
  jihad, 152
  Judicature Act, amendment, 149
  Judicial Service Commission,
    misconduct/incompetence, 150
  Majlis, impact, 149, 150
  Mohammed bin Salman visit, 156
  national auditor report, 137

234   *Index*

Parliament, Standing Orders
  (amendments), 149
political transition, 136
post-Cold War transition, 136
pre-democratic trajectory, 136
presidential hegemony, 148–151
pro-government events, attendance, 151
'progression through regression,'
  152–153
religious extremism, challenge, 151–152
Saudi Arabia, external influence,
  153–157
Sharia punishments, 152–153
Special Operations Unit (Star Force), 147
Transparency Maldives (diplomatic
  mission), 138
Xi Jinping visit, 154
Maldives democracy, 134
  crisis, 135–136
  denigration, 152
  impact, 146–157
  trajectory, 148
  transition, 136–137
  vulnerability, 153–154
Maldives National Defence Force,
  arrests, 147
Maldives Supreme Court, laywer
  suspension, 150
Maldivian Democracy Network (MDN),
  abolishment, 153
Maldivian Democratic Party (MDP), 151
  jihad, 152
  role, 137–138
Mandal, B.P. (power), 110
Mandal (backward caste cohorts), gap, 111
Mandali (collective of the marginals)
  (India), 110
Mandal, politicization, 111
Mangmi of Wangphu Gewog, removal
  (Bhutan), 90
Mangmi Sangye Tempa, removal
  (Bhutan), 88
Mani Dorji, election win (Bhutan), 89
Mann ki baat (India), 120
Manthan (churning), 112, 116
Maoists, armed anti-government forces
  (Jiang perception), 170
Marsyangdi Hydropower Station,
  construction (Nepal), 173
media, silencing, 58–59
Memescape, 119
Memorandum of Understanding (MOU),
  Maldive government signing, 156
militaristic ideologies, rise, 9

military authoritarianism, 13–14
Ministry of Women's Affairs, elimination, 44
minority groups, prohibition (liberal
  democracy component), 6
Modi hai to mumkinhai (with Modi
  present, anything is conceivable)
  (India), 112
Modi leher (Modi wave) (India), 112
Modi, Narendra, 111, 167
  agenda, 114
  humor, investment, 121
  impact, 112–116
  Neo-Hindutva, 114
  weak/nonexistent party democracy
    issue, 122
Mohamed, Abdullah, 147
Mohammed, Amir Dost, 36
Mohammed bin Salman, Maldives
  visits, 156
Molden, David (retirement), 86
monarchies
  absolute monarchy, 79
  Contractual Monarchy (Bhutan), 79
monopolistic partyarchal governance,
  establishment, 56
MPs, resignations/removals (Bhutan),
  85–86
Mubarak, Hosni, 136
Mufti, Mariam, 26, 185
Mugabe, Robert, 151
Muizzu, Mohamed, 155
Mujibur, Sheikh, 53
muktijudhher chetona (spirit of liberation
  war), term (usage), 68
Munda, Birsa, 125
Municipal Election Committees,
  creation, 39
Munir, Muhammad, 201
Murtazashvili, Jennifer Brick, 24, 31
Musharraf, Pervez, 186, 191, 196
  coup, 197
  martial law (1999), 200
  Provisional Constitution Order of
    1999, 192
Muslim Brotherhood (Egypt), 151–152
Muslim League, 196–197
Mutahida Quami Movement (MQM), 195

N
Narasiomha Rao, P.V. (control), 110–112
Naseem, Ahmed, 147–148
Naseem, Azra, 135–137
Naseem, Evan (murder), 138
Nasheed, Jr., Mohamed, 135

Index 235

Nasheed, Mohamed, 137–138, 146–149
  accusations, 152
National Assembly Act (2008) (Bhutan), 83
National Assembly, dissolution
  (Pakistan), 197
National Assembly houses, elimination, 44
National Assembly, impact, 34–35
national churches, transformation, 11
National Communist Party (NCP)
  (Nepal), 173
national-level politics (Afghanistan),
  35–37
National Register of Citizens (NRC), 116
National Security Council (2009),
  abolition (Pakistan), 193
National Solidarity Program (NSP), 40
  donor project, 35
  World Bank assessment, 40–41
National Unity Government, 19th
  Amendment adoption (Sri Lanka), 208
Nehru, Jawaharlal (socialist rhetoric),
  108–109
Neo-Hindutva, 118–119
neopatrimonialism, pervasiveness, 63–64
Neo-sanjeevani (India), 117
Nepal
  authoritarianism, 164
  backsliding, varieties, 168
  China card, playing, 172
  China, impact, 163
  Commission for Investigation of Abuse
    of Authority (CIAA), 178
  community-based organizations
    (CBOs), impact, 178
  Constituent Assembly (CA) elections,
    166–167
  Constituent Assembly (CA), setup,
    164–165
  democratic backsliding, 167–168,
    179–180
  democratic consolidation, 177–178
  democratic consolidation, con-
    sequences, 168–169
  democratic regression, historical signs,
    163–164
  Department of Money Laundering, 168
  Department of Revenue Investigation, 168
  electoral process, 169
  external influences, 163
  foreign direct investment (FDI), 173–174
  foreign involvement, 174–175
  geo-political rivalry, 174–180
  geopolitics, domestic leadership
    (interaction), 179

grassroots democracy, 167
high-quality democracy, recovery
  (absence), 179
ideological counterpart, 173
illiberal democracy, 167–168
India-friendliness, 177
India, role, 169–172
instabilities, 76
internal bickering, 166
internal dynamics, 163
internal war, 170
International Centre for Integrated
  Mountain Development (ICIMOD), 86
inter-party dynamics, influences, 171
local-level bodies, 167
Madhesh issues, 171
Maoists, India support (absence),
  170–171
marginalization, 170
Marsyangdi Hydropower Station,
  construction, 173
National Communist Party (NCP), 173
National Investigation Department, 168
no-confidence, motion (minority
  government collapse), 165–166
nongovernmental organizations
  (NGOs), impact, 178
oligarchy, 164–165
Panchayat system, 165
People's Movement, 165, 173
pliant leadership, 26
Pokhara International Regional Airport,
  construction, 173
political interference, 178
political leadership, subservience, 176
political pluralism, 169
politics, activity, 172–173
politics, political leadership examples, 177
politics, role, 169
Public Accounts Committee (PAC)
  corruption investigations, 169
Revolution of 1950, 164–165
royal coup, 166
'Second People's 'Movement,' 166
society, division, 174
stability, 165–166
strategic location, 178
United Marxist Leninist (UML) party,
  165–166, 173
Xi Jinping visit, 173
Nepal democracy
  breakdown, continuation, 166–167
  explanation, 167–169
  historical overview, 164–174

236 *Index*

impact, 168
securing, inability, 163
tryst, 163
ushering, 171
Non-Aligned Movement, 134
nongovernmental organizations (NGOs),
  impact, 178
North-East Provincial Council,
  establishment (Sri Lanka), 210–211
Northwest Frontier Province (NWFP),
  governance, 189
"Not Free" countries, 22

O
Official Secrets Act (Pakistan), 202
Oli, K.P., 168, 177
Oli, K.P. Sharma, 24
On Democracy (Dahl), 4, 174
Operation Fair Play (Pakistan), 191
opposition leaders, disqualification, 20
opposition movements, surge, 12–13
opposition parties, silencing, 58–59
Organisation of Islamic Cooperation
  (OIC), 134
Other Backward Classes (OBCs),
  assistance/impact (India), 109–111

P
Padma Bridge (mega project), 67
Pakistan
  58 2(b) system, 192
  actor-centered approach, 188
  Awami National Party (ANP), 195
  Basic Democracy, 192
  British Raj, legacy, 188–190
  Charter of Democracy (2006), 192
  civilian institutions, decline, 190–191
  civil-military relations, imbalance, 191
  clientelism, logic, 199
  constituency-development funds
    (CDFs), 192
  constitutional reform, military
    government plans, 192
  democratic institutions, weakness, 191
  democratization, 187
  democratization, challenges, 186
  developments, 76–77
  direct military-to-military transfers, 200
  economic/military assistance, long-term
    flow, 201
  Eighteenth Constitutional Amendment
    (2010), 193
  Eighth Amendment, 192
  election (2024), 198

electoral competition, uni-dimensional
  spectrum, 187–188
Federally Administrative Tribal Areas
  (FATA), universal suffrage
  (extension), 186
hybridity, multi-dimensional
  conception, 187–188
hybrid regime, 185–188
Information Management Wing (ISI), 194
international actors, strategic
  alliances, 191
international community, relationship,
  199–201
International Monetary Fund,
  financing, 201
intra-party elections, absence, 195
Islami Jamhoori Ittehad (IJI)
  alliance, 197
Jamaat-e-Islami (JI), 195
Jamiat-Ulema-e-Islam (JUI-F), 195
Joint Investigative Team, 202–203
judiciary, impact, 201–203
Lawyer's Movement, 202
leadership, crisis, 190–191
liberal democracy, 187–188
martial law administration, 191–192
martial law, imposition, 185–186
military-led regime, 186
Mutahida Quami Movement
  (MQM), 195
National Assembly, actions, 195
National Assembly, dissolution, 197
National Security Council (2009),
  abolition, 193
no-confidence motion, 198
non-regulation provinces, 189
Official Secrets Act, 202
Operation Fair Play, 191
opposition parties, shaping, 199
party factionalization, 197
party-switching, 197
political competition, 192
political parties, impact, 196
political parties, splintering, 196
politics, indirect/direct military
  intervention, 194
politics, tutelary control, 187
pre-poll rigging, 185
Provisional Constitution Order of
  1999, 192
regime hybridity, 187
Revival of Constitution Order, 192
rubber-stamp institution, role, 201
security, significance, 193–194

Index   237

self-sufficient politicians, dependence, 196
strategic depth, pursuit, 193
structural approaches, 188
structuralist approach, 188
tutelary democracy, 186–188
voluntarist approach, 188
weakly institutionalized political
    parties, 195–199
weak party organizations, 196
World Bank, financing, 201
Pakistan Democratic Movement
    (PDM), 198
Pakistan military, 190–194
capacity/expertise, enhancement, 200
regimes, United States (contribution), 200
rule, 15
War on Terror, relationship, 199
Pakistan Muslim League (PML-N),
    193–196
Pakistan Muslim League-Quaid
    (PML-Q), 195
Pakistan People's Party (PPP),
    193–196, 202
popularity, 197
Pakistan Tehreek-e-Insaf (PTI),
    overthrow, 23–24
Pakistan Tehrik-e-Insaaf (PTI), 193–194,
    196, 198, 203
decimation, 186–187
dharna (sit-in), 198
Palshikar, Suhas, 108
Panama Papers, allegations, 202
panchayati raj (local self-government),
    establishment, 106
Panchayat system (Nepal), 165
Panday, Devendra Raj, 176
partyarchy (Bangladesh), 56
party factionalization (Pakistan), 197
party-switching, FAFEN study, 197
Patel, Sardar, 125
Pema Gyamtsho (Director General
    selection), 86–87
Pema Rinzin, removal (Bhutan), 94
Penden Wangchuk, surrender (Bhutan), 95
people, divisions (inflaming), 19
Peoples' Alliance (Sri Lanka), 207
People's Democratic Party (PDP)
    (Bhutan), 84–85
People's Movement (Nepal), 165
performance legitimacy, 11
phishing, 120
Planning Commission, establishment
    (India), 109
Plattner, Marc F., 15

plausibility probe, 18
pluralism (liberal democracy component), 6
polarization, driving force, 17
political consolidation, problems,
    105–106
political democratization (1947–2014)
    (India), 108–112
political institutions, state-led debilitation/
    elimination, 51
political interference, 178
political parties, splintering, 196
political power, concentration (Kabul), 32
political protest, factor, 13
political rights, conceptual distinctiveness, 7
polyarchal democracy, 4–5
characteristics, defining, 5
polyarchy
criteria, 21
elements, 7
political system form, 5
positive secularism (India), 111
post-Soviet states, democratization, 12
post-World War II ascent, 15
power
constraints, 18
distribution/sharing, unwillingness, 45–46
relations, regulation, 3
Power, Timothy, 175
prachinsabhyata (ancient cultures)
    (India), 112
Praja-raja (subject and rulers) syndrome,
    impact (India), 109–0110
Prara-raja syndrome (India), 126
Preface to Democratic Theory, A (Dahl), 4
presidential hegemony, 20
Pressler Amendment, 200
prime ministerial system, creation, 55–56
prodemocracy movement, 14
'progression through regression,' 152–153
promissory coup (Bangladesh), 52–53
Provincial Reconstruction Teams (PRTs),
    impact, 41
Provisional Constitution Order of 1999
    (Pakistan), 192
pseudo-secularism (India), 111
Public Accounts Committee (PAC)
corruption investigations (Nepal), 169
public policy, crafting, 34–35
Punjab, governance, 189
Pushparajah, Nadarajah, 26, 207

R
Rahman, Abdur, 36
assassination, 53

238 Index

Rahman, Tarique (graft charge conviction), 63
Rajapaksa, Basil, 216–217
Rajapaksa, Chamal, 216
Rajapaksa, Gotabaya, 208, 216, 217, 220
Rajapaksa, Mahinda, 207–208, 215, 217–219
Rajapaksa, Mahindra, 167–168
Rajapaksa, Namal, 217
Ram Janmabhoomi movement (India), 111
rapid death (autocratization path), 20
Rashtra sadbhavana evam ekata (national goodwill and unity) (India), 116
Rashtriya Swayamsevak Sangh (RSS), support (distance), 113
Ratha-yatra movement (India), 111
recession, term (usage), 19
regression, term (usage), 19
religious groups, prohibition (liberal democracy component), 6
Reporters Without Borders, 23
Republican Afghanistan, celebration, 33–34
resurgent authoritarianism, 16–17
revivalist movements, impact (India), 106–107
Revival of Constitution Order (Pakistan), 192
Riaz, Ali, 13, 25, 51
"Rip Van Winkle" sentiment, 15
Road Act, violation (Bhutan), 87
Robinson, J.J., 135
Roopur Nuclear Power Plant (mega project), 67
Rose, Leo, 169
Royal Civil Service Commission (RCSC), impact (Bhutan), 95–97
rule of law
  absence, 76
  institutions, 208
  prevalence (Bhutan), 97–99
  protections, liberal democracy component, 6
Russia, authoritarian state, 175

S

Saheen Bagh protestors, 117
saidq (truthful), 202
Salafism, spread, 156
Sangh Parivar (BJP umbrella organization), 121
sankalp (Modi pledge), 112

sapno ka saudaagar (dream merchant) (India), 113
sarva-dharma samabhava (temperaments of tolerance), 122
Saudi Arabia
  external influence, 153–157
  Memorandum of Understanding (MOU), Maldive government signing, 156
Saward, Michael, 1, 2
sea line of communications (SLOC), 134
Second Backward Classes Commission, establishment (India), 109
second-try pattern, 14
semi-authoritarianism (Bangladesh), 56
Shah, Amit (BJP president), 114
  declaration, 115
  popularitiy, 116
Sharia punishments, 152–153
Sharif, Nawaz, 194, 202
  leadership, IJI split, 197
  resignation, call, 186
Sharif, Raheel, 198
Sharma, Abijit, 26, 163
Shastri, Lal Bahadur, 125
Shin, Doh Chull, 10
shuddhikaran (purge) (India), 114
Singh, Kalyan, 111
Singh, V.P., 110
Single Non-Transferable Voting system, 36
single non-transferable voting system (SNTV), impact, 32
Sinha, S.K., 66–67
Sirsena, Maithripala, 208, 215, 217
slow death (autocratization path), 20
smart cities, 120
snowballing (demonstration effects), 11
Sobhan, Zafar, 65
social democratization (1947–2014) (India), 108–112
social movements, impact (India), 106–107
Solih, Ibrahim Mohamed, 135
Sonam Tshering, surrender (Bhutan), 95–96
South Asia
  China, arrival, 174
  democracies, 207
  democracy level, decline, 23
  democratic trajectory, 15
  institutional sclerosis, 107
  situating, 22–24
  social media/meme landscapes, 113

Index 239

South Asian Association for Regional Cooperation (SAARC), 134, 172
Special Operations Unit (Star Force) (Maldives), 147
Sri Lanka
  Act of Parliament, 216
  amendments (17th/19th/21st), 211–216
  amendments (18th/20th), 216–221
  Constitutional Amendments, 207
  Constitutional Council, appointment, 213–214
  Constitutional Council, concept, 211–214
  Constitutional Council, restoration, 208
  Constitution (1978), impact, 210
  democracy, 207
  democratic backsliding, theoretical aspects, 208
  democratization, elements, 215–216
  developments, 76–77
  Elections Commission, 213
  governance reforms, 214–215
  liberal democracy, erosion, 210
  Liberation Tigers of Tamil Eelam (LTTE), conflict, 216
  Liberation Tigers of Tamil Eelam (LTTE), military defeat, 207
  National Unity Government, 19th Amendment adoption, 208
  North-East Provincial Council, establishment, 210–211
  Order Paper of Parliament, 216
  Parliamentary Council, 218
  People's Alliance, 207
  politicization, elimination, 207–208
  post-independent constitutional changes, 209
  post-independent constitutional order, 209–211
  premier-presidential system, 215
  president, authority (reduction), 214–215
  prime minister, constitutional status, 220
  Public Interest Law Foundation v. the Attorney-General, 213
  rebuilding, 217
  Republican Constitution, 209
  semi-presidentialism system, 215
  Soulbury Constitution, 209
  two-term limit, removal, 218–219
  undemocratic elements, 219–221
  United National Party (UNP), impact, 209
  'Urgent bill' procedure, 215–216
Sri Lanka Freedom Party (SLFP)

  amendments, 210
  Constitution enactment, 209
Sri Lanka Podujana Peramuna (SLPP), 217–218
state, control (liberal democracy component), 6
state-created parallel structures, 40–42
strategic depth, pursuit (Pakistan), 193
Strategic Forecast (2016), prediction, 51
strategic silencing, 58–59
structuralist approach (Pakistan), 188
substantive democracy, 3
Swachh Bharat Mission, announcement (India), 124
Swadeshi Jagran Manch, power (India), 113
swing states, impact, 19
Syiem, U Tirot Sing, 125

T
Taliban
  power, 23
  power, consolidation, 44–45
  rule, consequences, 44–45
Tandin Penjor, imprisonment (Bhutan), 94–95
techno-nationalism (India), 118–121
Thinlay Norbu, imprisonment (Bhutan), 94–95
Thinley Tobgye, arrest (Bhutan), 91–93
Third Wave, democratization, 10–15
Third Wave: Democratization in the Late Twentieth Century (Huntington), 8
Third Wave of Democracy, 54
Thompson, Dennis, 4
Thrompon Tsheten Dorji, candidacy disqualification (Bhutan), 90
Tilly, Charles, 2
transparency, absence, 76–77
Transparency International, Bangladesh corruption ranking, 63
Transparency Maldives (diplomatic mission), 138
Tshering Dorji, legal breach/removal (Bhutan), 91, 94
Tshogpon Jigme Tshulthrim (corruption case), 83–85, 97
tutelary democracy (Pakistan), 186–188
two-party system, emergence, 56–57
two-turnover test, 12

U
United Marxist Leninist (UML) party (Nepal), 165–166, 173
United National Party (UNP) (Sri Lanka)

240 Index

amendments, 210
impact, 209
United People's Freedom Alliance (UPFA),
impact, 216
United States
financial crisis, 76–77
intra-Afghan talks, peace agreement, 34
universalization, 11–12
Upadhyay, Deendayal (mantra), 112
upper caste resistance, lower caste outrage
(India), 110
Uttar Rai, Bhutan candidacy, 90

V

Vaipayee, Atal Bihari, 114
Vajpayee, Atal Behari, 113, 179
Vande Bharat program (India), 117
Varieties of Democracy Institute
(V-Dem), 16
democracy report, 22
electoral democracy indicators,
identification, 54
information, alternative sources
study, 108
Vasudhaivakutumbakum (mantra of
gratitude) (India), 117
Vejvoda, Ivan, 3
Vishwa Gutu (India), 118
voluntarist approach (Pakistan), 188
voter suppression plans (Bangladesh), 69
voting equality (democratic process
criterion), 4

W

Waheed, Abdullah, 152
Wahhabism, spread, 156
Wakhley, K.B., 95
Waldner, David, 19
Wangchuck, Jigme Singye (abdication), 78
Wani, Aijaz Ashraf, 1, 134
War on Terror, 199–201

waves, metaphor, 7–10
Way, Lucan A., 148
weakly institutionalized political parties
(Pakistan), 195–199
weak/nonexistent party democracy, issue
(India), 122
Western colonial powers, interference, 154
Western liberal democracy, universalization,
11–12
Westminster model, assessment, 108
Whitehead, Lawrence, 5, 7
Wickremesinghe, Ranil, 208, 215, 217
World Bank, financing, 201
*World Safe for Democracy: Liberal
Internationalism and the Crises of
Global Order* (Ikenberry), 9
World War I, democratization, 9

X

Xi Jinping
Maldives visit, 154
Nepal visit, 173
thought, 175

Y

Yameen, Abdullah, 148, 150–151
impact, 155–156
Yeshey Dorji (Bhutan)
arrest/detention, 91–94
surrender, 95–96
Yeshi Dorji, election/arrest (Bhutan),
88–89

Z

Zakaria, Fareed, 7
Zardari, Asif Ali, 202
Zarifi, Sam, 149
Zia, Khaleda, 13, 55, 56
persecution, 63
removal, idea, 57
Ziblatt, Daniel, 52

Printed in the United States
by Baker & Taylor Publisher Services